John Henry Bernard

Kant's Kritik of judgment

John Henry Bernard

Kant's Kritik of judgment

ISBN/EAN: 9783337739584

Printed in Europe, USA, Canada, Australia, Japan

Cover: Foto ©Thomas Meinert / pixelio.de

More available books at **www.hansebooks.com**

KANT'S

KRITIK OF JUDGMENT

TRANSLATED

WITH INTRODUCTION AND NOTES

BY

J. H. BERNARD, D.D.

FELLOW OF TRINITY COLLEGE, AND ARCHBISHOP KING'S LECTURER
IN DIVINITY IN THE UNIVERSITY OF DUBLIN

London

MACMILLAN AND CO.

AND NEW YORK

1892

CONTENTS

EDITOR'S INTRODUCTION

THERE are not wanting indications that public interest in the Critical Philosophy has been quickened of recent days in these countries, as well as in America. To lighten the toil of penetrating through the wilderness of Kant's long sentences, the English student has now many aids, which those who began their studies fifteen or twenty years ago did not enjoy. Translations, paraphrases, criticisms, have been published in considerable numbers; so that if it is not yet true that "he who runs may read," it may at least be said that a patient student of ordinary industry and intelligence has his way made plain before him. And yet the very number of aids is dangerous. Whatever may be the value of short and easy handbooks in other departments of science, it is certain that no man will become a philosopher, no man will even acquire a satisfactory knowledge of the history of philosophy, without personal and prolonged study of the *ipsissima verba* of the great masters of human thought. "Above all," said Schopenhauer, "my truth-seeking young friends, beware of letting our professors tell you

what is contained in the Kritik of the Pure Reason ";
and the advice has not become less wholesome with
the lapse of years. The fact, however, that many
persons have not sufficient familiarity with German
to enable them to study German Philosophy in the
original with ease, makes translations an educa-
tional necessity; and this translation of Kant's
Kritik of the faculty of Judgment has been undertaken in the hope that it may promote a more
general study of that masterpiece. If any reader
wishes to follow Schopenhauer's advice, he has only
to omit the whole of this prefatory matter and
proceed at once to the Author's laborious Introduction.

It is somewhat surprising that the Kritik of
Judgment has never yet been made accessible to
the English reader. Dr. Watson has indeed translated a few selected passages, so also has Dr. Caird
in his valuable account of the Kantian philosophy,
and I have found their renderings of considerable
service; but the space devoted by both writers to
the Kritik of Judgment is very small in comparison
with that given to the Kritiks of Pure and Practical
Reason. And yet the work is not an unimportant
one. Kant himself regarded it as the coping-stone
of his critical edifice; it even formed the point of
departure for his successors, Fichte, Schelling and
Hegel, in the construction of their respective
systems. Possibly the reason of its comparative
neglect lies in its repulsive style. Kant was never
careful of style, and in his later years he became

more and more enthralled by those technicalities and refined distinctions which deter so many from the Critical Philosophy even in its earlier sections. These "symmetrical architectonic amusements," as Schopenhauer called them, encumber every page of Kant's later writings, and they are a constant source of embarrassment to his unhappy translator. For, as every translator knows, no single word in one language exactly covers any single word in another ; and yet if Kant's distinctions are to be preserved it is necessary to select with more or less arbitrariness English equivalents for German technical terms, and retain them all through. Instances of this will be given later on ; I only remark here on the fact that Kant's besetting sin of over-technicality is especially conspicuous in this treatise.

Another fault—an old fault of Kant—apparent after reading even a few pages, is that repetitions are very frequent of the same thought in but slightly varied language. Arguments are repeated over and over again until they become quite wearisome ; and then when the reader's attention has flagged, and he is glancing cursorily down the page, some important new point is introduced without emphasis, as if the author were really anxious to keep his meaning to himself at all hazards. A book written in such fashion rarely attracts a wide circle of readers. And yet, not only did Goethe think highly of it, but it received a large measure of attention in France as well as in Germany on its first appearance. Originally published at Berlin in

1790, a Second Edition was called for in 1793; and
a French translation was made by Imhoff in 1796.
Other French versions are those by Keratry and
Weyland in 1823, and by Barni in 1846. This
last I have had before me while performing my
task, but I have not found it of much service; the
older French translations I have not seen. The
existence of these French versions, when taken in
connection with the absence until very recently of
any systematic account of the Kritik of Judgment
in English, may be perhaps explained by the lively
interest that was taken on the Continent in the
Philosophy of Art in the early part of the century;
whereas scientific studies on this subject received
little attention in England during the same period.

The student of the Kritik of Pure Reason will
remember how closely, in his Transcendental Logic,
Kant follows the lines of the ordinary logic of the
schools. He finds his whole plan ready made for
him, as it were; and he proceeds to work out the
metaphysical principles which underlie the process
of syllogistic reasoning. And as there are three
propositions in every syllogism, he points out that,
in correspondence with this triplicity, [the higher
faculties of the soul may be regarded as threefold.
The Understanding or the faculty of concepts
gives us our major premiss, as it supplies us in
the first instance with a general notion. By means
of the Judgment we see that a particular case comes
under the general rule, and by the Reason we draw
our conclusion. These, as three distinct move-

ments in the process of reasoning, are regarded by Kant as indicating three distinct faculties, with which the Analytic of Concepts, the Analytic of Principles, and the Dialectic are respectively concerned. The full significance of this important classification does not seem, however, to have occurred to Kant at the time, as we may see from the order in which he wrote his great books.[1] The first problem which arrests the attention of all modern philosophers is, of course, the problem of knowledge, its conditions and its proper objects. And in the Kritik of Pure Reason this is discussed, and the conclusion is reached that nature as phenomenon is the only object of which we can hope to acquire any exact knowledge. But it is apparent that there are other problems which merit consideration ; a complete philosophy includes practice as well as theory ; it has to do not only with logic, but with life. And thus the Kritik of Practical Reason was written, in which is unfolded the doctrine of man's freedom standing in sharp contrast with the necessity of natural law. Here, then, it seems at first sight as if we had covered the whole field of human activity. For we have investigated the sources of knowledge, and at the same time have pointed out the conditions of practical life, and have seen that the laws of freedom are just as true in their own sphere as are the laws of nature.

---

[1] Dr. Caird (*Critical Philosophy of Kant*, vol. ii. p. 406) has given an instructive account of the gradual development in Kant's mind of the main idea of the Kritik of Judgment.

But as we reflect on our mental states we find that here no proper account has been given of the phenomena of *feeling*, which play so large a part in experience. And this Kant saw before he had proceeded very far with the Kritik of Practical Reason ; and in consequence he adopted a threefold classification of the higher mental faculties based on that given by previous psychologists. Knowledge, feeling, desire, these are the three ultimate modes of consciousness, of which the second has not yet been described. And when we compare this with the former triple division which we took up from the Aristotelian logic, we see that the parallelism is significant. Understanding is *par excellence* the faculty of knowledge, and Reason the faculty of desire (these points are developed in Kant's first two Kritiks). And this suggests that the Judgment corresponds to the feeling of pleasure and pain ; it occupies a position intermediate between Understanding and Reason, just as, roughly speaking, the feeling of pleasure is intermediate between our perception of an object and our desire to possess it.

And so the Kritik of Judgment completes the whole undertaking of criticism ; its endeavour is to show that there are *a priori* principles at the basis of Judgment just as there are in the case of Understanding and of Reason ; that these principles, like the principles of Reason, are not constitutive but only regulative of experience, *i.e.* that they do not teach us anything positive about the characteristics of objects, but only indicate the conditions under which we find it necessary to view them; and lastly, that we are thus furnished with an *a priori* philosophy of pleasure.

The fundamental principle underlying the procedure of the Judgment is seen to be that of the purposiveness of Nature; nature is everywhere adapted to ends or purposes, and thus constitutes a κόσμος, a well-ordered whole. By this means, nature is regarded by us as if its particular empirical laws were not isolated and disparate, but connected and in relation, deriving their unity in seeming diversity from an intelligence which is at the source of nature. It is only by the assumption of such a principle that we can construe nature to ourselves; and the principle is then said to be a transcendental condition of the exercise of our judging faculty, but valid only for the reflective, not for the determinant Judgment. It gives us pleasure to view nature in this way; just as the contemplation of chaos would be painful.

But this purposiveness may be only formal and subjective, or real and objective. In some cases the purposiveness resides in the felt harmony and accordance of the form of the object with the cognitive faculties; in others the form of the object is judged to harmonise with the purpose in view in its existence. That is to say, in the one case we judge the form of the object to be purposive, as in the case of a flower, but could not explain any purpose served by it; in the other case we have a definite

b

notion of what it is adapted for. In the former case
the aesthetical Judgment is brought to bear, in the
latter the teleological: and it thus appears that the
Kritik of Judgment has two main divisions: it treats
first of the philosophy of Taste, the Beautiful and
the Sublime in Nature: and secondly, of the Teleology of nature's working. It is a curious literary
parallel that S. Augustine hints (*Confessions* iv. 15)
that he had written a book, *De Pulchro et Apto*, in
which these apparently distinct topics were combined: "pulchrum esse, quod per se ipsum:
aptum, autem, quod ad aliquid accommodatum
deceret." A beautiful object has no purpose
external to itself and the observer: but a useful
object serves further ends. Both, however, may be
brought under the higher category of things that are
reckoned *purposive* by the Judgment.

We have here then, in the first place, a basis for
an *a priori* Philosophy of Taste: and Kant works
out its details with great elaboration. He borrowed
little from the writings of his predecessors, but
struck out, as was ever his plan, a line of his own.
He quotes with approval from Burke's *Treatise on
the Sublime and Beautiful*, which was accessible to
him in a German translation: but is careful to
remark that it is as psychology, not as philosophy,
that Burke's work has value. He may have read
in addition Hutcheson's *Inquiry* which had also
been translated into German; and he was complete
master of Hume's opinions. Of other writers on
Beauty he only names Batteux and Lessing.

Batteux was a French writer of repute who had
attempted a twofold arrangement of the Arts as
they may be brought under Space and under Time
respectively, a mode of classification which would
naturally appeal to Kant. He does not seem,
however, to have read the ancient text-book
on the subject. Aristotle's *Poetics*, the principles
of which Lessing declared to be as certain as
Euclid.

Following the guiding thread of the categories, he
declares that the aesthetical judgment about Beauty
is according to *quality* disinterested: a point which
had been laid down by such different writers
as Hutcheson and Moses Mendelssohn. As to
quantity, the judgment about beauty gives universal
satisfaction, although it is based on no definite
concept. The universality is only subjective:
but still it is there. The maxim *Tribus que gustibus
voluptas* does not apply to the pleasure afforded by
a pure judgment about beauty. As to *relation*, the
characteristic of the object called beautiful is that it
betrays a purposiveness without definite purpose.
The pleasure is *a priori*, independent on the one
hand of the charms of sense or the emotions of mere
feeling, as Winckelmann had already declared: and
on the other hand is a pleasure quite distinct from
that taken which we feel when viewing perfection,
with which Wolff and Baumgarten had identified it.
By his distinction between free and dependent
beauty, which we also find in the pages of Hutcheson, Kant further develops his doctrine of the

freedom of the pure judgment of taste from the thraldom of concepts.

Finally, the satisfaction afforded by the contemplation of a beautiful object is a necessary satisfaction. This necessity is not, to be sure, theoretical like the necessity attaching to the Law of Causality; nor is it a practical necessity as is the need to assume the Moral Law as the guiding principle of conduct. But it may be called *exemplary*; that is, we may set up our satisfaction in a beautiful picture as setting an example to be followed by others. It is plain, however, that this can only be assumed under certain presuppositions. I We must presuppose the idea of a *sensus communis* or common sense in which all men share. As knowledge admits of being communicated to others, so also does the feeling for beauty. For the relation between the cognitive faculties requisite for Taste is also requisite for Intelligence or sound Understanding, and as we always presuppose the latter to be the same in others as in ourselves, so may we presuppose the former.

The analysis of the Sublime which follows that of the Beautiful is interesting and profound; indeed Schopenhauer regarded it as the best part of the Kritik of the Aesthetical Judgment. The general characteristics of our judgments about the Sublime are similar to those already laid down in the case of the Beautiful; but there are marked differences in the two cases. If the pleasure taken in beauty arises from a feeling of the purposiveness of the object in its relation to the subject, that in sublimity rather expresses a purposiveness of the subject in respect of the object. Nothing in nature is sublime; and the sublimity really resides in the mind and there alone. Indeed, as true Beauty is found, properly speaking, only in beauty of form, the idea of sublimity is excited rather by those objects which are formless and exhibit a violation of purpose.

A distinction not needed in the case of the Beautiful becomes necessary when we proceed to further analyse the Sublime. For in aesthetical judgments about the Beautiful the mind is in *restful* contemplation; but in the case of the Sublime a mental *movement* is excited (pp. 105 and 120). This movement, as it is pleasing, must involve a purposiveness in the harmony of the mental powers; and the purposiveness may be either in reference to the faculty of cognition or to that of desire. In the former case the sublime is called the Mathematical Sublime—the sublime of mere magnitude—the absolutely great; in the latter it is the sublime of power, the Dynamically Sublime. Gioberti, an Italian writer on the philosophy of Taste, has pushed this distinction so far as to find in it an explanation of the relation between Beauty and Sublimity. "The dynamical Sublime," he says, "creates the Beautiful; the mathematical Sublime contains it," a remark with which probably Kant would have no quarrel.

In both cases, however, we find that the feeling of the Sublime awakens in us a feeling of the supersensible destination of man. "The very capacity of conceiving the sublime," he tells us, "indicates a mental faculty that far surpasses every standard of sense." And to explain the necessity belonging to our judgments about the sublime, Kant points out that as we find ourselves compelled to postulate a *sensus communis* to account for the agreement of men in their appreciation of beautiful objects, so the principle underlying their consent in judging of the sublime is "the presupposition of the moral feeling in man." The feeling of the sublimity of our own moral destination is the necessary prerequisite for forming such judgments. The connection between Beauty and Goodness involved to a Greek in the double sense of the word καλόν is developed by Kant with keen insight. To feel interest in the beauty of Nature he regards as a mark of a moral disposition, though he will not admit that the same inference may be drawn as to the character of the art connoisseur (§ 42). But it is specially with reference to the connection between the capacity for appreciating the Sublime, and the moral feeling, that the originality of Kant's treatment becomes apparent.

The objects of nature, he continues, which we call sublime, inspire us with a feeling of pain rather than of pleasure ; as Lucretius has it—

> Me quaedam divina voluptas
> Percipit atque horror.

But this "horror" must not inspire actual fear. As no extraneous charm must mingle with the satisfaction felt in a beautiful object, if the judg-

ment about beauty is to remain pure; so in the
case of the sublime we must not be afraid of the
object which yet in certain aspects is fearful.

This conception of the feelings of sublimity
excited by the loneliness of an Alpine peak or the
grandeur of an earthquake is now a familiar one;
but it was not so in Kant's day. Switzerland had
not then become the recreation-ground of Europe;
and though natural beauty was a familiar topic with
poets and painters it was not generally recognised
that taste has also to do with the sublime. De
Saussure's *Travels*, Haller's poem *Die Alpen*, and
this work of Kant's mark the beginning of a new
epoch in our ways of looking at the sublime and
terrible aspects of Nature. And it is not a little
remarkable that the man who could write thus
feelingly about the emotions inspired by grand and
savage scenery, had never seen a mountain in
his life. The power and the insight of his
observations here are in marked contrast to the
poverty of some of his remarks about the characteristics of beauty. For instance, he puts forward the
curious doctrine that colour in a picture is only an
extraneous charm, and does not really add to the
beauty of the form delineated, nay rather distracts
the mind from it. His criticisms on this point, if
sound, would make Flaxman a truer artist than
Titian or Paolo Veronese. But indeed his discussion
of Painting or Music is not very appreciative; he
was, to the end, a creature of pure Reason.

Upon the analysis he gives of the Arts, little

need be said here. Fine Art is regarded as the
Art of Genius, "that innate mental disposition
through which Nature gives the rule to Art" (§ 46).
Art differs from Science in the absence of definite
concepts in the mind of the artist. It thus happens
that the great artist can rarely communicate his
methods ; indeed he cannot explain them even to
himself. *Poeta nascitur, non fit* ; and the same is
true in every form of fine art. Genius is, in short,
the faculty of presenting aesthetical Ideas ; an
aesthetical Idea being an intuition of the Imagination, to which no concept is adequate. And it
is by the excitation of such ineffable Ideas that a
great work of art affects us.] As Bacon tells us,
"that is the best part of Beauty which a picture
cannot express ; no, nor the first sight of the eye."
This characteristic of the artistic genius has been
noted by all who have thought upon art ; more is
present in its productions than can be perfectly
expressed in language. As Pliny said of Timanthus
the painter of Iphigenia, "In omnibus ejus operibus
intelligitur plus super quam pingitur." But this
genius requires to be kept in check by taste ; quite
in the spirit of the σωφροσύνη of the best Greek art,
Kant remarks that if in a work of art some feature
must be sacrificed, it is better to lose something of
genius than to violate the canons of taste. It is in
this self-mastery that "the sanity of true genius"
expresses itself.

The main question with which the Kritik of
Judgment is concerned is, of course, the question as

to the purposiveness, the *Zweckmässigkeit*, exhibited
by nature. That nature appears to be full of
purpose is mere matter of fact. It displays purposiveness in respect of our faculties of cognition,
in those of its phenomena which we designate
beautiful. And also in its organic products we
observe methods of operation which we can only
explain by describing them as processes in which
means are used to accomplish certain ends, as
processes that are *purposive.* ⟨In our observation
of natural phenomena, as Kuno Fischer puts it, we
judge their *forms* aesthetically, and their *life* teleologically.⟩

As regards the first kind of *Zweckmässigkeit*,
that which is *ohne Zweck*—the purposiveness of a
beautiful object which does not seem to be directed
to any external end—there are two ways in which we
may account for it. We may either say that it was
actually designed to be beautiful by the Supreme
Force behind Nature, or we may say that purposiveness is not really resident in nature, but that our
perception of it is due to the subjective needs of our
judging faculty. We have to contemplate beautiful
objects *as if* they were purposive, but they may not
be so in reality. And this latter idealistic doctrine is
what Kant falls back upon. He appeals in support
of it, to the phenomena of crystallisation (pp. 243
sqq.), in which many very beautiful forms seem
to be produced by merely mechanical processes.
The beauty of a rock crystal is apparently produced
without any forethought on the part of nature, and

he urges that we are not justified in asserting
dogmatically that any laws distinct from those of
mechanism are needed to account for beauty in
other cases. Mechanism can do so much ; may it
not do all ? And he brings forward as a consideration which ought to settle the question, the fact that
in judging of beauty " we invariably seek its gauge
in ourselves a priori " ; we do not learn from nature,
but from ourselves, what we are to find beautiful.
Mr. Kennedy in his Donnellan Lectures has here
pointed out several weak spots in Kant's armour. In
the first place, the fact that we seek the gauge of
beauty in our own mind "may be shown from his
own definition to be a necessary result of the very
nature of beauty." [1] For Kant tells us that the
aesthetical judgment about beauty always involves
"a reference of the representation to the subject" ;
and this applies equally to judgments about the
beautiful in Art and the beautiful in Nature. But
no one could maintain that from this definition it
follows that we are not compelled to postulate design
in the mind of the artist who paints a beautiful
picture. And thus as the fact that "we always seek
the gauge of beauty " in ourselves does not do away
with the belief in a designing mind when we are
contemplating works of art, it cannot be said to
exclude the belief in a Master Hand which moulded
the forms of Nature. As Cicero has it, nature is
"non artificiosa solum, sed plane artifex." But the
cogency of this reasoning, for the details of which I

[1] *Natural Theology and Modern Thought*, p. 158.

must refer the reader to Mr. Kennedy's pages, becomes more apparent when we reflect on that second form of purposiveness, viz. adaptation to definite ends, with which we meet in the phenomena of organic life.

If we watch, *e.g.*, the growth of a tree we perceive that its various parts are not isolated and unconnected, but that on the contrary they are only possible by reference to the idea of the whole. Each limb affects every other, and is reciprocally affected by it; in short "in such a product of nature every part not only exists *by means of* the other parts, but is thought as existing *for the sake of* the others and the whole" (p. 277). The operations of nature in organised bodies seem to be of an entirely different character from mere mechanical processes; we cannot construe them to ourselves except under the hypothesis that nature in them is working towards a designed end. The distinction between nature's "Technic" or purposive operation, and nature's Mechanism is fundamental for the explanation of natural law. The language of biology eloquently shows the impossibility of eliminating at least the *idea* of purpose from our investigations into the phenomena of life, growth, and reproduction. And Kant dismisses with scant respect that cheap and easy philosophy which would fain deny the distinctiveness of nature's purposive operation. A doctrine, like that of Epicurus, in which every natural phenomenon is regarded as the result of the blind drifting of atoms in accordance with purely mechanical laws,

really explains nothing, and least of all explains
that illusion in our teleological judgments which
leads us to assume purpose where really there is
none.

It has been urged by Kirchmann and others
that this distinction between Technic and Mechanism,
on which Kant lays so much stress, has been dis-
proved by the progress of modern science. The
doctrines, usually associated with the name of
Darwin, of Natural Selection and Survival of the
Fittest, quite sufficiently explain, it is said, on
mechanical principles the semblance of purpose with
which nature mocks us. The presence of order is
not due to any purpose behind the natural operation,
but to the inevitable disappearance of the disorderly.
It would be absurd, of course, to claim for Kant
that he anticipated the Darwinian doctrines of
development ; and yet passages are not wanting in
his writings in which he takes a view of the con-
tinuity of species with which modern science would
have little fault to find. "Nature organises itself
and its organised products in every species, no
doubt after one general pattern but yet with suitable
deviations, which self-preservation demands according to circumstances" (p. 279). "The analogy of
forms, which with all their differences seem to have
been produced according to a common original type,
strengthens our suspicions of an actual relationship
between them in their production from a common
parent. through the gradual approximation of one
animal genus to another—from those in which the

principle of purposes seems to be best authenticated, *i.e.* from man, down to the polype and again from this down to mosses and lichens, and finally to crude matter. And so the whole Technic of nature, which is so incomprehensible to us in organised beings that we believe ourselves compelled to think a different principle for it, seems to be derived from matter and its powers according to mechanical laws (like those by which it works in the formation of crystals) " (p. 337). Such a theory he calls " a daring venture of reason," and its coincidences with modern science are real and striking. But he is careful to add that such a theory, even if established, would not eliminate purpose from the universe; it would indeed suggest that certain special processes having the semblance of purpose may be elucidated on mechanical principles, but on the whole, purposive operation on the part of Mother Nature it would still be needful to assume (p. 338). "No finite Reason can hope to understand the production of even a blade of grass by mere mechanical causes" (p. 326). "It is absurd to hope that another Newton will arise in the future who shall make comprehensible by us the production of a blade of grass according to natural laws which no design has ordered" (p. 312).

Crude materialism thus affording no explanation of the purposiveness in nature, we go on to ask what other theories are logically possible. We may dismiss at once the doctrine of Hylozoism, according to which the purposes in nature are explained

in reference to a world-soul, which is the inner
principle of the material universe and constitutes its
life.   For such a doctrine is self-contradictory, inasmuch as lifelessness, *inertia*, is the essential characteristic of matter, and to talk of living matter is
absurd (p. 304).   A much more plausible system is
that of Spinoza, who aimed at establishing the ideality
of the principle of natural purposes.   He regarded
the world whole as a complex of manifold determinations inhering in a single simple substance; and
thus reduced our concepts of the purposive in nature
to our own consciousness of existing in an all-embracing Being.   But on reflection we see that this
does not so much explain as explain away the purposiveness of nature; it gives us an unity of inherence *in* one Substance, but not an unity of causal
dependence *on* one Substance (p. 303).   And this
latter would be necessary in order to explain the
unity of purpose which nature exhibits in its phenomenal working.   Spinozism, therefore, does not give
what it pretends to give ; it puts us off with a vague
and unfruitful unity of ground, when what we seek
is an unity that shall itself contain the causes of the
differences manifest in nature.

We have left then as the only remaining possible
doctrine, Theism, which represents natural purposes
as produced in accordance with the Will and Design
of an Intelligent Author and Governor of Nature.
This theory is, in the first place, "superior to all
other grounds of explanation" (p. 305), for it gives
a full solution of the problem before us and enables

us to maintain the reality of the *Zweckmässigkeit* of nature. "Teleology finds the consummation of its investigations only in Theology" (p. 311). To represent the world and the natural purposes therein as produced by an intelligent Cause is "completely satisfactory from every human point of view for both the speculative and practical use of our Reason" (p. 312). Thus the contemplation of natural purposes, *i.e.* the common Argument from Design, enables us to reach a highest Understanding as Cause of the world "in accordance with the principles of the reflective Judgment, *i.e. in accordance with the constitution of our human faculty of cognition*" (p. 416).

It is in this qualifying clause that Kant's negative attitude in respect of Theism betrays itself. He regards it as a necessary assumption for the guidance of scientific investigation, no less than for the practical needs of morals ; but he does not admit that we can claim for it objective validity. In the language of the Kritik of Pure Reason, the Idea of God furnishes a regulative, not a constitutive principle of Reason ; or as he prefers to put it in the present work, it is valid only for the reflective, not for the determinant Judgment. We are not justified, Kant maintains, in asserting dogmatically that God exists ; there is only permitted to us the limited formula "We cannot otherwise conceive the purposiveness which must lie at the basis of our cognition of the internal possibility of many natural things, than by representing it and the world in general as produced by an intelligent cause, *i.e.* a God" (p. 312).

We ask then, whence arises this impossibility of objective statement? It is in the true Kantian spirit to assert that no synthetical proposition can be made with reference to what lies above and behind the world of sense; but there is a difficulty in carrying out this principle into details. Kant's refusal to infer a designing Hand behind the apparent order of nature is based, he tells us, on the fact that the concept of a "natural purpose" is one that cannot be justified to the speculative Reason. For all we know it may only indicate our way of looking at things, and may point to no corresponding objective reality. That we are forced by the limited nature of our faculties to view nature as working towards ends, as purposive, does not prove that it is really so. We cannot justify such pretended insight into what is behind the veil.

It is to be observed, however, that precisely similar arguments might be · urged against our affirmation of purpose, design, will, as the spring of the actions of other human beings.[1] For let us consider why it is that, mind being assumed as the basis of our own individual consciousness, we go on to attribute minds of like character to other men. We see that the external behaviour of other men is similar to our own, and that the most reasonable way of accounting for such behaviour is to suppose

---

[1] I reproduce here in part a paper read before the Victoria Institute in April 1892.

that they have minds like ourselves, that they are possessed of an active and spontaneously energising faculty, which is the seat of their personality. But it is instructive to observe that neither on Kantian principles nor on any other can we *demonstrate* this ; to cross the chasm which separates one man's personality from another's requires a venture of faith just as emphatically as any theological formula. I can by no means *prove* to the determinant Judgment that the complex of sensations which I constantly experience, and which I call the Prime Minister, is anything more than a well-ordered machine. It is improbable that this is the case— highly improbable ; but the falsity of such an hypothesis cannot be proved in the same way that we would prove the falsity of the assertion that two and two make five. But then though the hypothesis cannot be thus ruled out of court by demonstration of its absurdity, it is not the simplest hypothesis, nor is it that one which best accounts for the facts. The assumption, on the other hand, that the men whom I meet every day have minds like my own, perfectly accounts for all the facts, and is a very simple assumption. It merely extends by induction the sphere of a force which I already know to exist. Or in other words, crude materialism not giving me an intelligent account of my own individual consciousness, I recognise mind, νοῦς, as a *vera causa*, as something which really does produce effects in the field of experience, and which therefore I may legitimately put forward as the cause of those actions

of other men which externally so much resemble my
own. But, as has been said before, this argument,
though entirely convincing to any sane person, is not
demonstrative ; in Kantian language and on Kantian
principles the reasoning here used would seem to be
valid only for the reflective and not for the determinant Judgment. If the principle of design or
conscious adaptation of means to ends be not a
constitutive principle of experience, but only a
regulative principle introduced to account for the
facts, what right have we to put it forward dogmatically as affording an explanation of the actions
of other human beings ?

It cannot be said that Kant's attempted answer
to such a defence of the Design Argument is quite
conclusive. In § 90 of the *Methodology* (p. 309) he
pleads that though it is perfectly legitimate to argue
by analogy from our own minds to the minds of
other men, nay further, although we may conclude
from those actions of the lower animals which
display plan, that they are not, as Descartes alleged,
mere machines—yet it is not legitimate to conclude
from the apparent presence of design in the operations of nature that a conscious mind directs those
operations. For, he argues, that in comparing the
actions of men and the lower animals, or in comparing
the actions of one man with those of another, we are
not pressing our analogy beyond the limits of experience. Men and beasts alike are finite living beings,
subject to the limitations of finite existence ; and
hence the law which governs the one series of

operations may be regarded by analogy as sufficiently explaining the other series. But the power at the basis of Nature is utterly above definition or comprehension, and we are going beyond our legitimate province if we venture to ascribe to it a mode of operation with which we are only conversant in the case of beings subject to the conditions of space and time. He urges in short that when speaking about man and his mind we thoroughly understand what we are talking about; but in speaking of the Mind of Deity we are dealing with something of which we have no experience, and of which therefore we have no right to predicate anything.

But it is apparent that, as has been pointed out, even when we infer the existence of another finite mind from certain observed operations, we are making an inference about something which is as mysterious an x as anything can be. Mind is not a thing that is subject to the laws and conditions of the world of sense; it is "*in* the world but not *of* the world." And so to infer the existence of the mind of any individual except myself is a quite different kind of inference from that by which, for example, we infer the presence of an electro-magnet in a given field. The action of the latter we understand to a large extent; but we do not understand the action of mind, which yet we know from daily experience of ourselves does produce effects in the phenomenal world, often permanent and important effects. Briefly, the action of mind upon matter (to use the ordinary phraseology for the sake of clearness) is—we may assume for our present purpose—an established fact. Hence the causality of mind is a *vera causa*; we bring it in to account for the actions of other human beings, and by precisely the same process of reasoning we invoke it to explain the operations of nature.

And it is altogether beside the point to urge, as Kant does incessantly, that in the latter case the intelligence inferred is *infinite*; in the former only *finite*. All that the Design Argument undertakes to prove is that mind lies at the basis of nature. It is quite beyond its province to say whether this mind is finite or infinite; and thus Kant's criticisms on p. 364 are somewhat wide of the mark. There is always a difficulty in any argument which tries to establish the operation of mind anywhere, for mind cannot be seen or touched or felt; but the difficulty is not peculiar to that particular form of argument with which theological interests are involved.

The real plausibility of this objection arises from a vague idea, often present to us when we speak of *infinite* wisdom or *infinite* intelligence, namely that the epithet *infinite* in some way alters the meaning of the attributes to which it is applied. But the truth is that the word *infinite*, when applied to wisdom or knowledge or any other intellectual or moral quality, can only properly have reference to the number of acts of wisdom or knowledge that we suppose to have been performed. The only sense in which we have any right to speak of *infinite*

wisdom is that it is that which performs an infinite
number of wise acts. And so when we speak of
infinite *intelligence*, we have not the slightest warrant,
either in logic or in common sense, for supposing
that such intelligence is not similar in kind to that
finite intelligence which we know in man.

To understand Kant's attitude fully, we must
also take into consideration the great weight that
he attaches to the Moral Argument for the existence of God. The positive side of his teaching on Theism is summed up in the following
sentence (p. 388) : "For the theoretical reflective
Judgment physical Teleology sufficiently proves
from the purposes of Nature an intelligent world-
cause ; for the practical Judgment moral Teleology
establishes it by the concept of a final purpose,
which it is forced to ascribe to creation." That
side of his system which is akin to Agnosticism
finds expression in his determined refusal to admit
anything more than this. The existence of God is
for him a "thing of faith"; and is not a fact of knowledge, strictly so called. "Faith" he holds (p. 409)
"is the moral attitude of Reason as to belief in
that which is unattainable by theoretical cognition.
It is therefore the permanent principle of the mind
to assume as true that which it is necessary to presuppose as condition of the possibility of the highest
moral final purpose." As he says elsewhere (Introduction to Logic, ix. p. 60), "That man is morally
unbelieving who does not accept that which, though
impossible to know, is *morally necessary* to suppose."

And as far as he goes a Theist may agree with
him, and he has done yeoman's service to Theism by
his insistence on the absolute impossibility of any
other working hypothesis as an explanation of the
phenomena of nature. But I have endeavoured to
indicate at what points he does not seem to me to
have gone as far as even his own declared principles
would justify him in going. If the existence of a
Supreme Mind be a "thing of faith," this may with
equal justice be said of the finite minds of the men
all around us; and his attempt to show that the
argument from analogy is here without foundation is
not convincing.

Kant, however, in the Kritik of Judgment is
sadly fettered by the chains that he himself had
forged, and frequently chafes under the restraints
they impose. He indicates more than once a point
of view higher than that of the Kritik of Pure Reason,
from which the phenomena of life and mind may be
contemplated. He had already hinted in that work
that the supersensible substrate of the ego and the
non-ego might be identical. " Both kinds of objects
differ from each other, not internally, but only so far
as the one *appears* external to the other; possibly
what is at the basis of phenomenal matter as a thing
in itself may not be so heterogeneous after all as we
imagine."[1] This hypothesis which remains a bare
undeveloped possibility in the earlier work is put
forward as a positive doctrine in the Kritik of Judgment. "There must," says Kant, "be a ground

---

[1] Kritik of *Pure Reason*. Dialectic, Bk. ii. chap. i. near the end.

of the *unity* of the supersensible, which lies at the basis of nature, with that which the concept of freedom practically contains" (Introduction, p. 12). That is to say, he maintains that to explain the phenomena of organic life and the purposiveness of nature we must hold that the world of sense is not disparate from and opposed to the world of thought, but that *nature is the development of freedom.* The connection of nature and freedom is suggested by, nay is involved in, the notion of natural adaptation : and although we can arrive at no knowledge of the supersensible substrate of both, yet such a common ground there must be. This principle is the starting point of the systems which followed that of Kant ; and the philosophy of later Idealism is little more than a development of the principle in its consequences.

He approaches the same doctrine by a different path in the Kritik of the Teleological Judgment (§ 77), where he argues that the distinction between the mechanical and the teleological working of nature, upon which so much stress has been justly laid, depends for its validity upon the peculiar character of our Understanding. When we give what may be called a mechanical elucidation of any natural phenomenon, we begin with its parts, and from what we know of them we explain the whole. But in the case of certain objects, *e.g.* organised bodies, this cannot be done. In their case we can only account for the parts by a reference to the whole. Now, were it possible for us to perceive a whole before its parts and derive the latter from the former,[1] then an organism would be capable of being understood and would be an object of knowledge in the strictest sense. But our Understanding is not able to do this, and its inadequacy for such a task leads us to conceive the possibility of an Understanding, not discursive like ours, but intuitive, for which knowledge of the whole would precede that of the parts. " It is at least possible to consider the material world as mere phenomenon, and to think as its substrate something like a thing in itself (which is not phenomenon), and to attach to this a corresponding intellectual intuition. Thus there would be, although incognisable by us, a supersensible real ground for nature, to which we ourselves belong " (p. 325). Hence, although Mechanism and Technic must not be confused and must ever stand side by side in our scientific investigation of natural law, yet must they be regarded as coalescing in a single higher principle incognisable by us. The ground of union is "the supersensible substrate of nature of which we can determine nothing positively, except that it is the being in itself of which we merely know the phenomenon." Thus, then, it appears that the whole force of Kant's main argument has proceeded upon an assumption, viz. the permanent opposition between Sense and Understanding, which the progress of the argument has shown to be unsound. " Kant seems," says Goethe,[2]

---

[1] Cf. Kuno Fischer, A Critique of Kant, p. 142.

[2] Quoted by Caird, Critical Philosophy of Kant, vol. ii. p. 507,

"to have woven a certain element of irony into his method. For, while at one time he seemed to be bent on limiting our faculties of knowledge in the narrowest way, at another time he pointed, as it were with a side gesture, beyond the limits which he himself had drawn." The fact of adaptation of means to ends observable in nature seems to break down the barrier between Nature and Freedom; and if we once relinquish the distinction between Mechanism and Technic in the operations of nature we are led to the Idea of an absolute Being, who manifests Himself by action which, though necessary, is yet the outcome of perfect freedom.

Kant, however, though he approaches such a position more than once, can never be said to have risen to it. He deprecates unceasingly the attempt to combine principles of nature with the principles of freedom as a task beyond the modest capacity of human reason; and while strenuously insisting on the practical force of the Moral Argument for the Being of God, which is found in the witness of man's conscience, will not admit that it can in any way be regarded as strengthening the theoretical arguments adduced by Teleology. The two lines of proof, he holds, are quite distinct; and nothing but confusion and intellectual disaster can result from the effort to combine them. The moral proof stands by itself, and it needs no such crutches as the argument from Design can offer. But, as

who reiterates this criticism all through his account of Kant's teaching.

Mr. Kennedy has pointed out in his acute criticism [1] of the Kantian doctrine of Theism, it would not be possible to combine a theoretical *disbelief* in God with a frank acceptance of the practical belief of His existence borne in upon us by the Moral Law. Kant himself admits this : "A dogmatical *unbelief*," he says (p. 411), "cannot subsist together with a moral maxim dominant in the mental attitude." That is, though the theoretical argument be incomplete, we cannot reject the conclusion to which it leads, for this is confirmed by the moral necessities of conscience.

Kant's position, then, seems to come to this, that though he never doubts the existence of God, he has very grave doubts that He can be theoretically known by man. *That* he is, is certain ; *what* he is, we cannot determine. It is a position not dissimilar to current Agnostic doctrines ; and as long as the antithesis between Sense and Understanding, between Matter and Mind, is insisted upon as expressing a real and abiding truth, Kant's reasoning can hardly be refuted with completeness. No doubt it may be urged that since the practical and theoretical arguments both arrive at the same conclusion, the cogency of our reasoning in the latter should confirm our trust in the former. But true conclusions may sometimes seem to follow from quite insufficient premises ; and Kant is thus justified in demanding that each argument shall be submitted to independent tests. I have en-

[1] *Natural Theology and Modern Thought,* p. 241.

deavoured to show above that he has not treated
the theoretical line of reasoning quite fairly, and that ·
he has underestimated its force ; but its value *as an
argument* is not increased by showing that another
entirely different process of thought leads to the
same result. And that the witness of conscience
affords the most powerful and convincing argument
for the existence of a Supreme Being, the source of
law as of love, is a simple matter of experience.
Induction, syllogism, analogy, do not really generate
belief in God, though they may serve to justify to
reason a faith that we already possess. The poet
has the truth of it :

> Wer Gott nicht fühlt in allen Lebenskreisen,
> Dem werdet Ihr Ihn nicht beweisen mit Beweisen.

I give at the end of this Introduction a Glossary
of the chief philosophical terms used by Kant; I
have tried to render them by the same English
equivalents all through the work, in order to preserve, as far as may be, the exactness of expression
in the original. I am conscious that this makes the
translation clumsy in many places, but have thought
it best to sacrifice elegance to precision. This
course is the more necessary to adopt, as Kant
cannot be understood unless his nice verbal distinctions be attended to. Thus *real* means quite a
different thing from *wirklich* ; *Hang* from *Neigung* ;
Rührung from *Affekt* or *Leidenschaft* ; *Anschauung*
from *Empfindung* or *Wahrnehmung* ; *Endzweck* from

letzter Zweck; *Idee* from *Vorstellung*; *Eigenschaft*
from *Attribut* or *Beschaffenheit*; *Schranke* from
Grenze; *überreden* from *überzeugen*, etc.   I am not
satisfied with "gratification" and "grief" as the
English equivalents for *Vergnügen* and *Schmerz*; but
it is necessary to distinguish these words from *Lust*
and *Unlust*, and "mental pleasure," "mental pain,"
which would nearly hit the sense, are awkward.
Again, the constant rendering of *schön* by beautiful
involves the expression "beautiful art" instead of the
more usual phrase "fine art."   *Purposive* is an ugly
word, but it has come into use lately; and its employment enables us to preserve the connection between
Zweck and *zweckmässig*.   I have printed *Judgment*
with a capital letter when it signifies the *faculty*,
with a small initial when it signifies the *act*, of
judging.   And in like manner I distinguish *Objekt*
from *Gegenstand*, by printing the word "Object"
when it represents the former with a large initial.

The text I have followed is, in the main, that
printed by Hartenstein; but occasionally Rosenkranz
preserves the better reading.   All important variants
between the First and Second Editions have been
indicated at the foot of the page.   A few notes have
been added, which are enclosed in square brackets,
to distinguish them from those which formed part of
the original work.   I have in general quoted Kant's
Introduction to Logic and *Kritik of Practical Reason*
in Dr. Abbott's translations.

My best thanks are due to Rev. J. H. Kennedy
and Mr. F. Purser for much valuable aid during

the passage of this translation through the press. And I am under even greater obligations to Mr. Mahaffy, who was good enough to read through the whole of the proof; by his acute and learned criticisms many errors have been avoided. Others I have no doubt still remain, but for these I must be accounted alone responsible.

J. H. BERNARD.

TRINITY COLLEGE, DUBLIN,
May 24, 1892.

GLOSSARY OF KANT'S PHILOSOPHICAL TERMS

Absicht ; *design.*
Achtung ; *respect.*
Affekt ; *affection.*
Angenehm ; *pleasant.*
Anschauung ; *intuition.*
Attribut ; *attribute.*
Aufklärung ; *enlightenment.*

Begehr ; *desire.*
Begriff ; *concept.*
Beschaffenheit ; *constitution* or *characteristic.*
Bestimmen ; *to determine.*

Darstellen ; *to present.*
Dasein ; *presence* or *being.*

Eigenschaft ; *property.*
Empfindung ; *sensation.*
Endzweck ; *final purpose.*
Erkenntniss ; *cognition* or *knowledge.*
Erklärung ; *explanation.*
Erscheinung ; *phenomenon.*
Existenz ; *existence.*

Fürwahrhalten ; *belief.*

Gebiet ; *realm.*
Gefühl ; *feeling.*
Gegenstand ; *object.*
Geist ; *spirit.*
Geniessen ; *enjoyment.*
Geschicklichkeit ; *skill.*
Geschmack ; *Taste.*

Gesetzmässigkeit ; *conformity to law.*
Gewalt ; *dominion* or *authority.*
Glaube ; *faith.*
Grenze ; *bound.*
Grundsatz ; *fundamental proposition* or *principle.*

Hang ; *propension.*

Idee ; *Idea.*

Leidenschaft ; *passion.*
Letzter Zweck ; *ultimate purpose.*
Lust ; *pleasure.*

Meinen ; *opinion.*

Neigung ; *inclination.*

Objekt ; *Object.*

Prinzip ; *principle.*

Real ; *real.*
Reich ; *kingdom.*
Reiz ; *charm.*
Rührung ; *emotion.*

Schein ; *illusion.*
Schmerz ; *grief.*
Schön ; *beautiful.*
Schranke ; *limit.*
Schwärmerei ; *fanaticism.*
Seele : *soul.*

Ueberreden ; *to persuade.*
Ueberschwänglich ; *transcendent.*
Ueberzeugen ; *to convince.*
Unlust ; *pain.*
Urtheil ; *judgment.*
Urtheilskraft ; *Judgment.*

Verbindung ; *combination.*
Vergnügen ; *gratification.*
Verknüpfung ; *connection.*
Vermögen ; *faculty.*
Vernunft ; *Reason.*
Vernünftelei ; *sophistry* or *subtlety.*
Verstand ; *Understanding* or *intelligence.*

Vorstellung ; *representation.*

Wahrnehmung ; *perception.*
Wesen ; *being.*
Willkühr ; *elective will.*
Wirklich ; *actual.*
Wohlgefallen ; *satisfaction.*

Zufriedenheit ; *contentment.*
Zweck ; *purpose.*
Zweckmässig ; *purposive.*
Zweckverbindung ; *purposive combination,* etc.

PREFACE

WE may call the faculty of cognition from principles *a priori*, *pure Reason*, and the inquiry into its possibility and bounds generally the Kritik of pure Reason, although by this faculty we only understand Reason in its theoretical employment, as it appears under that name in the former work ; without wishing to inquire into its faculty, as practical Reason, according to its special principles. That [Kritik] goes merely into our faculty of knowing things *a priori*, and busies itself therefore only with the *cognitive faculty* to the exclusion of the feeling of pleasure and pain and the faculty of desire ; and of the cognitive faculties it only concerns itself with *Understanding*, according to its principles *a priori*, to the exclusion of *Judgment* and *Reason* (as faculties alike belonging to theoretical cognition), because it is found in the sequel that no other cognitive faculty but the Understanding can furnish constitutive principles of cognition *a priori*. The Kritik, then, which sifts them all, as regards the share which each of the other faculties might pretend to have in the unmixed possession of knowledge from its own peculiar root, leaves nothing but what the *Understanding* prescribes *a priori* as law for nature as the complex of phenomena (whose form also is given *a priori*). It relegates all other pure con-

B

cepts under Ideas, which are transcendent for our theoretical faculty of cognition, but are not therefore useless or to be dispensed with. For they serve as regulative principles; partly to check the dangerous pretensions of Understanding, as if it (because it can furnish *a priori* the conditions of the possibility of all things which it can know) had thereby confined within these bounds the possibility of all things in general; and partly to lead it to the consideration of nature according to a principle of completeness, although it can never attain to this, and thus to further the final design of all knowledge.

It was then properly the *Understanding* which has its special realm in the *cognitive faculty*, so far as it contains constitutive principles of cognition *a priori*, which by the Kritik, generally called the Kritik of pure Reason, was to be placed in certain but sole possession against all other competitors. And so also to *Reason*, which contains constitutive principles *a priori* nowhere except simply in respect of the *faculty of desire*, should be assigned its place in the Kritik of practical Reason.

Whether now the *Judgment*, which in the order of our cognitive faculties forms a mediating link between Understanding and Reason, has also principles *a priori* for itself; whether these are constitutive or merely regulative (thus pointing out no special realm); and whether they give a rule *a priori* to the feeling of pleasure and pain, as the mediating link between the cognitive faculty and the faculty of desire (just as the Understanding prescribes laws *a priori* to the first, Reason to the second); these are the questions with which the present Kritik of Judgment is concerned.

A Kritik of pure Reason, *i.e.* of our faculty of judging *a priori* according to principles, would be incomplete, if the Judgment, which as a cognitive faculty also makes claim to such principles, were not treated as a particular part of it; although its principles in a system of pure Philosophy need form no particular part between the theoretical and the practical, but can be annexed when needful to one or both as occasion requires. For if such a system is one day to be completed under the general name of Metaphysic (which it is possible to achieve quite completely, and which is supremely important for the use of Reason in every reference), the soil for the edifice must be explored by Kritik as deep down as the foundation of the faculty of principles independent of experience, in order that it may sink in no part, for this would inevitably bring about the downfall of the whole.

We can easily infer from the nature of the Judgment (whose right use is so necessarily and so universally requisite, that by the name of sound Understanding nothing else but this faculty is meant), that it must be attended with great difficulties to find a principle peculiar to it; (some such it must contain *a priori* in itself, for otherwise it would not be set apart by the commonest Kritik as a special cognitive faculty). This principle must not be derived *a priori* from concepts, for these belong to the Understanding, and Judgment is only concerned with their application. It must, therefore, furnish of itself a concept, through which, properly speaking, no thing is cognised, but which only serves as a rule, though not an objective one to which it can adapt its judgment; because for this latter another faculty of Judgment would be requisite, in order to be able to distinguish whether [any given case] is or is not the case for the rule.

This perplexity about a principle (whether it is subjective or objective) presents itself mainly in those judgments that we call æsthetical, which concern the Beautiful and the Sublime of Nature or of Art. And, nevertheless, the critical investigation of a principle of Judgment in these is the most important part of a Kritik of this faculty. For although they do not by themselves contribute to the knowledge of things, yet they belong to the cognitive faculty alone, and point to an immediate reference of this faculty to the feeling of pleasure or pain according to some principle *a priori*; without confusing this with what may be the determining ground of the faculty of desire, which has its principles *a priori* in concepts of Reason.— In the logical judging of nature, experience exhibits a conformity to law in things, to the understanding or to the explanation of which the general concept of the sensible does not attain ; here the Judgment can only derive from itself a principle of the reference of the natural thing to the unknowable supersensible (a principle which it must only use from its own point of view for the cognition of nature). And so, though in this case such a principle *a priori* can and must be applied to the *cognition* of the beings of the world, and opens out at the same time prospects which are advantageous for the practical Reason, yet it has no immediate reference to the feeling of pleasure and pain. But this reference is precisely the puzzle in the principle of Judgment, which renders a special section for this faculty necessary in the Kritik : since the logical judging according to concepts (from which an immediate inference can never be drawn to the feeling of pleasure and pain) along with their critical limitation, has at all events been capable of being appended to the theoretical part of Philosophy.

The examination of the faculty of taste, as the æsthetical Judgment, is not here planned in reference to the formation or the culture of taste (for this will take its course in the future as in the past without any such investigations), but merely in a transcendental point of view. Hence, I trust that as regards the deficiency of the former purpose it will be judged with indulgence, though in the latter point of view it must be prepared for the severest scrutiny. But I hope that the great difficulty of solving a problem so involved by nature may serve as excuse for some hardly avoidable obscurity in its solution, if only it be clearly established that the principle is correctly stated. I grant that the mode of deriving the phenomena of the Judgment from it has not all the clearness which might be rightly demanded elsewhere, viz., in the case of cognition according to concepts ; but I believe that I have attained to it in the second part of this work.

Here then I end my whole critical undertaking. I shall proceed without delay to the doctrinal [part] in order to profit, as far as is possible, by the more favourable moments of my increasing years. It is obvious that in this [part] there will be no special section for the Judgment, because in respect of this faculty Kritik serves instead of Theory ; but, according to the division of Philosophy (and also of pure Philosophy) into theoretical and practical, the Metaphysic of Nature and of Morals will complete the undertaking.

INTRODUCTION

WE proceed quite correctly if, as usual, we divide
Philosophy, as containing the principles of the
rational cognition of things by means of concepts
(not merely, as logic does, principles of the form of
thought in general without distinction of objects),
into *theoretical* and *practical.* But then the concepts,
which furnish their object to the principles of this
rational cognition, must be specifically distinct ;
otherwise they would not justify a division, which
always presupposes a contrast between the principles
of the rational cognition belonging to the different
parts of a science.

Now there are only two kinds of concepts, and
these admit as many distinct principles of the
possibility of their objects, viz., *natural concepts*
and the *concept of freedom.* The former render
possible *theoretical* cognition according to principles
a priori; the latter in respect of this theoretical
cognition only supplies in itself a negative principle
(that of mere contrast), but on the other hand it
furnishes fundamental propositions which extend the
sphere of the determination of the will and are
therefore called practical. Thus Philosophy is
correctly divided into two parts, quite distinct in

their principles; the theoretical part or *Natural Philosophy*, and the practical part or *Moral Philosophy* (for that is the name given to the practical legislation of Reason in accordance with the concept of freedom). But up to the present a gross misuse of these expressions has prevailed, both in the division of the different principles and consequently also of Philosophy itself. For what is practical according to natural concepts has been identified with the practical according to the concept of freedom; and so with the like titles, 'theoretical' and 'practical' Philosophy, a division has been made, by which in fact nothing has been divided (for both parts might in such case have principles of the same kind).

The will, regarded as the faculty of desire, is in fact one of the many natural causes in the world, viz., that cause which acts in accordance with concepts. All that is represented as possible (or necessary) by means of a will is called practically possible (or necessary); as distinguished from the physical possibility or necessity of an effect, whose cause is not determined to causality by concepts (but in lifeless matter by mechanism and in animals by instinct). Here, in respect of the practical, it is left undetermined whether the concept which gives the rule to the causality of the will, is a natural concept or a concept of freedom.

But the last distinction is essential. For if the concept which determines the causality [of the will] is a natural concept, then the principles are *technically practical*; whereas, if it is a concept of freedom they are *morally practical*. And as the division of a rational science depends on the distinction between objects whose cognition needs distinct

principles, the former will belong to theoretical Philosophy (doctrine of Nature), but the latter alone
will constitute the second part, viz., practical Philosophy (doctrine of Morals).

All technically practical rules (*i.e.* the rules of art
and skill generally, or of sagacity regarded as skill
in exercising an influence over men and their wills),
so far as their principles rest on concepts, must be
reckoned only as corollaries to theoretical Philosophy.
For they concern only the possibility of things ac-
co ding to natural concepts, to which belong not
only the means which are to be met with in nature,
but also the will itself (as a faculty of desire and
consequently a natural faculty), so far as it can be
determined conformably to these rules by natural
motives. However, practical rules of this kind are
not called laws (like physical laws), but only precepts ; because the will does not stand merely under
the natural concept, but also under the concept of
freedom, in relation to which its principles are called
laws. These with their consequences alone constitute the second or practical part of Philosophy.

The solution of the problems of pure geometry
does not belong to a particular part of the science ;
mensuration does not deserve the name of practical,
in contrast to pure geometry, as a second part of
geometry in general; and just as little ought the
mechanical or chemical art of experiment or observation to be reckoned as a practical part of the
doctrine of Nature. Just as little, in fine, ought
housekeeping, farming, statesmanship, the art of
conversation, the prescribing of diet, the universal
doctrine of happiness itself, or the curbing of the
inclinations and checking of the affections for the
sake of happiness, to be reckoned as practical Philo-

sophy, or taken to constitute the second part of Philosophy in general. For all these contain only rules of skill (and are consequently only technically practical) for bringing about an effect that is possible according to the natural concepts of causes and effects, which, since they belong to theoretical Philosophy, are subject to those precepts as mere corollaries from it (viz., natural science), and can therefore claim no place in a special Philosophy called practical. On the other hand, the morally practical precepts, which are altogether based on the concept of freedom to the complete exclusion of the natural determining grounds of the will, constitute a quite special class. These, like the rules which nature obeys, are called simply laws, but they do not, like them, rest on sensuous conditions but on a supersensible principle; and accordingly they require for themselves a quite different part of Philosophy, called practical, corresponding to its theoretical part.

We hence see that a complex of practical precepts given by Philosophy does not constitute a distinct part of Philosophy, as opposed to the theoretical part, because these precepts are practical; for they might be that, even if their principles were derived altogether from the theoretical cognition of nature (as technically practical rules). [A distinct branch of Philosophy is constituted only] if their principle, as it is not borrowed from the natural concept which is always sensuously conditioned, rests on the supersensible, which alone makes the concept of freedom cognisable by formal laws. These precepts are then morally practical, *i.e.* not merely precepts or rules in this or that aspect, but, without any preceding reference to purposes and designs, are laws.

II. OF THE REALM OF PHILOSOPHY IN GENERAL

So far as our concepts have *a priori* application, so far extends the use of our cognitive faculty according to principles, and with it Philosophy.

But the complex of all objects, to which those concepts are referred, in order to bring about a knowledge of them where it is possible, may be subdivided according to the adequacy or inadequacy of our [cognitive] faculty with this design.

Concepts, so far as they are referred to objects, independently of the possibility or impossibility of the cognition of these objects, have their field which is determined merely according to the relation that their Object has to our cognitive faculty in general. The part of this field in which knowledge is possible for us is a ground or territory (*territorium*) for these concepts and the requisite cognitive faculty. The part of this territory, where they are legislative, is the realm (*ditio*) of these concepts and of the corresponding cognitive faculties. Empirical concepts have, therefore, their territory in nature, as the complex of all objects of sense, but no realm, only a dwelling-place (*domicilium*); for though they are produced in conformity to law they are not legislative, but the rules based on them are empirical and consequently contingent.

Our whole cognitive faculty has two realms, that of natural concepts and that of the concept of freedom; for through both it is legislative *a priori*. In accordance with this, Philosophy is divided into theoretical and practical. But the territory to which its realm extends and in which its legislation is *exercised*, is always only the complex of objects of all possible experience, so long as they are taken for

nothing more than mere phenomena ; for otherwise
no legislation of the Understanding in respect of
them is conceivable.

⟨ Legislation through natural concepts is carried
on by means of the Understanding and is theoretical.
Legislation through the concept of freedom is carried
on by the Reason and is merely practical.   It is only
in the practical [sphere] that the Reason can be
legislative ; in respect of theoretical cognition (of
nature) it can merely (as acquainted with law by the
Understanding) deduce from given laws consequences which always remain within [the limits of]
nature.   But on the other hand, Reason is not
always therefore *legislative*, where there are practical
rules, for they may be only technically practical.   ⟩

Understanding and Reason exercise, therefore,
two distinct legislations on one and the same
territory of experience, without prejudice to each
other.   The concept of freedom as little disturbs
the legislation of nature, as the natural concept influences the legislation through the former.— The
possibility of at least thinking without contradiction
the co-existence of both legislations, and of the corresponding faculties in the same subject, has been
shown in the Kritik of pure Reason ; whilst it has
annulled the objections to this [theory] by exposing
the dialectical illusion which they contain.

These two different realms then do not limit
each other in their legislation, though they perpetually do so in the world of sense.   That they
do not constitute *one* realm, arises from this, that
the natural concept represents its objects in intuition,
not as things in themselves, but as mere phenomena ;
the concept of freedom, on the other hand, represents in its Object a thing in itself, but not in

intuition. Hence, neither of them can furnish
a theoretical knowledge of its Object (or even of
the thinking subject) as a thing in itself; this would
be the supersensible, the Idea of which we must
indeed make the basis of the possibility of all these
objects of experience, but which we can never extend
or elevate into a cognition.

There is, then, an unbounded but also inacces-
sible field for our whole cognitive faculty—the field
of the supersensible—wherein we find no territory,
and, therefore, can have in it, for theoretical cognition, no realm either for concepts of Understanding
or Reason. · This field we must indeed occupy with
Ideas on behalf of the theoretical as well as the
practical use of Reason, but we can supply to them
in reference to the laws [arising] from the concept
of freedom no other than practical reality, by which
our theoretical cognition is not extended in the
slightest degree towards the supersensible.

Now even if an immeasurable gulf is fixed
between the sensible realm of the concept of nature
and the supersensible realm of the concept of freedom,
so that no transition is possible from the first to
the second (by means of the theoretical use of
Reason), just as if they were two different worlds
of which the first could have no influence upon
the second, yet the second is *meant* to have an influence upon the first. The concept of freedom is
meant to actualise in the world of sense the purpose
proposed by its laws, and consequently nature must
be so thought that the conformity to law of its form,
at least harmonises with the possibility of the
purposes to be effected in it according to laws of
freedom.— There must, therefore, be a ground of
the *unity* of the supersensible, which lies at the

basis of nature, with that which the concept of freedom practically contains; and the concept of this ground, although it does not attain either theoretically or practically to a knowledge of the same, and hence has no peculiar realm, nevertheless makes possible the transition from the mode of thought according to the principles of the one to that according to the principles of the other.

III. OF THE KRITIK OF JUDGMENT AS A MEANS OF COMBINING THE TWO PARTS OF PHILOSOPHY INTO A WHOLE.

The Kritik of the cognitive faculties, as regards what they can furnish *a priori*, has properly speaking no realm in respect of Objects, because it is not a doctrine, but only has to investigate whether and how, in accordance with the state of these faculties, a doctrine is possible by their means. Its field extends to all their pretensions, in order to confine them within their legitimate bounds. But what cannot enter into the division of Philosophy may yet enter, as a chief part, into the Kritik of the pure faculty of cognition in general, viz., if it contains principles which are available neither for theoretical nor for practical use.

The natural concepts, which contain the ground of all theoretical knowledge *a priori*, rest on the legislation of the Understanding.— The concept of freedom, which contains the ground of all sensuously-unconditioned practical precepts *a priori*, rests on the legislation of the Reason. Both faculties, therefore, besides being capable of application as regards their logical form to principles of whatever origin, have also as regards their content, their special

legislations above which there is no other (*a priori*) ;
and hence the division of Philosophy into theoretical
and practical is justified.

But in the family of the supreme cognitive
faculties there is a middle term between the Understanding and the Reason. This is the *Judgment*, of
which we have cause for supposing according to
analogy that it may contain in itself, if not a special
legislation, yet a special principle of its own to be
sought according to laws, though merely subjective
a priori. This principle, even if it have no field
of objects as its realm, yet may have somewhere a
territory with a certain character, for which no other
principle can be valid.

But besides (to judge by analogy) there is a
new ground for bringing the Judgment into connection with another arrangement of our representative faculties, which seems to be of even
greater importance than that of its relationship
with the family of the cognitive faculties. For all
faculties or capacities of the soul can be reduced to
three, which cannot be any further derived from one
common ground : the *faculty of knowledge*, the *feeling of pleasure and pain*, and the *faculty of desire*.[1]

---

[1] If we have cause for supposing that concepts which we use as
empirical principles stand in relationship with the pure cognitive
faculty *a priori*, it is profitable, because of this reference, to seek for
them a transcendental definition ; *i.e.*, a definition through pure categories, so far as these by themselves adequately furnish the distinction
of the concept in question from others. We here follow the example
of the mathematician who leaves undetermined the empirical data of
his problem, and only brings their relation in their pure synthesis
under the concepts of pure Arithmetic, and thus generalises the solution. Objection has been brought against a similar procedure of
mine (cf. the Preface to the Kritik of Practical Reason, *Abbott's Translation*, p. 94), and my definition of the faculty of desire has been
found fault with, viz., that it is [the being's] *faculty of becoming by
means of its representations the cause of the actuality of the objects of
these representations* ; for the desires might be mere *cravings*, and by

For the faculty of knowledge the Understanding is alone legislative, if (as must happen when it is considered by itself without confusion with the faculty of desire) this faculty is referred to nature as the faculty of *theoretical knowledge*; for in respect of nature (as phenomenon) it is alone possible for us to give laws by means of natural concepts *a priori*, *i.e.* by pure concepts of Understanding.— For the faculty of desire, as a supreme faculty according to the concept of freedom, the Reason (in which alone

means of these alone every one is convinced the Object cannot be produced.— But this proves nothing more than that there are desires in man, by which he is in contradiction with himself. For here he strives for the production of the Object by means of the representation *alone*, from which he can expect no result, because he is conscious that his mechanical powers (if I may so call those which are not psychological) which must be determined by that representation to bring about the Object (mediately) are either not competent, or even tend towards what is impossible ; *e.g.*, to reverse the past (*O mihi præteritos* . . . etc.), or to annihilate in the impatience of expectation the interval before the wished for moment.— Although in such fantastic desires we are conscious of the inadequacy (or even the unsuitability) of our representations for being *causes* of their objects, yet their reference as causes, and consequently the representation of their *causality*, is contained in every *wish* ; and this is peculiarly evident if the wish is an affection or *longing*. For these [longings] by their dilatation and contraction of the heart and consequent exhaustion of powers, prove that these powers are continually kept on the stretch by representations, but that they perpetually let the mind, having regard to the impossibility [of the desire], fall back in exhaustion. Even prayers [offered up] to avert great and (as far as one can see) unavoidable evils, and many superstitious means for attaining in a natural way impossible purposes, point to the causal reference of representations to their Objects ; a reference which cannot at all be checked by the consciousness of the inadequacy of the effort to produce the effect.— As to why there should be in our nature this propensity to desires which are consciously vain, that is an anthropologico-teleological problem. It seems that if we were not determined to the application of our powers before we were assured of the adequacy of our faculties to produce an Object, these powers would remain in great part unused. For we commonly learn to know our powers only by first making trial of them. This deception in the case of vain wishes is then only the consequence of a benevolent ordinance in our nature. [This note was added by Kant in the Second Edition.]

this concept has a place) is alone *a priori* legislative. Now between the faculties of knowledge and desire there is the feeling of pleasure, just as the Judgment mediates between the Understanding and the Reason. We may therefore suppose provisionally that the Judgment likewise contains in itself an *a priori* principle. And as pleasure or pain is necessarily combined with the faculty of desire (either preceding this principle as in the lower desires, or following it as in the higher, when the desire is determined by the moral law), we may also suppose that the Judgment will bring about a transition from the pure faculty of knowledge, the realm of natural concepts, to the realm of the concept of freedom, just as in its logical use it makes possible the transition from Understanding to Reason.

Although, then, Philosophy can be divided only into two main parts, the theoretical and the practical, and although all that we may be able to say of the special principles of Judgment must be counted as belonging in it to the theoretical part, *i.e.*, to rational cognition in accordance with natural concepts ; yet the Kritik of pure Reason, which must decide all this, as regards the possibility of the system before undertaking it, consists of three parts : the Kritik of pure Understanding, of pure Judgment, and of pure Reason, which faculties are called pure because they are legislative *a priori*.

IV. OF JUDGMENT AS A FACULTY LEGISLATING *A PRIORI*

Judgment in general is the faculty of thinking the particular as contained under the Universal. If the universal (the rule, the principle, the law) be

given, the Judgment which subsumes the particular
under it (even if, as transcendental Judgment, it
furnishes, *a priori*, the conditions in conformity with
which subsumption under that universal is alone possible) is *determinant*. But if only the particular be
given for which the universal has to be found, the
Judgment is merely *reflective.*

The determinant Judgment only subsumes under
universal transcendental laws given by the Understanding; the law is marked out for it, *a priori*, and
it has therefore no need to seek a law for itself
in order to be able to subordinate the particular in
nature to the universal.— But the forms of nature
are so manifold, and there are so many modifications of the universal transcendental natural concepts left undetermined by the laws given, *a priori*,
by the pure Understanding,—because these only
concern the possibility of a nature in general (as an
object of sense),—that there must be laws for these
[forms] also. These, as empirical, may be contingent
from the point of view of *our* Understanding, and yet,
if they are to be called laws (as the concept of a
nature requires), they must be regarded as necessary
in virtue of a principle of the unity of the manifold,
though it be unknown to us.— The reflective Judgment, which is obliged to ascend from the particular
in nature to the universal, requires on that account
a principle that it cannot borrow from experience,
because its function is to establish the unity of all
empirical principles under higher ones, and hence
to establish the possibility of their systematic subordination. Such a transcendental principle, then,
the reflective Judgment can only give as a law from
and to itself. It cannot derive it from outside
(because then it would be the determinant Judg-

ment), nor can it prescribe it to nature, because
reflection upon the laws of nature adjusts itself by
nature, and not nature by the conditions according
to which we attempt to arrive at a concept of it which
is quite contingent in respect of nature.

This principle can be no other than the following : As universal laws of nature have their ground
in our Understanding, which prescribes them to
nature (although only according to the universal
concept of it as nature) ; so particular empirical laws,
in respect of what is in them left undetermined by
these universal laws, must be considered in accordance with such a unity as they would have if an
Understanding (although not our Understanding)
had furnished them to our cognitive faculties, so as
to make possible a system of experience according
to particular laws of nature.   Not as if, in this
way, such an Understanding must be assumed as
actual (for it is only our reflective Judgment to
which this Idea serves as a principle—for reflecting,
not for determining) ; but this faculty thus gives a
law only to itself and not to nature.

Now the concept of an Object, so far as it contains the ground of the actuality of this Object, is the
purpose ; and the agreement of a thing with that
constitution of things, which is only possible according to purposes, is called the *purposiveness* of its
form.   Thus the principle of Judgment, in respect
of the form of things of nature under empirical laws
generally, is the *purposiveness of nature* in its variety.
That is, nature is represented by means of this concept, as if an Understanding contained the ground
of the unity of the variety of its empirical laws.

The purposiveness of nature is therefore a particular concept, *a priori*, which has its origin solely

in the reflective Judgment.   For we cannot ascribe
to natural products anything like a reference of
nature in them to purposes; we can only use this
concept to reflect upon such products in respect of
the connection of phenomena which is given in them
according to empirical laws. This concept is also
quite different from practical purposiveness (in
human art or in morals), though it is certainly
thought according to the analogy of these last.

V. THE PRINCIPLE OF THE FORMAL PURPOSIVENESS OF NATURE IS A TRANSCENDENTAL PRINCIPLE OF JUDGMENT.

A transcendental principle is one by means of
which is represented, *a priori*, the universal condition under which alone things can be in general
Objects of our cognition.   On the other hand, a
principle is called metaphysical if it represents the
a priori condition under which alone Objects, whose
concept must be empirically given, can be further
determined *a priori*.   Thus the principle of the
cognition of bodies as substances, and as changeable
substances, is transcendental, if thereby it is asserted
that their changes must have a cause; it is metaphysical if it asserts that their changes must have an
external cause.   For in the former case bodies need
only be thought by means of ontological predicates
(pure concepts of Understanding), *e.g.*, substance,
in order to cognise the proposition *a priori*; but in
the latter case the empirical concept of a body (as a
movable thing in space) must lie at the basis of the
proposition, although once this basis has been laid
down, it may be seen completely *a priori* that this
latter predicate (motion only by external causes)

belongs to body.— Thus, as I shall presently show,
the principle of the purposiveness of nature (in the
manifoldness of its empirical laws) is a transcendental principle. For the concept of Objects, so far as
they are thought as standing under this principle, is
only the pure concept of objects of possible empirical
cognition in general and contains nothing empirical.
On the other hand, the principle of practical purposiveness, which must be thought in the Idea of the
determination of a free *will*, is a metaphysical principle ; because the concept of a faculty of desire as
a will must be given empirically (*i.e.* does not belong
to transcendental predicates). Both principles are,
however, not empirical, but *a priori* ; because for
the combination of the predicate with the empirical
concept of the subject of their judgments no further
experience is needed, but it can be apprehended
completely *a priori.*

That the concept of a purposiveness of nature
belongs to transcendental principles can be sufficiently
seen from the maxims of the Judgment, which lie
at the basis of the investigation of nature *a priori*,
and yet do not go further than the possibility of
experience, and consequently of the cognition of
nature—not indeed nature in general, but nature
as determined through a variety of particular laws.
These maxims present themselves in the course
of this science often enough, though in a scattered
way, as sentences of metaphysical wisdom, whose
necessity we cannot demonstrate from concepts.
" Nature takes the shortest way (*lex parsimoniæ*) ;
at the same time it makes no leaps, either in the
course of its changes or in the juxta-position of
specifically different forms (*lex continui in natura*) ;
its great variety in empirical laws is yet unity

under a few principles (*principia præter necessitatem non sunt multiplicanda*)," etc.

If we propose to set forth the origin of these fundamental propositions and try it by the psychological method, we violate their sense. For they do not tell us what happens, *i.e.* by what rule our cognitive powers actually operate, and how we judge, but how we ought to judge ; and this logical objective necessity does not emerge if the principles are merely empirical. Hence that purposiveness of nature for our cognitive faculties and their use, which is plainly apparent from them, is a transcendental principle of judgments, and needs therefore also a Transcendental Deduction, by means of which the ground for so judging must be sought in the sources of cognition *a priori*.

We find in the grounds of the possibility of an experience in the very first place something necessary, viz., the universal laws without which nature in general (as an object of sense) cannot be thought ; and these rest upon the Categories, applied to the formal conditions of all intuition possible for us, so far as it is also given *a priori*. Now under these laws the Judgment is determinant, for it has nothing to do but to subsume under given laws. For example, the Understanding says that every change has its cause (universal law of nature); the transcendental Judgment has nothing further to do than to supply *a priori* the condition of subsumption under the concept of the Understanding placed before it, *i.e.* the succession [in time] of the determinations of one and the same thing. For nature in general (as an object of possible experience) that law is cognised as absolutely necessary.— But now the objects of empirical cognition are determined in many other ways than by that formal time-condition, or, at least as far as we can judge *a priori*, are determinable. Hence specifically different natures can be causes in an infinite variety of ways, as well as in virtue of what they have in common as belonging to nature in general ; and each of these modes must (in accordance with the concept of a cause in general) have its rule, which is a law and therefore brings necessity with it, although we do not at all comprehend this necessity, in virtue of the constitution and the limitations of our cognitive faculties. We must therefore think in nature, in respect of its merely empirical laws, a possibility of infinitely various empirical laws, which are, as far as our insight goes, contingent (cannot be cognised *a priori*), and in respect of which we judge nature, according to empirical laws and the possibility of the unity of experience (as a system according to empirical laws), to be contingent. But such an unity must be necessarily presupposed and assumed, for otherwise there would be no thoroughgoing connection of empirical cognitions in a whole of experience. The universal laws of nature no doubt furnish such a connection of things according to their kind as things of nature in general, but not specifically, as such particular beings of nature. Hence the Judgment must assume for its special use this principle *a priori*, that what in the particular (empirical) laws of nature is from the human point of view contingent, yet contains an unity of law in the combination of its manifold into an experience possible in itself—an unity not indeed to be fathomed by us, but yet thinkable. Consequently as the unity of law in a combination, which we cognise as contingent in itself,

although in conformity with a necessary design (a
need) of Understanding, is represented as the purposiveness of Objects (here of nature) ; so must the
Judgment, which in respect of things under possible
(not yet discovered) empirical laws is merely reflection, think of nature in respect of the latter according to a *principle of purposiveness* for our cognitive
faculty, which then is expressed in the above
maxims of the Judgment. This transcendental
concept of a purposiveness of nature is neither a
natural concept nor a concept of freedom, because it
ascribes nothing to the Object (of nature), but only
represents the peculiar way in which we must
proceed in reflection upon the objects of nature
in reference to a thoroughly connected experience,
and is consequently a subjective principle (maxim)
of the Judgment. Hence, as if it were a lucky
chance favouring our design, we are rejoiced (properly speaking, relieved of a want), if we meet with
such systematic unity under merely empirical laws ;
although we must necessarily assume that there
is such a unity without our comprehending it or
being able to prove it.

In order to convince ourselves of the correctness
of this Deduction of the concept before us, and the
necessity of assuming it as a transcendental principle
of cognition, just consider the magnitude of the
problem. The problem, which lies *a priori* in our
Understanding, is to make a connected experience
out of given perceptions of a nature containing at all
events an infinite variety of empirical laws. The
Understanding is, no doubt, in possession *a priori*
of universal laws of nature, without which nature
could not be an object of experience ; but it needs
in addition a certain order of nature in its particular

rules, which can only be empirically known and
which are, as regards the Understanding, contingent.
These rules, without which we could not proceed
from the universal analogy of a possible experience
in general to the particular, must be thought by it
as laws (*i.e.* as necessary), for otherwise they would
not constitute an order of nature; although their
necessity can never be cognised or comprehended
by it. ⌊Although, therefore, the Understanding
can determine nothing *a priori* in respect of Objects,
it must, in order to trace out these empirical so-called
laws, place at the basis of all reflection upon Objects
an *a priori* principle, viz., that a cognisable order
of nature is possible in accordance with these laws.⌋
The following propositions express some such principle. There is in nature a subordination of genera
and species comprehensible by us. Each one
approximates to some other according to a common
principle, so that a transition from one to another and
so on to a higher genus may be possible. Though
it seems at the outset unavoidable for our Understanding to assume different kinds of causality for
the specific differences of natural operations, yet
these different kinds may stand under a small
number of principles, with the investigation of which
we have to busy ourselves. This harmony of
nature with our cognitive faculty is presupposed
a priori by the Judgment, on behalf of its reflection
upon nature in accordance with its empirical laws;
whilst the Understanding at the same time cognises
it objectively as contingent, and it is only the Judgment that ascribes it to nature as a transcendental
purposiveness (in relation to the cognitive faculty of
the subject). For without this presupposition we
should have no order of nature in accordance with

empirical laws, and consequently no guiding thread
for an experience ordered by these in all their variety,
or for an investigation of them.

For it might easily be thought that, in spite of
all the uniformity of natural things according to the
universal laws, without which we should not have
the form of an empirical cognition in general, the
specific variety of the empirical laws of nature including their effects might yet be so great, that it
would be impossible for our Understanding, to
detect in nature a comprehensible order; to divide
its products into genera and species, so as to use
the principles which explain and make intelligible
one for the explanation and comprehension of
another; or out of such confused material (strictly
we should say, so infinitely various and not to be
measured by our faculty of comprehension) to make
a connected experience.

The Judgment has therefore also in itself a
principle *a priori* of the possibility of nature, but
only in a subjective aspect; by which it prescribes,
not to nature (autonomy), but to itself (heautonomy)
a law for its reflection upon nature. This we might
call the *law of the specification of nature* in respect
of its empirical laws. The Judgment does not
cognise this *a priori* in nature, but assumes it on
behalf of a natural order cognisable by our Understanding in the division which it makes of the
universal laws of nature when it wishes to subordinate
to these the variety of particular laws. If then we
say that nature specifies its universal laws according
to the principles of purposiveness for our cognitive
faculty, *i.e.* in accordance with the necessary business
of the human Understanding of finding the universal
for the particular which perception offers it, and again

of finding connection for the diverse (which however is a universal for each species) in the unity of
a principle,—we thus neither prescribe to nature a
law, nor do we learn one from it by observation
(although such a principle may be confirmed by this
means). For it is not a principle of the determinant
but merely of the reflective Judgment. We only
require that, be nature disposed as it may as regards
its universal laws, investigation into its empirical
laws may be carried on in accordance with that principle and the maxims founded thereon, because it is
only so far as that holds that we can make any
progress with the use of our Understanding in
experience, or gain knowledge.

VI. OF THE COMBINATION OF THE FEELING OF
PLEASURE WITH THE CONCEPT OF THE PUR-
POSIVENESS OF NATURE.

The conceived harmony of nature in the variety
of its particular laws with our need of finding
universality of principles for it, must be judged as
contingent in respect of our insight, but yet at the
same time as indispensable for the needs of our
Understanding, and consequently as a purposiveness
by which nature is harmonised with our design,
which, however, has only knowledge for its aim.
The universal laws of the Understanding, which
are at the same time laws of nature, are just as
necessary (although arising from spontaneity) as the
material laws of motion. Their production presupposes no design on the part of our cognitive
faculty, because it is only by means of them that
we, in the first place, attain a concept of what the
cognition of things (of nature) is, and attribute them

necessarily to nature as Object of our cognition in general. But, so far as we can see, it is contingent that the order of nature according to its particular laws, in all its variety and heterogeneity possibly at least transcending our comprehension, should be actually conformable to these [laws]. The discovery of this [order] is the business of the Understanding which is designedly borne towards a necessary purpose, viz., the bringing of unity of principles into nature, which purpose then the Judgment must ascribe to nature, because the Understanding cannot here prescribe any law to it.

The attainment of that design is bound up with the feeling of pleasure, and since the condition of this attainment is a representation *a priori*,—as here a principle for the reflective Judgment in general,— therefore the feeling of pleasure is determined by a ground *a priori* and valid for every man, and that merely by the reference of the Object to the cognitive faculty, the concept of purposiveness here not having the least reference to the faculty of desire. It is thus quite distinguished from all practical purposiveness of nature.

In fact, although from the agreement of perceptions with laws in accordance with universal natural concepts (the categories), we do not and cannot find in ourselves the slightest effect upon the feeling of pleasure, because the Understanding necessarily proceeds according to its nature without any design ; yet, on the other hand, the discovery that two or 'more empirical heterogeneous laws of nature may be combined under one principle comprehending them both, is the ground of a very marked pleasure, often even of an admiration, which does not cease, though we may be already quite

familiar with the objects of it. We no longer find, it
is true, any marked pleasure in the comprehensibility
of nature and in the unity of its divisions into genera
and species, by which all empirical concepts are
possible, through which we cognise it according to
its particular laws.   But this pleasure has certainly
been present at one time, and it is only because the
commonest experience would be impossible without
it that it is gradually confounded with mere cognition
and no longer arrests particular attention.   There is
then something in our judgments upon nature which
makes us attentive to its purposiveness for our Understanding—an endeavour to bring, where possible, its
dissimilar laws under higher ones, though still always
empirical—and thus, if successful, makes us feel pleasure in that harmony of these with our cognitive
faculty, which harmony we regard as merely contingent. On the other hand, a representation of nature
would altogether displease, by which it should be
foretold to us that in the smallest investigation
beyond the commonest experience we should meet
with a heterogeneity of its laws, which would make the
union of its particular laws under universal empirical
laws impossible for our Understanding. For this
would contradict the principle of the subjectively-
purposive specification of nature in its genera, and
also of our reflective Judgment in respect of such
principle.

This presupposition of the Judgment is, however,
at the same time so indeterminate as to how far that
ideal purposiveness of nature for our cognitive
faculty should be extended, that if we were told that
a deeper or wider knowledge of nature derived from
observation must lead at last to a variety of laws,
which no human Understanding could reduce to a

principle, we should at once acquiesce. But still
we more gladly listen to one who offers hope that
the more we know nature internally, and can compare
it with external members now unknown to us, the
more simple shall we find it in its principles, and that
the further our experience reaches the more uniform
shall we find it amid the apparent heterogeneity of
its empirical laws. For it is a mandate of our
Judgment to proceed according to the principle of
the harmony of nature with our cognitive faculty so
far as that reaches, without deciding (because it is
not the determinant Judgment which gives us this
rule) whether or not it is bounded anywhere. For
although in respect of the rational use of our cognitive
faculty we can determine such bounds, this is not
possible in the empirical field.

VII. OF THE ÆSTHETICAL REPRESENTATION OF THE PURPOSIVENESS OF NATURE.

That which in the representation of an Object
is merely subjective, *i.e.* which decides its reference
to the subject, not to the object, is its æsthetical
character ; but that which serves or can be used
for the determination of the object (for cognition),
is its logical validity. In the cognition of an object
of sense both references present themselves. In
the sense - representation of external things the
quality of space wherein we intuite them is the
merely subjective [element] of my representation
(by which it remains undecided what they may be in
themselves as Objects), on account of which reference
the object is thought thereby merely as phenomenon.
But space, notwithstanding its merely subjective
quality, is at the same time an ingredient in the

cognition of things as phenomena. *Sensation*, again (*i.e.* external sensation), expresses the merely subjective [element] of our representations of external things, but it is also the proper material (reale) of them (by which something existing is given), just as space is the mere form *a priori* of the possibility of their intuition. Nevertheless, however, sensation is also employed in the cognition of external Objects. But the subjective [element] in a representation *which cannot be an ingredient of cognition*, is the *pleasure* or *pain* which is bound up with it; for through it I cognise nothing in the object of the representation, although it may be the effect of some cognition. Now the purposiveness of a thing, so far as it is represented in perception, is no characteristic of the Object itself (for such cannot be perceived), although it may be inferred from a cognition of things. The purposiveness, therefore, which precedes the cognition of an Object, and which, even without our wishing to use the representation of it for cognition, is, at the same time, immediately bound up with it, is that subjective [element] which cannot be an ingredient in cognition. Hence the object is only called purposive, when its representation is immediately combined with the feeling of pleasure; and this very representation is an æsthetical representation of purposiveness.— We have only to ask whether there is, in general, such a representation of purposiveness.

If pleasure is bound up with the mere apprehension (*apprehensio*) of the form of an object of intuition, without reference to a concept for a definite cognition, then the representation is thereby not referred to the Object, but simply to the subject ; and the pleasure can express nothing else than

its harmony with the cognitive faculties which come
into play in the reflective Judgment, and so far as
they are in play ; and hence can only express a
subjective formal purposiveness of the Object. For
that apprehension of forms in the Imagination can
never take place without the reflective Judgment,
though undesignedly, at least comparing them with
its faculty of referring intuitions to concepts. If
now in this comparison the Imagination (as the
faculty of *a priori* intuitions) is placed by means
of a given representation undesignedly in agreement with the Understanding, as the faculty of
concepts, and thus a feeling of pleasure is aroused,
the object must then be regarded as purposive for
the reflective Judgment. Such a judgment is an
æsthetical judgment upon the purposiveness of the
Object, which does not base itself upon any present
concept of the object, nor does it furnish any such.
In the case of an object whose form (not the matter
of its representation, or sensation), in the mere
reflection upon it (without reference to any concept
to be obtained of it), is judged as the ground of
a pleasure in the representation of such an Object,
this pleasure is judged as bound up with the representation necessarily ; and, consequently, not only
for the subject which apprehends this form, but for
every judging being in general. The object is then
called beautiful ; and the faculty of judging by
means of such a pleasure (and, consequently, with
universal validity) is called Taste. For since
the ground of the pleasure is placed merely in the
form of the object for reflection in general—and,
consequently, in no sensation of the object, and
also without reference to any concept which anywhere involves design—it is only the conformity

to law in the empirical use of the Judgment in
general (unity of the Imagination with the Understanding) in the subject, with which the representation of the Object in reflection, whose conditions
are universally valid *a priori*, harmonises. And
since this harmony of the object with the faculties
of the subject is [only] contingent, it brings about the
representation of its purposiveness [only] in respect
of the cognitive faculties of the subject.

Here now is a pleasure, which, like all pleasure
or pain that is not produced through the concept of
freedom (*i.e.* through the preceding determination
of the higher faculties of desire by pure Reason);
can never be comprehended from concepts, as necessarily bound up with the representation of an object.
It must always be cognised as combined with this
only by means of reflective perception; and, consequently, like all empirical judgments, it can declare
no objective necessity and lay claim to no *a priori*
validity. But the judgment of taste also claims,
as every other empirical judgment does, to be valid
for all men; and in spite of its inner contingency
this is always possible. The strange and irregular
thing is that it is not an empirical concept, but a
feeling of pleasure (consequently not a concept at
all), which by the judgment of taste is attributed to
every one, just as if it were a predicate bound up
with the cognition of the Object, and which is connected with the representation thereof.

A singular judgment of experience, *e.g.*, when
we perceive a moveable drop of water in an ice-
crystal, may justly claim that every other person
should find it the same; because we have formed
this judgment, according to the universal conditions
of the determinant faculty of Judgment, under the

laws of a possible experience in general. Just in the same way he who feels pleasure in the mere reflection upon the form of an object without respect to any concept, although this judgment be empirical and singular, justly claims the agreement of all men ; because the ground of this pleasure is found in the universal, although subjective, condition of reflective judgments, viz., the purposive harmony of an object (whether a product of nature or of art) with the mutual relations of the cognitive faculties (the Imagination and the Understanding), a harmony which is requisite for every empirical cognition. The pleasure, therefore, in the judgment of taste is dependent on an empirical representation, and cannot be bound up *a priori* with any concept (we cannot determine *a priori* what object is or is not according to taste ; that we must find out by experiment). But the pleasure is the determining ground of this judgment only because we are conscious that it rests merely on reflection and on the universal though only subjective conditions of the harmony of that reflection with the cognition of Objects in general, for which the form of the Object is purposive.

Thus the reason why judgments of taste according to their possibility are subjected to a Kritik is that they presuppose a principle *a priori*, although this principle is neither one of cognition for the Understanding nor of practice for the Will, and therefore is not in any way determinant *a priori*.

Susceptibility to pleasure from reflection upon the forms of things (of Nature as well as of Art), indicates not only a purposiveness of the Objects in relation to the reflective Judgment, conformably to the concept of nature in the subject ; but also

conversely a purposiveness of the subject in respect
of the objects according to their form or even their
formlessness, in virtue of the concept of freedom.
Hence the æsthetical judgment is not only related
as a judgment of taste to the beautiful, but also
as springing from a spiritual feeling is related to
the *sublime* ; and thus the Kritik of the æsthetical
Judgment must be divided into two corresponding
sections.

VIII. OF THE LOGICAL REPRESENTATION OF THE PURPOSIVENESS OF NATURE

Purposiveness may be represented in an object
given in experience on a merely subjective ground,
as the harmony of its form,—in the *apprehension*
(*apprehensio*) of it prior to any concept,—with the
cognitive faculties, in order to unite the intuition
with concepts for a cognition generally. Or it
may be represented objectively as the harmony
of the form of the object with the possibility of the
thing itself, according to a concept of it which
precedes and contains the ground of this form.
We have seen that the representation of purposiveness of the first kind rests on the immediate
pleasure in the form of the object in the mere
reflection upon it. But the representation of purposiveness of the second kind, since it refers the
form of the Object, not to the cognitive faculties
of the subject in the apprehension of it, but to a
definite cognition of the object under a given concept,
has nothing to do with a feeling of pleasure in
things, but only with the Understanding in its judgment upon them. If the concept of an object is
given, the business of the Judgment in the use of
the concept for cognition consists in *presentation*

(*exhibitio*), *i.e.* in setting a corresponding intuition beside the concept. This may take place either through our own Imagination, as in Art when we realise a preconceived concept of an object which is a purpose of ours ; or through Nature in its Technic (as in organised bodies) when we supply to it our concept of its purpose in order to judge of its products. In the latter case it is not merely the *purposiveness* of nature in the form of the thing that is represented, but this its product is represented as a *natural purpose.*— Although our concept of a subjective purposiveness of nature in its forms according to empirical laws is not a concept of the Object, but only a principle of the Judgment for furnishing itself with concepts amid the immense variety of nature (and thus being able to ascertain its own position), yet we thus ascribe to nature as it were a regard to our cognitive faculty according to the analogy of purpose. Thus we can regard *natural beauty* as the *presentation* of the concept of the formal (merely subjective) purposiveness, and *natural purposes* as the presentation of the concept of a real (objective) purposiveness. The former of these we judge of by Taste (æsthetical, by the medium of the feeling of pleasure), the latter by Understanding and Reason (logical, according to concepts).

On this is based the division of the Kritik of Judgment into the Kritik of *æsthetical* and of *teleological* Judgment. By the first we understand the faculty of judging of the formal purposiveness (otherwise called subjective) of Nature by means of the feeling of pleasure or pain ; by the second the faculty of judging its real (objective) purposiveness by means of Understanding and Reason.

In a Kritik of Judgment the part containing the
æsthetical Judgment is essential, because this alone
contains a principle which the Judgment places quite
a priori at the basis of its reflection upon nature ;
viz., the principle of a formal purposiveness of nature,
according to its particular (empirical) laws, for our
cognitive faculty, without which the Understanding
could not find itself in nature.   On the other hand no
reason *a priori* could be specified,—and even the
possibility of a reason would not be apparent from
the concept of nature as an object of experience
whether general or particular,—why there should be
objective purposes of nature, *i.e.* things which are
only possible as natural purposes ; but the Judgment, without containing such a principle *a priori* in
itself, in given cases (of certain products), in order
to make use of the concept of purposes on behalf
of Reason, would only contain the rule according
to which that transcendental principle already has
prepared the Understanding to apply to nature the
concept of a purpose (at least as regards its form).

But the transcendental principle which represents
a purposiveness of nature (in subjective reference to
our cognitive faculty) in the form of a thing as a
principle by which we judge of nature, leaves it
quite undetermined where and in what cases I have
to judge of a product according to a principle of
purposiveness, and not rather according to universal
natural laws.   It leaves it to the *æsthetical* Judgment
to decide by taste the harmony of this product (of
its form) with our cognitive faculty (so far as this
decision rests not on any agreement with concepts
but on feeling).   On the other hand, the Judgment
teleologically employed furnishes conditions determinately under which something (*e.g.* an organised

body) is to be judged according to the Idea of a purpose of nature ; but it can adduce no fundamental proposition from the concept of nature as an object of experience authorising it to ascribe to nature *a priori* a reference to purposes, or even indeterminately to assume this of such products in actual experience. The reason of this is that we must have many particular experiences, and consider them under the unity of their principle, in order to be able to cognise, even empirically, objective purposiveness in a certain object.—— The æsthetical Judgment is therefore a special faculty for judging of things according to a rule, but not according to concepts. The teleological Judgment is not a special faculty, but only the reflective Judgment in general, so far as it proceeds, as it always does in theoretical cognition, according to concepts ; but in respect of certain objects of nature according to special principles. viz., of a merely reflective Judgment, and not of a Judgment that determines Objects. Thus as regards its application it belongs to the theoretical part of Philosophy ; and on account of its special principles which are not determinant, as they must be in Doctrine, it must constitute a special part of Kritik. On the other hand, the æsthetical Judgment contributes nothing towards the knowledge of its objects, and thus must be reckoned as belonging to the Kritik of the judging subject and its cognitive faculties, *only* so far as they are susceptible of *a priori* principles, of whatever other use (theoretical or practical) they may be. This is the propædeutic of all Philosophy.

IX. OF THE CONNECTION OF THE LEGISLATION OF UN-
DERSTANDING WITH THAT OF REASON BY MEANS
OF THE JUDGMENT

The Understanding legislates *a priori* for nature
as an Object of sense—for a theoretical knowledge
of it in a possible experience. Reason legislates *a
priori* for freedom and its peculiar causality; as the
supersensible in the subject, for an unconditioned
practical knowledge. The realm of the natural
concept under the one legislation and that of the
concept of freedom under the other are entirely
removed from all mutual influence which they might
have on one another (each according to its fundamental laws) by the great gulf that separates the
supersensible from phenomena. The concept of
freedom determines nothing in respect of the
theoretical cognition of nature; and the natural concept determines nothing in respect of the practical
laws of freedom. So far then it is not possible to
throw a bridge from the one realm to the other.
But although the determining grounds of causality
according to the concept of freedom (and the
practical rules which it contains) are not resident
in nature, and the sensible cannot determine the
supersensible in the subject, yet this is possible
conversely (not, to be sure, in respect of the cognition of nature, but as regards the effects of the supersensible upon the sensible). This in fact is involved
in the concept of a causality through freedom, the
effect of which is to take place in the world according to its formal laws. The word *cause*, of course,
when used of the supersensible only signifies the
ground which determines the causality of natural

things to an effect in accordance with their proper
natural laws, although harmoniously with the formal
principle of the laws of Reason. Although the
possibility of this cannot be comprehended, yet the
objection of a contradiction alleged to be found in
it can be sufficiently answered.[1]— The effect in
accordance with the concept of freedom is the final
purpose which (or its phenomenon in the world of
sense) ought to exist ; and the condition of the
possibility of this is presupposed in nature (in the
nature of the subject as a sensible being, that is, as
man). The Judgment presupposes this *a priori*
and without reference to the practical ; and thus
furnishes the mediating concept between the concepts of nature and that of freedom. It makes
possible the transition from the conformity to law
in accordance with the former to the final purpose
in accordance with the latter, and this by the concept of a *purposiveness* of nature. For thus is
cognised the possibility of the final purpose which
alone can be actualised in nature in harmony with
its laws.

The Understanding by the possibility of its *a*

---

[1] One of the various pretended contradictions in this whole
distinction of the causality of nature from that of freedom is this.
It is objected that if I speak of *obstacles* which nature opposes to
causality according to (moral) laws of freedom or of the *assistance* it
affords, I am admitting an *influence* of the former upon the latter.
But if we try to understand what has been said, this misinterpretation is very easy to avoid. The opposition or assistance is not
between nature and freedom, but between the former as phenomenon
and the *effects* of the latter as phenomena in the world of sense.
The causality of freedom itself (of pure and practical Reason) is the
causality of a natural cause subordinated to nature (*i.e.* of the
subject considered as man and therefore as phenomenon). The
intelligible, which is thought under freedom, contains the ground of
the *determination* of this [natural cause] in a further inexplicable way
(just as that intelligible does which constitutes the supersensible substrate of nature).

priori laws for nature, gives a proof that nature is only cognised by us as phenomenon; and implies at the same time that it has a supersensible substrate, though it leaves this quite *undetermined*. The Judgment by its *a priori* principle for the judging of nature according to its possible particular laws, makes the supersensible substrate (both in us and without us) *determinable by means of the intellectual faculty*. But the Reason by its practical *a priori* law *determines* it; and thus the Judgment makes possible the transition from the realm of the natural concept to that of the concept of freedom.

As regards the faculties of the soul in general, in their higher aspect, as containing an autonomy; the Understanding is that which contains the *constitutive* principles *a priori* for the *cognitive faculty* (the theoretical cognition of nature). For the *feeling of pleasure and pain* there is the Judgment, independently of concepts and sensations which relate to the determination of the faculty of desire and can thus be immediately practical. For the *faculty of desire* there is the Reason which is practical without the mediation of any pleasure whatever. It determines for the faculty of desire, as a superior faculty, the final purpose which carries with it the pure intellectual satisfaction in the Object.— The concept formed by Judgment of a purposiveness of nature belongs to natural concepts, but only as a regulative principle of the cognitive faculty; although the æsthetical judgment upon certain objects (of Nature or Art) which occasions it is, in respect of the feeling of pleasure or pain, a constitutive principle. The spontaneity in the play of the cognitive faculties, the harmony of which contains the ground of this pleasure, makes the above concept [of the purposiveness of nature] fit to be the mediating link between the realm of the natural concept and that of the concept of freedom in its effects ; whilst at the same time it promotes the sensibility of the mind to moral feeling.— The following table may facilitate the review of all the higher faculties according to their systematic unity.[1]

All the faculties of the mind

Cognitive faculties.		Faculties of desire.
	Feeling of pleasure and pain.	
	Cognitive faculties	
Understanding.	Judgment.	Reason.
	A priori principles	
Conformity to law.	Purposiveness.	Final purpose.
	Application to	
Nature.	Art.	Freedom.

[1] It has been thought a doubtful point that my divisions in pure Philosophy should always be threefold. But that lies in the nature of the thing. If there is to be an *a priori* division it must be either *analytical*, according to the law of contradiction, which is always twofold (*quodlibet ens est aut A aut non A*) ; or it is *synthetical*. And if in this latter case it is to be derived from *a priori concepts* (not as in Mathematic from the intuition corresponding to the concept), the division must necessarily be trichotomy. For according to what is requisite for synthetical unity in general there must be (1) a condition, (2) a conditioned, and (3) the concept which arises from the union of the conditioned with its condition.

THE KRITIK OF JUDGMENT

PART I

KRITIK OF THE ÆSTHETICAL JUDGMENT

FIRST DIVISION

ANALYTIC OF THE ÆSTHETICAL JUDGMENT

FIRST BOOK

ANALYTIC OF THE BEAUTIFUL

FIRST MOMENT

OF THE JUDGMENT OF TASTE [1] ACCORDING TO QUALITY

§ 1. *The judgment of taste is æsthetical*

In order to distinguish whether anything is beautiful or not, we refer the representation not by the Understanding to the Object for cognition, but by the Imagination (perhaps in conjunction with the Understanding) to the subject, and its feeling of pleasure or pain. The judgment of taste is therefore not a judgment of cognition, and is consequently not logical but æsthetical, by which we understand that whose determining ground can be

[1] The definition of taste which is laid down here is that it is the faculty of judging of the beautiful. But the analysis of judgments of taste must show what is required in order to call an object beautiful. The moments, to which this Judgment has regard in its reflection, I have sought in accordance with the guidance of the logical functions of judgment (for in a judgment of taste a reference to the Understanding is always involved). I have considered the moment of quality first, because the æsthetical judgment upon the beautiful first pays attention to it.

no other than subjective. Every reference of representations, even that of sensations, may be objective (and then it signifies the real [element] of an empirical representation) ; save only the reference to the feeling of pleasure and pain, by which nothing in the Object is signified, but through which there is a feeling in the subject, as it is affected by the representation.

To apprehend a regular, purposive building by means of one's cognitive faculty (whether in a clear or a confused way of representation) is something quite different from being conscious of this representation as connected with the sensation of satisfaction. Here the representation is altogether referred to the subject and to its feeling of life, under the name of the feeling of pleasure or pain. This establishes a quite separate faculty of distinction and of judgment, adding nothing to cognition, but only comparing the given representation in the subject with the whole faculty of representations, of which the mind is conscious in the feeling of its state. Given representations in a judgment can be empirical (consequently, æsthetical) ; but the judgment which is formed by means of them is logical, provided they are referred in the judgment to the Object. Conversely, if the given representations are rational, but are referred in a judgment simply to the subject (to its feeling), the judgment is so far always æsthetical.

§ 2. *The satisfaction which determines the judgment of taste is disinterested*

The satisfaction which we combine with the representation of the existence of an object is called interest. Such satisfaction always has reference to the faculty of desire, either as its determining ground or as necessarily connected with its determining ground. ⟨Now when the question is if a thing is beautiful, we do not want to know whether anything depends or can depend on the existence of the thing either for myself or for any one else, but how we judge it by mere observation (intuition or reflection).⟩ If any one asks me if I find that palace beautiful which I see before me, I may answer: I do not like things of that kind which are made merely to be stared at.   Or I can answer like that Iroquois *Sachem* who was pleased in Paris by nothing more than by the cook-shops.   Or again after the manner of *Rousseau* I may rebuke the vanity of the great who waste the sweat of the people on such superfluous things.   In fine I could easily convince myself that if I found myself on an uninhabited island without the hope of ever again coming among men, and could conjure up just such a splendid building by my mere wish, I should not even give myself the trouble if I had a sufficiently comfortable hut.   This may all be admitted and approved; but we are not now talking of this.   We wish only to know if this mere representation of the object is accompanied in me with satisfaction, however indifferent I may be as regards the existence of the object of this representation.   We easily see that in saying it is *beautiful* and in showing that I have taste, I am concerned, not with that in which I depend on the existence of the object, but with that which I make out of this representation in myself.   Every one must admit that a judgment about beauty, in which the least interest mingles, is very partial and is not a pure judgment of taste.   We must not be in the least prejudiced in

favour of the existence of the things, but be quite
indifferent in this respect, in order to play the judge
in things of taste.

We cannot, however, better elucidate this proposition, which is of capital importance, than by
contrasting the pure disinterested[1] satisfaction in
judgments of taste, with that which is bound up with
an interest, especially if we can at the same time be
certain that there are no other kinds of interest than
those which are to be now specified.

§ 3. *The satisfaction in the* PLEASANT *is bound up with interest*

That which pleases the senses in sensation is
PLEASANT.   Here the opportunity presents itself of
censuring a very common confusion of the double
sense which the word sensation can have, and of
calling attention to it.   All satisfaction (it is said or
thought) is itself sensation (of a pleasure).   Consequently everything that pleases is pleasant because
it pleases (and according to its different degrees or
its relations to other pleasant sensations it is *agreeable, lovely, delightful, enjoyable*, etc.)   But if this
be admitted, then impressions of Sense which
determine the inclination, fundamental propositions
of Reason which determine the Will, mere reflective
forms of intuition which determine the Judgment,
are quite the same, as regards the effect upon the
feeling of pleasure.   For this would be pleasantness

---

[1] A judgment upon an object of satisfaction may be quite *disinterested*, but yet very *interesting, i.e.* not based upon an interest, but
bringing an interest with it : of this kind are all pure moral judgments.   Judgments of taste, however, do not in themselves establish
any interest.   Only in society is it *interesting* to have taste : the
reason of this will be shown in the sequel.

in the sensation of one's state, and since in the
end all the operations of our faculties must issue in
the practical and unite in it as their goal, we could
suppose no other way of estimating things and their
worth than that which consists in the gratification
that they promise.   It is of no consequence at all
how this is attained, and since then the choice of
means alone could make a difference, men could
indeed blame one another for stupidity and in-
discretion, but never for baseness and wickedness.
For thus they all, each according to his own way of
seeing things, seek one goal, that is, gratification.

If a determination of the feeling of pleasure or
pain is called sensation, this expression signifies
something quite different from what I mean when I
call the representation of a thing (by sense, as a
receptivity belonging to the cognitive faculty)
sensation.   For in the latter case the representation
is referred to the Object, in the former simply to the
subject, and is available for no cognition whatever,
not even for that by which the subject *cognises* itself.

In the above elucidation we understand by the
word sensation, an objective representation of sense ;
and in order to avoid misinterpretation, we shall call
that, which must always remain merely subjective
and can constitute absolutely no representation of
an object, by the ordinary term "feeling."   The
green colour of the meadows belongs to *objective*
sensation, as a perception of an object of sense ; the
pleasantness of this belongs to *subjective* sensation
by which no object is represented, *i.e.* to feeling,
by which the object is considered as an Object of
satisfaction (which does not furnish a cognition of it).

Now that a judgment about an object, by which
I describe it as pleasant, expresses an interest in it,

E

is plain from the fact that by sensation it excites a
desire for objects of that kind; consequently the
satisfaction presupposes not the mere judgment
about it, but the relation of its existence to my state,
so far as this is affected by such an Object.   Hence
we do not merely say of the pleasant, *it pleases*; but,
it gratifies.   I give to it no mere assent, but inclination is aroused by it; and in the case of what is
pleasant in the most lively fashion, there is no judgment at all upon the character of the Object, for
those [persons] who always lay themselves out for
enjoyment (for that is the word describing intense
gratification) would fain dispense with all judgment.

§ 4. *The satisfaction in the* GOOD *is bound up with interest*

Whatever by means of Reason pleases through
the mere concept is GOOD.   That which pleases only
as a means we call *good for something* (the useful);
but that which pleases for itself is *good in itself*.   In
both there is always involved the concept of a
purpose, and consequently the relation of Reason to
the (at least possible) volition, and thus a satisfaction
in the *presence* of an Object or an action, *i.e.* some
kind of interest.

In order to find anything good, I must always
know what sort of a thing the object ought to be, *i.e.*
I must have a concept of it.   But there is no need
of this, to find a thing beautiful.   Flowers, free
delineations, outlines intertwined with one another
without design and called [conventional] foliage,
have no meaning, depend on no definite concept,
and yet they please.   The satisfaction in the beautiful must depend on the reflection upon an object,

leading to any concept (however indefinite) ; and it is thus distinguished from the pleasant which rests entirely upon sensation. ⟩

It is true, the Pleasant seems in many cases to be the same as the Good. Thus people are accustomed to say that all gratification (especially if it lasts) is good in itself; which is very much the same as to say that lasting pleasure and the good are the same. But we can soon seé that this is merely a confusion of words ; for the concepts which properly belong to these expressions can in no way be interchanged. The pleasant, which, as such, represents the object simply in relation to Sense, must first be brought by the concept of a purpose under principles of Reason, in order to call it good, as an object of the Will. But that there is [involved] a quite different relation to satisfaction in calling that which gratifies at the same time *good*, may be seen from the fact that in the case of the good the question always is, whether it is mediately or immediately good (useful or good in itself) ; but on the contrary in the case of the pleasant there can be no question about this at all, for the word always signifies something which pleases immediately. (The same is applicable to what I call beautiful.)

Even in common speech men distinguish the Pleasant from the Good. Of a dish which stimulates the taste by spices and other condiments we say unhesitatingly that it is pleasant, though it is at the same time admitted not to be good ; for though it immediately *delights* the senses, yet mediately, *i.e.* considered by Reason which looks to the after results, it displeases. Even in the judging of health we may notice this distinction. It is immediately pleasant to every one possessing it (at least negatively, *i.e.* as

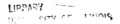

the absence of all bodily pains). But in order to say that it is good, it must be considered by Reason with reference to purposes ; viz., that it is a state which makes us fit for all our business. Finally in respect of happiness every one believes himself entitled to describe the greatest sum of the pleasantness of life (as regards both their number and their duration) as a true, even as the highest, good. However Reason is opposed to this. Pleasantness is enjoyment. And if we were concerned with this alone, it would be foolish to be scrupulous as regards the means which procure it for us, or [to care] whether it is obtained passively by the bounty of nature or by our own activity and work. But Reason can never be persuaded that the existence of a man who merely lives for *enjoyment* (however busy he may be in this point of view), has a worth in itself ; even if he at the same time is conducive as a means to the best enjoyment of others, and shares in all their gratifications by sympathy. Only what he does, without reference to enjoyment, in full freedom and independently of what nature can procure for him passively, gives an [absolute [1]] worth to his presence [in the world] as the existence of a person ; and happiness, with the whole abundance of its pleasures, is far from being an unconditioned good.[2]

However, notwithstanding all this difference between the pleasant and the good, they both agree in this that they are always bound up with an interest in their object ; so are not only the pleasant

---

[1] [Second Edition.]

[2] An obligation to enjoyment is a manifest absurdity. Thus the obligation to all actions which have merely enjoyment for their aim can only be a pretended one ; however spiritually it may be conceived (or decked out), even if it is a mystical, or so-called heavenly, enjoyment.

(§ 3), and the mediate good (the useful) which is pleasing as a means towards pleasantness somewhere, but also that which is good absolutely and in every aspect, viz., moral good, which brings with it the highest interest. For the good is the Object of will (*i.e.* of a faculty of desire determined by Reason). But to wish for something, and to have a satisfaction in its existence, *i.e.* to take an interest in it, are identical.

§ 5. *Comparison of the three specifically different kinds of satisfaction*

The pleasant and the good have both a reference to the faculty of desire ; and they bring with them— the former a satisfaction pathologically conditioned (by impulses, *stimuli*)—the latter a pure practical satisfaction, which is determined not merely by the representation of the object, but also by the represented connection of the subject with the existence of the object. [It is not merely the object that pleases, but also its existence.[1]] On the other hand, the judgment of taste is merely *contemplative* ; *i.e.* it is a judgment which, indifferent as regards the existence of an object, compares its character with the feeling of pleasure and pain. But this contemplation itself is not directed to concepts ; for the judgment of taste is not a cognitive judgment (either theoretical or practical), and thus is not *based* on concepts, nor has it concepts as its *purpose*.

The Pleasant, the Beautiful, and the Good, designate then, three different relations of representations to the feeling of pleasure and pain, in reference to which we distinguish from each other objects or methods of representing them. And the expressions

[1] [Second Edition.]

corresponding to each, by which we mark our complacency in them, are not the same. (That which GRATIFIES a man is called *pleasant*; that which merely PLEASES him is *beautiful*; that which is ESTEEMED [or *approved*[1]] by him, *i.e.* that to which he accords an objective worth, is *good*.)Pleasantness concerns irrational animals also; but Beauty only concerns men, *i.e.* animal, but still rational, beings— not merely *quâ* rational (*e.g.* spirits), but *quâ* animal also; and the Good concerns every rational being in general. This is a proposition which can only be completely established and explained in the sequel. We may say that of all these three kinds of satisfaction, that of taste in the Beautiful is alone a disinterested and *free* satisfaction; for no interest, either of Sense or of Reason, here forces our assent. Hence we may say of satisfaction that it is related in the three aforesaid cases to *inclination*, to *favour*, or to *respect*. Now *favour* is the only free satisfaction. An object of inclination, and one that is proposed to our desire by a law of Reason, leave us no freedom in forming for ourselves anywhere an object of pleasure. All interest presupposes or generates a want; and, as the determining ground of assent, it leaves the judgment about the object no longer free.

As regards the interest of inclination in the case of the Pleasant, every one says that hunger is the best sauce, and everything that is eatable is relished by people with a healthy appetite; and thus a satisfaction of this sort shows no choice directed by taste. It is only when the want is appeased that we can distinguish which of many men has or has not taste. In the same way there may be manners

---

[1] [Second Edition.]

(conduct) without virtue, politeness without good-will, decorum without modesty, etc. For where the moral law speaks there is no longer, objectively, a free choice as regards what is to be done ; and to display taste in its fulfilment (or in judging of another's fulfilment of it) is something quite different from manifesting the moral attitude of thought. For this involves a command and generates a want, whilst moral taste only plays with the objects of satisfaction, without attaching itself to one of them.

EXPLANATION OF THE BEAUTIFUL RESULTING FROM THE FIRST MOMENT

Taste is the faculty of judging of an object or a method of representing it by an *entirely disinterested* satisfaction or dissatisfaction. The object of such satisfaction is called *beautiful*.[1]

SECOND MOMENT

OF THE JUDGMENT OF TASTE, VIZ., ACCORDING TO QUANTITY

§ 6. *The beautiful is that which apart from concepts is represented as the object of a universal satisfaction*

This explanation of the beautiful can be derived

---

[1] [Ueberweg points out (*Hist. of Phil.*, ii. 528, Eng. Trans.) that Mendelssohn had already called attention to the disinterestedness of our satisfaction in the Beautiful. " It appears," says Mendelssohn, " to be a particular mark of the beautiful, that it is contemplated with quiet satisfaction, that it pleases, even though it be not in our possession, and even though we be never so far removed from the desire to put it to our use." But, of course, as Ueberweg remarks, Kant's conception of disinterestedness extends far beyond the idea of merely not desiring to possess the object.]

from the preceding explanation of it as the object of
an entirely disinterested satisfaction.   For the fact
of which every one is conscious, that the satisfaction
is for him quite disinterested, implies in his judgment a ground of satisfaction for all men.   For
since it does not rest on any inclination of the
subject (nor upon any other premeditated interest),
but since the person who judges feels himself quite
free as regards the satisfaction which he attaches to
the object, he cannot find the ground of this satisfaction in any private conditions connected with his
own subject; and hence it must be regarded as
grounded on what he can presuppose in every other
person.   Consequently he must believe that he has
reason for attributing a similar satisfaction to every
one.   He will therefore speak of the beautiful, as if
beauty were a characteristic of the object and the
judgment logical (constituting a cognition of the
Object by means of concepts of it); although it is
only æsthetical and involves merely a reference of
the representation of the object to the subject.   For
it has this similarity to a logical judgment that we
can presuppose its validity for all men.   But this
universality cannot arise from concepts; for from
concepts there is no transition to the feeling of
pleasure or pain (except in pure practical laws,
which bring an interest with them such as is not
bound up with the pure judgment of taste).   Consequently the judgment of taste, accompanied with the
consciousness of separation from all interest, must
claim validity for every man, without this universality
depending on Objects.   That is, there must be
bound up with it a title to subjective universality.

§ 7. *Comparison of the Beautiful with the Pleasant and the Good by means of the above characteristic*

As regards the Pleasant every one is content that his judgment, which he bases upon private feeling, and by which he says of an object that it pleases him, should be limited merely to his own person. Thus he is quite contented that if he says "Canary wine is pleasant," another man may correct his expression and remind him that he ought to say "It is pleasant *to me*." And this is the case not only as regards the taste of the tongue, the palate, and the throat, but for whatever is pleasant to any one's eyes and ears. To one violet colour is soft and lovely, to another it is washed out and dead. One man likes the tone of wind instruments, another that of strings. To strive here with the design of reproving as incorrect another man's judgment which is different from our own, as if the judgments were logically opposed, would be folly. As regards the pleasant therefore the fundamental proposition is valid, *every one has his own taste* (the taste of Sense).

The case is quite different with the Beautiful. It would (on the contrary) be laughable if a man who imagined anything to his own taste, thought to justify himself by saying: "This object (the house we see, the coat that person wears, the concert we hear, the poem submitted to our judgment) is beautiful *for me*." For he must not call it *beautiful* if it merely pleases him. Many things may have for him charm and pleasantness; no one troubles himself at that; but if he gives out anything as beautiful, he supposes in others the same satisfaction—he

judges not merely for himself, but for every one, and
speaks of beauty as if it were a property of things.
Hence he says "the *thing* is beautiful"; and he does
not count on the agreement of others with this his
judgment of satisfaction, because he has found this
agreement several times before, but he *demands* it of
them.   He blames them if they judge otherwise and
he denies them taste, which he nevertheless requires
from them.   Here then we cannot say that each man
has his own particular taste.   For this would be as
much as to say that there is no taste whatever; *i.e.*
no æsthetical judgment, which can make a rightful
claim upon every one's assent.

At the same time we find as regards the Pleasant
that there is an agreement among men in their
judgments upon it, in regard to which we deny Taste
to some and attribute it to others; by this not
meaning one of our organic senses, but a faculty
of judging in respect of the pleasant generally.
Thus we say of a man who knows how to entertain
his guests with pleasures (of enjoyment for all
the senses), so that they are all pleased, "he has
taste."   But here the universality is only taken
comparatively; and there emerge rules which are
only *general* (like all empirical ones), and not *universal*; which latter the judgment of Taste upon
the beautiful undertakes or lays claim to.   It is a
judgment in reference to sociability, so far as this
rests on empirical rules.   In respect of the Good
it is true that judgments make rightful claim to
validity for every one; but the Good is represented
only *by means of a concept* as the Object of a
universal satisfaction, which is the case neither with
the Pleasant nor with the Beautiful.

§ 8. *The universality of the satisfaction is represented
in a judgment of Taste only as subjective*

This particular determination of the universality
of an æsthetical judgment, which is to be met with in
a judgment of taste, is noteworthy, not indeed for
the logician, but for the transcendental philosopher.
It requires no small trouble to discover its origin,
but we thus detect a property of our cognitive
faculty which without this analysis would remain
unknown.

First, we must be fully convinced of the fact
that in a judgment of taste (about the Beautiful)
the satisfaction in the object is imputed to *every one*,
without being based on a concept (for then it would
be the Good). Further, this claim to universal
validity so essentially belongs to a judgment by
which we describe anything as *beautiful*, that if
this were not thought in it, it would never come
into our thoughts to use the expression at all,
but everything which pleases without a concept
would be counted as pleasant. In respect of the
latter every one has his own opinion ; and no one
assumes in another, agreement with his judgment
of taste, which is always the case in a judgment
of taste about beauty. I may call the first the taste
of Sense, the second the taste of Reflection ; so
far as the first lays down mere private judgments,
and the second judgments supposed to be generally
valid (public), but in both cases æsthetical (not practical) judgments about an object merely in respect
of the relation of its representation to the feeling
of pleasure and pain. Now here is something
strange. As regards the taste of Sense not only

does experience show that its judgment (of pleasure or pain connected with anything) is not valid universally, but every one is content not to impute agreement with it to others (although actually there is often found a very extended concurrence in these judgments). On the other hand, the taste of Reflection has its claim to the universal validity of its judgments (about the beautiful) rejected often enough, as experience teaches; although it may find it possible (as it actually does) to represent judgments which can demand this universal agreement. In fact it imputes this to every one for each of its judgments of taste, without the persons that judge disputing as to the possibility of such a claim; although in particular cases they cannot agree as to the correct application of this faculty.

Here we must, in the first place, remark that a universality which does not rest on concepts of Objects (not even on empirical ones) is not logical but æsthetical, *i.e.* it involves no objective quantity of the judgment but only that which is subjective. For this I use the expression *general validity* which signifies the validity of the reference of a representation not to the cognitive faculty, but to the feeling of pleasure and pain for every subject. (We can avail ourselves also of the same expression for the logical quantity of the judgment, if only we prefix *objective* to "universal validity," to distinguish it from that which is merely subjective and æsthetical.)

A judgment with *objective universal validity* is also always valid subjectively; *i.e.* if the judgment holds for everything contained under a given concept, it holds also for every one who represents an object by means of this concept. But from a *subjective universal validity, i.e.* æsthetical and resting on no concept, we cannot infer that which is logical; because that kind of judgment does not extend to the Object. But therefore the æsthetical universality which is ascribed to a judgment must be of a particular kind, because it does not unite the predicate of beauty with the concept of the *Object*, considered in its whole logical sphere, and yet extends it to the whole sphere of judging persons.

In respect of logical quantity all judgments of taste are *singular* judgments. For because I must refer the object immediately to my feeling of pleasure and pain, and that not by means of concepts, they cannot have the quantity of objective generally valid judgments. Nevertheless if the singular representation of the Object of the judgment of taste in accordance with the conditions determining the latter, were transformed by comparison into a concept, a logically universal judgment could result therefrom. *E.g.* I describe by a judgment of taste the rose, that I see, as beautiful. But the judgment which results from the comparison of several singular judgments, " Roses in general are beautiful " is no longer described simply as æsthetical, but as a logical judgment based on an æsthetical one. Again the judgment " The rose is pleasant " (to use) is, although æsthetical and singular, not a judgment of Taste but of Sense. It is distinguished from the former by the fact that the judgment of Taste carries with it an *æsthetical quantity* of universality, *i.e.* of validity for every one ; which cannot be found in a judgment about the Pleasant. It is only judgments about the Good which—although they also determine satisfaction in an object,—have logical and not merely æsthetical universality ; for they are valid of the

Object, as cognitive of it, and thus are valid for every one.

If we judge Objects merely according to concepts, then all representation of beauty is lost. Thus there can be no rule according to which any one is to be forced to recognise anything as beautiful. We cannot press [upon others] by the aid of any reasons or fundamental propositions our judgment that a coat, a house, or a flower is beautiful. People wish to submit the Object to their own eyes, as if the satisfaction in it depended on sensation ; and yet if we then call the object beautiful, we believe that we speak with a universal voice, and we claim the assent of every one, although on the contrary all private sensation can only decide for the observer himself and his satisfaction.

We may see now that in the judgment of taste nothing is postulated but such a *universal voice*, in respect of the satisfaction without the intervention of concepts ; and thus the *possibility* of an æsthetical judgment that can, at the same time, be regarded as valid for every one. The judgment of taste itself does not *postulate* the agreement of every one (for that can only be done by a logically universal judgment because it can adduce reasons) ; it only *imputes* this agreement to every one, as a case of the rule in respect of which it expects, not confirmation by concepts, but assent from others. The universal voice is, therefore, only an Idea (we do not yet inquire upon what it rests). It may be uncertain whether or not the man, who believes that he is laying down a judgment of taste, is, as a matter of fact, judging in conformity with that Idea ; but that he refers his judgment thereto, and, consequently, that it is intended to be a judgment of taste, he

announces by the expression "beauty." He can
be quite certain of this for himself by the mere
consciousness of the separating off everything belonging to the Pleasant and the Good from the
satisfaction which is left ; and this is all for which he
promises himself the agreement of every one—a claim
which would be justifiable under these conditions,
provided only he did not often make mistakes, and
thus lay down an erroneous judgment of taste.

§ 9. *Investigation of the question whether in the
judgment of taste the feeling of pleasure precedes
or follows the judging of the object*

The solution of this question is the key to the
Kritik of Taste, and so is worthy of all attention.

If the pleasure in the given object precedes,
and it is only its universal communicability that is
to be acknowledged in the judgment of taste about
the representation of the object, there would be a
contradiction. For such pleasure would be nothing
different from the mere pleasantness in the sensation,
and so in accordance with its nature could have only
private validity, because it is immediately dependent
on the representation through which the object *is
given.*

Hence, it is the universal capability of communication of the mental state in the given representation which, as the subjective condition of
the judgment of taste, must be fundamental, and
must have the pleasure in the object as its consequent. But nothing can be universally communicated except cognition and representation, so
far as it belongs to cognition. For it is only thus
that this latter can be objective ; and only through

this has it a universal point of reference, with which the representative power of every one is compelled to harmonise. If the determining ground of our judgment as to this universal communicability of the representation is to be merely subjective, *i.e.* is conceived independently of any concept of the object, it can be nothing else than the state of mind, which is to be met with in the relation of our representative powers to each other, so far as they refer a given representation to *cognition in general.*

The cognitive powers, which are involved by this representation, are here in free play, because no definite concept limits them to a definite[1] rule of cognition. Hence, the state of mind in this representation must be a feeling of the free play of the representative powers in a given representation with reference to a cognition in general. Now a representation by which an object is given, that is to become a cognition in general, requires *Imagination*, for the gathering together the manifold of intuition, and *Understanding*, for the unity of the concept uniting the representations. This state of *free play* of the cognitive faculties in a representation by which an object is given, must be universally communicable; because cognition, as the determination of the Object with which given representations (in whatever subject) are to agree, is the only kind of representation which is valid for every one.

The subjective universal communicability of the mode of representation in a judgment of taste, since it is to be possible without presupposing a definite concept, can refer to nothing else than the state of mind in the free play of the Imagination

---

[1] [First Edition has *particular*.]

and the Understanding (so far as they agree with each other, as is requisite for *cognition in general*). We are conscious that this subjective relation, suitable for cognition in general, must be valid for every one, and thus must be universally communicable, just as if it were a definite cognition, resting always on that relation as its subjective condition.

This merely subjective (æsthetical) judging of the object, or of the representation by which it is given, precedes the pleasure in the same, and is the ground of this pleasure in the harmony of the cognitive faculties ; but on that universality of the subjective conditions for judging of objects is alone based the universal subjective validity of the satisfaction bound up by us with the representation of the object that we call beautiful.

That the power of communicating one's state of mind, even though only in respect of the cognitive faculties, carries a pleasure with it ; this we can easily show from the natural propension of man towards sociability (empirical and psychological). But this is not enough for our design. The pleasure that we feel is, in a judgment of taste, necessarily imputed by us to every one else ; as if, when we call a thing beautiful, it is to be regarded as a characteristic of the object which is determined in it according to concepts ; though beauty, without a reference to the feeling of the subject, is nothing by itself. But we must reserve the examination of this question until we have answered that other : "If and how æsthetical judgments are possible *a priori* ?"

We now occupy ourselves with the easier question, in what way we are conscious of a mutual subjective harmony of the cognitive powers with

F

one another in the judgment of taste; is it
æsthetically by mere internal sense and sensation?
or is it intellectually by the consciousness of our
designed activity, by which we bring them into
play?

If the given representation, which occasions the
judgment of taste, were a concept uniting Understanding and Imagination in the judging of the
object, into a cognition of the Object, the consciousness of this relation would be intellectual
(as in the objective schematism of the Judgment of
which the Kritik[1] treats). But then the judgment
would not be laid down in reference to pleasure and
pain, and consequently would not be a judgment of
taste. But the judgment of taste, independently of
concepts, determines the Object in respect of
satisfaction and of the predicate of beauty.
Therefore that subjective unity of relation can only
make itself known by means of sensation. The
excitement of both faculties (Imagination and
Understanding) to indeterminate, but yet, through
the stimulus of the given sensation, harmonious
activity, viz., that which belongs to cognition in
general, is the sensation whose universal communicability is postulated by the judgment of taste. An
objective relation can only be thought, but yet, so
far as it is subjective according to its conditions,
can be felt in its effect on the mind; and, of a
relation based on no concept (like the relation of the
representative powers to a cognitive faculty in
general), no other consciousness is possible than
that through the sensation of the effect, which
consists in the more lively play of both mental powers
(the Imagination and the Understanding) when

[1] [I.e. The Kritik of *Pure Reason*, Analytic, bk. ii. c. i.]

animated by mutual agreement. A representation which, as individual and apart from comparison with others, yet has an agreement with the conditions of universality which it is the business of the Understanding to supply, brings the cognitive faculties into that proportionate accord which we require for all cognition, and so regard as holding for every one who is determined to judge by means of Understanding and Sense in combination (*i.e.* for every man).

EXPLANATION OF THE BEAUTIFUL RESULTING FROM THE SECOND MOMENT

The *beautiful* is that which pleases universally without [requiring] a concept.

THIRD MOMENT

OF JUDGMENTS OF TASTE, ACCORDING TO THE RELATION OF THE PURPOSES WHICH ARE BROUGHT INTO CONSIDERATION IN THEM.

§ 10. *Of purposiveness in general*

If we wish to explain what a purpose is according to its transcendental determinations (without presupposing anything empirical like the feeling of pleasure) [we say that] the purpose is the object of a concept, in so far as the concept is regarded as the cause of the object (the real ground of its possibility) ; and the causality of a *concept* in respect of its *Object* is its purposiveness (*forma finalis*). Where then not merely the cognition of an object, but the object itself (its form and existence) is thought as an effect only possible by means of the concept of this latter, there we think a purpose. The representation of the effect is here the determining ground of its cause and precedes it. The consciousness of the causality of a representation, for *maintaining* the subject in the same state, may here generally denote what we call pleasure ; while on the other hand pain is that representation which contains the ground of the determination of the state of representations into their opposite [of restraining or removing them [1]].

The faculty of desire, so far as it is determinable to act only through concepts, *i.e.* in conformity with the representation of a purpose, would be the Will. But an Object, or a state of mind, or even an action, is called purposive, although its possibility does not necessarily presuppose the representation of a purpose, merely because its possibility can be explained and conceived by us only so far as we assume for its ground a causality according to purposes, *i.e.* in accordance with a will which has regulated it according to the representation of a certain rule. There can be, then, purposiveness without [2] purpose, so far as we do not place the causes of this form in a Will, but yet can only make the explanation of its possibility intelligible to ourselves by deriving it from a Will. Again, we are not always forced to regard what we observe (in respect of its possibility) from the point

---

[1] [Second Edition. Mr. Herbert Spencer expresses much more concisely what Kant has in his mind here. "Pleasure . . . is a feeling which we seek to bring into consciousness and retain there : pain is . . . a feeling which we seek to get out of consciousness and to keep out." *Principles of Psychology*, § 125.]

[2] [The editions of Hartentstein and Kirchmann omit *ohne* before *zweck*, which makes havoc of the sentence. It is correctly printed by Rosenkranz.]

of view of Reason.   Thus we can at least observe a purposiveness according to form, without basing it on a purpose (as the material of the *nexus finalis*), and remark it in objects, although only by reflection.

§ 11. *The judgment of taste has nothing at its basis but the* form *of the purposiveness of an object* (*or of its mode of representation*)

Every purpose, if it be regarded as a ground of satisfaction, always carries with it an interest—as the determining ground of the judgment—about the object of pleasure.   Therefore no subjective purpose can lie at the basis of the judgment of taste. But also the judgment of taste can be determined by no representation of an objective purpose, *i.e.* of the possibility of the object itself in accordance with principles of purposive combination, and consequently by no concept of the good ; because it is an æsthetical and not a cognitive judgment.   It therefore has to do with no *concept* of the character and internal or external possibility of the object by means of this or that cause, but merely with the relation of the representative powers to one another, so far as they are determined by a representation.

⋅ Now this relation in the determination of an object as beautiful is bound up with the feeling of pleasure, which is declared by the judgment of taste to be valid for every one ; hence a pleasantness, [merely] accompanying the representation, can as little contain the determining ground [of the judgment] as the representation of the perfection of the object and the concept of the good can.   Therefore it can be nothing else than the subjective purposiveness in the

representation of an object without any purpose
(either objective or subjective) ; and thus it is the
mere form of purposiveness in the representation by
which an object is *given* to us, so far as we are
conscious of it, which constitutes the satisfaction
that we without a concept judge to be universally
communicable ; and, consequently, this is the determining ground of the judgment of taste.

§ 12. *The judgment of taste rests on* a priori *grounds*

To establish *a priori* the connection of the
feeling of a pleasure or pain as an effect, with any
representation whatever (sensation or concept) as its
cause, is absolutely impossible ; for that would be a
[particular][1] causal relation which (with objects of
experience) can always only be cognised *a posteriori*,
and through the medium of experience itself. We
actually have, indeed, in the Kritik of practical
Reason, derived from universal moral concepts
a priori the feeling of respect (as a special and
peculiar modification of feeling which will not
strictly correspond either to the pleasure or the
pain that we get from empirical objects). But
there we could go beyond the bounds of experience
and call in a causality which rested on a supersensible attribute of the subject, viz., freedom. And
even there, properly speaking, it was not this *feeling*
which we derived from the Idea of the moral as
cause, but merely the determination of the will.
But the state of mind which accompanies any
determination of the will is in itself a feeling of
pleasure and identical with it, and therefore does

[1] [First Edition.]

not follow from it as its effect. This last must only be assumed if the concept of the moral as a good precede the determination of the will by the law ; for in that case the pleasure that is bound up with the concept could not be derived from it as from a mere cognition.

Now the case is similar with the pleasure in æsthetical judgments, only that here it is merely contemplative and does not bring about an interest in the Object, whilst on the other hand in the moral judgment it is practical.[1] The consciousness of the mere formal purposiveness in the play of the subject's cognitive powers, in a representation through which an object is given, is the pleasure itself ; because it contains a determining ground of the activity of the subject in respect of the excitement of its cognitive powers, and therefore an inner causality (which is purposive) in respect of cognition in general without however being limited to any definite cognition ; and consequently contains a mere form of the subjective purposiveness of a representation in an æsthetical judgment. This pleasure is in no way practical, neither like that arising from the pathological ground of pleasantness, nor that from the intellectual ground of the presented good. But yet it involves causality, viz., of *maintaining* without further design the state of the representation itself and the occupation of the cognitive powers. We *linger*

---

[1] [Cf. *Metaphysic of Morals*, Introd. I. "The pleasure which is necessarily bound up with the desire (of the object whose representation affects feeling) may be called *practical* pleasure, whether it be cause or effect of the desire. On the contrary, the pleasure which is not necessarily bound up with the desire of the object, and which, therefore, is at bottom not a pleasure in the existence of the Object of the representation, but clings to the representation only, may be called mere contemplative pleasure or *passive satisfaction*. The feeling of the latter kind of pleasure we call *taste*."]

over the contemplation of the beautiful, because this
contemplation strengthens and reproduces itself,
which is analogous to (though not of the same kind
as) that lingering which takes place when a [physical]
charm in the representation of the object repeatedly
arouses the attention, the mind being passive.

§ 13. *The pure judgment of taste is independent of charm and emotion*

Every interest spoils the judgment of taste and
takes from its impartiality, especially if the purposiveness is not, as with the interest of Reason,
placed before the feeling of pleasure but grounded
on it.   This last always happens in an æsthetical
judgment upon anything so far as it gratifies or
grieves us.   Hence judgments so affected can lay
no claim at all to a universally valid satisfaction, or
at least so much the less claim, in proportion as
there are sensations of this sort among the determining grounds of taste.   That taste is always
barbaric which needs a mixture of *charms* and
emotions in order that there may be satisfaction, and
still more so if it make these the measure of its
assent.

Nevertheless charms are often not only taken
account of in the case of beauty (which properly
speaking ought merely to be concerned with form) as
contributory to the æsthetical universal satisfaction ;
but they are passed off as in themselves beauties,
and thus the matter of satisfaction is substituted for
the form.   This misconception, however, which like
so many others, has something true at its basis, may
be removed by a careful determination of these
concepts.

A judgment of taste on which charm and emotion

have no influence (although they may be bound up
with the satisfaction in the beautiful),—which therefore has as its determining ground merely the purposiveness of the form,—is a *pure judgment of taste*.

§ 14. *Elucidation by means of examples*

Æsthetical judgments can be divided just like
theoretical (logical) judgments into empirical and
pure. The first assert pleasantness or unpleasantness ; the second assert the beauty of an object or
of the manner of representing it. The former are
judgments of Sense (material æsthetical judgments) ;
the latter [as formal [1]] are alone strictly judgments
of Taste.

A judgment of taste is therefore pure, only so
far as no merely empirical satisfaction is mingled
with its determining ground. But this always
happens if charm or emotion have any share in the
judgment by which anything is to be described as
beautiful.

Now here many objections present themselves,
which fallaciously put forward charm not merely as
a necessary ingredient of beauty, but as alone
sufficient [to justify] a thing's being called beautiful.
A mere colour, *e.g.* the green of a grass plot, a mere
tone (as distinguished from sound and noise) like
that of a violin, are by most people described as
beautiful in themselves ; although both seem to have
at their basis merely the matter of representations,
viz., simply sensation, and therefore only deserve to
be called pleasant. But we must at the same time
remark that the sensations of colours and of tone
have a right to be regarded as beautiful only in so

[1] [Second Edition.]

far as they are *pure*. This is a determination which
concerns their form, and is the only [element] of
these representations which admits with certainty of
universal communicability; for we cannot assume
that the quality of sensations is the same in all
subjects, and we can hardly say that the pleasantness
of one colour or the tone of one musical instrument
is judged preferable to that of another in the same [1]
way by every one.

If we assume with *Euler* that colours are iso-
chronous vibrations (*pulsus*) of the æther, as sounds
are of the air in a state of disturbance, and,—
what is the most important,— that the mind
not only perceives by sense the effect of these in
exciting the organ, but also perceives by reflection
the regular play of impressions (and thus the form of
the combination of different representations)—which
I very much doubt [2]—then colours and tone cannot
be reckoned as mere sensations, but as the formal
determination of the unity of a manifold of sensations, and thus as beauties.

But "pure" in a simple mode of sensation means
that its uniformity is troubled and interrupted by no
foreign sensation, and it belongs merely to the form;
because here we can abstract from the quality of
that mode of sensation (abstract from the colours
and tone, if any, which it represents). Hence all
simple colours, so far as they are pure, are regarded
as beautiful; composite colours have not this advantage, because, as they are not simple, we have no
standard for judging whether they should be called
pure or not.

---

[1] [First Edition has *gleiche*; Second Edition has *solche*.]
[2] [First Edition has *nicht zweifle* for *sehr zweifle*; but this was
apparently only a misprint.]

But as regards the beauty attributed to the object on account of its form, to suppose it to be capable of augmentation through the charm of the object is a common error, and one very prejudicial to genuine, uncorrupted, well-founded taste. We can doubtless add these charms to beauty, in order to interest the mind by the representation of the object, apart from the bare satisfaction [received]; and thus they may serve as a recommendation of taste and its cultivation, especially when it is yet crude and un-exercised. But they actually do injury to the judgment of taste if they draw attention to themselves as the grounds for judging of beauty. So far are they from adding to beauty that they must only be admitted by indulgence as aliens; and provided always that they do not disturb the beautiful form, in cases when taste is yet weak and unexercised.

In painting, sculpture, and in all the formative arts —in architecture, and horticulture, so far as they are beautiful arts—the *delineation* is the essential thing; and here it is not what gratifies in sensation but what pleases by means of its form that is fundamental for taste. The colours which light up the sketch belong to the charm; they may indeed enliven[1] the object for sensation, but they cannot make it worthy of contemplation and beautiful. In most cases they are rather limited by the requirements of the beautiful form; and even where charm is permissible it is ennobled solely by this.

Every form of the objects of sense (both of external sense and also mediately of internal) is either *figure* or *play*. In the latter case it is either play of figures (in space, viz., pantomime and dancing), or the mere play of sensations (in time).

---

[1] [*Belebt machen*; First Edition had *beliebt.*]

The *charm* of colours or of the pleasant tones of an
instrument may be added ; but the *delineation* in the
first case and the composition in the second constitute the proper object of the pure judgment of taste.
To say that the purity of colours and of tones, or
their variety and contrast, seems to add to beauty,
does not mean that they supply a homogeneous
addition to our satisfaction in the form because they
are pleasant in themselves ; but they do so, because
they make the form more exactly, definitely, and
completely, intuitible, and besides by their charm
[excite the representation, whilst they[1]] awaken and
fix our attention on the object itself.

Even what we call *ornaments* [parerga[2]], *i.e.*
those things which do not belong to the complete
representation of the object internally as elements
but only externally as complements, and which
augment the satisfaction of taste, do so only by their
form ; as for example [the frames of pictures,[3] or]
the draperies of statues or the colonnades of palaces.
But if the ornament does not itself consist in beautiful form, and if it is used as a golden frame is used,
merely to recommend the painting by its *charm*, it
is then called *finery* and injures genuine beauty.

Emotion, that is a sensation in which pleasantness is produced by means of a momentary checking and a consequent more powerful outflow of the
vital force, does not belong at all to beauty. But
sublimity [with which the feeling of emotion is
bound up[4]] requires a different standard of judgment from that which is at the foundation of taste :
and thus a pure judgment of taste has for its determining ground neither charm nor emotion, in a word,

---

[1] [Second Edition.]   [2] [Second Edition.]
[3] [Second Edition.]   [4] [Second Edition.]

no sensation as the material of the æsthetical judgment.

§ 15. *The judgment of taste is quite independent of the concept of perfection*

Objective purposiveness can only be cognised by means of the reference of the manifold to a definite purpose, and therefore only through a concept. From this alone it is plain that the Beautiful, the judging of which has at its basis a merely formal purposiveness, *i.e.* a purposiveness without purpose, is quite independent of the concept of the Good ; because the latter presupposes an objective purposiveness, *i.e.* the reference of the object to a definite purpose.

Objective purposiveness is either external, *i.e.* the *utility*, or internal, *i.e.* the *perfection* of the object. That the satisfaction in an object, on account of which we call it beautiful, cannot rest on the representation of its utility, is sufficiently obvious from the two preceding sections ; because in that case it would not be an immediate satisfaction in the object, which is the essential condition of a judgment about beauty. But objective internal purposiveness, *i.e.* perfection, comes nearer to the predicate of beauty ; and it has been regarded by celebrated philosophers[1] as the same as beauty, with the proviso, *if it is thought in a confused way*. It is of the greatest importance in a Kritik of Taste to decide whether beauty can thus actually be resolved into the concept of perfection.

[1] [Kant probably refers here to Baumgarten (1714-1762), who was the first writer to give the name of Æsthetics to the Philosophy of Taste. He defined beauty as " perfection apprehended through the senses." Kant is said to have used as a text-book at lectures a work by Meier, a pupil of Baumgarten's, on this subject.]

To judge of objective purposiveness we always need not only the concept of a purpose, but (if that purposiveness is not to be external utility but internal) the concept of an internal purpose which shall contain the ground of the internal possibility of the object. Now as a purpose in general is that whose *concept* can be regarded as the ground of the possibility of the object itself; so, in order to represent objective purposiveness in a thing, the concept of *what sort of thing it is to be* must come first. The agreement of the manifold in it with this concept (which furnishes the rule for combining the manifold) is the *qualitative perfection* of the thing. Quite different from this is *quantitative* perfection, the completeness of a thing after its kind, which is a mere concept of magnitude (of totality).[1] In this *what the thing ought to be* is conceived as already determined, and it is only asked if it has *all* its requisites. The formal [element] in the representation of a thing, *i.e.* the agreement of the manifold with a unity (it being undetermined what this ought to be), gives to cognition no objective purposiveness whatever. For since abstraction is made of this unity as *purpose* (what the thing ought to be), nothing remains but the subjective purposiveness of the representations in the mind of the intuiting subject. And this, although it furnishes a certain purposiveness of the representative state of the

[1] [Cf. Preface to the *Metaphysical Elements of Ethics*, v. : "The word *perfection* is liable to many misconceptions. It is sometimes understood as a concept belonging to Transcendental Philosophy ; viz. the concept of the *totality* of the manifold, which, taken together, constitutes a Thing ; sometimes, again, it is understood as belonging to *Teleology*, so that it signifies the agreement of the characteristics of a thing with a *purpose*. Perfection in the former sense might be called *quantitative* (material), in the latter *qualitative* (formal) perfection."]

subject, and so a facility of apprehending a given form by the Imagination, yet furnishes no perfection of an Object, since the Object is not here conceived by means of the concept of a purpose.   For example, if in a forest I come across a plot of sward, round which trees stand in a circle, and do not then represent to myself a purpose, viz. that it is intended to serve for country dances, not the least concept of perfection is furnished by the mere form.   But to represent to oneself a formal *objective* purposiveness without purpose, *i.e.* the mere form of a *perfection* (without any matter and without the *concept* of that with which it is accordant, even if it were merely the idea of conformity to law in general[1]) is a veritable contradiction.

Now the judgment of taste is an æsthetical judgment, *i.e.* such as rests on subjective grounds, the determining ground of which cannot be a concept, and consequently cannot be the concept of a definite purpose.   Therefore by means of beauty, regarded as a formal subjective purposiveness, there is in no way thought a perfection of the object, as a purposiveness alleged to be formal, but which is yet objective. And thus to distinguish between the concepts of the Beautiful and the Good, as if they were only different in logical form, the first being a confused, the second a clear concept of perfection, but identical in content and origin, is quite fallacious. For then there would be no *specific* difference between them, but a judgment of taste would be as much a cognitive judgment as the judgment by which a thing is described as good ; just as when the ordinary man says that fraud is unjust he bases

---

[1] [The words *even if . . . general* were added in the Second Edition.]

his judgment on confused grounds, whilst the philosopher bases it on clear grounds, but both on identical principles of Reason. I have already, however, said that an æsthetical judgment is unique of its kind, and gives absolutely no cognition (not even a confused cognition) of the Object ; this is only supplied by a logical judgment. On the contrary, it simply refers the representation, by which an Object is given, to the subject ; and brings to our notice no characteristic of the object, but only the purposive form in the determination of the representative powers which are occupying themselves therewith. The judgment is called æsthetical just because its determining ground is not a concept, but the feeling (of internal sense) of that harmony in the play of the mental powers, so far as it can be felt in sensation. On the other hand, if we wish to call confused concepts and the objective judgment based on them, æsthetical, we will have an Understanding judging sensibly or a Sense representing its Objects by means of concepts [both of which are contradictory.[1]] The faculty of concepts, be they confused or clear, is the Understanding ; and although Understanding has to do with the judgment of taste, as an æsthetical judgment (as it has with all judgments), yet it has to do with it not as a faculty by which an object is cognised, but as the faculty which determines the judgment and its representation (without any concept) in accordance with its relation to the subject and the subject's internal feeling, in so far as this judgment may be possible in accordance with a universal rule.

[1] [Second Edition.]

§ 16. *The judgment of taste, by which an object is declared to be beautiful under the condition of a definite concept, is not pure*

There are two kinds of beauty; free beauty (*pulchritudo vaga*) or merely dependent beauty (*pulchritudo adhaerens*). The first presupposes no concept of what the object ought to be ; the second does presuppose such a concept and the perfection of the object in accordance therewith. The first is called the (self-subsistent) beauty of this or that thing ; the second, as dependent upon a concept (conditioned beauty), is ascribed to objects which come under the concept of a particular purpose.

Flowers are free natural beauties. Hardly any one but a botanist knows what sort of a thing a flower ought to be ; and even he, though recognising in the flower the reproductive organ of the plant, pays no regard to this natural purpose if he is passing judgment on the flower by Taste. There is then at the basis of this judgment no perfection of any kind, no internal purposiveness, to which the collection of the manifold is referred. Many birds (such as the parrot, the humming bird, the bird of paradise), and many sea shells are beauties in themselves, which do not belong to any object determined in respect of its purpose by concepts, but please freely and in themselves. So also delineations *à la grecque*, foliage for borders or wall-papers, mean nothing in themselves ; they represent nothing—no Object under a definite concept,—and are free beauties. We can refer to the same class what are called in music phantasies (*i.e.* pieces without any theme), and in fact all music without words.

G

In the judging of a free beauty (according to the mere form) the judgment of taste is pure. There is presupposed no concept of any purpose, which the manifold of the given object is to serve, and which therefore is to be represented in it. By such a concept the freedom of the Imagination which disports itself in the contemplation of the figure would be only limited.

But human beauty (*i.e.* of a man, a woman, or a child), the beauty of a horse, or a building (be it church, palace, arsenal, or summer-house) presupposes a concept of the purpose which determines what the thing is to be, and consequently a concept of its perfection; it is therefore adherent beauty. Now as the combination of the Pleasant (in sensation) with Beauty, which properly is only concerned with form, is a hindrance to the purity of the judgment of taste; so also is its purity injured by the combination with Beauty of the Good (viz. that manifold which is good for the thing itself in accordance with its purpose).

We could add much to a building which would immediately please the eye, if only it were not to be a church. We could adorn a figure with all kinds of spirals and light but regular lines, as the New Zealanders do with their tattooing, if only it were not the figure of a human being. And again this could have much finer features and a more pleasing and gentle cast of countenance provided it were not intended to represent a man, much less a warrior.

Now the satisfaction in the manifold of a thing in reference to the internal purpose which determines its possibility is a satisfaction grounded on a concept; but the satisfaction in beauty is such as presupposes no concept, but is immediately bound up with the

representation through which the object is given
(not through which it is thought).   If now the judgment of Taste in respect of the beauty of a thing is
made dependent on the purpose in its manifold, like
a judgment of Reason, and thus limited, it is no longer
a free and pure judgment of Taste.

It is true that taste gains by this combination of
æsthetical with intellectual satisfaction, inasmuch as
it becomes fixed ; and though it is not universal, yet
in respect to certain purposively determined Objects
it becomes possible to prescribe rules for it.   These,
however, are not rules of taste, but merely rules
for the unification of Taste with Reason, *i.e.* of the
Beautiful with the Good, by which the former
becomes available as an instrument of design in
respect of the latter.   Thus the tone of mind which
is self-maintaining and of subjective universal validity
is subordinated to the way of thinking which can be
maintained only by painful resolve, but is of objective
universal validity.   Properly speaking, however, perfection gains nothing by beauty or beauty by
perfection ; but, when we compare the representation by which an object is given to us with the
Object (as regards what it ought to be) by means
of a concept, we cannot avoid considering along with
it the sensation in the subject.   And thus when
both states of mind are in harmony our *whole faculty*
of representative power gains.

A judgment of taste, then, in respect of an object
with a definite internal purpose, can only be pure,
if either the person judging has no concept of this
purpose, or else abstracts from it in his judgment.
Such a person, although forming an accurate judgment of taste in judging of the object as free beauty,
would yet by another who considers the beauty in

it only as a dependent attribute (who looks to the purpose of the object) be blamed, and accused of false taste ; although both are right in their own way, the one in reference to what he has before his eyes, the other in reference to what he has in his thought. By means of this distinction we can settle many disputes about beauty between judges of taste ; by showing that the one is speaking of free, the other of dependent, beauty,—that the first is making a pure, the second an applied, judgment of taste.

§ 17. *Of the Ideal of beauty*

There can be no objective rule of taste which shall determine by means of concepts what is beautiful. For every judgment from this source is æsthetical ; *i.e.* the feeling of the subject, and not a concept of the Object, is its determining ground. To seek for a principle of taste which shall furnish, by means of definite concepts, a universal criterion of the beautiful, is fruitless trouble ; because what is sought is impossible and self-contradictory. The universal communicability of sensation (satisfaction or dissatisfaction) without the aid of a concept— the agreement, as far as is possible, of all times and peoples as regards this feeling in the representation of certain objects—this is the empirical criterion, although weak and hardly sufficing for probability, of the derivation of a taste, thus confirmed by examples, from the deep-lying general grounds of agreement in judging of the forms under which objects are given.

Hence, we consider some products of taste as *exemplary.* Not that taste can be acquired by imitating others ; for it must be an original faculty. He who imitates a model shows, no doubt, in so far as he attains to it, skill ; but only shows taste in so far as he can judge of this model itself.[1]   It follows from hence that the highest model, the archetype of taste, is a mere Idea, which every one must produce in himself; and according to which he must judge every Object of taste, every example of judgment by taste, and even the taste of every one. *Idea* properly means a rational concept, and *Ideal* the representation of an individual being, regarded as adequate to an Idea.[2]   Hence that archetype of taste, which certainly rests on the indeterminate Idea that Reason has of a maximum, but which cannot be represented by concepts, but only in an individual presentation, is better called the Ideal of the beautiful. Although we are not in possession of this, we yet strive to produce it in ourselves. But it can only be an Ideal of the Imagination, because it rests on a presentation and not on concepts, and the Imagination is the faculty of presentation.— How do we arrive at such an Ideal of beauty ? *A priori*, or empirically ? Moreover, what species of the beautiful is susceptible of an Ideal ?

First, it is well to remark that the beauty for

---

[1] Models of taste as regards the arts of speech must be composed in a dead and learned language. The first, in order that they may not suffer that change which inevitably comes over living languages, in which noble expressions become flat, common ones antiquated, and newly created ones have only a short circulation. The second, because learned languages have a grammar which is subject to no wanton change of fashion, but the rules of which are preserved unchanged.

[2] [This distinction between an *Idea* and an *Ideal*, as also the further contrast between Ideals of the Reason and Ideals of the Imagination, had already been given by Kant in the Kritik of *Pure Reason*, Dialectic, bk. ii. c. iii. § 1.]

which an Ideal is to be sought cannot be *vague*
beauty, but is *fixed* by a concept of objective
purposiveness ; and thus it cannot appertain to the
Object of a quite pure judgment of taste, but to
that of a judgment of taste which is in part intellectual. That is, in whatever grounds of judgment an Ideal is to be found, an Idea of Reason
in accordance with definite concepts must lie at
its basis ; which determines *a priori* the purpose
on which the internal possibility of the object rests.
An Ideal of beautiful flowers, of a beautiful piece
of furniture, of a beautiful view, is inconceivable.
But neither can an Ideal be represented of a beauty
dependent on definite purposes, *e.g.* of a beautiful
dwelling-house, a beautiful tree, a beautiful garden,
etc. ; presumably because their purpose is not
sufficiently determined and fixed by the concept,
and thus the purposiveness is nearly as free as
in the case of *vague* beauty. The only being which
has the purpose of its existence in itself is *man*, who
can determine his purposes by Reason ; or, where
he must receive them from external perception, yet
can compare them with essential and universal
purposes, and can judge this their accordance
æsthetically. This *man* is, then, alone of all objects
in the world, susceptible of an Ideal of *beauty* ; as
it is only *humanity* in his person, as an intelligence,
that is susceptible of the Ideal of *perfection*.

But there are here two elements. *First*, there
is the æsthetical *normal Idea*, which is an individual
intuition (of the Imagination), representing the
standard of our judgment [upon man] as a thing
belonging to a particular animal species. *Secondly*,
there is the *rational Idea* which makes the purposes
of humanity, so far as they cannot be sensibly

represented, the principle for judging of a figure
through which, as their phenomenal effect, those
purposes are revealed.   The normal Idea of the
figure of an animal of a particular race must take its
elements from experience.   But the greatest
purposiveness in the construction of the figure,
that would be available for the universal standard
of æsthetical judgment upon each individual of this
species—the image which is as it were designedly
at the basis of nature's Technic, to which only
the whole race and not any isolated individual is
adequate — this lies merely in the Idea of the
judging [subject].   And this, with its proportions,
as an æsthetical Idea, can be completely presented
in concreto in a model.   In order to make intelligible
in some measure (for who can extract her whole
secret from nature?) how this comes to pass, we
shall attempt a psychological explanation.

We must remark that, in a way quite incomprehensible by us, the Imagination can not only recall,
on occasion, the signs for concepts long past,
but can also reproduce the image of the figure
of the object out of an unspeakable number of
objects of different kinds or even of the same kind.
Further, if the mind is concerned with comparisons,
the Imagination can, in all probability, actually
though unconsciously let one image glide into
another, and thus by the concurrence of several of
the same kind come by an average, which serves as
the common measure of all.   Every one has seen a
thousand full-grown men.   Now if you wish to
judge of their normal size, estimating it by means of
comparison, the Imagination (as I think) allows a
great number of images (perhaps the whole
thousand), to fall on one another.   If I am allowed

to apply here the analogy of optical presentation,
it is in the space where most of them are combined
and inside the contour, where the place is illumi-
nated with the most vivid colours, that the *average
size* is cognisable; which, both in height and
breadth, is equally far removed from the extreme
bounds of the greatest and smallest stature. And
this is the stature of a beautiful man. (We could
arrive at the same thing mechanically, by adding
together all thousand magnitudes, heights, breadths,
and thicknesses, and dividing the sum by a thousand. But the Imagination does this by means
of a dynamical effect, which arises from the various
impressions of such figures on the organ of internal
sense.) If now in a similar way for this average
man we seek the average head, for this head
the average nose, etc., such figure is at the basis
of the normal Idea in the country where the
comparison is instituted. Thus necessarily under
these empirical conditions a negro must have a
different normal Idea of the beauty of the [human
figure] from a white man, a Chinaman a different
normal Idea from a European, etc. And the same
is the case with the model of a beautiful horse or
dog (of a certain breed).— This *normal Idea* is not
derived from proportions got from experience [and
regarded] *as definite rules*; but in accordance with
it rules for judging become in the first instance
possible. It is the image for the whole race, which
floats among all the variously different intuitions of
individuals, which nature takes as archetype in her
productions of the same species, but which appears
not to be fully reached in any individual case. It is
by no means the whole *archetype of beauty* in the
race, but only the form constituting the indis-

pensable condition of all beauty, and thus merely *correctness* in the [mental] presentation of the race. It is, like the celebrated *Doryphorus* of *Polycletus*,[1] the *rule* (*Myron's*[2] Cow might also be used thus for its kind). It can therefore contain nothing specifically characteristic, for otherwise it would not be the *normal Idea* for the race. Its presentation pleases, not by its beauty, but merely because it contradicts no condition, under which alone a thing of this kind can be beautiful. The presentation is merely correct.[3]

We must yet distinguish the *normal Idea* of the beautiful from the *Ideal*, which latter, on grounds already alleged, we can only expect in the *human* figure. In this the Ideal consists in the expression of the *moral*, without which the object would not please universally and thus positively (not merely negatively in an accurate presentation). The visible expression of moral Ideas that rule men

---

[1] [Polycletus of Argos flourished about 430 B.C. His statue of the *Spearbearer* (*Doryphorus*), afterwards became known as the *Canon*; because in it the artist was supposed to have embodied a perfect representation of the ideal of the human figure.]

[2] [This was a celebrated statue executed by Myron, a Greek sculptor, contemporary with Polycletus. It is frequently mentioned in the Greek Anthology.]

[3] It will be found that a perfectly regular countenance, such as a painter might wish to have for a model, ordinarily tells us nothing ; because it contains nothing characteristic, and therefore rather expresses the Idea of the race than the specific [traits] of a person. The exaggeration of a characteristic of this kind, *i.e.* such as does violence to the normal Idea (the purposiveness of the race) is called *caricature*. Experience also shows that these quite regular countenances commonly indicate internally only a mediocre man ; presumably (if it may be assumed that external nature expresses the proportions of internal) because, if no mental disposition exceeds that proportion which is requisite in order to constitute a man free from faults, nothing can be expected of what is called *genius*, in which nature seems to depart from the ordinary relations of the mental powers on behalf of some special one.

inwardly, can indeed only be got from experience ; but to make its connection with all which our Reason unites with the morally good in the Idea of the highest purposiveness,—goodness of heart, purity, strength, peace, etc.,—visible as it were in bodily manifestation (as the effect of that which is internal), requires a union of pure Ideas of Reason with great imaginative power, even in him who wishes to judge of it, still more in him who wishes to present it.   The correctness of such an Ideal of beauty is shown by its permitting no sensible charm to mingle with the satisfaction in the Object and yet allowing us to take a great interest therein.   This shows that a judgment in accordance with such a standard can never be purely æsthetical, and that a judgment in accordance with an Ideal of beauty is not a mere judgment of taste.

EXPLANATION OF THE BEAUTIFUL
DERIVED FROM THIS THIRD MOMENT

Beauty is the form of the *purposiveness* of an object, so far as this is perceived in it *without any representation of a purpose.*[1]

---

[1] It might be objected to this explanation that there are things, in which we see a purposive form without cognising any purpose in them, like the stone implements often got from old sepulchral tumuli with a hole in them as if for a handle.   These, although they plainly indicate by their shape a purposiveness of which we do not know the purpose, are nevertheless not described as beautiful.   But if we regard a thing as a work of art, that is enough to make us admit that its shape has reference to some design and definite purpose. And hence there is no immediate satisfaction in the contemplation of it.   On the other hand a flower, *e.g.* a tulip, is regarded as beautiful ; because in perceiving it we find a certain purposiveness which, in our judgment, is referred to no purpose at all.

FOURTH MOMENT

OF THE JUDGMENT OF TASTE, ACCORDING TO THE
MODALITY OF THE SATISFACTION IN THE OBJECT

§ 18. *What the modality in a judgment of taste is*

I can say of every representation that it is at
least *possible* that (as a cognition) it should be bound
up with a pleasure. Of a representation that I
call *pleasant* I say that it *actually* excites pleasure
in me. But the *beautiful* we think as having a
necessary-reference to satisfaction. Now this necessity is of a peculiar kind. It is not a theoretical
objective necessity; in which case it would be
cognised *a priori* that every one *will feel* this satisfaction in the object called beautiful by me. It is
not a practical necessity; in which case, by concepts of a pure rational will serving as a rule for
freely acting beings, the satisfaction is the necessary
result of an objective law and only indicates that we
absolutely (without any further design) ought to
act in a certain way. But the necessity which is
thought in an æsthetical judgment can only be called
exemplary; *i.e.* a necessity of the assent of *all* to a
judgment which is regarded as the example of a
universal rule that we cannot state. Since an æsthetical judgment is not an objective cognitive judgment, this necessity cannot be derived from definite
concepts, and is therefore not apodictic. Still less
can it be inferred from the universality of experience
(of a complete agreement of judgments as to the
beauty of a certain object). For not only would

experience hardly furnish sufficiently numerous vouchers for this; but also, on empirical judgments we can base no concept of the necessity of these judgments.

§ 19. *The subjective necessity, which we ascribe to the judgment of taste, is conditioned*

The judgment of taste requires the agreement of every one; and he who describes anything as beautiful claims that every one *ought* to give his approval to the object in question and also describe it as beautiful. The *ought* in the æsthetical judgment is therefore pronounced in accordance with all the data which are required for judging and yet is only conditioned. We ask for the agreement of every one else, because we have for it a ground that is common to all; and we could count on this agreement, provided we were always sure that the case was correctly subsumed under that ground as rule of assent.

§ 20. *The condition of necessity which a judgment of taste asserts is the Idea of a common sense*

If judgments of taste (like cognitive judgments) had a definite objective principle, then the person who lays them down in accordance with this latter would claim an unconditioned necessity for his judgment. If they were devoid of all principle, like those of the mere taste of sense, we would not allow them in thought any necessity whatever. Hence they must have a subjective principle which determines what pleases or displeases only by feeling and not by concepts, but yet with universal validity. But such a principle could only be regarded as a *common sense*, which is essentially different from common Understanding which people sometimes call common Sense (*sensus communis*); for the latter does not judge by feeling but always by concepts, although ordinarily only as by obscurely represented principles.

Hence it is only under the presupposition that there is a common sense (by which we do not understand an external sense, but the effect resulting from the free play of our cognitive powers)—it is only under this presupposition, I say, that the judgment of taste can be laid down.

§ 21. *Have we ground for presupposing a common sense?*

Cognitions and judgments must, along with the conviction that accompanies them, admit of universal communicability; for otherwise there would be no harmony between them and the Object, and they would be collectively a mere subjective play of the representative powers, exactly as scepticism desires. But if cognitions are to admit of communicability, so must also the state of mind,—*i.e.* the accordance of the cognitive powers with a cognition generally, and that proportion of them which is suitable for a representation (by which an object is given to us) in order that a cognition may be made out of it— admit of universal communicability. For without this as the subjective condition of cognition, cognition as an effect could not arise. This actually always takes place when a given object by means of Sense excites the Imagination to collect the manifold, and the Imagination in its turn excites the Understanding to bring about a unity of this collective process in concepts. But this accordance of the cognitive

powers has a different proportion according to the
variety of the Objects which are given. However, it
must be such that this internal relation, by which one
mental faculty is excited by another, shall be generally the most beneficial for both faculties in respect
of cognition (of given objects); and this accordance
can only be determined by feeling (not according to
concepts). Since now this accordance itself must
admit of universal communicability, and consequently
also our feeling of it (in a given representation), and
since the universal communicability of ¯a feeling
presupposes a common sense, we have grounds for
assuming this latter. And this common sense is
assumed without relying on psychological observations, but simply as the necessary condition of the
universal communicability of our knowledge, which
is presupposed in every Logic and in every principle of knowledge that is not sceptical.

§ 22. *The necessity of the universal agreement that
is thought in a judgment of taste is a subjective
necessity, which is represented as objective under
the presupposition of a common sense*

In all judgments by which we describe anything
as beautiful, we allow no one to be of another
opinion; without however grounding our judgment
on concepts but only on our feeling, which we therefore place at its basis not as a private, but as a
common, feeling. Now this common sense cannot
be grounded on experience; for it aims at justifying
judgments which contain an *ought*. It does not say
that every one *will* agree with my judgment, but
that he *ought*. And so common sense, as an
example of whose judgment I here put forward my

judgment of taste and on account of which I attribute to the latter an *exemplary* validity, is a mere ideal norm, under the supposition of which I have a right to make into a rule for every one a judgment that accords therewith, as well as the satisfaction in an Object expressed in such judgment. For the principle, which concerns the agreement of different judging persons, although only subjective, is yet assumed as subjectively universal (an Idea necessary for every one); and thus can claim universal assent (as if it were objective) provided we are sure that we have correctly subsumed [the particulars] under it.

This indeterminate norm of a common sense is actually presupposed by us; as is shown by our claim to lay down judgments of taste. Whether there is in fact such a common sense, as a constitutive principle of the possibility of experience, or whether a yet higher principle of Reason makes it only into a regulative principle for producing in us a common sense for higher purposes: whether therefore Taste is an original and natural faculty, or only the Idea of an artificial one yet to be acquired, so that a judgment of taste with its assumption of a universal assent in fact, is only a requirement of Reason for producing such harmony of sentiment; whether the ought, *i.e.* the objective necessity of the confluence of the feeling of any one man with that of every other, only signifies the possibility of arriving at this accord, and the judgment of taste only affords an example of the application of this principle: these questions we have neither the wish nor the power to investigate as yet; we have now only to resolve the faculty of taste into its elements in order to unite them at last in the Idea of a common sense.

EXPLANATION OF THE BEAUTIFUL RESULTING FROM THE FOURTH MOMENT

The *beautiful* is that which without any concept is cognised as the object of a *necessary* satisfaction.

GENERAL REMARK ON THE FIRST SECTION OF THE ANALYTIC

If we seek the result of the preceding analysis we find that everything runs up into this concept of Taste, that it is a faculty for judging an object in reference to the Imagination's *free conformity to law*. Now if in the judgment of taste the Imagination must be considered in its freedom, it is in the first place not regarded as reproductive, as it is subject to the laws of association, but as productive and spontaneous (as the author of arbitrary forms of possible in- tuition). And although in the apprehension of a given object of sense it is tied to a definite form of this Object, and so far has no free play (such as that of poetry) yet it may readily be conceived that the object can furnish it with such a form containing a collection of the manifold, as the Imagination itself, if it were left free, would project in accordance with the *conformity to law of the Understanding* in general. But that the *imaginative power* should be *free* and yet *of itself conformed to law, i.e.* bringing autonomy with it, is a contradiction. The Under- standing alone gives the law. If, however, the Imagination is compelled to proceed according to a definite law, its product in respect of form is deter- mined by concepts as to what it ought to be. But then, as is above shown, the satisfaction is not that in the Beautiful, but in the Good (in perfection, at any rate in mere formal perfection) ; and the judgment is not a judgment of taste.   Hence it is a conformity to law without a law ; and a subjective agreement of the Imagination and Understanding, —without such an objective agreement as there is when the representation is referred to a definite concept of an object,—can subsist along with the free conformity to law of the Understanding (which is also called purposiveness without purpose) and with the peculiar feature of a judgment of taste.

Now geometrically regular figures, such as a circle, a square, a cube, etc., are commonly adduced by critics of taste as the simplest and most indisputable examples of beauty ; and yet they are called regular, because we can only represent them by regarding them as mere presentations of a definite concept which prescribes the rule for the figure (according to which alone it is possible).   One of these two must be wrong, either that judgment of the critic which ascribes beauty to the said figures, or ours, which regards purposiveness apart from a concept as requisite for beauty.

Hardly any one will say that a man must have taste in order that he should find more satisfaction in a circle than in a scrawled outline, in an equilateral and equiangular quadrilateral than in one which is oblique, irregular, and as it were deformed, for this belongs to the ordinary Understanding and is not Taste at all. Where, *e.g.*, our design is to judge of the size of an area, or to make intelligible the relation of the parts of it, when divided, to one another and to the whole, then regular figures and those of the simplest kind are needed, and the satisfaction does not rest immediately on the aspect of the figure, but on its availability for

all kinds of possible designs. A room whose walls
form oblique angles, or a parterre of this kind, even
every violation of symmetry in the figure of animals
(*e.g.* being one-eyed), of buildings, or of flower beds,
displeases, because it contradicts the purpose of the
thing, not only practically in respect of a definite
use of it, but also when we pass judgment on it as
regards any possible design. This is not the case
in the judgment of taste, which when pure combines satisfaction or dissatisfaction,—without any
reference to its use or to a purpose,—with the mere
consideration of the object.

The regularity which leads to the concept of an
object is indeed the indispensable condition (*conditio
sine qua non*) for grasping the object in a single
representation and determining the manifold in its
form. This determination is a purpose in respect of
cognition, and in reference to this it is always bound
up with satisfaction (which accompanies the execution of every, even problematical, design). There is
here, however, merely the approval of the solution
satisfying a problem, and not a free and indefinite
purposive entertainment of the mental powers with
what we call beautiful, where the Understanding is
at the service of Imagination and not *vice versa*.

In a thing that is only possible by means of design,
—a building, or even an animal,—the regularity
consisting in symmetry must express the unity
of the intuition that accompanies the concept of
purpose, and this regularity belongs to cognition.
But where only a free play of the representative
powers (under the condition, however, that the
Understanding is to suffer no shock thereby) is to
be kept up, in pleasure gardens, room decorations,
all kinds of tasteful furniture, etc., regularity that

shows constraint is avoided as much as possible. Thus in the English taste in gardens, or in bizarre taste in furniture, the freedom of the Imagination is pushed almost near to the grotesque, and in this separation from every constraint of rule we have the case, where taste can display its greatest perfection in the enterprises of the Imagination.

All ·stiff regularity (such as approximates to mathematical regularity) has something in it repugnant to taste ; for our entertainment in the contemplation of it lasts for no length of time, but it rather, in so far as it has not expressly in view cognition or a definite practical purpose, produces weariness. On the other hand that with which Imagination can play in an unstudied and purposive manner is always new to us, and one does not get tired of looking at it. *Marsden* in his description of Sumatra makes the remark that the free beauties of nature surround the spectator everywhere and thus lose their attraction for him.[1] On the other hand a pepper-garden, where the stakes on which this plant twines itself form parallel rows, had much attractiveness for him, if he met with it in the middle of a forest. And he hence infers that wild beauty, apparently irregular, only pleases as a variation from the regular beauty of which one has seen enough. But he need only have made the experiment of spending one day in a pepper-garden, to have been convinced that, if the Understanding has put itself in accordance with the order that it always needs by means of regularity, the object will not entertain for long,—nay rather it will impose a burdensome constraint upon the Imagination. On

---

[1] [See *The History of Sumatra*, by W. Marsden (London, 1783), p. 113.]

the other hand, nature, which there is prodigal in its variety even to luxuriance, that is subjected to no constraint of artificial rules, can supply constant food for taste.— Even the song of birds, which we can bring under no musical rule, seems to have more freedom, and therefore more for taste, than a song of a human being which is produced in accordance with all the rules of music ; for we very much sooner weary of the latter, if it is repeated often and at length. Here, however, we probably confuse our participation in the mirth of a little creature that we love, with the beauty of its song ; for if this were exactly imitated by man (as sometimes the notes of the nightingale are)[1] it would seem to our ear quite devoid of taste.

Again, beautiful objects are to be distinguished from beautiful views of objects (which often on account of their distance cannot be more clearly cognised). In the latter case taste appears not so much in what the Imagination *apprehends* in this field, as in the impulse it thus gets to *fiction*, *i.e.* in the peculiar fancies with which the mind entertains itself, whilst it is continually being aroused by the variety which strikes the eye. An illustration is afforded, *e.g.*, by the sight of the changing shapes of a fire on the hearth or of a rippling brook ; neither of these has beauty, but they bring with them a charm for the Imagination, because they entertain it in free play.

[1] [Cf. § 42 *infra*.]

§ 23. *Transition from the faculty which judges of the Beautiful to that which judges of the Sublime*

The Beautiful and the Sublime agree in this, that both please in themselves. Further, neither presupposes a judgment of sense nor a judgment logically determined, but a judgment of reflection. Consequently the satisfaction [belonging to them] does not depend on a sensation, as in the case of the Pleasant, nor on a definite concept, as in the case of the Good; but it is nevertheless referred to concepts although indeterminate ones. And so the satisfaction is connected with the mere presentation [of the object] or with the faculty of presentation; so that in the case of a given intuition this faculty or the Imagination is considered as in agreement with the *faculty of concepts* of Understanding or Reason, regarded as promoting these latter. Hence both kinds of judgments are *singular*, and yet announce themselves as universally valid for every subject; although they lay claim merely to the feeling of pleasure and not to any cognition of the object.

But there are also remarkable differences between the two. The Beautiful in nature is connected with the form of the object, which consists in having [definite] boundaries. The Sublime, on the other hand, is to be found in a formless object, so far as in it or by occasion of it *boundlessness* is represented, and yet its totality is also present to thought. Thus the Beautiful seems to be regarded as the presentation of an indefinite concept of Understanding; the Sublime as that of a like concept of Reason. Therefore the satisfaction in the one case is bound up with the representation of *quality*, in the other with that of *quantity*. And the latter satisfaction is quite different in kind from the former, for this [the Beautiful[1]] directly brings with it a feeling of the furtherance of life, and thus is compatible with charms and with the play of the Imagination. But the other [the feeling of the Sublime[2]] is a pleasure that arises only indirectly; viz. it is produced by the feeling of a momentary checking of the vital powers and a consequent stronger outflow of them, so that it seems to be regarded as emotion,—not play, but earnest in the exercise of the Imagination. —Hence it is incompatible with [physical] charm; and as the mind is not merely attracted by the object but is ever being alternately repelled, the satisfaction in the sublime does not so much involve a positive pleasure as admiration or respect, which rather deserves to be called negative pleasure.

But the inner and most important distinction between the Sublime and Beautiful is, certainly, as follows. (Here, as we are entitled to do, we only bring under consideration in the first instance the sublime in natural Objects; for the sublime of Art is always limited by the conditions of agreement with Nature). Natural beauty (which is inde-

---

[1] [Second Edition.]   [2] [Second Edition.]

pendent) brings with it a purposiveness in its
form by which the object seems to be, as it were,
pre-adapted to our Judgment, and thus constitutes
in itself an object of satisfaction.   On the other
hand, that which excites in us, without any reasoning about it, but in the mere apprehension of it,
the feeling of the sublime, may appear as regards
its form to violate purpose in respect of the Judgment, to be unsuited to our presentative faculty,
and, as it were, to do violence to the Imagination ;
and yet it is judged to be only the more sublime.

Now we may see from this that in general we
express ourselves incorrectly if we call any *object of
nature* sublime, although we can quite correctly call
many objects of nature beautiful.   For how can
that be marked by an expression of approval, which
is apprehended in itself as ·being a violation of
purpose ? ｜All that we can say is that the object
is fit for the presentation of a sublimity which can
be found in the mind ; for no sensible form can
contain the sublime properly so-called.   This concerns only Ideas of the Reason, which, although no
adequate presentation is possible for them, by this
inadequateness that admits of sensible presentation,
are aroused and summoned into the mind.｜ Thus the
wide ocean, disturbed by the storm, cannot be called
sublime.   Its aspect is horrible ; and the mind must
be already filled with manifold Ideas if it is to be
determined by such an intuition to a feeling itself sublime, as it is incited to abandon sensibility and to busy
itself with Ideas that involve higher purposiveness.

Independent natural beauty discovers to us a
Technic of nature, which represents it as a system
in accordance with laws, the principle of which we
do not find in the whole of our faculty of Under-

standing. That principle is the principle of purposiveness, in respect of the use of our Judgment in regard to phenomena ; [which requires] that these must not be judged as merely belonging to nature in its purposeless mechanism, but also as belonging to something analogous to art. It, therefore, actually extends, not indeed our cognition of natural Objects, but our concept of nature ; [which is now not regarded] as mere mechanism but as art. This leads to profound investigations as to the possibility of such a form. But in what we are accustomed to call sublime there is nothing at all that leads to particular objective principles and forms of nature corresponding to them ; so far from it that for the most part nature excites the Ideas of the sublime in its chaos or in its wildest and most irregular disorder and desolation, provided size and might are perceived. Hence, we see that the concept of the Sublime is not nearly so important or rich in consequences as the concept of the Beautiful ; and that in general it displays nothing purposive in nature itself, but only in that possible use of our intuitions of it by which there is produced in us a feeling of a purposiveness quite independent of nature. We must seek a ground external to ourselves for the Beautiful of nature ; but seek it for the Sublime merely in ourselves and in our attitude of thought which introduces sublimity into the representation of nature. This is a very needful preliminary remark, which quite separates the Ideas of the sublime from that of a purposiveness of *nature*, and makes the theory of the sublime a mere appendix to the æsthetical judging of that purposiveness ; because by means of it no particular form is represented in nature, but there is only developed a purposive use which the Imagination makes of its representation.

§ 24. *Of the divisions of an investigation into the feeling of the sublime*

As regards the division of the moments of the æsthetical judging of objects in reference to the feeling of the sublime, the Analytic can proceed according to the same principle as was adapted in the analysis of judgments of taste. [For as an act of the æsthetical reflective Judgment, the satisfaction in the Sublime must be represented just as in the case of the Beautiful,—according to *quantity* as universally valid, according to *quality* as devoid of *interest*, according to *relation* as subjective purposiveness, and according to *modality* as necessary.] And so the method here will not diverge from that of the preceding section ; unless, indeed, we count it a difference that in the case where the æsthetical Judgment is concerned with the form of the object we began with the investigation of its quality, but here, in view of the formlessness which may belong to what we call sublime, we will begin with quantity, as the first moment of the æsthetical judgment as to the sublime. The reason for this may be seen from the preceding paragraph.

But the analysis of the Sublime involves a division not needed in the case of the Beautiful, viz., a division into the *mathematically* and the *dynamically sublime*.

For the feeling of the Sublime brings with it as its characteristic feature a *movement* of the mind bound up with the judging of the object, while in the case of the Beautiful taste presupposes and maintains the mind in *restful* contemplation. Now this movement ought to be judged as subjectively purposive (because the sublime pleases us), and thus it is referred through the Imagination either to the *faculty of cognition* or of *desire*. In either reference the purposiveness of the given representation ought to be judged only in respect of this *faculty* (without purpose or interest); but in the first case it is ascribed to the Object as a *mathematical* determination of the Imagination, in the second as *dynamical*. And hence we have this twofold way of representing the sublime.

A.—Of the Mathematically Sublime.

§ 25. *Explanation of the term "sublime"*

We call that *sublime* which is *absolutely great*. But to be great, and to be a great something are quite different concepts (*magnitudo* and *quantitas*). In like manner to *say simply* (*simpliciter*) that anything is *great* is quite different from saying that it is *absolutely great* (*absolute, non comparative magnum*). The latter is *what is great beyond all comparison.*— What now is meant by the expression that anything is great or small or of medium size? It is not a pure concept of Understanding that is thus signified; still less is it an intuition of Sense, and just as little is it a concept of Reason, because it brings with it no principle of cognition. It must therefore be a concept of Judgment or derived from one; and a subjective purposiveness of the representation in reference to the Judgment must lie at its basis. That anything is a magnitude (*quantum*) may be cognised from the thing itself, without any comparison of it with other things ; viz., if there is a multiplicity of the homogeneous constituting one thing. But to cognise *how great* it is always requires some other magnitude as a measure. But because the judging of magnitude depends not merely on multiplicity (number), but also on the magnitude of the unit (the measure), and since, to judge of the magnitude of this latter again requires another as measure with which it may be compared, we see that the determination of the magnitude of phenomena can supply no absolute concept whatever of magnitude, but only a comparative one.

If now I say simply that anything is great, it appears that I have no comparison in view, at least none with an objective measure ; because it is thus not determined at all how great the object is. But although the standard of comparison is merely subjective, yet the judgment none the less claims universal assent ; "this man is beautiful," and " he is tall," are judgments not limited merely to the judging subject, but, like theoretical judgments, demanding the assent of every one.

In a judgment by which anything is designated simply as great, it is not merely meant that the object has a magnitude, but that this magnitude is superior to that of many other objects of the same kind, without, however, any exact determination of this superiority. Thus there is always at the basis of our judgment a standard which we assume as the same for every one ; this, however, is not available for any logical (mathematically definite) judging of magnitude, but only for æsthetical judging of the same, because it is a merely subjective standard lying at the basis of the reflective judgment upon magnitude. It may be empirical, as, *e.g.*, the average size of the men known to us, of animals of a certain kind, trees, houses, mountains, etc. Or it may be a standard given *a priori*, which through the defects of the judging subject is limited by the subjective conditions of presentation *in concreto*; as, *e.g.*, in the practical sphere, the greatness of a certain virtue, or of the public liberty and justice in a country; or, in the theoretical sphere, the greatness of the accuracy or the inaccuracy of an observation or measurement that has been made, etc.

Here it is remarkable that, although we have no interest whatever in an Object,—*i.e.* its existence is indifferent to us,—yet its mere size, even if it is considered as formless, may bring a satisfaction with it that is universally communicable, and that consequently involves the consciousness of a subjective purposiveness in the use of our cognitive faculty. This is not indeed a satisfaction in the Object (because it may be formless), as in the case of the Beautiful, in which the reflective Judgment finds itself purposively determined in reference to cognition in general; but [a satisfaction] in the extension of the Imagination by itself.

If (under the above limitation) we say simply of an object "it is great," this is no mathematically definite judgment but a mere judgment of reflection upon the representation of it, which is subjectively purposive for a certain use of our cognitive powers in the estimation of magnitude; and we always then bind up with the representation a kind of respect, as also a kind of contempt for what we simply call "small." Further, the judging of things as great or

small extends to everything, even to all their characteristics; thus we describe beauty as great or
small. The reason of this is to be sought in the
fact that whatever we present in intuition according
to the precept of the Judgment (and thus represent
æsthetically) is always a phenomenon and thus a
quantum.

But if we call anything not only great, but absolutely great in every point of view (great beyond all
comparison), *i.e.* sublime, we soon see that it is not
permissible to seek for an adequate standard of this
outside itself, but merely in itself. It is a magnitude which is like itself alone. It follows hence
that the sublime is not to be sought in the things of
nature, but only in our Ideas; but in which of them
it lies must be reserved for the Deduction.

The foregoing explanation can be thus expressed:
*the sublime is that in comparison with which every-
thing else is small.* Here we easily see that nothing
can be given in nature, however great it is judged
by us to be, which could not if considered in another
relation be reduced to the infinitely small; and conversely there is nothing so small, which does not
admit of extension by our Imagination to the greatness of a world, if compared with still smaller
standards. Telescopes have furnished us with
abundant material for making the first remark,
microscopes for the second. Nothing, therefore,
which can be an object of the senses, is, considered
on this basis, to be called sublime. But because there
is in our Imagination a striving towards infinite
progress, and in our Reason a claim for absolute
totality, regarded as a real Idea, therefore this very
inadequateness for that Idea in our faculty for
estimating the magnitude of things of sense, excites

in us the feeling of a supersensible faculty. And
it is not the object of sense, but the use which the
Judgment naturally makes of certain objects on
behalf of this latter feeling, that is absolutely great ;
and in comparison every other use is small. [Consequently it is the state of mind produced by a certain
representation with which the reflective Judgment
is occupied, and not the Object, that is to be called
sublime.

We can therefore append to the preceding
formulas explaining the sublime this other : *the sublime is that, the mere ability to think which, shows a
faculty of the mind surpassing every standard of Sense.*

§ 26. *Of that estimation of the magnitude of natural things which is requisite for the Idea of the Sublime*

The estimation of magnitude by means of concepts of number (or their signs in Algebra) is mathematical ; but that [performed] by mere intuition (by
the measurement of the eye) is æsthetical. Now we
can come by definite concepts of *how great* a thing is,
[only][1] by numbers, of which the unit is the measure
(at all events by series of numbers progressing to
infinity) ; and so far all logical estimation of magnitude is mathematical. But since the magnitude of
the measure must then be assumed known, and this
again is only to be estimated mathematically by
means of numbers,—the unit of which must be another [smaller] measure,—we can never have a first
or fundamental measure, and therefore can never
have a definite concept of a given magnitude. So
the estimation of the magnitude of the fundamental
measure must consist in this, that we can immedi-

---

[1] [Second Edition.]

ately apprehend it in intuition and use it by the Imagination for the presentation of concepts of number. That is, all estimation of the magnitude of the objects of nature is in the end æsthetical (*i.e.* subjectively and not objectively determined).

Now for the mathematical estimation of magnitude there is, indeed, no maximum (for the power of numbers extends to infinity); but for its æsthetical estimation there is always a maximum, and of this I say that if it is judged as the absolute measure than which no greater is possible subjectively (for the judging subject), it brings with it the Idea of the sublime and produces that emotion which no mathematical estimation of its magnitude by means of numbers can bring about (except so far as that æsthetical fundamental measure remains vividly in the Imagination). For the former only presents relative magnitude by means of comparison with others of the same kind; but the latter presents magnitude absolutely, so far as the mind can grasp it in an intuition.

In receiving a quantum into the Imagination by intuition, in order to be able to use it for a measure or as a unit for the estimation of magnitude by means of numbers, there are two operations of the Imagination involved: *apprehension* (*apprehensio*) and *comprehension* (*comprehensio æsthetica*). As to apprehension there is no difficulty, for it can go on *ad infinitum*; but comprehension becomes harder the further apprehension advances, and soon attains to its maximum, viz., the greatest possible æsthetical fundamental measure for the estimation of magnitude. For when apprehension has gone so far that the partial representations of sensuous intuition at first apprehended begin to vanish in the Imagination, whilst this ever proceeds to the apprehension of others, then it loses as much on the one side as it gains on the other; and in comprehension there is a maximum beyond which it cannot go.

Hence can be explained what *Savary*[1] remarks in his account of Egypt, viz., that we must keep from going very near the Pyramids just as much as we keep from going too far from them, in order to get the full emotional effect from their size. For if we are too far away, the parts to be apprehended (the stones lying one over the other) are only obscurely represented, and the representation of them produces no effect upon the æsthetical judgment of the subject. But if we are very near, the eye requires some time to complete the apprehension of the tiers from the bottom up to the apex; and then the first tiers are always partly forgotten before the Imagination has taken in the last, and so the comprehension of them is never complete.— The same thing may sufficiently explain the bewilderment or, as it were, perplexity which, it is said, seizes the spectator on his first entrance into St. Peter's at Rome. For there is here a feeling of the inadequacy of his Imagination for presenting the Ideas of a whole, wherein the Imagination reaches its maximum, and, in striving to surpass it, sinks back into itself, by which, however, a kind of emotional satisfaction is produced.

I do not wish to speak as yet of the ground of this satisfaction, which is bound up with a representation from which we should least of all expect it, viz., a representation which makes us remark its inadequacy and consequently its subjective want of purposiveness for the Judgment in the estimation of

---

[1] [*Lettres sur l'Egypte*, par M. Savary, Amsterdam, 1787.]

magnitude.   I only remark that if the æsthetical judgment is *pure* (i.e. *mingled with no teleological judgment* or judgment of Reason) and is to be given as a completely suitable example of the Kritik of the *æsthetical* Judgment, /we must not exhibit the sublime in products of art (*e.g.*, buildings, pillars, etc.) where human purpose determines the form as well as the size : nor yet in things of nature *the concepts of which bring with them a definite purpose* (*e.g.*, animals with a known natural destination); but in rude nature (and in this only in so far as it does not bring with it any charm or emotion produced by actual danger) merely as containing magnitude./ For in this kind of representation nature contains nothing monstrous (either magnificent or horrible); the magnitude that is apprehended may be increased as much as you wish provided it can be comprehended in a whole by the Imagination.   An object is *monstrous* if by its size it destroys the purpose which constitutes the concept of it.   But the mere presentation of a concept is called *colossal,* which is almost too great for any presentation (bordering on the relatively monstrous); because the purpose of the presentation of a concept is made hard [to carry out] by the intuition of the object being almost too great for our faculty of apprehension.— A pure judgment upon the sublime must, however, have no purpose of the Object as its determining ground, if it is to be æsthetical and not mixed up with any judgment of Understanding or Reason.

Because everything which is to give disinterested pleasure to the merely reflective Judgment must bring with the representation of it, subjective

and, as subjective, universally valid purposiveness—
although no purposiveness of the *form* of the object
lies (as in the case of the Beautiful) at the ground of
the judgment—the question arises "what is this
subjective purposiveness?" And how does it come
to be prescribed as the norm by which a ground for
universally valid satisfaction is supplied in the mere
estimation of magnitude, even in that which is
forced up to the point where our faculty of Imagination is inadequate for the presentation of the concept
of magnitude?

In the process of combination requisite for the
estimation of magnitude, the Imagination proceeds
of itself to infinity without anything hindering it;
but the Understanding guides it by means of concepts
of number, for which it must furnish the schema.
And in this procedure, as belonging to the logical
estimation of magnitude, there is indeed something
objectively purposive,—in accordance with the concept of a purpose (as all measurement is),—but nothing
purposive and pleasing for the æsthetical Judgment.
There is also in this designed purposiveness nothing
which would force us to push the magnitude of the
measure, and consequently the *comprehension* of the
manifold in an intuition, to the bounds of the faculty
of Imagination, or as far as ever this can reach in its
presentations. For in the estimation of magnitude
by the Understanding (Arithmetic) we only go to a
certain point whether we push the comprehension
of the units up to the number 10 (as in the decimal
scale) or only up to 4 (as in the quaternary scale);
the further production of magnitude proceeds by
combination or, if the quantum is given in intuition,
by apprehension, but merely by way of progression
not of comprehension) in accordance with an as-

sumed principle of progression.   In this mathematical estimation of magnitude the Understanding is
equally served and contented whether the Imagination
chooses for unit a magnitude that we can take in
in a glance, *e.g.*, a foot or rod, or a German mile or
even the earth's diameter,—of which the apprehension is indeed possible, but not the comprehension in
an intuition of the Imagination (not possible by *comprehensio æsthetica*, although quite possible by
comprehensio logica in a concept of number).   In
both cases the logical estimation of magnitude goes
on without hindrance to infinity.

But now the mind listens to the voice of Reason
which, for every given magnitude,—even for those
that can never be entirely apprehended, although (in
sensible representation) they are judged as entirely
given,— requires totality.   Reason consequently
desires comprehension in *one* intuition, and so the
[joint] *presentation* of all these members of a pro-
gressively increasing series.   It does not even exempt
the infinite (space and past time) from this requirement ; it rather renders it unavoidable to think the
infinite (in the judgment of common Reason) as
entirely given (according to its totality).

But the infinite is absolutely (not merely comparatively) great.   Compared with it everything
else (of the same kind of magnitudes) is small.   And
what is most important is that to be able only to
think it as *a whole* indicates a faculty of mind which
surpasses every standard of Sense.   For [to represent it sensibly] would require a comprehension
having for unit a standard bearing a definite relation,
expressible in numbers, to the infinite ; which is
impossible.   Nevertheless, *the bare capability of
thinking* this infinite without contradiction requires in

the human mind a faculty itself supersensible. For
it is only by means of this faculty and its Idea of a
noumenon, — which admits of no intuition, but
which yet serves as the substrate for the intuition
of the world, as a mere phenomenon, — that the
infinite of the world of sense, in the pure intellectual
estimation of magnitude, can be *completely* comprehended *under* one concept, although in the mathematical estimation of magnitude by means of *concepts
of number* it can never be completely thought. The
faculty of being able to think the infinite of supersensible intuition as given (in its intelligible substrate), surpasses every standard of sensibility, and
is great beyond all comparison even with the
faculty of mathematical estimation ; not of course in
a theoretical point of view and on behalf of the
cognitive faculty, but as an extension of the mind
which feels itself able in another (practical) point of
view to go beyond the limits of sensibility.

Nature is therefore sublime in those of its
phenomena, whose intuition brings with it the Idea
of its infinity. This last can only come by the inadequacy of the greatest effort of our Imagination to
estimate the magnitude of an object. But now in
mathematical estimation of magnitude the Imagination is equal to providing a sufficient measure for
every object ; because the numerical concepts of the
Understanding, by means of progression, can make
any measure adequate to any given magnitude.
Therefore it must be the *æsthetical* estimation of
magnitude in which the effort towards comprehension surpasses the power of the Imagination. Here
it is felt that we can comprehend in a whole of
intuition the progressive apprehension, and at the
same time we perceive the inadequacy of this faculty,

unbounded in its progress, for grasping and using any fundamental measure available for the estimation of magnitude with the easiest application of the Understanding. Now the proper unchangeable fundamental measure of nature is its absolute whole ; which, regarding nature as a phenomenon, would be infinity comprehended. But since this fundamental measure is a self-contradictory concept (on account of the impossibility of the absolute totality of an endless progress), that magnitude of a natural Object, on which the Imagination fruitlessly spends its whole faculty of comprehension, must carry our concept of nature to a supersensible substrate (which lies at its basis and also at the basis of our faculty of thought). As this, however, is great beyond all standards of sense, it makes us judge as *sublime*, not so much the object, as our own state of mind in the estimation of it.

Therefore, just as the æsthetical Judgment in judging the Beautiful refers the Imagination in its free play to the *Understanding*, in order to harmonise it with the *concepts* of the latter in general (without any determination of them) ; so does the same faculty when judging a thing as Sublime refer itself to the *Reason* in order that it may subjectively be in accordance with its *Ideas* (no matter what they are) :—*i.e.* that it may produce a state of mind conformable to them and compatible with that brought about by the influence of definite (practical) Ideas upon feeling.

We hence see also that true sublimity must be sought only in the mind of the [subject] judging, not in the natural Object, the judgment upon which occasions this state. Who would call sublime, *e.g.*, shapeless mountain masses piled in wild disorder

upon each other with their pyramids of ice, or the
gloomy raging sea ?   But the mind feels itself raised
in its own judgment if, while contemplating them
without any reference to their form, and abandoning
itself to the Imagination and to the Reason—which
although placed in combination with the Imagination
without any definite purpose, merely extends it—it
yet finds the whole power of the Imagination inadequate to its Ideas.

Examples of the mathematically Sublime of
nature in mere intuition are all the cases in
which we are given, not so much a larger numerical
concept as a large unit for the measure of the
Imagination (for shortening the numerical series).
A tree, [the height of] which we estimate with
reference to the height of a man, at all events gives
a standard for a mountain ; and if this were a mile
high, it would serve as unit for the number ex-
pressive of the earth's diameter, so that the latter
might be made intuitible.   The earth's diameter
[would supply a unit] for the known planetary
system ; this again for the milky way ; and the
immeasurable number of milky way systems called
nebulæ,—which presumably constitute a system of
the same kind among themselves—lets us expect
no bounds here.   Now the Sublime in the æsthetical
judging of an immeasurable whole like this lies
not so much in the greatness of the number [of
units], as in the fact that in our progress we ever
arrive at yet greater units.   To this the systematic
division of the universe contributes, which represents
every magnitude in nature as small in its turn ; and
represents our Imagination with its entire freedom
from bounds, and with it Nature, as a mere nothing
in comparison with the Ideas of Reason, if it is

sought to furnish a presentation which shall be adequate to them.

§ 27. *Of the quality of the satisfaction in our judgments upon the Sublime*

The feeling of our incapacity to attain to an Idea, *which is a law for us*, is RESPECT. Now the Idea of the comprehension of every phenomenon that can be given us in the intuition of a whole, is an Idea prescribed to us by a law of Reason, which recognises no other measure, definite, valid for every one, and invariable, than the absolute whole. But our Imagination, even in its greatest efforts, in respect of that comprehension, which we expect from it, of a given object in a whole of intuition (and thus with reference to the presentation of the Idea of Reason), exhibits its own limits and inadequacy; although at the same time it shows that its destination is to make itself adequate to this Idea regarded as a law. Therefore the feeling of the Sublime in nature is respect for our own destination, which by a certain subreption we attribute to an Object of nature (conversion of respect for the Idea of humanity in our own subject into respect for the object). This makes intuitively evident the superiority of the rational determination of our cognitive faculties to the greatest faculty of our Sensibility.

The feeling of the Sublime is therefore a feeling of pain, arising from the want of accordance between the æsthetical estimation of magnitude formed by the Imagination and the estimation of the same formed by Reason. There is at the same time a pleasure thus excited, arising from the corre-

spondence with rational Ideas of this very judgment
of the inadequacy of our greatest faculty of Sense ;/
in so far as it is a law for us to strive after these
Ideas. ' In fact it is for us a law (of Reason), and
belongs to our destination, to estimate as small, in
comparison with Ideas of Reason, everything which
nature, regarded as an object of Sense, contains
that is great for us ; and that which arouses in us
the feeling of this supersensible destination agrees
with that law.   Now the greatest effort of the
Imagination in the presentation of the unit for the
estimation of magnitude indicates a reference to
something *absolutely great*; and consequently a
reference to the law of Reason, which bids us take
this alone as our highest measure of magnitude.
Therefore the inner perception of the inadequacy
of all sensible standards for rational estimation of
magnitude indicates a correspondence with rational
laws; it involves a pain, which arouses in us the
feeling of our supersensible destination, according
to which it is purposive and therefore pleasurable
to find every standard of Sensibility inadequate to
the Ideas of Understanding.

The mind feels itself *moved* in the representation of the Sublime in nature ; whilst in æsthetical
judgments about the Beautiful it is in *restful*
contemplation.   This movement may (especially in
its beginnings) be compared to a vibration, *i.e.* to a
quickly alternating attraction towards, and repulsion
from, the same Object.   The transcendent (towards
which the Imagination is impelled in its apprehension
of intuition) is for the Imagination like an abyss in
which it fears to lose itself; but for the rational
Idea of the supersensible it is not transcendent but
in conformity with law to bring about such an

effort of the Imagination, and consequently here there is the same amount of attraction as there was of repulsion for the mere Sensibility. But the judgment itself always remains in this case only æsthetical, because, without having any determinate concept of the Object at its basis ; it merely represents the subjective play of the mental powers (Imagination and Reason) as harmonious through their very contrast. For just as Imagination and *Understanding*, in judging of the Beautiful, generate a subjective purposiveness of the mental powers by means of their harmony, so [in this* case[1]] Imagination and *Reason* do so by means of their conflict. That is, they bring about a feeling that we possess pure self-subsistent Reason, or a faculty for the estimation of magnitude, whose superiority can be made intuitively evident only by the inadequacy of that faculty [Imagination] which is itself unbounded in the presentation of magnitudes (of sensible objects).

The measurement of a space (regarded as apprehension) is at the same time a description of it, and thus an objective movement in the act of Imagination and a progress. On the other hand, the comprehension of the manifold in the unity,—not of thought but of intuition,—and consequently the comprehension of the successively apprehended [elements] in one glance, is a regress, which annihilates the condition of time in this progress of the Imagination and makes *coexistence* intuitible.[2] It is therefore (since the time-series is a condition of the internal sense and

---

[1] [Second Edition.]

[2] [With this should be compared the similar discussion in the Kritik of *Pure Reason*, Dialectic, bk. ii. c. ii. § 1, *On the System of Cosmological Ideas.*]

of an intuition) a subjective movement of the Imagination, by which it does violence to the internal sense ; this must be the more noticeable, the greater the quantum is which the Imagination comprehends in one intuition. The effort, therefore, to receive in one single intuition a measure for magnitude that requires a considerable time to apprehend, is a kind of representation, which, subjectively considered, is contrary to purpose : but objectively, as requisite for the estimation of magnitude, it is purposive. Thus that very violence which is done to the subject through the Imagination is judged as purposive *in reference to the whole determination* of the mind.

The *quality* of the feeling of the Sublime is that it is a feeling of pain in reference to the faculty by which we judge æsthetically of an object, which pain, however, is represented at the same time as purposive. This is possible through the fact that the very incapacity in question discovers the consciousness of an unlimited faculty of the same subject, and that the mind can only judge of the latter æsthetically by means of the former.

In the logical estimation of magnitude the impossibility of ever arriving at absolute totality, by means of the progress of the measurement of things of the sensible world in time and space, was cognised as objective, *i.e.* as an impossibility of *thinking* the infinite as entirely given ; and not as merely subjective or that there was only an incapacity to *grasp* it. For there we have not to do with the degree of comprehension in an intuition, regarded as a measure, but everything depends on a concept of number. But in æsthetical estimation of magnitude the concept of number must disappear or be changed, and the comprehension of the Imagination in reference to the unit of measure (thus avoiding the concepts of a law of the successive production of concepts of magnitude) is alone purposive for it.— If now a magnitude almost reaches the limit of our faculty of comprehension in an intuition, and yet the Imagination is invited by means of numerical magnitudes (in respect of which we are conscious that our faculty is unbounded) to æsthetical comprehension in a greater unit, then we mentally feel ourselves confined æsthetically within bounds. But nevertheless the pain in regard to the necessary extension of the Imagination for accordance with that which is unbounded in our faculty of Reason, viz. the Idea of the absolute whole, and consequently the very unpurposiveness of the faculty of Imagination for rational Ideas and the arousing of them, are represented as purposive. Thus it is that the æsthetical judgment itself is subjectively purposive for the Reason as the source of Ideas, *i.e.* as the source of an intellectual comprehension for which all æsthetical comprehension is small; and there accompanies the reception of an object as sublime a pleasure, which is only possible through the medium of a pain.

B.—Of the Dynamically Sublime in Nature

§ 28. *Of Nature regarded as Might*

Might is that which is superior to great hindrances. It is called *dominion* if it is superior to the resistance of that which itself possesses might. Nature considered in an æsthetical judgment as might that has no dominion over us, is *dynamically sublime.*

If nature is to be judged by us as dynamically sublime, it must be represented as exciting fear (although it is not true conversely that every object which excites fear is regarded in our æsthetical judgment as sublime). For in æsthetical judgments (without the aid of concepts) superiority to hindrances can only be judged according to the greatness of the resistance. Now that which we are driven to resist is an evil, and, if we do not find our faculties a match for it, is an object of fear. Hence nature can be regarded by the æsthetical Judgment as might, and consequently as dynamically sublime, only so far as it is considered an object of fear.

But we can regard an object as *fearful*, without being afraid *of* it ; viz. if we judge of it in such a way that we merely *think* a case in which we would wish to resist it, and yet in which all resistance would be altogether vain. Thus the virtuous man fears God without being afraid of Him ; because to wish to resist Him and His commandments, he thinks is a case that *he* need not apprehend. But in every such case that he thinks as not impossible, he cognises Him as fearful.

He who fears can form no judgment about the Sublime in nature ; just as he who is seduced by inclination and appetite can form no judgment about the Beautiful. The former flies from the sight of an object which inspires him with awe ; and it is impossible to find satisfaction in a terror that is seriously felt. Hence the pleasurableness arising from the cessation of an uneasiness is *a state of joy*. But this, on account of the deliverance from danger [which is involved], is a state of joy when conjoined with the resolve that we shall no more be exposed to the danger ; we cannot willingly look back upon our sensations [of danger], much less seek the occasion for them again.

Bold, overhanging, and as it were threatening, rocks ; clouds piled up in the sky, moving with lightning flashes and thunder peals ; volcanoes in all their violence of destruction ; hurricanes with their track of devastation ; the boundless ocean in a state of tumult ; the lofty waterfall of a mighty river, and such like ; these exhibit our faculty of resistance as insignificantly small in comparison with their might.   But the sight of them is the more attractive, the more fearful it is, provided only that we are in security ; and we willingly call these objects sublime, because they raise the energies of the soul above their accustomed height, and discover in us a faculty of resistance of a quite different kind, which gives us courage to measure ourselves against the apparent almightiness of nature.

Now, in the immensity of nature, and in the insufficiency of our faculties to take in a standard proportionate to the æsthetical estimation of the magnitude of its *realm*, we find our own limitation ; although at the same time in our rational faculty we find a different, non-sensuous standard, which has that infinity itself under it as a unity, in comparison with which everything in nature is small, and thus in our mind we find a superiority to nature even in its immensity.   And so also the irresistibility of its might, while making us recognise our own [physical [1]] impotence, considered as beings of nature, discloses to us a faculty of judging independently of, and a superiority over, nature ; on which is based a kind of self-preservation, entirely different from that which can be attacked and brought into danger by

[1] [Second Edition.]

external nature. Thus, humanity in our person remains unhumiliated, though the individual might have to submit to this dominion. In this way nature is not judged to be sublime in our æsthetical judgments, in so far as it excites fear ; but because it calls up that power in us (which is not nature) of regarding as small the things about which we are solicitous (goods, health, and life), and of regarding its might (to which we are no doubt subjected in respect of these things), as nevertheless without any dominion over us and our personality to which we must bow where our highest fundamental propositions, and their assertion or abandonment, are concerned. Therefore nature is here called sublime merely because it elevates the Imagination to a presentation of those cases in which the mind can make felt the proper sublimity of its destination, in comparison with nature itself.

This estimation of ourselves loses nothing through the fact that we must regard ourselves as safe in order to feel this inspiriting satisfaction ; and that hence, as there is no seriousness in the danger, there might be also (as might seem to be the case) just as little seriousness in the sublimity of our spiritual faculty. For the satisfaction here concerns only the *destination* of our faculty which discloses itself in such a case, so far as the tendency to this destination lies in our nature, whilst its development and exercise remain incumbent and obligatory. [And in this there is truth [and reality], however conscious the man may be of his present actual powerlessness, when he turns his reflection to it.

No doubt this principle seems to be too farfetched and too subtly reasoned, and consequently seems to go beyond [the scope of] an æsthetical judgment; but observation of men proves the opposite, and shows that it may lie at the root of the most ordinary judgments, although we are not always conscious of it. For what is that which is, even to the savage, an object of the greatest admiration ? It is a man who shrinks from nothing, who fears nothing, and therefore does not yield to danger, but rather goes to face it vigorously with the most complete deliberation. Even in the most highly civilised state this peculiar veneration for the soldier remains, though only under the condition that he exhibit all the virtues of peace, gentleness, compassion, and even a becoming care for his own person ; because even by these it is recognised that his mind is unsubdued by danger. Hence whatever disputes there may be about the superiority of the respect which is to be accorded them, in the comparison of a statesman and a general, the æsthetical judgment decides for the latter. War itself, if it is carried on with order and with a sacred respect for the rights of citizens, has something sublime in it, and makes the disposition of the people who carry it on thus, only the more sublime, the more numerous are the dangers to which they are exposed, and in respect of which they behave with courage. On the other hand, a long peace generally brings about a predominant commercial spirit, and along with it, low selfishness, cowardice, and effeminacy, and debases the disposition of the people.[1]

It appears to conflict with this solution of the concept of the sublime, so far as sublimity is ascribed to might, that we are accustomed to

[1] [Cf. § 83, *infra.*]

represent God as presenting Himself in His wrath and yet in His sublimity, in the tempest, the storm, the earthquake, etc. ; and that it would be foolish and criminal to imagine a superiority of our minds over these works of His, and, as it seems, even over the designs of such might. Hence it would appear that no feeling of the sublimity of our own nature, but rather subjection, abasement, and a feeling of complete powerlessness, is a fitting state of mind in the presence of such an object, and this is generally bound up with the Idea of it during natural phenomena of this kind. In religion in general, prostration, adoration with bent head, with contrite, anxious demeanour and voice, seems to be the only fitting behaviour in presence of the Godhead ; and hence most peoples have adopted and still observe it. But this state of mind is far from being necessarily bound up with the Idea of the *sublimity* of a religion and its object. The man who is actually afraid, because he finds reasons for fear in himself, whilst conscious by his culpable disposition of offending against a Might whose will is irresistible and at the same time just, is not in the frame of mind for admiring the divine greatness. For this a mood of calm contemplation and a quite free judgment are needed. Only if he is conscious of an upright disposition pleasing to God do those operations of might serve to awaken in him the Idea of the sublimity of this Being, for then he recognises in himself a sublimity of disposition conformable to His will ; and thus he is raised above the fear of such operations of nature, which he no longer regards as outbursts of His wrath. Even humility, in the shape of a stern judgment upon his own faults,—which otherwise, with a consciousness of good intentions, could be easily palliated from the frailty of human nature,—is a sublime state of mind, consisting in a voluntary subjection of himself to the pain of remorse, in order that the causes of this may be gradually removed. In this way religion is essentially distinguished from superstition. The latter establishes in the mind, not reverence for the Sublime, but fear and apprehension of the all-powerful Being to whose will the terrified man sees himself subject, without according Him any high esteem. From this nothing can arise but a seeking of favour, and flattery, instead of a religion which consists in a good life.[1]

Sublimity, therefore, does not reside in anything of nature, but only in our mind, in so far as we can become conscious that we are superior to nature within, and therefore also to nature without us (so far as it influences us). Everything that excites this feeling in us, *e.g.*, the *might* of nature which calls forth our forces, is called then (although improperly) sublime. Only by supposing this Idea in ourselves, and in reference to it, are we capable of attaining to the Idea of the sublimity of that Being, which produces respect in us, not merely by the might that it displays in nature, but rather by means of the faculty which resides in us of judging it fearlessly and of regarding our destination as sublime in respect of it.

---

[1] [In the *Philosophical Theory of Religion*, pt. i. *sub fin.* (Abbott's Translation, p. 360), Kant, as here, divides "all religions into two classes—*favour-seeking* religion (mere worship) and *moral* religion, that is, the religion *of a good life*;" and he concludes that "amongst all the public religions that have ever existed the Christian alone is moral."]

§ 29. *Of the modality of the judgment upon the*
sublime in nature

There are numberless beautiful things in nature
about which we can assume and even expect, without being widely mistaken, the harmony of every
one's judgment with our own. But in respect of
our judgment upon the sublime in nature, we cannot
promise ourselves so easily the accordance of others.
For a far greater culture, as well of the æsthetical
Judgment as of the cognitive faculties which lie
at its basis, seems requisite in order to be able
to pass judgment on this peculiarity of natural
objects.

That the mind be attuned to feel the sublime
postulates a susceptibility of the mind for Ideas.
For in the very inadequacy of nature to these
latter, and thus only by presupposing them and by
straining the Imagination to use nature as a schema
for them, is to be found that which is terrible to
sensibility and yet is attractive. [It is attractive]
because Reason exerts a dominion over sensibility
in order to extend it in conformity with its proper
realm (the practical) and to make it look out
into the Infinite, which is for it an abyss. In
fact, without development of moral Ideas, that
which we, prepared by culture, call sublime, presents
itself to the uneducated man merely as terrible.
In the indications of the dominion of nature in
destruction, and in the great scale of its might,
in comparison with which his own is a vanishing
quantity, he will only see the misery, danger, and
distress which surround the man who is exposed to
it. So the good, and indeed intelligent, Savoyard

peasant (as Herr von *Saussure*[1] relates) unhesitatingly called all lovers of snow-mountains fools.
And who knows, whether he would have been so
completely wrong, if Saussure had undertaken
the danger to which he exposed himself merely, as
most travellers do, from amateur curiosity, or that
he might be able to give a pathetic account of them ?
But his design was the instruction of men ; and
this excellent man gave the readers of his Travels,
soul-stirring sensations such as he himself had, into
the bargain.

But although the judgment upon the Sublime
in nature needs culture (more than the judgment
upon the Beautiful), it is not therefore primarily
produced by culture and introduced in a merely
conventional way into society. Rather has it its root
in human nature, even in that which, alike with
common Understanding, we can impute to and
expect of every one, viz. in the tendency to the
feeling for (practical) Ideas, *i.e.* to what is moral.

Hereon is based the necessity of that agreement
of the judgment of others about the sublime with
our own which we include in the latter. For
just as we charge with want of *taste* the man who
is indifferent when passing judgment upon an object
of nature that we regard as beautiful ; so we say
of him who remains unmoved in the presence of
that which we judge to be sublime, he has no *feeling*. But we claim both from every man, and we
presuppose them in him if he has any culture at
all ; only with the difference, that we expect the
former directly of every one, because in it the Judgment refers the Imagination merely to the Under-

[1] [*Voyages dans les Alpes*, par H. B. de Saussure ; vol. i. was
published at Neuchatel in 1779 ; vol. ii. at Geneva in 1786.]

standing, the faculty of concepts ; but the latter, because in it the Imagination is related to the Reason, the faculty of Ideas, only under a subjective presupposition (which, however, we believe we are authorised in imputing to every one), viz. the presupposition of the moral feeling [in man.[1]] Thus it is that we ascribe necessity to this æsthetical judgment also.

In this modality of æsthetical judgments, viz., in the necessity claimed for them, lies an important moment of the Kritik of Judgment. For it enables us to recognise in them an *a priori* principle, and raises them out of empirical psychology, in which otherwise they would remain buried amongst the feelings of gratification and grief (only with the unmeaning addition of being called *finer* feelings). Thus it enables us too to place the Judgment among those faculties that have *a priori* principles at their basis, and so to bring it into Transcendental Philosophy.

GENERAL REMARK UPON THE EXPOSITION OF THE ÆSTHETICAL REFLECTIVE JUDGMENT

In reference to the feeling of pleasure an object is to be classified as either *pleasant*, or *beautiful*, or *sublime*, or *good* (absolutely), (*jucundum, pulchrum, sublime, honestum*).

The *pleasant*, as motive of desire, is always of one and the same kind, no matter whence it comes and however specifically different the representation (of sense, and sensation objectively considered) may be. Hence in judging its influence on the mind, account is taken only of the number of its

[1] [Second Edition.]

charms (simultaneous and successive), and so only of the mass, as it were, of the pleasant sensation ; and this can be made intelligible only by *quantity*. It has no reference to culture, but belongs to mere enjoyment.— On the other hand, the *beautiful* requires the representation of a certain *quality* of the Object, that can be made intelligible and reduced to concepts (although it is not so reduced in an æsthetical judgment) ; and it cultivates us, in that it teaches us to attend to the purposiveness in the feeling of pleasure.— The *sublime* consists merely in the *relation* by which the sensible in the representation of nature is judged available for a possible supersensible use.— The *absolutely good*, subjectively judged according to the feeling that it inspires (the Object of the moral feeling), as capable of determining the powers of the subject through the representation of an *absolutely compelling* law, is specially distinguished by the *modality* of a necessity that rests *a priori* upon concepts. This necessity involves not merely a *claim*, but a *command* for the assent of every one, and belongs in itself to the pure intellectual, rather than to the æsthetical Judgment ; and is by a determinant and not a mere reflective judgment ascribed not to Nature but to Freedom. But the *determinability of the subject* by means of this Idea, and especially of a subject that can feel *hindrances* in sensibility, and at the same its superiority to them by their subjugation—involving a *modification of its state—i.e.* the moral feeling, is yet so far cognate to the æsthetical Judgment and its formal conditions that it can serve to represent the conformity to law of action from duty as æsthetical, *i.e.* as sublime or even as beautiful, without losing

purity. This would not be so, if we were to put it in
natural combination with the feeling of the pleasant.

If we take the result of the foregoing exposition
of the two kinds of æsthetical judgments, there
arise therefrom the following short explanations :

The *Beautiful* is what pleases in the mere
judgment (and therefore not by the medium of
sensation in accordance with a concept of the Understanding). It follows at once from this that it
must please apart from all interest.

The *Sublime* is what pleases immediately through
its opposition to the interest of sense.

Both, as explanations of æsthetical universally
valid judging, are referred to subjective grounds ;
in the one case to grounds of sensibility, in favour of
the contemplative Understanding ; in the other case
in opposition to sensibility, but on behalf of the purposes of practical Reason. Both, however, united
in the same subject, are purposive in reference to
the moral feeling. The Beautiful prepares us to
love disinterestedly something, even nature itself ;
the Sublime prepares us to esteem something highly
even in opposition to our own (sensible) interest.

We may describe the Sublime thus : it is an
object (of nature) *the representation of which determines the mind to think the unattainability of nature
regarded as a presentation of Ideas.*

Literally taken and logically considered, Ideas
cannot be presented. But if we extend our empirical representative faculty (mathematically or
dynamically) to the intuition of nature, Reason
infallibly intervenes, as the faculty expressing the
independence of absolute totality,[1] and generates the

---

[1] [*Als Vermögen der Independenz der absoluten Totalität*, a
curious phrase.]

unsuccessful effort of the mind to make the representation of the senses adequate to these [Ideas]. This effort,—and the feeling of the unattainability of the Idea by means of the Imagination,—is itself a presentation of the subjective purposiveness of our mind in the employment of the Imagination for its supersensible destination ; and forces us, subjectively, to *think* nature itself in its totality as a presentation of something supersensible, without being able *objectively* to arrive at this presentation.

For we soon see that nature in space and time entirely lacks the unconditioned, and, consequently, that absolute magnitude, which yet is desired by the most ordinary Reason. It is by this that we are reminded that we only have to do with nature as phenomenon, and that it must be regarded as the mere presentation of a nature in itself (of which Reason has the Idea). But this Idea of the supersensible, which we can no further determine,—so that we cannot *know* but only *think* nature as its presentation,—is awakened in us by means of an object, whose æsthetical appreciation strains the Imagination to its utmost bounds, whether of extension (mathematical) or of its might over the mind (dynamical). And this judgment is based upon a feeling of the mind's destination, which entirely surpasses the realm of the former (*i.e.* upon the moral feeling), in respect of which the representation of the object is judged as subjectively purposive.

In fact, a feeling for the Sublime in nature cannot well be thought without combining therewith a mental disposition which is akin to the Moral. And although the immediate pleasure in the Beautiful of nature likewise presupposes and cultivates a

certain *liberality* in our mental attitude, *i.e.* a satisfaction independent of mere sensible enjoyment, yet
freedom is thus represented as in *play* rather than
in that law-directed *occupation* which is the genuine
characteristic of human morality, in which Reason
must exercise dominion over Sensibility. But in
æsthetical judgments upon the Sublime this dominion is represented as exercised by the Imagination,
regarded as an instrument of Reason.

The satisfaction in the Sublime of nature is
then only *negative* (whilst that in the Beautiful is
positive); viz., a feeling that the Imagination is
depriving itself of its freedom, while it is purposively
determined according to a different law from that
of its empirical employment. It thus acquires an
extension and a might greater than it sacrifices,—
the ground of which, however, is concealed from
itself; whilst yet it *feels* the sacrifice or the
deprivation and, at the same time, the cause to
which it is subjected. *Astonishment*, that borders
upon terror, the dread and the holy awe which
seizes the observer at the sight of mountain peaks
rearing themselves to heaven, deep chasms and
streams raging therein, deep-shadowed solitudes that
dispose one to melancholy meditations—this, in the
safety in which we know ourselves to be, is not
actual fear, but only an attempt to feel fear by
the aid of the Imagination; that we may feel the
might of this faculty in combining with the mind's
repose the mental movement thereby excited, and
being thus superior to internal nature,—and therefore
to external,—so far as this can have any influence
on our feeling of well-being. For the Imagination
by the laws of Association makes our state of contentment dependent on physical [causes]; but it also,

by the principles of the Schematism of the Judgment (being so far, therefore, ranked under freedom), is the instrument of Reason and its Ideas, and, as such, has might to maintain our independence of natural influences, to regard as small what in reference to them is great, and so to place the absolutely great only in the proper destination of the subject. The raising of this reflection of the æsthetical Judgment so as to be adequate to Reason (though without a definite concept of Reason) represents the object as subjectively purposive, even by the objective want of accordance between the Imagination in its greatest extension and the Reason (as the faculty of Ideas).

We must here, generally, attend to what has been already noted, that in the Transcendental Æsthetic of Judgment we must speak solely of pure æsthetical judgments ; consequently our examples are not to be taken from such beautiful or sublime objects of Nature as presuppose the concept of a purpose. For, if so, the purposiveness would be either teleological, or would be based on mere sensations of an object (gratification or grief) ; and thus would be in the former case not æsthetical, in the latter not merely formal. If then we call the sight of the starry heaven *sublime*, we must not place at the basis of our judgment concepts of worlds inhabited by rational beings, and regard the bright points, with which we see the space above us filled, as their suns moving in circles purposively fixed with reference to them ; but we must regard it, just as we see it, as a distant, all-embracing, vault. Only under such a representation can we range that sublimity which a pure æsthetical judgment ascribes to this object. And in the same way, if we are to call the sight of the ocean sublime, we must not *think* of it as we [ordinarily] do, as implying all kinds of knowledge (that are not contained in immediate intuition). For example, we sometimes think of the ocean as a vast kingdom of aquatic creatures; or as the great source of those vapours that fill the air with clouds for the benefit of the land ; or again as an element which, though dividing continents from each other, yet promotes the greatest communication between them : but these furnish merely teleological judgments. To call the ocean sublime we must regard it as poets do, merely by what strikes the eye ; if it is at rest, as a clear mirror of water only bounded by the heaven ; if it is restless, as an abyss threatening to overwhelm everything. The like is to be said of the Sublime and Beautiful in the human figure. We must not regard as the determining grounds of our judgment the concepts of the purposes which all our limbs serve, and we must not allow this coincidence to *influence* our æsthetical judgment (for then it would no longer be pure) ; although it is certainly a necessary condition of æsthetical satisfaction that there should be no conflict between them. Æsthetical purposiveness is the conformity to law of the Judgment in its *freedom*. The satisfaction in the object depends on the relation in which we wish to place the Imagination ; always provided that it by itself entertains the mind in free occupation. If, on the other hand, the judgment be determined by anything else,—whether sensation or concept,—although it may be conformable to law, it cannot be the act of a *free* Judgment.

If then we speak of intellectual beauty or sublimity, these expressions are, *first*, not quite accurate, because beauty and sublimity are æsthetical modes of representation, which would not be found in us at all if we were pure intelligences (or even regarded ourselves as such in thought). *Secondly*, although both, as objects of an intellectual (moral) satisfaction, are so far compatible with æsthetical satisfaction that they *rest* upon no interest, yet they are difficult to unite with it, because they are meant to *produce* an interest. This, if its presentation is to harmonise with the satisfaction in the æsthetical judgment, could only arise by means of a sensible interest that we combine with it in the presentation ; and thus damage would be done to the intellectual purposiveness, and it would lose its purity.

The object of a pure and unconditioned intellectual satisfaction is the Moral Law in that might which it exercises in us over all mental motives *that precede it*. This might only makes itself æsthetically known to us through sacrifices (which causing a feeling of deprivation, though on behalf of internal freedom, in return discloses in us an unfathomable depth of this supersensible faculty, with consequences extending beyond our ken) ; thus the satisfaction on the æsthetical side (in relation to sensibility) is negative, *i.e.* against this interest, but regarded from the intellectual side it is positive and combined with an interest. Hence it follows that the intellectual, in itself purposive, (moral) good, æsthetically judged, must be represented as sublime rather than beautiful, so that it rather awakens the feeling of respect (which disdains charm) than that of love and familiar inclination ; for human nature does not attach itself to this good spontaneously, but only by the authority which Reason exercises over Sensibility. Conversely also, that which we call sublime in nature, whether external or internal (*e.g.* certain affections), is only represented as a might in the mind to

overcome [*certain*]¹ hindrances of the Sensibility by
means of moral fundamental propositions, and only
thus does it interest.

I will dwell a moment on this latter point. The
Idea of the Good conjoined with [strong] affection
is called *enthusiasm*. This state of mind seems to be
sublime, to the extent that we commonly assert that
nothing great could be done without it. Now every
affection² is blind, either in the choice of its purpose,
or, if this be supplied by Reason, in its accomplishment; for it is a mental movement which makes it
impossible to exercise a free deliberation about
fundamental propositions so as to determine ourselves thereby. It can therefore in no way deserve
the approval of the Reason. Nevertheless, æsthetically, enthusiasm is sublime, because it is a tension
of forces produced by Ideas, which give an impulse
to the mind, that operates far more powerfully and
lastingly than the impulse arising from sensible
representations. But (which seems strange) the
absence of affection (*apatheia, phlegma in significatu
bono*) in a mind that vigorously follows its unalter-
able principles is sublime, and in a far preferable
way, because it has also on its side the satisfaction

---

¹ [Second Edition.]

² *Affections* are specifically different from *passions*. The former
are related merely to feeling; the latter belong to the faculty of
desire, and are inclinations which render difficult or impossible all
determination of the [elective] will by principles. The former are
stormy and unpremeditated; the latter are steady and deliberate;
thus indignation in the form of wrath is an affection, but in the form
of hatred (revenge) is a passion. The latter can never and in no
reference be called sublime; because while in an affection the
freedom of the mind is *hindered*, in a passion it is abolished. [Cf.
Preface to the *Metaphysical Elements of Ethics*, § xvi., where this
distinction is more fully drawn out. Affection is described as *hasty*;
and passion is defined as the sensible *appetite* grown into a permanent
inclination.]

of pure Reason.[1] A mental state of this kind is
alone called noble ; and this expression is subsequently applied to things, *e.g.* a building, a garment,
literary style, bodily presence, etc., when these do not
so much arouse *astonishment* (the affection produced
by the representation of novelty exceeding our
expectations), as *admiration* (astonishment that does
not cease when the novelty disappears) ; and this
is the case when Ideas agree in their presentation undesignedly and artlessly with the æsthetical
satisfaction.

Every affection of the STRENUOUS kind (viz. that
excites the consciousness of our power to overcome
every obstacle—*animi strenui*) is *æsthetically sublime*,
e.g. wrath, even despair (*i.e.* the despair of *indignation*, not of *faintheartedness*). But affections of the
LANGUID kind (which make the very effort of resistance an object of pain—*animum languidum*) have
nothing *noble* in themselves, but they may be reckoned
under the sensuously beautiful. *Emotions*, which may
rise to the strength of affections, are very different.
We have both *spirited* and *tender* emotions. The
latter, if they rise to [strong] affections, are worthless ;
the propensity to them is called *sentimentality*. A
sympathetic grief that will not admit of consolation,
or one referring to imaginary evils to which we
deliberately surrender ourselves—being deceived by
fancy—as if they were actual, indicates and produces
a tender,[2] though weak, soul—which shows a beautiful side and which can be called fanciful, though not
enthusiastic. Romances, lacrymose plays, shallow

---

[1] [In the Preface to the *Metaphysical Elements of Ethics*, § xvii.,
Kant gives the term *moral apathy* to that freedom from the sway of
the affections, which is distinguished from indifference to them.]

[2] [Reading *weiche* with Rosenkranz ; Hartenstein and Kirchmann have *weise*, which yields no sense.]

moral precepts, which toy with (falsely) so-called
moral dispositions, but in fact make the heart languid, insensible to the severe precept of duty, and
incapable of all respect for the worth of humanity in
our own person, and for the rights of men (a very
different thing from their happiness), and in general
incapable of all steady principle; even a religious
discourse,[1] which recommends a cringing, abject
seeking of favour and ingratiation of ourselves, which
proposes the abandonment of all confidence in our own
faculties in opposition to the evil within us, instead
of a sturdy resolution to endeavour to overcome our
inclinations by means of those powers which with all
our frailty yet remain to us; that false humility
which sets the only way of pleasing the Supreme
Being in self-depreciation, in whining hypocritical
repentance and in a mere passive state of mind—
these are not compatible with any frame of mind
that can be counted beautiful, still less with one
which is to be counted sublime.

But even stormy movements of mind which may
be connected under the name of edification with
Ideas of religion, or—as merely belonging to culture
—with Ideas containing a social interest, can in no
way, however they strain the Imagination, lay claim
to the honour of being *sublime* presentations, unless
they leave after them a mental mood which, although only indirectly, has influence upon the mind's
consciousness of its strength, and its resolution in
reference to that which involves pure intellectual
purposiveness (the supersensible). For otherwise
all these emotions belong only to *motion*, which one
would fain enjoy for the sake of health. The
pleasant exhaustion, consequent upon such dis-

[1] [Cf. p. 129 supra.]

turbance produced by the play of the affections, is
an enjoyment of our wellbeing arising from the
restored equilibrium of the various vital forces.
This in the end amounts to the same thing as that
state which Eastern voluptuaries find so delightful,
when they get their bodies as it were kneaded and
all their muscles and joints softly pressed and bent ;
only that in this case the motive principle is for the
most part external, in the other case it is altogether
internal.   Many a man believes himself to be edified
by a sermon, when indeed there is no edification at
all (no system of good maxims) ; or to be improved
by a tragedy, when he is only glad at his ennui being
happily dispelled.   So the Sublime must always have
reference to the *disposition, i.e.* to the maxims which
furnish to the intellectual [part] and to the Ideas of
Reason a superiority over sensibility.

　We need not fear that the feeling of the sublime
will lose by so abstract a mode of presentation,—
which is quite negative in respect of what is sensible,
—for the Imagination, although it finds nothing beyond the sensible to which it can attach itself, yet
feels itself unbounded by this removal of its limitations; and thus that very abstraction is a presentation
of the Infinite, which can be nothing but a mere
negative presentation, but which yet expands the
soul.   Perhaps there is no sublimer passage in the
Jewish Law than the command, *Thou shalt not
make to thyself any graven image, nor the likeness
of anything which is in heaven or in the earth or
under the earth,* etc.   This command alone can
explain the enthusiasm that the Jewish people in
their moral period felt for their religion, when they
compared themselves with other peoples ; or explain
the pride which Mahommedanism inspires.   The

same is true of the moral law and of the tendency to morality in us.   It is quite erroneous to fear that if we deprive this [tendency] of all that can recommend it to sense it will only involve a cold lifeless assent and no moving force or emotion.   It is quite the other way, for where the senses see nothing more before them, and the unmistakable and indelible Idea of morality remains, it would be rather necessary to moderate the impetus of an unbounded Imagination, to prevent it from rising to enthusiasm, than through fear of the powerlessness of these Ideas to seek aid for them in images and childish ritual.   Thus governments have willingly allowed religion to be abundantly provided with the latter accompaniments; and seeking thereby to relieve their subjects of trouble, they have also sought to deprive them of the faculty of extending their spiritual powers beyond the limits that are arbitrarily assigned to them, and by means of which they can be the more easily treated as mere passive [1] beings.

This pure, elevating, merely negative presentation of morality brings with it, on the other hand, no danger of *fanaticism*, which is *a belief in our capacity of seeing something beyond all bounds of sensibility*, *i.e.* of dreaming in accordance with fundamental propositions (or of going mad with Reason); and this is so just because this presentation is merely negative.   For the *inscrutableness of the Idea of Freedom* quite cuts it off from any positive presentation; but the moral law is in itself sufficiently and originally determinant in us, so that it does not permit us to cast a glance at any ground of determination external to itself.   If enthusiasm is comparable to *madness*, fanaticism is comparable to

[1] [Kirchmann has *positiv*; but this is probably a mere misprint.]

monomania ; of which the latter is least of all compatible with the sublime, because in its detail it is
ridiculous.   In enthusiasm, regarded as an affection,
the Imagination is without bridle ; in fanaticism,
regarded as an inveterate, brooding passion, it is
without rule.   The first is a transitory accident
which sometimes befalls the soundest Understanding ; the second is a disease which unsettles it.

Simplicity (purposiveness without art) is as it
were the style of Nature in the sublime, and so also
of Morality which is a second (supersensible) nature ;
of which we only know the laws without being able
to reach by intuition that supersensible faculty in
ourselves which contains the ground of the legislation.

Now the satisfaction in the Beautiful, like that in
the Sublime, is not alone distinguishable from other
æsthetical judgments by its universal *communicability*, but also because it acquires an interest through
this very property in reference to society (in which
this communication is possible).   We must, however,
remark that *separation from all society* is regarded
as sublime, if it rests upon Ideas that overlook all
sensible interest.   To be sufficient for oneself, and
consequently to have no need of society, without at
the same time being unsociable, *i.e.* without flying
from it, is something bordering on the sublime ;
as is any dispensing with wants.   On the other
hand, to fly from men from *misanthropy*, because we
bear ill-will to them, or from *anthropophoby* (shyness),
because we fear them as foes, is partly hateful, partly
contemptible.   There is indeed a misanthropy (very
improperly so-called), the tendency to which frequently appears with old age in many right-thinking
men ; which is philanthropic enough as far as *good-*

L

will to men is concerned, but which through long and
sad experience is far removed from *satisfaction* with
men.   Evidence of this is afforded by the propensity
to solitude, the fantastic wish for a secluded country
seat, or (in the case of young persons) by the dream
of the happiness of passing one's life with a little
family upon some island unknown to the rest of the
world ; a dream of which story-tellers or writers
of Robinsonades know how to make good use.
Falsehood, ingratitude, injustice, the childishness
of the purposes regarded by ourselves as important and great, in the pursuit of which men
inflict upon each other all imaginable evils, are so
contradictory to the Idea of what men might be if
they would, and conflict so with our lively wish to
see them better, that, in order that we may not hate
them (since we cannot love them), the renunciation
of all social joys seems but a small sacrifice.   This
sadness—not the sadness (of which sympathy is the
cause) for the evils which fate brings upon others,
—but for those things which men do to one another
(which depends upon an antipathy in fundamental
propositions), is sublime, because it rests upon
Ideas, whilst the former can only count as beautiful.—   The brilliant and thorough *Saussure*,[1] in his
account of his Alpine travels, says of one of the
Savoy mountains, called *Bonhomme*, "There reigns
there a certain *insipid sadness*."   He therefore
recognised an *interesting* sadness, that the sight of
a solitude might inspire, to which men might wish
to transport themselves that they might neither hear
nor experience any more of the world ; which, however, would not be quite so inhospitable that it would
offer only an extremely painful retreat.—   I make

---

[1] [L.c. vol. ii. p. 181.]

this remark solely with the design of indicating
again that even depression (not dejected sadness)
may be counted among the *sturdy* affections, if it
has its ground in moral Ideas.   But if it is grounded
on sympathy and, as such, is amiable, it belongs
merely to the *languid* affections.   [I make this
remark] to call attention to the state of mind which
is *sublime* only in the first case.

We can now compare the above Transcendental
Exposition of æsthetical judgments with the Physiological worked out by *Burke* and by many clear-
headed men among us, in order to see whither a
merely empirical exposition of the Sublime and
Beautiful leads.   *Burke*, who deserves to be regarded as the most important author who adopts
this mode of treatment, infers by this method "that
the feeling of the Sublime rests on the impulse towards self-preservation and on *fear*, *i.e.* on a pain,
which not going as far as actually to derange the parts
of the body, produces movements which, since they
purify the finer or grosser vessels of dangerous or
troublesome stoppages, are capable of exciting pleasant sensations ; not indeed pleasure, but a kind of
satisfying horror, a certain tranquillity tinged with
terror."[1]   The Beautiful, which he founded on love

---

[1] [See Burke, *On the Sublime and Beautiful*, Part IV., Sect.
vii. "If the pain and terror are so modified as not to be actually
noxious ; if the pain is not carried to violence, and the terror is not
conversant about the present destruction of the person, as these
emotions clear the parts, whether fine or gross, of a dangerous and
troublesome incumbrance, they are capable of producing delight ;
not pleasure, but a sort of delightful horror, a sort of tranquillity
tinged with terror ; which, as it belongs to self-preservation, is one
of the strongest of all the passions."   Kant quotes from the German
version published at Riga in 1773.   This was a free translation made
from Burke's fifth edition.]

(which he wishes to keep quite separate from desire), he reduces to "the relaxing, slackening, and enervating of the fibres of the body, and a consequent weakening, languor, and exhaustion, a fainting, dissolving, and melting away for enjoyment."[1] And he confirms this explanation not only by cases in which the Imagination in combination with the Understanding can excite in us the feeling of the Beautiful or of the Sublime, but by cases in which it is combined with sensation.— As psychological observations, these analyses of the phenomena of our mind are exceedingly beautiful, and afford rich material for the favourite investigations of empirical anthropology. It is also not to be denied that all representations in us, whether, objectively viewed, they are merely sensible or are quite intellectual, may yet subjectively be united to gratification or grief, however imperceptible either may be; because they all affect the feeling of life, and none of them, so far as it is a modification of the subject, can be indifferent. And so, as Epicurus maintained, all *gratification* or *grief* may ultimately be corporeal, whether it arises from the representations of the Imagination or the Understanding; because life without a feeling of bodily organs would be merely a consciousness of existence, without any feeling of well-being or the reverse, *i.e.* of the furthering or the checking of the vital powers. For the mind is by itself alone life (the principle of life), and

---

[1] [See Burke, l.c.. Part IV., Sect. xix. "Beauty acts by relaxing the solids of the whole system. There are all the appearances of such a relaxation; and a relaxation somewhat below the natural tone seems to me to be the cause of all positive pleasure. Who is a stranger to that manner of expression so common in all times and in all countries, of being softened, relaxed, enervated, dissolved, melted away by pleasure?"]

hindrances or furtherances must be sought outside it and yet in the man, consequently in union with his body.

If, however, we place the satisfaction in the object altogether in the fact that it gratifies us by charm or emotion, we must not assume that any *other* man agrees with the æsthetical judgment which *we* pass; for as to these each one rightly consults his own individual sensibility. But in that case all censorship of taste would disappear, except indeed the example afforded by the accidental agreement of others in their judgments were regarded as *commanding* our assent; and this principle we should probably resist, and should appeal to the natural right of subjecting the judgment, which rests on the immediate feeling of our own well-being, to our own sense and not to that of any other man.

If then the judgment of taste is not to be valid merely *egoistically*, but according to its inner nature,— *i.e.* on account of itself and not on account of the examples that others give of their taste,—to be necessarily valid *pluralistically*, if we regard it as a judgment which may exact the adhesion of every one; then there must lie at its basis some *a priori* principle (whether objective or subjective) to which we can never attain by seeking out the empirical laws of mental changes. For these only enable us to know how we judge, but do not prescribe to us how we ought to judge. They do not supply an *unconditioned* command,[1] such as judgments of taste presuppose, inasmuch as they require that the satisfaction be *immediately* connected with the representation. Thus the empirical exposition of

[1] [Reading *Gebot* with Hartenstein and Rosenkranz; Kirchmann has *Gesetz*.]

æsthetical judgments may be a beginning of a collection of materials for a higher investigation; but a transcendental discussion of this faculty is also possible, and is an essential part of the Kritik of Taste.   For if it had not *a priori* principles, it could not possibly pass sentence on the judgments of others, and it could not approve or blame them with any appearance of right.

The remaining part of the Analytic of the Æsthetical Judgment contains first the

DEDUCTION OF [PURE[1]] ÆSTHETICAL JUDGMENTS

§ 30. *The Deduction of æsthetical judgments on the objects of nature must not be directed to what we call Sublime in nature, but only to the Beautiful.*

The claim of an æsthetical judgment to universal validity for every subject requires, as a judgment resting on some *a priori* principle, a Deduction (or legitimatising of its pretensions) in addition to its Exposition; if it is concerned with satisfaction or dissatisfaction in the *form of the Object*.   Of this kind are judgments of taste about the Beautiful in Nature.   For in that case the purposiveness has its ground in the Object and in its figure, although it does not indicate its reference to other objects in accordance with concepts (for a cognitive judgment), but merely has to do in general with the apprehension of this form, so far as it shows itself conformable to the *faculty* of concepts and of the presentation (which is identical with the apprehension)

[1] [Second Edition.]

of them in the mind. We can thus, in respect of the Beautiful in nature, suggest many questions touching the cause of this purposiveness of their forms, *e.g.*, to explain why nature has scattered abroad beauty with such profusion, even in the depth of the ocean, where the human eye (for which alone that purposiveness exists) but seldom penetrates.

But the Sublime in nature—if we are passing upon it a pure æsthetical judgment, not mixed up with any concepts of perfection or objective purposiveness, in which case it would be a teleological judgment—may be regarded as quite formless or devoid of figure, and yet as the object of a pure satisfaction ; and it may display a subjective purposiveness in the given representation. And we ask if, for an æsthetical judgment of this kind,—over, and above the Exposition of what is thought in it,— a Deduction also of its claim to any (subjective) *a priori* principle may be demanded.

To which we may answer that the Sublime in nature is improperly so called, and that properly speaking the word should only be applied to a state of mind, or rather to its foundation in human nature. The apprehension of an otherwise formless and unpurposive object gives merely the occasion, through which we become conscious of such a state ; the object is thus *employed* as subjectively purposive, but is not judged as such *in itself* and on account of its form (it is, as it were, a *species finalis accepta, non data*). Hence our Exposition of judgments concerning the Sublime in nature was at the same time their Deduction. For when we analysed the reflection of the Judgment in such acts, we found in them a purposive relation of the cognitive faculties, which must be ascribed ultimately to the faculty of purposes (the will), and hence is itself purposive *a priori*. This then immediately involves the Deduction, *i.e.* the justification of the claim of such a judgment to universal and necessary validity.

We shall therefore only have to seek for the deduction of judgments of Taste, *i.e.* of judgments about the Beauty of natural things ; we shall thus treat satisfactorily the problem with which the whole faculty of æsthetical Judgment is concerned.

§ 31. *Of the method of deduction of judgments of Taste*

A Deduction, *i.e.* the guarantee of the legitimacy of a class of judgments, is only obligatory if the judgment lays claim to necessity. This it does, if it demands even subjective universality or the agreement of every one, although it is not a judgment of cognition but only one of pleasure or pain in a given object ; *i.e.* it assumes a subjective purposiveness thoroughly valid for every one, which must not be based on any concept of the thing, because the judgment is one of taste.

We have before us in the latter case no cognitive judgment—neither a theoretical one based on the concept of a *Nature* in general formed by the Understanding, nor a (pure) practical one based on the Idea of *Freedom*, as given *a priori* by Reason. Therefore we have to justify *a priori* the validity neither of a judgment which represents what a thing is, nor of one which prescribes that I ought to do something in order to produce it. We have merely to prove for the Judgment generally the *universal validity* of a singular judgment that expresses the subjective purposiveness of an empirical representation of the form of an object ; in order to explain how it is possible that a thing can please in the mere act of judging it (without sensation or concept), and how the satisfaction of one man can be proclaimed as a rule for every other ; just as the act of judging of an object for the sake of a *cognition* in general has universal rules.

If now this universal validity is not to be based on any collecting of the suffrages of others, or on any questioning of them as to the kind of sensations they have, but is to rest, as it were, on an autonomy of the judging subject in respect of the feeling of pleasure (in the given representation), *i.e.* on his own taste, and yet is not to be derived from concepts ; then a judgment like this—such as the judgment of taste is, in fact—has a twofold logical peculiarity. *First*, there is its *a priori* universal validity, which is not a logical universality in accordance with concepts, but the universality of a singular judgment. *Secondly*, it has a necessity (which must always rest on *a priori* grounds), which however does not depend on any *a priori* grounds of proof, through the representation of which the assent that every one concedes to the judgment of taste could be exacted.

The explanation of these logical peculiarities, wherein a judgment of taste is different from all cognitive judgments—if we at the outset abstract from all content, viz., from the feeling of pleasure, and merely compare the æsthetical form with the form of objective judgments as logic prescribes it —is sufficient by itself for the deduction of this singular faculty. We shall then represent and elucidate by examples these characteristic properties of taste.

§ 32. *First peculiarity of the judgment of Taste*

The judgment of taste determines its object in respect of satisfaction (in its beauty) with an accompanying claim for the assent of *every one*, just as if it were objective.

To say that "this flower is beautiful" is the same as to assert its proper claim to satisfy every one. By the pleasantness of its smell it has no such claim. A smell which one man enjoys gives another a headache. Now what are we to presume from this except that beauty is to be regarded as a property of the flower itself, which does not accommodate itself to any diversity of persons or of their sensitive organs, but to which these must accommodate themselves if they are to pass any judgment upon it? And yet this is not so. For a judgment of taste consists in calling a thing beautiful just because of that characteristic in respect of which it accommodates itself to our mode of apprehension.

Moreover, it is required of every judgment which is to prove the taste of the subject, that the subject shall judge by himself, without needing to grope about empirically among the judgments of others, and acquaint himself previously as to their satisfaction or dissatisfaction with the same object; thus his judgment should be pronounced *a priori*, and not be a mere imitation because the thing actually gives universal pleasure. However, we ought to think that an *a priori* judgment must contain a concept of the Object, for the cognition of which it contains the principle ; but the judgment of taste is not based upon concepts at all, and is in general not a cognitive but an æsthetical judgment.

Thus a young poet does not permit himself to be dissuaded out of his conviction that his poem is beautiful, by the judgment of the public or of his friends ; and if he gives ear to them he does so, not because he now judges differently, but because, although (in regard to him) the whole public has false taste, in his desire for applause he finds reason for accommodating himself to the common error (even against his judgment). It is only at a later time, when his Judgment has been sharpened by exercise, that he voluntarily departs from his former judgments ; just as he proceeds with those of his judgments which rest upon Reason. Taste [merely][1] claims autonomy. To make the judgments of others the determining grounds of his own would be heteronomy.

That we, and rightly, recommend the works of the ancients as models and call their authors classical, thus forming among writers a kind of noble class who give laws to the people by their example, seems to indicate *a posteriori* sources of taste, and to contradict the autonomy of taste in every subject. But we might just as well say that the old mathematicians, —who are regarded up to the present day as supplying models not easily to be dispensed with for the supreme profundity and elegance of their synthetical methods,—prove that our Reason is only imitative, and that we have not the faculty of producing from it in combination with intuition rigid proofs by means of the construction of concepts.[2] There is

---

[1] [Second Edition.]
[2] [Cf. Kritik of *Pure Reason*, Methodology, c. I, § I. " The

no use of our powers, however free, no use of
Reason itself (which must create all its judgments
a priori from common sources) which would not
give rise to faulty attempts, if every subject had
always to begin anew from the rude basis of his
natural state, and if others had not preceded him
with their attempts.   Not that these make mere
imitators of those who come after them, but rather
by their procedure they put others on the track
of seeking in themselves principles and so of pursu-
ing their own course, often a better one.   Even in
religion—where certainly every one has to derive
the rule of his conduct from himself, because he
remains responsible for it and cannot shift the
blame of his transgressions upon others, whether
his teachers or his predecessors—there is never
as much accomplished by means of universal precepts, either obtained from priests or philosophers
or got from oneself, as by means of an example
of virtue or holiness which, exhibited in history,
does not dispense with the autonomy of virtue
based on the proper and original Idea of morality
(*a priori*), or change it into a mechanical imitation.
Following, involving something precedent, not
" imitation," is the right expression for all influence
that the products of an exemplary author may
have upon others.   And this only means that we
draw from the same sources as our predecessor
did, and learn from him only the way to avail
ourselves of them.   But of all faculties and talents
Taste, because its judgment is not determinable by
concepts and precepts, is just that one which most
needs examples of what has in the progress of culture

construction of a concept is the *a priori* presentation of the corresponding intuition."]

received the longest approval; that it may not
become again uncivilised and return to the crudeness
of its first essays.   —

§ 33. *Second peculiarity of the judgment of Taste*

The judgment of taste is not determinable by
grounds of proof, just as if it were merely *subjective*.

If a man, *in the first place*, does not find a building, a prospect, or a poem beautiful, a hundred voices
all highly praising it will not force his inmost agreement. He may indeed feign that it pleases him in
order that he may not be regarded as devoid of
taste; he may even begin to doubt whether he has
formed his taste on a knowledge of a sufficient
number of objects of a certain kind (just as one,
who believes that he recognises in the distance as a
forest, something which all others regard as a town,
doubts the judgment of his own sight). But he
clearly sees that the agreement of others gives no
valid proof of the judgment about beauty. Others
might perhaps see and observe for him; and what
many have seen in one way, although he believes
that he has seen it differently, might serve him as
an adequate ground of proof of a theoretical and
consequently logical judgment. But that a thing
has pleased others could never serve as the basis
of an æsthetical judgment. A judgment of others
which is unfavourable to ours may indeed rightly
make us scrutinise our own carefully, but it can
never convince us of its incorrectness. There is
therefore no empirical *ground of proof* which would
force a judgment of taste upon any one.

Still less, *in the second place*, can an *a priori*
proof determine according to definite rules a judg-

ment about beauty. If a man reads me a poem of his or brings me to a play, which does not on the whole suit my taste, he may bring forward in proof of the beauty of his poem *Batteux*[1] or *Lessing* or still more ancient and famous critics of taste, and all the rules laid down by them ; certain passages which displease me may agree very well with rules of beauty (as they have been put forth by these writers and are universally recognised) : but I stop my ears, I will listen to no arguments and no reasoning ; and I will rather assume that these rules of the critics are false, or at least that they do not apply to the case in question, than admit that my judgment should be determined by grounds of proof *a priori.* For it is to be a judgment of Taste and not of Understanding or Reason.

It seems that this is one of the chief reasons why this æsthetical faculty of judgment has been given the name of Taste. For though a man enumerate to me all the ingredients of a dish, and remark that each is separately pleasant to me and further extol with justice the wholesomeness of this particular food—yet am I deaf to all these reasons ; I try the dish with *my* tongue and my palate, and thereafter (and not according to universal principles) do I pass my judgment.

In fact the judgment of Taste always takes the form of a singular judgment about an Object. The Understanding can form a universal judgment by comparing the Object in point of the satisfaction it affords with the judgment of others upon it : *e.g.* "all tulips are beautiful." But then this is not a judgment of taste but a logical judgment, which

---

[1] [Charles Batteux (1713-1780), author of *Les Beaux Arts reduits à un même principe.*]

takes the relation of an Object to taste as the predicate of things of a certain species. That judgment, however, in which I find an individual given tulip beautiful, *i.e.* in which I find my satisfaction in the object to be universally valid, is alone a judgment of taste. Its peculiarity consists in the fact that, although it has merely subjective validity, it claims the assent of *all* subjects, exactly as it would do if it were an objective judgment resting on grounds of knowledge, that could be established by a proof.

§ 34. *There is no objective principle of Taste possible*

By a principle of taste I mean a principle under the condition of which we could subsume the concept of an object and thus infer by means of a syllogism that the object is beautiful. But that is absolutely impossible. For I must immediately feel pleasure in the representation of the Object, and of that I can be persuaded by no grounds of proof whatever.] Although, as *Hume* says,[1] all critics can reason more plausibly than cooks, yet the same fate awaits them. They cannot expect the determining ground of their judgment [to be derived] from the force of the proofs, but only from the reflection of the subject upon its own proper state

---

[1] [Essay XVIII, *The Sceptic.* "Critics can reason and dispute more plausibly than cooks or perfumers. We may observe, however, that this uniformity among human kind, hinders not, but that there is a considerable diversity in the sentiments of beauty and worth, and that education, custom, prejudice, caprice, and humour, frequently vary our taste of this kind. . . . Beauty and worth are merely of a relative nature, and consist in an agreable sentiment, produced by an object in a particular mind, according to the peculiar structure and constitution of that mind."]

(of pleasure or pain), all precepts and rules being rejected.

But although critics can and ought to pursue their reasonings so that our judgments of taste may be corrected and extended, it is not with a view to set forth the determining ground of this kind of æsthetical judgments in a universally applicable formula, which is impossible; but rather to investigate the cognitive faculties and their exercise in these judgments, and to explain by examples the reciprocal subjective purposiveness, the form of which, as has been shown above, in a given representation, constitutes the beauty of the object. Therefore the Kritik of Taste is only subjective as regards the representation through which an object is given to us; viz. it is the art or science of reducing to rules the reciprocal relation between the Understanding and the Imagination in the given representation (without reference to any preceding sensation or concept). That is, it is the art or science of reducing to rules their accordance or discordance, and of determining the conditions of this. It is an *art*, if it only shows this by examples; it is a *science* if it derives the possibility of such judgments from the nature of these faculties, as cognitive faculties in general. We have here, in Transcendental Kritik, only to do with the latter. It should develop and justify the subjective principle of taste, as an *a priori* principle of the Judgment. This Kritik, as an art, merely seeks to apply, in the judging of objects, the physiological (here psychological), and therefore empirical rules, according to which taste actually proceeds (without taking any account of their possibility); and it criticises the products of beautiful art just as, regarded as a science, it criticises the faculty by which they are judged.

§ 35. *The principle of Taste is the subjective principle of Judgment in general*

The judgment of taste is distinguished from a logical judgment in this, that the latter subsumes a representation under the concept of the Object, while the former does not subsume it under any concept ; because otherwise the necessary universal agreement [in these judgments] would be capable of being compelled by proofs.   Nevertheless it is like the latter in this, that it claims universality and necessity, though not according to concepts of the Object, and consequently a merely subjective necessity.   Now, because the concepts in a judgment constitute its content (what belongs to the cognition of the Object), but the judgment of taste is not determinable by concepts, it is based only on the subjective formal condition of a judgment in general. The subjective condition of all judgments is the faculty of Judgment itself.   This when used with reference to a representation by which an object is given, requires the accordance of two representative powers : viz. Imagination (for the intuition and comprehension of the manifold) and Understanding (for the concept as a representation of the unity of this comprehension).   Now because no concept of the Object lies here at the basis of the judgment, it can only consist in the subsumption of the Imagination itself (in the case of a representation by which an object is given) under the conditions that the Understanding requires to pass from intuition to concepts.   That is, because the freedom of the

M

Imagination consists in the fact that it schematises without any concept, [the judgment of taste must rest on a mere sensation of the reciprocal activity of the Imagination in its *freedom* and the Understanding with its *conformity to law*. It must therefore rest on a feeling, which makes us judge the object by the purposiveness of the representation (by which an object is given) in respect of the furtherance of the cognitive faculty in its free play] Taste, then, as subjective Judgment, contains a principle of subsumption, not of intuitions under concepts, but of the *faculty* of intuitions or presentations (*i.e.* the Imagination) under the *faculty* of the concepts (*i.e.* the Understanding); so far as the former *in its freedom* harmonises with the latter *in its conformity to law*.

In order to discover this ground of legitimacy by a deduction of the judgments of taste we can only take as a clue the formal peculiarities of this kind of judgments, and consequently can only consider their logical form.

§ 36. *Of the problem of a Deduction of judgments of Taste*

The concept of an Object in general can immediately be combined with the perception of an object, containing its empirical predicates, so as to form a cognitive judgment; and it is thus that a judgment of experience is produced.[1] At the basis of this lie *a priori* concepts of the synthetical unity of the manifold of intuition, by which the

---

[1] [For the distinction, an important one in Kant, between judgments of experience and judgments of perception, see his *Prolegomena*, § 18. Cf. *Kant's Critical Philosophy for English Readers*, vol. i. p. 116.]

manifold is thought as the determination of an Object. These concepts (the Categories) require a Deduction, which is given in the Kritik of pure Reason ; and by it we can get the solution of the problem, how are synthetical *a priori* cognitive judgments possible ? This problem concerns then the *a priori* principles of the pure Understanding and its theoretical judgments.

But with a perception there can also be combined a feeling of pleasure (or pain) and a satisfaction, that accompanies the representation of the Object and serves instead of its predicate ; thus there can result an æsthetical non-cognitive judgment. At the basis of such a judgment—if it is not a mere judgment of sensation but a formal judgment of reflection, which imputes the same satisfaction necessarily to every one,—must lie some *a priori* principle ; which may be merely subjective (if an objective one should prove impossible for judgments of this kind), but also as such may need a Deduction, that we may thereby comprehend how an æsthetical judgment can lay claim to necessity. On this is founded the problem with which we are now occupied, how are judgments of taste possible ? This problem then has to do with the *a priori* principles of the pure faculty of Judgment in *æsthetical* judgments ; *i.e.* judgments in which it has not (as in theoretical ones) merely to subsume under objective concepts of Understanding, and in which it is subject to a law, but in which it is, itself, subjectively, both object and law.

This problem then may be thus represented : how is a judgment possible, in which merely from *our own* feeling of pleasure in an object, independently of its concept, we judge that this pleasure attaches to the representation of the same Object *in every other subject*, and that *a priori* without waiting for the accordance of others?

It is easy to see that judgments of taste are synthetical, because they go beyond the concept and even beyond the intuition of the Object, and add to that intuition as predicate something that is not a cognition, viz. a feeling of pleasure (or pain). Although the predicate (of the *personal* pleasure bound up with the representation) is empirical, nevertheless, as concerns the required assent of *every one* the judgments are *a priori*, or desire to be regarded as such; and this is already involved in the expressions of this claim. Thus this problem of the Kritik of Judgment belongs to the general problem of transcendental philosophy, how are synthetical *a priori* judgments possible?

§ 37. *What is properly asserted a priori of an object in a judgment of Taste*

That the representation of an object is immediately bound up with pleasure can only be internally perceived, and if we did not wish to indicate anything more than this it would give a merely empirical judgment. For I cannot combine a definite feeling (of pleasure or pain) with any representation except where there is at bottom an *a priori* principle in the Reason determining the Will. In that case the pleasure (in the moral feeling) is the consequence of the principle, but cannot be compared with the pleasure in taste, because it requires a definite concept of a law; and the latter pleasure, on the contrary, must be bound up with the mere act of judging, prior to all concepts. ⌊Hence also all judgments of taste are singular judgments, because they do not combine their predicate of satisfaction with a concept, but with a given individual empirical representation.

And so it is not the pleasure, but the *universal validity of this pleasure*, perceived as mentally bound up with the mere judgment upon an object, which is represented *a priori* in a judgment of taste as a universal rule for the Judgment and valid for every one. It is an empirical judgment [to say] that I perceive and judge an object with pleasure. But it is an *a priori* judgment [to say] that I find it beautiful, *i.e.* I attribute this satisfaction necessarily to every one.

§ 38. *Deduction of judgments of Taste*

If it be admitted that in a pure judgment of taste the satisfaction in the object is combined with the mere act of judging its form, it is nothing else than its subjective purposiveness for the Judgment which we feel to be mentally combined with the representation of the object. The Judgment, as regards the formal rules of its action, apart from all matter (whether sensation or concept), can only be directed to the subjective conditions of its employment in general (it is applied[1] neither to a particular mode of sense nor to a particular concept of the Understanding); and consequently to that subjective [element] which we can pre-suppose in all men (as requisite for possible cognition in general). Thus the agreement of a representation with these conditions of the Judgment must be capable of being assumed as valid *a priori* for every one. *I.e.* we

---

[1] [First Edition has "limited."]

may rightly impute to every one the pleasure or the
subjective purposiveness of the representation for
the relation between the cognitive faculties in the
act of judging a sensible object in general.[1]

Remark

This deduction is thus easy, because it has no
need to justify the objective reality of any concept,
for Beauty is not a concept of the Object and the
judgment of taste is not cognitive. It only maintains
that we are justified in pre-supposing universally in
every man those subjective conditions of the Judgment which we find in ourselves ;} and further, that
we have rightly subsumed the given Object under
these conditions. The latter has indeed unavoidable
difficulties which do not beset the logical Judgment.
There we subsume under concepts, but in the
æsthetical Judgment under a merely sensible relation between the Imagination and Understanding
mutually harmonising in the representation of the
form of the Object,—in which case the subsumption
may easily be deceptive. Yet the legitimacy of
the claim of the Judgment in counting upon universal assent is not thus annulled ; it reduces itself

---

[1] In order to be justified in claiming universal assent for an
æsthetical judgment that rests merely on subjective grounds, it is
sufficient to assume, (1) that the subjective conditions of the
Judgment, as regards the relation of the cognitive powers thus put
into activity to a cognition in general, are the same in all men.
This must be true, because otherwise men would not be able to
communicate their representations or even their knowledge. (2)
The judgment must merely have reference to this relation (consequently to the *formal condition* of the Judgment) and be pure, *i.e.*
not mingled either with concepts of the Object or with sensations, as
determining grounds. If there has been any mistake as regards
this latter condition, then there is only an inaccurate application of
the privilege, which a law gives us, to a particular case ; but that
does not destroy the privilege itself in general.

merely to judging as valid for every one the correctness of the principle from subjective grounds.
For as to the difficulty or doubt concerning the
correctness of the subsumption under that principle,
it makes the legitimacy of the claim of an æsthetical
judgment in general to such validity and the principle of the same, as little doubtful, as the alike
(though neither so commonly nor readily) faulty
subsumption of the logical Judgment under its
principle can make the latter, an objective principle,
doubtful.   But if the question were to be, how is
it possible to assume nature *a priori* to be a complex of objects of taste ? this problem has reference
to Teleology, because it must be regarded as a
purpose of nature essentially belonging to its concept to exhibit forms that are purposive for our
Judgment.   But the correctness of this latter assumption is very doubtful, whereas the efficacy of
natural beauties is patent to experience.

§ 39. *Of the communicability of a Sensation*

If sensation, as the real in perception, is related
to knowledge, it is called sensation of the senses ;
and its specific quality may be represented as generally communicable in a uniform way, if we assume
that every one has senses like our own.   But this
cannot at all be presupposed of any single sensation.
To a man who is deficient in the sense of smell,
this kind of sensation cannot be communicated ;
and even if it is not wholly deficient, we cannot
be certain that he gets exactly the same sensation
from a flower that we have.   But even more must
we represent men as differing in respect of the
pleasantness or *unpleasantness* involved in the sen-

sation from the same object of sense; and it is
absolutely not to be required that every man should
take pleasure in the same objects. Pleasure of this
kind, because it comes into the mind through the
senses, in respect of which therefore we are passive,
we may call the pleasure of *enjoyment*.

Satisfaction in an action because of its moral
character is on the other hand not the pleasure of
enjoyment, but of spontaneity and its accordance
with the Idea of its destination. But this feeling,
called moral, requires concepts, and presents not free
purposiveness, but purposiveness that is conformable
to law; it therefore admits of being universally
communicated only by means of Reason, and, if the
pleasure is to be homogeneous for every one, by
very definite practical concepts of Reason.

Pleasure in the Sublime in nature, regarded as
a pleasure of rational contemplation, also makes
claim to universal participation; but it presupposes,
besides, a different feeling, viz. that of our supersensible destination, which, however obscurely, has a
moral foundation. But that other men will take
account of it, and will find a satisfaction in the consideration of the wild greatness of nature (that
certainly cannot be ascribed to its aspect, which is
rather terrifying), I am not absolutely justified in
supposing. Nevertheless, in consideration of the
fact that on every suitable occasion regard should be
had to these moral dispositions, I can impute such
satisfaction to every man, but only by means of the
moral law which on its side again is based on
concepts of Reason.

On the contrary, pleasure in the Beautiful is
neither a pleasure of enjoyment nor of a law-abiding activity, nor even of rational contemplation in

accordance with Ideas, but of mere reflection. Without having as rule any purpose or fundamental proposition, this pleasure accompanies the ordinary apprehension of an object by the Imagination, as faculty of intuition, in relation with the Understanding, as faculty of concepts, by means of a procedure of the Judgment which it must also exercise on behalf of the commonest experience; only that in the latter case it is in order to perceive an empirical objective concept, in the former case (in æsthetical judgments) merely to perceive the accordance of the representation with the harmonious (subjectively purposive) activity of both cognitive faculties in their freedom, *i.e.* to feel with pleasure the mental state produced by the representation. This pleasure must necessarily depend for every one on the same conditions, for they are subjective conditions of the possibility of a cognition in general; and the proportion between these cognitive faculties requisite for Taste is also requisite for that ordinary sound Understanding which we have to presuppose in every one. Therefore he who judges with taste (if only he does not go astray in this act of consciousness and mistake matter for form or charm for beauty) may impute to every one subjective purposeiveness, *i.e.* his satisfaction in the Object, and may assume his feeling to be universally communicable and that without the mediation of concepts.

§ 40. *Of Taste as a kind of* sensus communis

We often give to the Judgment, if we are considering the result rather than the act of its reflection, the name of a sense, and we speak of a sense of truth, or of a sense of decorum, of justice, etc. And yet we know, or at least we ought to know, that these concepts cannot have their place in Sense, and further, that Sense has not the least capacity for expressing universal rules ; but that no representation of truth, fitness, beauty, or justice, and so forth, could come into our thoughts if we could not rise beyond Sense to higher faculties of cognition. *The common Understanding of men*, which, as the mere healthy (not yet cultivated) Understanding, we regard as the least to be expected from any one claiming the name of man, has therefore the doubtful honour of being given the name of common sense (*sensus communis*) ; and in such a way that by the name *common* (not merely in our language, where the word actually has a double signification, but in many others) we understand *vulgar*, that which is everywhere met with, the possession of which indicates absolutely no merit or superiority.

But under the *sensus communis* we must include the Idea of a sense *common to all, i.e.* of a faculty of judgment, which in its reflection takes account (*a priori*) of the mode of representation of all other men in thought ; in order *as it were* to compare its judgment with the collective Reason of humanity, and thus to escape the illusion arising from the private conditions that could be so easily taken for objective, which would injuriously affect the judgment. This is done by comparing our judgment with the possible rather than the actual judgments of others, and by putting ourselves in the place of any other man, by abstracting from the limitations which contingently attach to our own judgment. This, again, is brought about by leaving aside as much as possible the matter of our representative state, *i.e.* sensation, and simply having respect to the formal peculiarities of our representation or representative state. Now this operation of reflection seems perhaps too artificial to be attributed to the faculty called *common* sense; but it only appears so, when expressed in abstract formulæ. In itself there is nothing more natural than to abstract from charm or emotion if we are seeking a judgment that is to serve as a universal rule.

The following Maxims of common human Understanding do not properly come in here, as parts of the Kritik of Taste; but yet they may serve to elucidate its fundamental propositions. They are: 1° to think for oneself; 2° to put ourselves in thought in the place of every one else; 3° always to think consistently. The first is the maxim of *unprejudiced* thought; the second of *enlarged* thought; the third of *consecutive* thought.[1] The first is the maxim of a never *passive* Reason. The tendency to such passivity, and therefore to heteronomy of the Reason, is called *prejudice*; and the greatest prejudice of all is to represent nature as not subject to the rules that the Understanding places at its basis by means of its own essential law, *i.e.* is *superstition*. Deliverance from superstition is called *enlightenment*;[2] because although this name belongs to deliverance from prejudices in general,

---

[1] [Kant lays down these three maxims in his *Introduction to Logic*, § vii, as "general rules and conditions of the avoidance of error."]

[2] We soon see that although enlightenment is easy *in thesi*, yet *in hypothesi* it is difficult and slow of accomplishment. For not to be passive as regards Reason, but to be always self-legislative, is indeed quite easy for the man who wishes only to be in accordance with his essential purpose, and does not desire to know what is beyond his Understanding. But since we can hardly avoid seeking this, and there are never wanting others who promise with much confidence that they are able to satisfy our curiosity, it must be very hard to maintain in or restore to the mind (especially the mind of the public) that bare negative which properly constitutes enlightenment.

yet superstition specially (*in sensu eminenti*) deserves to be called a prejudice. For the blindness
in which superstition places us, which it even im-
poses on us as an obligation, makes the need of
being guided by others, and the consequent passive
state of our Reason, peculiarly noticeable. As
regards the second maxim of the mind, we are
otherwise wont to call him limited (*borné*, the
opposite of *enlarged*) whose talents attain to no
great use (especially as regards intensity.) But
here we are not speaking of the faculty of cognition,
but of the *mode of thought* which makes a purposive
use thereof. However small may be the area or the
degree to which a man's natural gifts reach, yet it
indicates a man of *enlarged thought* if he disregards
the subjective private conditions of his own judgment, by which so many others are confined, and
reflects upon it from a *universal standpoint* (which
he can only determine by placing himself at the
standpoint of others). The third maxim, viz. that
of *consecutive* thought, is the most difficult to attain,
and can only be attained by the combination of both
the former, and after the constant observance of
them has grown into a habit. We may say that
the first of these maxims is the maxim of Understanding, the second of Judgment, and the third of
Reason.

I take up again the threads interrupted by this
digression, and I say that Taste can be called *sensus
communis* with more justice than sound Understanding can ; and that the æsthetical Judgment
rather than the intellectual may bear the name
of a sense common to all,[1] if we are willing to use

---

[1] We may designate Taste as *sensus communis æstheticus*, common
Understanding as *sensus communis logicus*.

the word "sense" of an effect of mere reflection upon the mind : for then we understand by sense the feeling of pleasure. We could even define Taste as the faculty of judging of that which makes *universally communicable*, without the mediation of a concept, our feeling in a given representation.

The skill that men have in communicating their thoughts requires also a relation between the Imagination and the Understanding in order to associate intuitions with concepts, and concepts again with those concepts, which then combine in a cognition. But in that case the agreement of the two mental powers is *according to law*, under the constraint of definite concepts. Only where the Imagination in its freedom awakens the Understanding, and is put by it into regular play without the aid of concepts, does the representation communicate itself not as a thought but as an internal feeling of a purposive state of the mind.

Taste is then the faculty of judging *a priori* of the communicability of feelings that are bound up with a given representation (without the mediation of a concept).

If we could assume that the mere universal communicability of a feeling must carry in itself an interest for us with it (which, however, we are not justified in concluding from the character of a merely reflective Judgment), we should be able to explain why the feeling in the judgment of taste comes to be imputed to every one, so to speak, as a duty.

§ 41. *Of the empirical interest in the Beautiful*

That the judgment of taste by which something

is declared beautiful must have no interest *as its determining ground* has been sufficiently established above. But it does not follow that after it has been given as a pure æsthetical judgment, no interest can be combined with it. This combination, however, can only be indirect, *i.e.* taste must first of all be represented as combined with something else, in order that we may unite with the satisfaction of mere reflection upon an object a *pleasure in its existence* (as that wherein all interest consists). For here also in æsthetical judgments what we say in cognitive judgments (of things in general) is valid ; *a posse ad esse non valet consequentia*. This something else may be empirical, viz. an inclination proper to human nature, or intellectual, as the property of the Will of being capable of *a priori* determination by Reason. Both these involve a satisfaction in the presence of an Object, and so can lay the foundation for an interest in what has by itself pleased without reference to any interest whatever.

Empirically the Beautiful interests only in *society*. If we admit the impulse to society as natural to man, and his fitness for it, and his propension towards it, *i.e. sociability*, as a requisite for man as a being destined for society, and so as a property belonging to *humanity*, we cannot escape from regarding taste as a faculty for judging everything in respect of which we can communicate our *feeling* to all other men, and so as a means of furthering that which every one's natural inclination desires.

A man abandoned by himself on a desert island would adorn neither his hut nor his person ; nor would he seek for flowers, still less would he grow plants, in order to adorn himself therewith. It is

only in society that it occurs to him to be not merely
a man, but a refined man after his kind (the beginning of civilisation). For such do we judge him
to be who is both inclined and apt to communicate
his pleasure to others, and who is not contented
with an Object if he cannot feel satisfaction in it in
common with others. Again, every one expects and
requires from every one else this reference to universal communication [of pleasure], as it were from an
original compact dictated by humanity itself. Thus,
doubtless, in the beginning only those things which
attracted the senses, *e.g.*, colours for painting
oneself (roucou among the Carabs and cinnabar
among the Iroquois), flowers, mussel shells,
beautiful feathers, etc.,—but in time beautiful forms
also (*e.g.* in their canoes, and clothes, etc.), which
bring with them no gratification, or satisfaction of
enjoyment—were important in society, and were
combined with great interest. Until at last
(civilisation, having reached its highest point, makes)
out of this almost the main business of refined inclination ; and sensations are only regarded as of
worth in so far as they can be universally communicated. Here, although the pleasure which every
one has in such an object is inconsiderable and in
itself without any marked interest, yet the Idea of
its universal communicability increases its worth in
an almost infinite degree.

But this interest that indirectly attaches to the
Beautiful through our inclination to society, and
consequently is empirical, is of no importance for us
now ; because we have only to look to what may
have a reference, although only indirectly, to the
judgment of taste *a priori*. For if an interest
should also be detected as bound up with this form,

taste would detect for our faculty of judging a means of passing from sense-enjoyment to moral feeling; and so not only would we be the better guided in employing taste purposively, but there would be thus presented a link in the chain of the human faculties *a priori*, on which all legislation must depend. [We can only say thus much about the empirical interest in objects of taste and in taste itself. Since it is subservient to inclination, however refined the latter may be, it may easily be confounded with all the inclinations and passions, which attain their greatest variety and highest degree in society; and the interest in the Beautiful, if it is grounded thereon, can only furnish a very ambiguous transition from the Pleasant to the Good. But whether this can or cannot be furthered by taste, taken in its purity, is what we now have to investigate.

§ 42. *Of the intellectual interest in the Beautiful*

With the best intentions those persons who refer all activities, to which their inner natural dispositions impel men, to the final purpose of humanity, viz., the morally good, have regarded the taking an interest in the Beautiful in general as a mark of good moral character. But it is not without reason that they have been contradicted by others who rely on experience; for this shows that connoisseurs in taste not only often, but generally, are given up to idle, capricious, and mischievous passions, and that they could perhaps make less claim than others to any superiority of attachment to moral principles. Thus it would seem that the feeling for the Beautiful is not only (as actually is the case) specifically different from the Moral feeling ; but that the interest which can be bound up with it is hardly compatible with moral interest, and certainly has no inner affinity therewith.

Now I admit at once that the interest in the *Beautiful of Art* (under which I include the artificial use of natural beauties for adornment and so for vanity) furnishes no proof whatever of a disposition attached to the morally good or even inclined thereto. But on the other hand, I maintain that to take an *immediate interest* in the Beauty of Nature (not merely to have taste in judging it) is always a mark of a good soul ; and that when this interest is habitual it at least indicates a frame of mind favourable to the moral feeling, if it is voluntarily bound up with the *contemplation of nature*. It is to be remembered, however, that I here speak strictly of the beautiful *forms* of Nature, and I set aside the *charms*, that she is wont to combine so abundantly with them ; because, though the interest in the latter is indeed immediate, it is only empirical.

He who by himself (and without any design of communicating his observations to others) regards the beautiful figure of a wild flower, a bird, an insect, etc., with admiration and love—who would not willingly miss it in Nature, although it may bring him some damage, who still less wants any advantage from it—*he* takes an immediate and also an intellectual interest in the beauty of Nature. *I.e.* it is not merely the form of the product of nature which pleases him, but its very presence pleases him, the charms of sense having no share in this pleasure and no purpose whatever being combined with it.

N

But it is noteworthy that if we secretly deceived this lover of the beautiful by planting in the ground artificial flowers (which can be manufactured exactly like natural ones), or by placing artificially carved birds on the boughs of trees, and he discovered the deceit, the immediate interest that he previously took in them would disappear at once; though, perhaps, a different interest, viz. the interest of vanity in adorning his chamber with them for the eyes of others, would take its place. This thought then must accompany our intuition and reflection on beauty, viz. that nature has produced it; and on this alone is based the immediate interest that we take in it. Otherwise, there remains a mere judgment of taste, either devoid of all interest, or bound up with a mediate interest, viz. in that it has reference to society; which latter [interest] furnishes no certain indications of a morally good disposition.

This superiority of natural to artificial beauty in that it alone arouses an immediate interest, although as regards form the former may be surpassed by the latter, harmonises with the refined and thorough mental attitude of all men who have cultivated their moral feeling. If a man who has taste enough to judge of the products of beautiful Art with the greatest accuracy and refinement willingly leaves a chamber where are to be found those beauties that minister to vanity or to any social joys, and turns to the beautiful in Nature in order to find, as it were, delight for his spirit in a train of thought that he can never completely evolve, we will regard this choice of his with veneration, and attribute to him a beautiful soul, to which no connoisseur or lover [of Art] can lay claim on account of the interest he takes in his [artistic] objects.— What now is the difference in our estimation of these two different kinds of Objects, which in the judgment of mere taste it is hard to compare in point of superiority?

We have a faculty of mere æsthetical Judgment by which we judge forms without the aid of concepts, and find a satisfaction in this mere act of judgment; this we make into a rule for every one, without this judgment either being based on or producing any interest.— On the other hand, we have also a faculty of intellectual Judgment which determines an *a priori* satisfaction for the mere forms of practical maxims (so far as they are in themselves qualified for universal legislation); this we make into a law for every one, without our judgment being based on any interest whatever, *though in this case it produces such an interest.* The pleasure or pain in the former judgment is called that of taste, in the latter, that of moral feeling.

But it also interests Reason that the Ideas (for which in moral feeling it arouses an immediate interest) should have objective reality; *i.e.* that nature should at least show a trace or give an indication that it contains in itself a ground for assuming a regular agreement of its products with our entirely disinterested satisfaction (which we recognise *a priori* as a law for every one, without being able to base it upon proofs). Hence Reason must take an interest in every expression on the part of nature of an agreement of this kind. Consequently, the mind cannot ponder upon the beauty of *Nature* without finding itself at the same time interested therein. But this interest is akin to moral, and he who takes such an interest in the beauties of nature can do so only in so far as he previously has firmly established his interest in the morally good. If, therefore, the beauty of Nature interests a man immediately we have reason for attributing to him, at least, a basis for a good moral disposition.

It will be said that this account of æsthetical judgments, as akin to the moral feeling, seems far too studied to be regarded as the true interpretation of that cipher through which Nature speaks to us figuratively in her beautiful forms. However, in the first place, this immediate interest in .the beautiful is actually not common ; but is peculiar to those whose mental disposition either has already been cultivated in the direction of the good or is eminently susceptible of such cultivation. In that case the analogy between the pure judgment of taste which, independently of any interest, causes us to feel a satisfaction, and also represents it *a priori* as suitable to humanity in general, and the moral judgment that does the same thing from concepts without any clear, subtle, and premeditated reflection—this analogy leads to a similar immediate interest in the objects of the former as in those of the latter ; only that in the one case the interest is free, in the other it is based on objective laws. To this is to be added our admiration for Nature, which displays itself in its beautiful products as Art, not merely by chance, but as it were designedly, in accordance with a regular arrangement, and as purposiveness without purpose. This latter, as we never meet with it outside ourselves, we naturally seek in ourselves ; and, in fact, in that which constitutes the ultimate purpose of our being, viz. our moral destination. (Of this question as to the

ground of the possibility of such natural purposiveness we shall first speak in the Teleology.)

It is easy to explain why the satisfaction in the
pure æsthetical judgment in the case of beautiful Art
is not combined with an immediate interest as it is
in the case of beautiful Nature. For the former is
either such an imitation of the latter that it reaches
the point of deception and then produces the same
effect as natural beauty (for which it is taken) ; or
it is an art obviously directed designedly·to our
satisfaction. In the latter case the satisfaction in the
product would, it is true, be brought about immediately by taste, but it would be only a mediate interest
in the cause lying at its root, viz. an art that can
only interest by means of its purpose and never in
itself. It will, perhaps, be said that this is also
the case, if an Object of nature interests us by its
beauty only so far as it is associated with a moral
Idea. But it is not the Object itself which immediately interests us, but its character in virtue
of which it is qualified for such association, which
therefore essentially belongs to it.

The charms in beautiful Nature, which are so
often found, as it were, fused with beautiful forms,
may be referred to modifications either of light
(colours) or of sound (tones). For these are the only
sensations that imply not merely a sensible feeling
but also reflection upon the form of these modifications
of Sense ; and thus they involve in themselves as
it were a language by which nature speaks to us,
which thus seems to have a higher sense. Thus the
white colour of lilies seems to determine the mind
to Ideas of innocence ; and the seven colours in
order from the red to the violet seem to suggest the
Ideas of (1) Sublimity, (2) Intrepidity, (3) Candour,

(4) Friendliness, (5) Modesty, (6) Constancy, (7) Tenderness. The song of birds proclaims gladsomeness and contentment with existence. At least so we interpret nature, whether it have this design or not. But the interest which we here take in beauty has only to do with the beauty of Nature; it vanishes altogether as soon as we notice that we are deceived and that it is only Art—vanishes so completely that taste can no longer find the thing beautiful or sight find it charming. What is more highly praised by poets than the bewitching and beautiful note of the nightingale in a lonely copse on a still summer evening by the soft light of the moon? And yet we have instances of a merry host, where no such songster was to be found, deceiving to their great contentment the guests who were staying with him to enjoy the country air, by hiding in a bush a mischievous boy who knew how to produce this sound exactly like nature (by means of a reed or a tube in his mouth). But as soon as we are aware that it is a cheat, no one will remain long listening to the song which before was counted so charming. And it is just the same with the songs of all other birds. It must be Nature or be regarded as Nature, if we are to take an immediate *interest* in the Beautiful as such; and still more is this the case if we can require that others should take an interest in it too. This happens as a matter of fact when we regard as coarse and ignoble the mental attitude of those persons who have no *feeling* for beautiful Nature (for thus we describe a susceptibility to interest in its contemplation), and who confine themselves to eating and drinking—to the mere enjoyments of sense.

§ 43. *Of Art in general*

(1). *Art* is distinguished from Nature, as doing (*facere*) is distinguished from acting or working generally (*agere*), and as the product or result of the former is distinguished as *work* (*opus*) from the working (*effectus*) of the latter.

By right we ought only to describe as Art, production through freedom, *i.e.* through a will that places Reason at the basis of its actions. For although we like to call the product of bees (regularly built cells of wax) a work of art, this is only by way of analogy : as soon as we feel that this work of theirs is based on no proper rational deliberation, we say that it is a product of Nature (of instinct), and as Art only ascribe it to their Creator.

If, as sometimes happens, in searching through a bog we come upon a bit of shaped wood, we do not say : this is a product of Nature, but, of Art. Its producing cause has conceived a purpose to which the plank owes its form. Elsewhere too we should see art in everything which is made so that a representation of it in its cause must have preceded its actual existence (as even in the case of the bees), though without the effect of it even being capable of being *thought*. But if we call anything absolutely a work of art in order to distinguish it from a natural effect, we always understand by that a work of man.

(2). *Art* regarded as human skill differs from *science* (as *can* from *know*) as a practical faculty does from a theoretical, as Technic does from Theory (as mensuration from geometry). And so what we *can* do, as soon as we merely *know* what ought to be done and therefore are sufficiently cognisant of the desired effect, is not called Art. Only that which a man, even if he knows it completely, may not therefore have the skill to accomplish, belongs to Art. *Camper*[1] describes very exactly how the best shoes must be made, but he certainly could not make one.[2]

(3). *Art* also differs from *handicraft*; the first is called *free*, the other may be called mercenary. We regard the first as if it could only prove purposive as play, *i.e.* as occupation that is pleasant in itself. But the second is regarded as if it could only be compulsorily imposed upon one as work, *i.e.* as occupation which is unpleasant (a trouble) in itself, and which is only attractive on account of its effect (*e.g.*, the wage). Whether or not in the grade of the professions we ought to count watchmakers as artists, but smiths only as handicraftsmen, would require another point of view from which to judge than that which we are here taking up; viz. [we should have to consider] the proportion of talents which must be assumed requisite in these several occupations. Whether or not, again, under the so-called seven free arts some may be included which ought to be classed as sciences, and many that are akin rather to handicraft, I shall not here discuss. But it is not inexpedient to recall that in all free arts there is yet requisite something compulsory, or, as it is called, *mechanism*, without which the

[1] [Peter Camper (1722-1789), a celebrated naturalist and comparative anatomist; for some years professor at Groningen.]

[2] In my country a common man, if you propose to him such a problem as that of Columbus with his egg, says, *that is not art, it is only science.* *I.e.* if we *know* how, we can *do* it; and he says the same of all the pretended arts of jugglers. On the other hand, he will not refuse to apply the term art to the performance of a rope-dancer.

spirit, which must be free in art and which alone inspires the work, would have no body and would evaporate altogether; *e.g.*, in poetry there must be an accuracy and wealth of language, and also prosody and measure. [It is not inexpedient, I say, to recall this], for many modern educators believe that the best way to produce a free art is to remove it from all constraint, and thus to change it from work into mere play.

§ 44. *Of beautiful Art*

There is no Science of the Beautiful, but only a Kritik of it ; and there is no such thing as beautiful Science, but only beautiful Art. For as regards the first point, if it could be decided scientifically, *i.e.* by proofs, whether a thing was to be regarded as beautiful or not, the judgment upon beauty would belong to science and would not be a judgment of taste. And as far as the second point is concerned, a science which should be beautiful as such is a nonentity. For if in such a science we were to ask for grounds and proofs, we would be put off with tasteful phrases (bon-mots). — The source of the common expression, *beautiful science*, is without doubt nothing else than this, as it has been rightly remarked, that for beautiful art in its entire completeness much science is requisite ; *e.g.* a knowledge of ancient languages, a learned familiarity with classical authors, history, a knowledge of antiquities, etc. And hence these historical sciences, because they form the necessary preparation and basis for beautiful art, and also partly because under them is included the knowledge of the products of beautiful art (rhetoric and poetry), have come to be called beautiful sciences by a transposition of words.

If art which is adequate to the *cognition* of a possible object performs the actions requisite therefor merely in order to make it actual, it is *mechanical* art; but if it has for its immediate design the feeling of pleasure, it is called *æsthetical* art. This is again either *pleasant* or *beautiful*. It is the first, if its purpose is that the pleasure should accompany the representations [of the object] regarded as mere *sensations*; it is the second if they are regarded as *modes of cognition*.

Pleasant arts are those that are directed merely to enjoyment. Of this class are all those charming arts that can gratify a company at table; *e.g.* the art of telling stories in an entertaining way, of starting the company in frank and lively conversation, of raising them by jest and laugh to a certain pitch of merriment;[1] when, as people say, there may be a great deal of gossip at the feast, but no one will be answerable for what he says, because they are only concerned with momentary entertainment, and not with any permanent material for reflection or subsequent discussion. (Among these are also to be reckoned the way of arranging the table for enjoyment, and, at great feasts, the management of the music. This latter is a wonderful thing. It is meant to dispose to gaiety the minds of the guests, regarded solely as a pleasant noise, without any one paying the least attention to its composition; and it favours the free conversation of each with his neighbour.)

---

[1] [Kant was accustomed to say that the talk at a dinner table should always pass through these three stages—narrative, discussion, and jest; and punctilious in this, as in all else, he is said to have directed the conversation at his own table accordingly (Wallace's *Kant*, p. 39).]

Again, to this class belong all games which bring with them no further interest than that of making the time pass imperceptibly.

On the other hand, beautiful art is a mode of representation which is purposive for itself, and which, although devoid of [definite] purpose, yet furthers the culture of the mental powers in reference to social communication.

The universal communicability of a pleasure carries with it in its very concept that the pleasure is not one of enjoyment, from mere sensation, but must be derived from reflection ; and thus æsthetical art, as the art of beauty, has for standard the reflective Judgment and not sensation.

§ 45. *Beautiful Art is an art, in so far as it seems like nature*

In a product of beautiful art we must become conscious that it is Art and not Nature ; but yet the purposiveness in its form must seem to be as free from all constraint of arbitrary rules as if it were a product of mere nature. On this feeling of freedom in the play of our cognitive faculties, which must at the same time be purposive, rests that pleasure which alone is universally communicable, without being based on concepts. Nature is beautiful because it looks like Art ; and Art can only be called beautiful if we are conscious of it as Art while yet it looks like Nature.

For whether we are dealing with natural or with artificial beauty we can say generally: *That is beautiful which pleases in the mere act of judging it* (not in the sensation of it, or by means of a concept). Now art has always a definite design of producing

something. But if this something were bare sensation (something merely subjective), which is to be
accompanied with pleasure, the product would please
in the act of judgment only by mediation of sensible
feeling. And again, if the design were directed
towards the production of a definite Object, then,
if this were attained by art, the Object would only
please by means of concepts. But in both cases the
art would not please *in the mere act of judging; i.e.*
it would not please as beautiful, but as mechanical.

Hence the purposiveness in the product of beautiful art, although it is designed, must not seem to be
designed; *i.e.* beautiful art must *look* like nature,
although we are conscious of it as art. But a
product of art appears like nature when, although its
agreement with the rules, according to which alone
the product can become what it ought to be, is *punctiliously* observed, yet this is not *painfully* apparent;
[the form of the schools does not obtrude itself]¹—it
shows no trace of the rule having been before the eyes
of the artist and having fettered his mental powers.

§ 46. *Beautiful Art is the art of genius*

Genius is the talent (or natural gift) which gives
the rule to Art. Since talent, as the innate productive
faculty of the artist, belongs itself to Nature, we may
express the matter thus : *Genius* is the innate mental
disposition (*ingenium*) *through which* Nature gives
the rule to Art.

Whatever may be thought of this definition,
whether it is merely arbitrary or whether it is
adequate to the concept that we are accustomed to
combine with the word *genius* (which is to be

¹ [Second Edition.]

examined in the following paragraphs), we can prove already beforehand that according to the signification of the word here adopted, beautiful arts must necessarily be considered as arts of *genius*.

For every art presupposes rules by means of which in the first instance a product, if it is to be called artistic, is represented as possible. But the concept of beautiful art does not permit the judgment upon the beauty of a product to be derived from any rule, which has a *concept* as its determining ground, and therefore has at its basis a concept of the way in which the product is possible. Therefore, beautiful art cannot itself devise the rule according to which it can bring about its product. But since at the same time a product can never be called Art without some precedent rule, Nature in the subject must (by the harmony of its faculties) give the rule to Art; *i.e.* beautiful Art is only possible as a product of Genius.

We thus see (1) that genius is a *talent* for producing that for which no definite rule can be given; it is not a mere aptitude for what can be learnt by a rule. Hence *originality* must be its first property. (2) But since it also can produce original nonsense, its products must be models, *i.e.* *exemplary* ; and they consequently ought not to spring from imitation, but must serve as a standard or rule of judgment for others. (3) It cannot describe or indicate scientifically how it brings about its products, but it gives the rule just as nature does. / Hence the author of a product for which he is indebted to his genius does not know himself how he has come by his Ideas ; and he has not the power to devise the like at pleasure or in accordance with a plan, and to communicate it to others in precepts that will enable them to produce similar products.   (Hence it is probable that the word genius is derived from *genius*, that peculiar guiding and guardian spirit given to a man at his birth, from whose suggestion these original Ideas proceed.) (4) Nature by the medium of genius does not prescribe rules to Science, but to Art; and to it only in so far as it is to be beautiful Art.

§ 47. *Elucidation and confirmation of the above explanation of Genius*

Every one is agreed that genius is entirely opposed to the *spirit of imitation*.   Now since learning is nothing but imitation, it follows that the greatest ability and teachableness (capacity) regarded *quâ* teachableness, cannot avail for genius. Even if a man thinks or composes for himself, and does not merely take in what others have taught, even if he discovers many things in art and science, this is not the right ground for calling such a (perhaps great) *head*, a genius (as opposed to him who because he can only learn and imitate is called a *shallow-pate*).   For even these things could be learned, they lie in the natural path of him who investigates and reflects according to rules ; and they do not differ specifically from what can be acquired by industry through imitation.   Thus we can readily learn all that *Newton* has set forth in his immortal work on the Principles of Natural Philosophy, however great a head was required to discover it ; but we cannot learn to write spirited poetry, however express may be the precepts of the art and however excellent its models.   The reason is that *Newton* could make all his steps, from the

first elements of geometry to his own great and
profound discoveries, intuitively plain and definite
as regards consequence, not only to himself but to
every one else.   But a *Homer* or a *Wieland* cannot
show how his Ideas, so rich in fancy and yet so full
of thought, come together in his head, simply
because he does not know and therefore cannot
teach others.   In Science then the greatest
discoverer only differs in degree from his laborious
imitator and pupil ; but he differs specifically from
him whom Nature has gifted for beautiful Art.
And in this there is no depreciation of those great
men to whom the human race owes so much
gratitude, as compared with nature's favourites in
respect of the talent for beautiful art.   For in the
fact that the former talent is directed to the ever-
advancing greater perfection of knowledge and
every advantage depending on it, and at the same
time to the imparting this same knowledge to
others—in this it has a great superiority over [the
talent of] those who deserve the honour of being
called geniuses.   For art stands still at a certain
point ; a boundary is set to it beyond which it
cannot go, which presumably has been reached long
ago and cannot be extended further.   Again,
artistic skill cannot be communicated ; it is imparted
to every artist immediately by the hand of nature ;
and so it dies with him, until nature endows another
in the same way, so that he only needs an example
in order to put in operation in a similar fashion the
talent of which he is conscious.

    If now it is a natural gift which must prescribe
its rule to art (as beautiful art), of what kind is this
rule ?   It cannot be reduced to a formula and serve
as a precept, for then the judgment upon the

beautiful would be determinable according to
concepts; but the rule must be abstracted from the
fact, *i.e.* from the product, on which others may try
their own talent by using it as a model, not to be
copied but to be *imitated.* How this is possible is
hard to explain. The Ideas of the artist excite like
Ideas in his pupils if nature has endowed them with
a like proportion of their mental powers. Hence
models of beautiful art are the only means of
handing down these Ideas to posterity. This
cannot be done by mere descriptions, especially not
in the case of the arts of speech, and in this latter
classical models are only to be had in the old dead
languages, now preserved only as "the learned
languages."

Although mechanical and beautiful art are very
different, the first being a mere art of industry and
learning and the second of genius, yet there is no
beautiful art in which there is not a mechanical
element that can be comprehended by rules and
followed accordingly, and in which therefore there
must be something *scholastic* as an essential
condition. For [in every art] some purpose must
be conceived; otherwise we could not ascribe the
product to art at all, it would be a mere product of
chance. But in order to accomplish a purpose,
definite rules from which we cannot dispense
ourselves are requisite. Now since the originality
of the talent constitutes an essential (though not the
only) element in the character of genius, shallow
heads believe that they cannot better show themselves to be full-blown geniuses than by throwing
off the constraint of all rules; they believe, in effect,
that one could make a braver show on the back of
a wild horse than on the back of a trained animal.

Genius can only furnish rich *material* for products of beautiful art; its execution and its *form* require talent cultivated in the schools, in order to make such a use of this material as will stand examination by the Judgment. But it is quite ridiculous for a man to speak and decide like a genius in things which require the most careful investigation by Reason.   One does not know whether to laugh more at the impostor who spreads such a mist round him that we cannot clearly use our Judgment and so use our Imagination the more, or at the public which naïvely imagines that his inability to cognise clearly and to comprehend the masterpiece before him arises from new truths crowding in on him in such abundance that details (duly weighed definitions and accurate examination of fundamental propositions) seem but clumsy work.

§ 48. *Of the relation of Genius to Taste*

For *judging* of beautiful objects as such *taste* is requisite; but for beautiful art, *i.e.* for the *production* of such objects, *genius* is requisite.

If we consider genius as the talent for beautiful art (which the special meaning of the word implies) and in this point of view analyse it into the faculties which must concur to constitute such a talent, it is necessary in the first instance to determine exactly the difference between natural beauty, the judging of which requires only Taste, and artificial beauty, the possibility of which (to which reference must be made in judging such an object) requires Genius.

A natural beauty is a *beautiful thing*; artificial beauty is a *beautiful representation* of a thing.

In order to judge of a natural beauty as such

I need not have beforehand a concept of what sort
of thing the object is to be ; *i.e.* I need not know
its material purposiveness (the purpose), but its
mere form pleases by itself in the act of judging
it without any knowledge of the purpose. /But if
the object is given as a product of art, and as such
is to be declared beautiful, then, because art always
supposes a purpose in the cause (and its causality),
there must be at bottom in the first instance a
concept of what the thing is to be.] And as the
agreement of the manifold in a thing with its inner
destination, its purpose, constitutes the perfection
of the thing, it follows that in judging of artificial
beauty the perfection of the thing must be taken
into account ; but in judging of natural beauty
(as *such*) there is no question at all about this.—
It is true that in judging of objects of nature, especially objects endowed with life, *e.g.* a man or a horse,
their objective purposiveness also is commonly taken
into consideration in judging of their beauty ; but
then the judgment is no longer purely æsthetical,
i.e. a mere judgment of taste. Nature is no longer
judged inasmuch as it appears like art, but in so
far as it *is* actual (although superhuman) art ; and
the teleological judgment serves as the basis and
condition of the æsthetical, as a condition to which
the latter must have respect. In such a case, *e.g.* if
it is said "that is a beautiful woman," we think
nothing else than this : nature represents in her
figure the purposes in view in the shape of a woman's
figure. For we must look beyond the mere form to
a concept, if the object is to be thought in such a
way by means of a logically conditioned æsthetical
judgment.

Beautiful art shows its superiority in this, that

it describes as beautiful things which may be in
nature ugly or displeasing.[1] The Furies, diseases,
the devastations of war, etc., may [even regarded
as calamitous],[2] be described as very beautiful, as
they are represented in a picture. There is only
one kind of ugliness which cannot be represented
in accordance with nature, without destroying all
æsthetical satisfaction and consequently artificial
beauty; viz. that which excites *disgust*. For in
this singular sensation, which rests on mere imagination, the object is represented as it were obtruding
itself for our enjoyment while we strive against it
with all our might. And the artistic representation
of the object is no longer distinguished from the
nature of the object itself in our sensation, and thus
it is impossible that it can be regarded as beautiful.
The art of sculpture again, because in its products
art is almost interchangeable with nature, excludes
from its creations the immediate representation of
ugly objects; *e.g.* it represents death by a beautiful
genius, the warlike spirit by Mars, and permits
[all such things] to be represented only by an
allegory or attribute[3] that has a pleasing effect,
and thus only indirectly by the aid of the interpretation of Reason, and not for the mere æsthetical
Judgment.

---

[1] [Cf. Aristotle's *Poetics*, c. iv. p. 1448 b: ἃ γὰρ αὐτὰ λυπηρῶς
ὁρῶμεν, τούτων τὰς εἰκόνας τὰς μάλιστα ἠκριβωμένας χαίρομεν θεω-
ροῦντες οἷον θηρίων τε μορφὰς τῶν ἀτιμοτάτων καὶ νεκρῶν. Cf. also
Rhetoric, I. 11, p. 1371 b; and Burke on the *Sublime and Beautiful*,
Part I. § 16. Boileau (*L'art poétique*, chant 3), makes a similar observation:

> " Il n'est point de serpent ni de monstre odieux
> Qui, par l'art imité, ne puisse plaire aux yeux.
> D'un pinceau délicat l'artifice agréable
> Du plus affreux objet fait un objet aimable."]

[2] [Second Edition.]   [3] [Cf. p. 199 *infra*.]

So much for the beautiful representation of an object, which is properly only the form of the presentation of a concept, by means of which this latter is communicated universally.— But to give this form to the product of beautiful art, mere taste is requisite. By taste the artist estimates his work after he has exercised and corrected it by manifold examples from art or nature ; and after many, often toilsome, attempts to content himself he finds that form which satisfies him. Hence this form is not, as it were, a thing of inspiration or the result of a free swing of the mental powers, but of a slow and even painful process of improvement, by which he seeks to render it adequate to his thought, without detriment to the freedom of the play of his powers.

But taste is merely a judging and not a productive faculty ; and what is appropriate to it is therefore not a work of beautiful art. It can only be a product belonging to useful and mechanical art or even to science, produced according to definite rules that can be learned and must be exactly followed. But the pleasing form that is given to it is only the vehicle of communication, and a mode, as it were, of presenting it, in respect of which we remain free to a certain extent, although it is combined with a definite purpose. Thus we desire that table appointments, a moral treatise, even a sermon, should have in themselves this form of beautiful art, without it seeming to be *sought* : but we do not therefore call these things works of beautiful art. Under the latter class are reckoned a poem, a piece of music, a picture gallery, etc. ; and in some works of this kind asserted to be works of beautiful art we find genius without taste, while in others we find taste without genius.

§ 49. *Of the faculties of the mind that constitute Genius*

We say of certain products of which we expect that they should at least in part appear as beautiful art, they are without *spirit*[1]; although we find nothing to blame in them on the score of taste. A poem may be very neat and elegant, but without spirit. A history may be exact and well arranged, but without spirit. A festal discourse may be solid and at the same time elaborate, but without spirit. Conversation is often not devoid of entertainment, but it is without spirit: even of a woman we say that she is pretty, an agreeable talker, and courteous, but without spirit. What then do we mean by spirit?

Spirit, in an æsthetical sense, is the name given to the animating principle of the mind. But that by means of which this principle animates the soul, the material which it applies to that [purpose], is what puts the mental powers purposively into swing, *i.e.* into such a play as maintains itself and strengthens the mental powers in their exercise.

Now I maintain that this principle is no other than the faculty of presenting *æsthetical Ideas*. And by an æsthetical Idea I understand that representation of the Imagination which occasions much thought, without, however, any definite thought, *i.e.* any *concept*, being capable of being adequate to it; it consequently cannot be completely compassed and made intelligible by language.— We easily see that it is the counterpart (pendant) of a *rational Idea*; which

---

[1] [In English we would rather say " without *soul* "; but I prefer to translate *Geist* consistently by *spirit*, to avoid the confusion of it with *Seele*.]

conversely is a concept to which no *intuition* (or representation of the Imagination) can be adequate.

The Imagination (as a productive faculty of cognition) is very powerful in creating another nature, as it were, out of the material that actual nature gives it. We entertain ourselves with it when experience becomes too commonplace, and by it we remould experience, always indeed in accordance with analogical laws, but yet also in accordance with principles which occupy a higher place in Reason (laws too which are just as natural to us as those by which Understanding comprehends empirical nature). Thus we feel our freedom from the law of association (which attaches to the empirical employment of Imagination), so that the material supplied to us by nature in accordance with this law can be worked up into something different which surpasses nature.

Such representations of the Imagination we may call *Ideas*, partly because they at least strive after something which lies beyond the bounds of experience, and so seek to approximate to a presentation of concepts of Reason (intellectual Ideas), thus giving to the latter the appearance of objective reality,— but especially because no concept can be fully adequate to them as internal intuitions. The poet ventures to realise to sense, rational Ideas of invisible beings, the kingdom of the blessed, hell, eternity, creation, etc. ; or even if he deals with things of which there are examples in experience,—*e.g.* death, envy and all vices, also love, fame, and the like,— he tries, by means of Imagination, which emulates the play of Reason in its quest after a maximum, to go beyond the limits of experience and to present them to Sense with a completeness of which there is no example in nature. This is properly speaking the art of the poet, in which the faculty of æsthetical Ideas can manifest itself in its entire strength. But this faculty, considered in itself, is properly only a talent (of the Imagination).

If now we place under a concept a representation of the Imagination belonging to its presentation, but which occasions in itself more thought than can ever be comprehended in a definite concept, and which consequently æsthetically enlarges the concept itself in an unbounded fashion, the Imagination is here creative, and it brings the faculty of intellectual Ideas (the Reason) into movement; *i.e.* by a representation more thought (which indeed belongs to the concept of the object) is occasioned than can in it be grasped or made clear.

Those forms which do not constitute the presentation of a given concept itself but only, as approximate representations of the Imagination, express the consequences bound up with it and its relationship to other concepts, are called (æsthetical) *attributes* of an object, whose concept as a rational Idea cannot be adequately presented. Thus Jupiter's eagle with the lightning in its claws is an attribute of the mighty king of heaven, as the peacock is of his magnificent queen. They do not, like *logical attributes*, represent what lies in our concepts of the sublimity and majesty of creation, but something different, which gives occasion to the Imagination to spread itself over a number of kindred representations, that arouse more thought than can be expressed in a concept determined by words. They furnish an *æsthetical Idea*, which for that rational Idea takes the place of logical presentation; and thus as their proper office they enliven the mind by opening out to it the prospect into an illimitable field of kindred representations.   But beautiful art does this not only in the case of painting or sculpture (in which the term "attribute" is commonly employed) : poetry and rhetoric also get the spirit that animates their works simply from the æsthetical attributes of the object, which accompany the logical and stimulate the Imagination, so that it thinks more by their aid, although in an undeveloped way, than could be comprehended in a concept and therefore in a definite form of words.—   For the sake of brevity I must limit myself to a few examples only.

When the great King[1] in one of his poems expresses himself as follows :

> " Oui, finissons sans trouble et mourons sans regrets,
> En laissant l'univers comblé de nos bienfaits.
> Ainsi l'astre du jour au bout de sa carrière,
> Répand sur l'horizon une douce lumière ;
> Et les derniers rayons qu'il darde dans les airs,
> Sont les derniers soupirs qu'il donne à l'univers ; "

he quickens his rational Idea of a cosmopolitan disposition at the end of life by an attribute which the Imagination (in remembering all the pleasures of a beautiful summer day that are recalled at its close by a serene evening) associates with that representation, and which excites a number of sensations and secondary representations for which no expression is found.   On the other hand, an intellectual concept may serve conversely as an attribute for a representation of sense and so can quicken this latter by means of the Idea of the supersensible ; but only by

---

[1] [Barni quotes these lines as occurring in one of Frederick the Great's French poems : " Epître au maréchal Keith, sur les vaines terreurs de la mort et les frayeurs d'une autre vie ; " but I have not been able to verify his reference.   Kant here translates them into German.]

the æsthetical [element], that subjectively attaches
to the concept of the latter, being here employed.
Thus, for example, a certain poet[1] says, in his
description of a beautiful morning :

> " The sun arose
> As calm from virtue springs."

The consciousness of virtue, if we substitute it in
our thoughts for a virtuous man, diffuses in the mind
a multitude of sublime and restful feelings and a
boundless prospect of a joyful future, to which no
expression that is measured by a definite concept
completely attains.[2]

In a word the æsthetical Idea is a representation
of the Imagination associated with a given concept,
which is bound up with such a multiplicity of partial
representations in its free employment, that for it no
expression marking a definite concept can be found ;
and such a representation, therefore, adds to a
concept much ineffable thought, the feeling of which
quickens the cognitive faculties, and with language,
which is the mere letter, binds up spirit also.

The mental powers, therefore, whose union (in a
certain relation) constitutes *genius* are Imagination
and Understanding. In the employment of the
Imagination for cognition it submits to the constraint
of the Understanding and is subject to the limitation

---

[1] [I have not been able to identify this poet.]

[2] Perhaps nothing more sublime was ever said and no sublimer
thought ever expressed than the famous inscription on the Temple of
Isis (Mother *Nature*): " I am all that is and that was and that shall
be, and no mortal hath lifted my veil." *Segner* availed himself of
this Idea in a *suggestive* vignette prefixed to his Natural Philosophy,
in order to inspire beforehand the pupil whom he was about to lead
into that temple with a holy awe, which should dispose his mind to
serious attention. [J. A. de Segner (1704-1777) was Professor of
Natural Philosophy at Göttingen, and the author of several scientific
works of repute.]

of being conformable to the concept of the latter.
On the contrary, in an æsthetical point of view it is
free to furnish unsought, over and above that agreement with a concept, abundance of undeveloped
material for the Understanding; to which the
Understanding paid no regard in its concept, but
which it applies, though not objectively for cognition, yet subjectively to quicken the cognitive powers
and therefore also indirectly to cognitions. Thus
genius properly consists in the happy relation
[between these faculties], which no science can teach
and no industry can learn, by which Ideas are found
for a given concept; and on the other hand, we thus
find for these Ideas the *expression*, by means of
which the subjective state of mind brought about by
them, as an accompaniment of the concept, can be
communicated to others. The latter talent is properly speaking what is called spirit; for to express
the ineffable element in the state of mind implied by
a certain representation and to make it universally
communicable—whether the expression be in speech
or painting or statuary—this requires a faculty of
seizing the quickly passing play of Imagination and
of unifying it in a concept (which is even on that
account original and discloses a new rule that could
not have been inferred from any preceding principles
or examples), that can be communicated without any
constraint [of rules].[1]

If after this analysis we look back to the explanation given above of what is called *genius*, we find :
first, that it is a talent for Art; not for Science, in
which clearly known rules must go beforehand and
determine the procedure. *Secondly*, as an artistic

[1] [Second Edition.]

talent it presupposes a definite concept of the product, as the purpose, and therefore Understanding; but it also presupposes a representation (although an indeterminate one) of the material, *i.e.* of the intuition, for the presentment of this concept; and, therefore, a relation between the Imagination and the Understanding. *Thirdly*, it shows itself not so much in the accomplishment of the proposed purpose in a presentment of a definite *concept*, as in the enunciation or expression of *æsthetical Ideas*, which contain abundant material for that very design; and consequently it represents the Imagination as free from all guidance of rules and yet as purposive in reference to the presentment of the given concept. Finally, in the *fourth* place, the unsought undesigned subjective purposiveness in the free accordance of the Imagination with the legality of the Understanding presupposes such a proportion and disposition of these faculties as no following of rules, whether of science or of mechanical imitation, can bring about, but which only the nature of the subject can produce.

In accordance with these suppositions genius is the exemplary originality of the natural gifts of a subject in the *free* employment of his cognitive faculties. In this way the product of a genius (as regards what is to be ascribed to genius and not to possible learning or schooling) is an example, not to be imitated (for then that which in it is genius and constitutes the spirit of the work would be lost), but to be followed, by another genius; whom it awakens to a feeling of his own originality and whom it stirs so to exercise his art in freedom from the constraint of rules, that thereby a new rule is gained for art, and thus his talent shows itself to be exemplary. But because a genius is a favourite of nature and must be regarded by us as a rare phenomenon, his example produces for other good heads a school, *i.e.* a methodical system of teaching according to rules, so far as these can be derived from the peculiarities of the products of his spirit. For such persons beautiful art is so far imitation, to which nature through the medium of a genius supplied the rule.

But this imitation becomes a mere *aping*, if the scholar *copies* everything down to the deformities, which the genius must have let pass only because he could not well remove them without weakening his Idea. This mental characteristic is meritorious only in the case of a genius. A certain *audacity* in expression—and in general many a departure from common rules—becomes him well, but it is in no way worthy of imitation; it always remains a fault in itself which we must seek to remove, though the genius is as it were privileged to commit it, because the inimitable rush of his spirit would suffer from over-anxious carefulness. *Mannerism* is another kind of aping, viz. of mere *peculiarity* (originality) in general; by which a man separates himself as far as possible from imitators, without however possessing the talent to be at the same time *exemplary*.— There are indeed in general two ways (*modi*) in which such a man may put together his notions of expressing himself; the one is called a *manner* (*modus æstheticus*), the other a *method* (*modus logicus*). They differ in this, that the former has no other standard than the *feeling* of unity in the presentment, but the latter follows definite *principles*; hence the former alone avails for beautiful art. But an artistic product is said to show *mannerism* only when the

exposition of the artist's Idea is *founded* on its very
singularity, and is not made appropriate to the Idea
itself. The ostentatious (*précieux*), contorted, and
affected [manner, adopted] to differentiate oneself
from ordinary persons (though devoid of spirit) is
like the behaviour of a man of whom we say, that
he hears himself talk, or who stands and moves
about as if he were on a stage in order to be stared
at; this always betrays a bungler.

§ 50. *Of the combination of Taste with Genius in the products of beautiful Art*

To ask whether it is more important for the
things of beautiful art that Genius or Taste should
be displayed, is the same as to ask whether in it
more depends on Imagination or on Judgment.
Now, since in respect of the first an art is rather
said to be *full of spirit*, but only deserves to be
called a *beautiful* art on account of the second;
this latter is at least, as its indispensable condition
(*conditio sine qua non*), the most important thing
to which one has to look in the judging of art as
beautiful art. Abundance and originality of Ideas
are less necessary to beauty than the accordance
of the Imagination in its freedom with the conformity
to law of the Understanding. For all the abundance
of the former produces in lawless freedom nothing
but nonsense; on the other hand, the Judgment
is the faculty by which it is adjusted to the
Understanding.

Taste, like the Judgment in general, is the
discipline (or training) of Genius; it clips its wings,
it makes it cultured and polished; but, at the same
time, it gives guidance as to where and how far

it may extend itself, if it is to remain purposive. And while it brings clearness and order into the multitude of the thoughts [of genius], it makes the Ideas susceptible of being permanently and, at the same time, universally assented to, and capable of being followed by others, and of an ever-progressive culture. If, then, in the conflict of these two properties in a product something must be sacrificed, it should be rather on the side of genius ; and the Judgment, which in the things of beautiful art gives its decision from its own proper principles, will rather sacrifice the freedom and wealth of the Imagination than permit anything prejudicial to the Understanding.

For beautiful art, therefore, *Imagination, Understanding, Spirit,* and *Taste* are requisite.[1]

§ 51. *Of the division of the beautiful arts*

We may describe beauty in general (whether natural or artificial) as the *expression* of æsthetical Ideas ; only that in beautiful Art this Idea must be occasioned by a concept of the Object ; whilst in beautiful Nature the mere reflection upon a given intuition, without any concept of what the object is to be, is sufficient for the awakening and communicating of the Idea of which that Object is regarded as the *expression.*

If, then, we wish to make a division of the

---

[1] The three former faculties are *united* in the first instance by means of the fourth. Hume gives us to understand in his *History of England* that although the English are inferior in their productions to no people in the world as regards the evidences they display of the three former properties, *separately* considered, yet they must be put after their neighbours the French as regards that which unites these properties. [In his *Observations on the Beautiful and Sublime,* § iv. *sub init.,* Kant remarks that the English have the keener sense of the *sublime,* the French of the *beautiful.*]

beautiful arts, we cannot choose a more convenient
principle, at least tentatively, than the analogy of
art with the mode of expression of which men
avail themselves in speech, in order to communicate
to one another as perfectly as possible not merely
their concepts but also their sensations.[1]— This is
done by *word*, *deportment*, and *tone* (articulation,
gesticulation, and modulation).   It is only by the
combination of these three kinds of expression that
communication between the speaker [and his hearers]
can be complete.   For thus thought, intuition, and
sensation are transmitted to others simultaneously
and conjointly.

_There are, therefore, only three kinds of beautiful
arts ; the arts of *speech*, the *formative* arts, and the
art of the *play of sensations* (as external sensible
impressions).] We may also arrange a division by
dichotomy ; thus beautiful art may be divided
into the art of expression of thoughts and of intuitions ; and these further subdivided in accordance
with their form or their matter (sensation).   But
this would appear to be too abstract, and not so
accordant with ordinary concepts.

(1) The arts of SPEECH are *rhetoric* and *poetry*.
Rhetoric is the art of carrying on a serious business
of the Understanding as if it were a free play of
the Imagination ; *poetry*, the art of conducting a
free play of the Imagination as if it were a serious
business of the Understanding.

The *orator*, then, promises a serious business,
and in order to entertain his audience conducts it
as if it were a mere *play* with Ideas.   The *poet*

---

[1] The reader is not to judge this scheme for a possible division
of the beautiful arts as a deliberate theory.   It is only one of various
attempts which we may and ought to devise.

merely promises an entertaining play with Ideas,
and yet it has the same effect upon the Understanding as if he had only intended to carry on
its business. The combination and harmony of
both cognitive faculties, Sensibility and Understanding, which cannot dispense with one another,
but which yet cannot well be united without constraint and mutual prejudice, must appear to be undesigned and so to be brought about by themselves :
otherwise it is not *beautiful* art. Hence, all that
is studied and anxious must be avoided in it, for
beautiful art must be free art in a double sense.
It is not a work like a mercenary employment the
greatness of which can be judged according to a
definite standard, which can be attained or paid
for ; and again, though the mind is here occupied,
it feels itself thus contented and aroused, without
looking to any other purpose (independently of
reward).

The orator therefore gives something which he
does not promise, viz. an entertaining play of the
Imagination ; but he also fails to supply what he
did promise, which is indeed his announced business, viz. the purposive occupation of the Understanding. On the other hand, the poet promises
little and announces a mere play with Ideas ; but
he supplies something which is worth occupying
ourselves with, because he provides in this play
food for the Understanding, and by the aid of
Imagination gives life to his concepts. [Thus the
orator on the whole gives less, the poet more, than
he promises.]¹

(2) The FORMATIVE arts, or those by which expression is found for Ideas in *sensible intuition* (not

¹ [Second Edition.]

by representations of mere Imagination that are
aroused by words), are either arts of *sensible truth* or
of *sensible illusion*.   The former is called *Plastic*, the
latter *Painting*.   Both express Ideas by figures in
space ; the former makes figures cognisable by two
senses, sight and touch (although not by the latter
as far as beauty is concerned) ; the latter only by
one, the first of these.   The æsthetical Idea (the
archetype or original image) is fundamental for both
in the Imagination, but the figure which expresses
this (the ectype or copy) is either given 'in its
bodily extension (as the object itself exists), or as it
paints itself on the eye (according to its appearance
when projected on a flat surface).   In the first case
the condition given to reflection may be either the
reference to an actual purpose or only the semblance
of it.

   To *Plastic*, the first kind of beautiful formative
Art, belong *Sculpture* and *Architecture*.   The *first*
presents corporeally concepts of things, *as they
might have existed in nature* (though as beautiful art
it has regard to æsthetical purposiveness).   The
second is the art of presenting concepts of things
that are possible *only through Art*, and whose form
has for its determining ground not nature but an
arbitrary purpose, with the view of presenting them
with æsthetical purposiveness.   In the latter the
chief point is a certain *use* of the artistic object, by
which condition the æsthetical Ideas are limited.
In the former the main design is the mere *expression*
of æsthetical Ideas.   Thus statues of men, gods,
animals, etc., are of the first kind ; but temples,
splendid buildings for public assemblies, even
dwelling - houses, triumphal arches, columns, mau-
soleums, and the like, erected in honourable remem-

brance, belong to Architecture. Indeed all house
furniture (upholsterer's work and such like things
which are for use) may be reckoned under this art ;
because the suitability of a product for a certain use is
the essential thing in an *architectural work*. On the
other hand, a mere *piece of sculpture*, which is simply
made for show and which is to please in itself, is as
a corporeal presentation a mere imitation of nature,
though with a reference to æsthetical Ideas ; in it
sensible truth is not to be carried so far that the
product ceases to look like art and looks like a product of the elective will.

Painting, as the second kind of formative art,
which presents a *sensible illusion* artificially combined
with Ideas. I would divide into the art of the
beautiful *depicting of nature* and that of the beautiful
arrangement of its products. The first is *painting
proper*, the second is the art of *landscape gardening*.
The first gives only the illusory appearance of
corporeal extension ; the second gives this in
accordance with truth, but only the appearance of
utility and availableness for other purposes than the
mere play of the Imagination in the contemplation
of its forms.[1] This latter is nothing else than the

[1] That landscape gardening may be regarded as a species of
the art of painting, although it presents its forms corporeally, seems
strange. But since it actually takes its forms from nature (trees,
shrubs, grasses, and flowers from forest and field—at least in the first
instance), and so far is not an art like Plastic ; and since it also has
no concept of the object and its purpose (as in Architecture) con-
ditioning its arrangements, but involves merely the free play of the
Imagination in contemplation,—it so far agrees with mere æsthetical
painting which has no definite theme (which arranges sky, land, and
water, so as to entertain us by means of light and shade only).—In
general the reader is only to judge of this as an attempt to combine
the beautiful arts under one principle, viz. that of the expression of
æsthetical Ideas (according to the analogy of speech), and not to
regard it as a definitive analysis of them.

ornamentation of the soil with a variety of those
things (grasses, flowers, shrubs. trees, even ponds,
hillocks, and dells) which nature presents to an
observer, only arranged differently and in conformity
with certain Ideas. But, again, the beautiful arrangement of corporeal things is only apparent to the eye,
like painting ; the sense of touch cannot supply any
intuitive presentation of such a form.   Under painting in the wide sense I would reckon the decoration
of rooms by the aid of tapestry, bric-a-brac, and all
beautiful furniture which is merely available to be
looked at : and the same may be said of the art of
tasteful dressing (with rings, snuff-boxes, etc.).   For
a bed of various flowers, a room filled with various
ornaments (including under this head even ladies'
finery), make at a fête a kind of picture ; which. like
pictures properly so called (that are not intended to
teach either history or natural science). has in view
merely the entertainment of the Imagination in free
play with Ideas. and the occupation of the æsthetical
Judgment without any definite purpose.   The
detailed work in all this decoration may be quite
distinct in the different cases and may require
very different artists : but the judgment of taste
upon whatever is beautiful in these various arts is
always determined in the same way : viz. it only
judges the forms (without any reference to a
purpose) as they present themselves to the eye
either singly or in combination. according to the
effect they produce upon the Imagination.—   But
that formative art may be compared (by analogy)
with deportment in speech is justified by the fact
that the spirit of the artist supplies by these figures
a bodily expression to his thought and its mode. and
makes the thing itself as it were speak in mimic

language. This is a very common play of our
fancy, which attributes to lifeless things a spirit
suitable to their form by which they speak to us.

(3) The art of the BEAUTIFUL PLAY OF SENSA-
TIONS (externally produced), which admits at the
same time of universal communication, can be concerned with nothing else than the proportion of the
different degrees of the disposition (tension) of the
sense, to which the sensation belongs, i.e. with its tone.
In this far-reaching signification of the word it may
be divided into the artistic play of the sensations of
hearing and sight, i.e. into *Music* and the *Art of
colour.*— It is noteworthy that these two senses,
besides their susceptibility for impressions so far as
these are needed to gain concepts of external objects,
are also capable of a peculiar sensation bound up
therewith, of which we cannot strictly decide whether
it is based on sense or reflection. This susceptibility
may sometimes be wanting, although in other respects
the sense, as regards its use for the cognition of
objects, is not at all deficient but is peculiarly fine.
That is, we cannot say with certainty whether
colours or tones (sounds) are merely pleasant sensations or whether they form in themselves a beautiful play of sensations, and as such bring with them
in aesthetical judgment a satisfaction in the form [of
the object]. If we think of the velocity of the
vibrations of light, or in the second case of the air,
which probably far surpasses all our faculty of
judging immediately in perception the time interval
between them, we must believe that it is only the
effect of these vibrations upon the elastic parts of
our body that is felt, but that the *time interval*
between them is not remarked or brought into judgment ; and thus that only pleasantness and not

beauty of composition is bound up with colours and
tones.   But on the other hand, *first*, we think of
the mathematical [element] which enables us to
pronounce on the proportion between these oscilla-
tions in music and thus to judge of them ; and by
analogy with which we easily may judge of the
distinctions between colours.   *Secondly*, we recall
instances (although they are rare) of men who with
the best sight in the world cannot distinguish
colours, and with the sharpest hearing cannot distinguish tones ; whilst for those who can do this
the perception of an altered quality (not merely of
the degree of sensation) in the different intensities
in the scale of colours and tones is definite ; and
further, the very number of these is fixed by *intelligible* differences.   Thus we may be compelled
to see that both kinds of sensations are to be
regarded not as mere sensible impressions, but as
the effects of a judgment passed upon the form in
the play of divers sensations. ᵕThe difference in our
definition, according as we adopt the one or the
other opinion in judging of the grounds of Music,
would be just this : either, as we have done, we
must explain it as the beautiful play of sensations
(of hearing), or else as a play of *pleasant* sensations.
According to the former mode of explanation music
is represented altogether as a *beautiful* art ; according to the latter, as a *pleasant* art (at least in part).

§ 52. *Of the combination of beautiful arts in one and the same product*

Rhetoric may be combined with a pictorial presentation of its subjects and objects in a *theatrical
piece*; poetry may be combined with music in a

song, and this again with pictorial (theatrical) presentation in an *opera*; the play of sensations in
music may be combined with the play of figures in
the *dance*, and so on.   Even the presentation of the
sublime, so far as it belongs to beautiful art, may
combine with beauty in a *tragedy in verse*, in a
didactic poem, in an *oratorio* ; and in these combinations beautiful art is yet more artistic.   Whether it
is also more beautiful may in some of these cases be
doubted (since so many different kinds of satisfaction cross one another).   Yet in all beautiful art the
essential thing is the form, which is purposive as
regards our observation and judgment, where the
pleasure is at the same time cultivation and disposes
the spirit to Ideas, and consequently makes it susceptible of still more of such pleasure and entertainment.   The essential element is not the matter
of sensation (charm or emotion), which has only to
do with enjoyment; this leaves behind nothing in
the Idea, and it makes the spirit dull, the object
gradually distasteful, and the mind, on account of
its consciousness of a disposition that conflicts with
purpose in the judgment of Reason, discontented
with itself and peevish.

If the beautiful arts are not brought into more or
less close combination with moral Ideas, which alone
bring with them a self-sufficing satisfaction, this latter
fate must ultimately be theirs.   They then serve only
as a distraction, of which we are the more in need the
more we avail ourselves of them to disperse the discontent of the mind with itself; so that we thus render
ourselves ever more useless and ever more discontented.   The beauties of nature are generally of most
benefit in this point of view; if we are early accustomed to observe, appreciate, and admire them.

§ 53. *Comparison of the respective æsthetical worth of the beautiful arts*

Of all the arts *poetry* (which owes its origin almost entirely to genius and will least be guided by precept or example) maintains the first rank. It expands the mind by setting the Imagination at liberty ; and by offering within the limits of a given concept amid the unbounded variety of possible forms accordant therewith, that which unites the presentment of this concept with a wealth of thought, to which no verbal expression is completely adequate ; and so rising æsthetically to Ideas. It strengthens the mind by making it feel its faculty—free, spontaneous and independent of natural determination—of considering and judging nature as a phenomenon in accordance with aspects which it does not present in experience either for Sense or Understanding, and therefore of using it on behalf of, and as a sort of schema for, the supersensible. It plays with illusion, which it produces at pleasure, but without deceiving by it : for it declares its exercise to be mere play, which however can be purposively used by the Understanding.— Rhetoric, in so far as this means the art of persuasion, *i.e.* of deceiving by a beautiful show (*ars oratoria*), and not mere elegance of speech (eloquence and style), is a Dialectic, which borrows from poetry only so much as is needful to win minds to the side of the orator before they have formed a judgment, and to deprive them of their freedom ; it cannot therefore be recommended either for the law courts or for the pulpit. For if we are dealing with civil law, with the rights of individual persons, or with

lasting instruction and determination of people's
minds to an accurate knowledge and a conscientious
observance of their duty, it is unworthy of so
important a business to allow a trace of any luxuriance of wit and imagination to appear, and still less
any trace of the art of talking people over and of
captivating them for the advantage of any chance
person.   For although this art may sometimes be
directed to legitimate and praiseworthy designs, it
becomes objectionable, when in this way maxims and
dispositions are spoiled in a subjective point of view,
though the action may objectively be lawful.   It is
not enough to do what is right ; we should practise
it solely on the ground that it is right.   Again, the
mere concept of this species of matters of human
concern, when clear and combined with a lively
presentation of it in examples, without any offence
against the rules of euphony of speech or propriety
of expression, has by itself for Ideas of Reason (which
collectively constitute eloquence), sufficient influence
upon human minds ; so that it is not needful to add
the machinery of persuasion, which, since it can be
used equally well to beautify or to hide vice and
error, cannot quite lull the secret suspicion that one
is being artfully overreached.   In poetry everything proceeds with honesty and candour.   It
declares itself to be a mere entertaining play of the
Imagination, which wishes to proceed as regards
form in harmony with the laws of the Understanding ; and it does not desire to steal upon and
ensnare the Understanding by the aid of sensible
presentation.[1]

[1] I must admit that a beautiful poem has always given me a pure
gratification ; whilst the reading of the best discourse, whether of
a Roman orator or of a modern parliamentary speaker or of a

After poetry, *if we are to deal with charm and mental movement*, I would place that art which comes nearest to the art of speech and can very naturally be united with it, viz. *the art of tone.* For although it speaks by means of mere sensations without concepts, and so does not, like poetry, leave anything over for reflection, it yet moves the mind in a greater variety of ways and more intensely, although only transitorily. It is, however, rather enjoyment than cultivation (the further play of thought that is excited by its means is merely the effect of an, as it were, mechanical association); and in the judgment of Reason it has less worth than any other of the beautiful arts. Hence, like all enjoyment, it desires constant change, and does not bear frequent repetition without producing weariness.) Its charm, which admits of universal communication, appears to rest on this, that every expression of speech has in its context a tone appropriate to the sense. This tone indicates more or less an affection of the speaker, and produces it also in the hearer; which affection excites in its turn in the hearer the Idea that is expressed

preacher, has always been mingled with an unpleasant feeling of disapprobation of a treacherous art, which means to move men in important matters like machines to a judgment that must lose all weight for them on quiet reflection. Readiness and accuracy in speaking (which taken together constitute Rhetoric) belong to beautiful art; but the art of the orator (*ars oratoria*), the art of availing oneself of the weaknesses of men for one's own designs (whether these be well meant or even actually good does not matter) is worthy of no *respect*. Again, this art only reached its highest point, both at Athens and at Rome, at a time when the state was hastening to its ruin and true patriotic sentiment had disappeared. The man who along with a clear insight into things has in his power a wealth of pure speech, and who with a fruitful Imagination capable of presenting his Ideas unites a lively sympathy with what is truly good, is the *vir bonus dicendi peritus*, the orator without art but of great impressiveness, as *Cicero* has it; though he may not always remain true to this ideal.

in speech by the tone in question. Thus as modulation is as it were a universal language of sensations intelligible to every man, the art of tone employs it by itself alone in its full force, viz. as a language of the affections, and thus communicates universally according to the laws of association the æsthetical Ideas naturally combined therewith. Now these æsthetical Ideas are not concepts or determinate thoughts. Hence the form of the composition of these sensations (harmony and melody) only serves instead of the form of language, by means of their proportionate accordance, to express the æsthetical Idea of a connected whole of an unspeakable wealth of thought, corresponding to a certain theme which produces the dominating affection in the piece. This can be brought mathematically under certain rules, because it rests in the case of tones on the relation between the number of vibrations of the air in the same time, so far as these tones are combined simultaneously or successively. To this mathematical form, although not represented by determinate concepts, alone attaches the satisfaction that unites the mere reflection upon such a number of concomitant or consecutive sensations with this their play, as a condition of its beauty valid for every man. It is this alone which permits Taste to claim in advance a rightful authority over every one's judgment.

But in the charm and mental movement produced by Music, Mathematic has certainly not the slightest share. It is only the indispensable condition (*conditio sine qua non*) of that proportion of the impressions in their combination and in their alternation by which it becomes possible to gather them together and prevent them from destroying one another, and to harmonise them so as to produce a continual

movement and animation of the mind, by means of
affections consonant therewith, and thus a delightful
personal enjoyment.

If, on the other hand, we estimate the worth of
the Beautiful Arts by the culture they supply to the
mind, and take as a standard the expansion of the
faculties which must concur in the Judgment for
cognition, Music will have the lowest place among
them (as it has perhaps the highest among those arts
which are valued for their pleasantness), because it
merely plays with sensations. The formative arts
are far before it in this point of view; for in putting
the Imagination in a free play, which is also accordant with the Understanding, they at the same time
carry on a serious business. This they do by producing a product that serves for concepts as a
permanent self-commendatory vehicle for promoting
their union with sensibility and thus, as it were,
the urbanity of the higher cognitive powers. These
two species of art take quite different courses; the
first proceeds from sensations to indeterminate Ideas,
the second from determinate Ideas to sensations.
The latter produce *permanent*, the former only
transitory impressions. The Imagination can recall
the one and entertain itself pleasantly therewith;
but the other either vanish entirely, or if they are
recalled involuntarily by the Imagination they are
rather wearisome than pleasant.[1] Besides, there
attaches to music a certain want of urbanity from the
fact that, chiefly from the character of its instruments, it extends its influence further than is desired
(in the neighbourhood), and so as it were obtrudes
itself, and does violence to the freedom of others

[1] [From this to the end of the paragraph, and the next note,
were added in the Second Edition.]

who are not of the musical company. The Arts which appeal to the eyes do not do this ; for we need only turn our eyes away, if we wish to avoid being impressed. The case of music is almost like that of the delight derived from a smell that diffuses itself widely. The man who pulls his perfumed handkerchief out of his pocket attracts the attention of all round him, even against their will, and he forces them, if they are to breathe at all, to enjoy the scent ; hence this habit has gone out of fashion.[1]

Among the formative arts I would give the palm to painting ; partly because as the art of delineation it lies at the root of all the other formative arts, and partly because it can penetrate much further into the region of Ideas, and can extend the field of intuition in conformity with them further than the others can.

§ 54. *Remark*

As we have often shown, there is an essential difference between *what satisfies simply in the act of judging it*, and that which *gratifies* (pleases in sensation). We cannot ascribe the latter [kind of satisfaction] to every one, as we can the former. Gratification (the causes of which may even be

---

[1] Those who recommend the singing of spiritual songs at family prayers do not consider that they inflict a great hardship upon the public by such *noisy* (and therefore in general pharisaical) devotions ; for they force the neighbours either to sing with them or to abandon their meditations. [Kant suffered himself from such annoyances, which may account for the asperity of this note. At one period he was disturbed by the devotional exercises of the prisoners in the adjoining jail. In a letter to the burgomaster " he suggested the advantage of closing the windows during these hymn-singings, and added that the warders of the prison might probably be directed to accept less sonorous and neighbour-annoying chants as evidence of the penitent spirit of their captives " (Wallace's *Kant*, p. 42).]

situate in Ideas) appears always to consist in a feeling
of the furtherance of the whole life of the man, and
consequently, also of his bodily well-being, *i.e.* his
health ; so that *Epicurus*, who gave out that all
gratification was at bottom bodily sensation, may,
perhaps, not have been wrong, but only misunderstood himself when he reckoned intellectual and
even practical satisfaction under gratification. If
we have this distinction in view we can explain
how a gratification may dissatisfy the man who
sensibly feels it (*e.g.* the joy of a needy but well-
meaning man at becoming the heir of an affec-
tionate but penurious father) ; or how a deep grief
may satisfy the person experiencing it (the sorrow
of a widow at the death of her excellent husband) ;
or how a gratification can in addition satisfy (as in
the sciences that we pursue) ; or how a grief (*e.g.*
hatred, envy, revenge) can moreover dissatisfy.
The satisfaction or dissatisfaction here depends on
Reason, and is the same as *approbation* or *disapprobation* ; but gratification and grief can only rest
on the feeling or prospect of a possible (on whatever
grounds) *well-being* or *its opposite*.

All changing free play of sensations (that have
no design at their basis) gratifies, because it furthers
the feeling of health. In the judgment of Reason
we may or may not have any satisfaction in its
object or even in this gratification ; and this latter
may rise to the height of an affection, although
we take no interest in the object, at least none
that is proportionate to the degree of the gratification. We may subdivide this free play of sensations
into the *play of fortune* [games of chance], the *play
of tone* [music], and the *play of thought* [wit]. The
first requires an *interest*, whether of vanity or of

selfishness; which, however, is not nearly so great as the interest that attaches to the way in which we are striving to procure it. The *second* requires merely the change of *sensations*, all of which have a relation to affection, though they have not the degree of affection, and excite æsthetical Ideas. The *third* springs merely from the change of representations in the Judgment; by it, indeed, no thought that brings an interest with it is produced, but yet the mind is animated thereby.

How much gratification games must afford, without any necessity of placing at their basis an interested design, all our evening parties show; for hardly any of them can be carried on without a game. But the affections of hope, fear, joy, wrath, scorn, are put in play by them, alternating every moment; and they are so vivid that by them, as by a kind of internal motion, all the vital processes of the body seem to be promoted, as is shown by the mental vivacity excited by them, although nothing is gained or learnt thereby. But as the beautiful does not enter into games of chance, we will here set it aside. On the other hand, music and that which excites laughter are two different kinds of play with æsthetical Ideas, or of representations of the Understanding through which ultimately nothing is thought, which can give lively gratification merely by their changes. Thus we recognise pretty clearly that the animation in both cases is merely bodily, although it is excited by Ideas of the mind; and that the feeling of health produced by a motion of the intestines corresponding to the play in question makes up that whole gratification of a gay party, which is regarded as so refined and so spiritual. It is not the judging the harmony in tones or

sallies of wit,—which serves only in combination
with their beauty as a necessary vehicle,—but the
furtherance of the vital bodily processes, the affection
that moves the intestines and the diaphragm, in
a word, the feeling of health (which without such
inducements one does not feel) that makes up the
gratification felt by us ; so that we can thus reach
the body through the soul and use the latter as the
physician of the former.

In music this play proceeds from bodily sensations to æsthetical Ideas (the Objects of our
affections), and then from these back again to the
body with redoubled force.   In the case of jokes
(the art of which, just like music, should rather be
reckoned as pleasant than beautiful) the play begins
with the thoughts which together occupy the body,
so far as they admit of sensible expression ; and
as the Understanding stops suddenly short at this
presentment, in which it does not find what it expected, we feel the effect of this slackening in the
body by the oscillation of the organs, which promotes
the restoration of equilibrium and has a favourable
influence upon health.

In everything that is to excite a lively convulsive
laugh there must be something absurd (in which the
Understanding, therefore, can find no satisfaction).
*Laughter is an affection arising from the sudden
transformation of a strained expectation into nothing.*
This transformation, which is certainly not enjoyable
to the Understanding, yet indirectly gives it very
active enjoyment for a moment.   Therefore its
cause must consist in the influence of the representation upon the body, and the reflex effect of
this upon the mind ; not, indeed, through the
representation being objectively an object of grati-

fication? (for how could a delusive expectation gratify?), but simply through it as a mere play of representations bringing about an equilibrium of the vital powers in the body.

Suppose this story to be told: An Indian at the table of an Englishman in Surat, when he saw a bottle of ale opened and all the beer turned into froth and overflowing, testified his great astonishment with many exclamations. When the Englishman asked him, "What is there in this to astonish you so much?" he answered, "I am not at all astonished that it should flow out, but I do wonder how you ever got it in." At this story we laugh, and it gives us hearty pleasure; not because we deem ourselves cleverer than this ignorant man, or because of anything in it that we note as satisfactory to the Understanding, but because our expectation was strained [for a time] and then was suddenly dissipated into nothing. Again: The heir of a rich relative wished to arrange for an imposing funeral, but he lamented that he could not properly succeed; "for" (said he) "the more money I give my mourners to look sad the more cheerful they look." When we hear this story we laugh loud, and the reason is that an expectation is suddenly transformed into nothing. We must note well that it does not transform itself into the positive opposite of an expected object—for then there would still be something, which might even be a cause of grief—but it must be transformed into nothing. For if a man arouses great expectations in us when telling a story, and at the end we see its falsehood immediately, it displeases us; e.g. the story of the people

---

* [The First Edition adds "as in the case of a man who gets the news of a great commercial success."]

whose hair in consequence of great grief turned gray in one night. But if a wag, to repair the effect of this story describes very circumstantially the grief of the merchant returning from India to Europe with all his wealth in merchandise who was forced to throw it overboard in a heavy storm, and who grieved thereat so much that his wig turned gray the same night—we laugh and it gives us gratification. For we treat our own mistake in the case of an object otherwise indifferent to us, or rather the Idea which we are following out as we treat a ball which we knock to and fro for a time, though our only serious intention is to seize it and hold it fast. It is not the mere dismissal of a liar or a simpleton that arouses our gratification; for the latter story told with assumed seriousness would set a whole company in a roar of laughter while the former would ordinarily not be regarded as worth attending to.

It is remarkable that in all such cases the jest must contain something that is capable of deceiving for a moment. Hence, when the illusion is dissipated, the mind turns back to try it once again, and thus through a rapidly alternating tension and relaxation it is jerked back and put into a state of oscillation. This, because the strain on the cord as it were is suddenly (and not gradually) relaxed, must occasion a mental movement and an inner bodily movement harmonising therewith, which continues involuntarily and fatigues, even while cheering us (the effects of a motion conducive to health).

For if we admit that with all our thoughts is harmonically combined a movement in the organs of the body, we will easily comprehend how to this sudden transposition of the mind, now to one now to another standpoint in order to contemplate its object, may correspond an alternating tension and relaxation of the elastic portions of our intestines, which communicates itself to the diaphragm (like that which ticklish people feel). In connection with this the lungs expel the air at rapidly succeeding intervals, and thus bring about a movement beneficial to health; which alone, and not what precedes it in the mind, is the proper cause of the gratification in a thought that at bottom represents nothing.— *Voltaire* said that heaven had given us two things to counterbalance the many miseries of life, *hope* and *sleep*.[1] He could have added *laughter*, if the means of exciting it in reasonable men were only as easily attainable, and the requisite wit or originality of humour were not so rare, as the talent is common of imagining things which *break one's head*, as mystic dreamers do, or which *break one's neck*, as your genius does, or which *break one's heart*, as sentimental romance-writers (and even moralists of the same kidney) do.

We may therefore, as it seems to me, readily concede to *Epicurus* that all gratification, even that which is occasioned through concepts, excited by æsthetical Ideas, is *animal, i.e.* bodily sensation; without the least prejudice to the *spiritual* feeling of respect for moral Ideas, which is not gratification at all but an esteem for self (for humanity in us), that raises us above the need of gratification, and

---

[1] [*Henriade, Chant* 7, sub init.
    "Du Dieu qui nous créa la clémence infinie,
    Pour adoucir les maux de cette courte vie,
    A placé parmi nous deux êtres bienfaisants,
    De la terre à jamais aimables habitants,
    Soutiens dans les travaux, trésors dans l'indigence :
    L'un est le doux sommeil, et l'autre est l'espérance."]

even without the slightest prejudice to the less noble
[satisfactions] of *taste*.

We find a combination of these two last in
naiveté, which is the breaking out of the sincerity
originally natural to humanity in opposition to that
art of dissimulation which has become a second
nature. We laugh at the simplicity that does not
understand how to dissemble ; and yet we are
delighted with the simplicity of the nature which
thwarts that art. We look for the commonplace
manner of artificial utterance devised with foresight
to make a fair show ; and behold ! it is the
unspoiled innocent nature which we do not expect
to find, and which he who displays it did not think
of disclosing. That the fair but false show which
generally has so much influence upon our judgment
is here suddenly transformed into nothing, so that,
as it were, the rogue in us is laid bare, produces a
movement of the mind in two opposite directions,
which gives a wholesome shock to the body. But
the fact that something infinitely better than all
assumed manner, viz. purity of disposition (or at
least the tendency thereto), is not quite extinguished
yet in human nature, blends seriousness and high
esteem with this play of the Judgment. But because it is only a transitory phenomenon and the
veil of dissimulation is soon drawn over it again,
there is mingled therewith a compassion which is
an emotion of tenderness ; this, as play, readily
admits of combination with a good-hearted laugh,
and ordinarily is actually so combined, and withal is
wont to compensate him who supplies the material
therefor for the embarrassment which results from
not yet being wise after the manner of men.— An
art that is to be *naive* is thus a contradiction ; but

the representation of naiveté in a fictitious personage is quite possible, and is a beautiful though a rare art. Naiveté must not be confounded with open-hearted simplicity, which does not artificially spoil nature solely because it does not understand the art of social intercourse.

The *humorous* manner again may be classified as that which, as exhilarating us, is near akin to the gratification that proceeds from laughter; and belongs to the originality of spirit, but not to the talent of beautiful art. *Humour* in the good sense means the talent of being able voluntarily to put oneself into a certain mental disposition, in which everything is judged quite differently from the ordinary method (reversed, in fact), and yet in accordance with certain rational principles in such a frame of mind. He who is involuntarily subject to such mutations is called *a man of humours* [launisch]; but he who can assume them voluntarily and purposively (on behalf of a lively presentment brought about by the aid of a contrast that excites a laugh)—he and his exposition are called *humorous* [launigt]. This manner, however, belongs rather to pleasant than to beautiful art, because the object of the latter must always show proper worth in itself, and hence requires a certain seriousness in the presentation, as taste does in the act of judging.

§ 55

A faculty of Judgment that is to be dialectical must in the first place be rationalising, *i.e.* its judgments must claim universality[1] and that *a priori*; for it is in the opposition of such judgments that Dialectic consists. Hence the incompatibility of æsthetical judgments of Sense (about the pleasant and the unpleasant) is not dialectical. And again, the conflict between judgments of Taste, so far as each man depends merely on his own taste, forms no Dialectic of taste; because no one proposes to make his own judgment a universal rule. There remains therefore no other concept of a Dialectic which has to do with taste than that of a Dialectic of the *Kritik* of taste (not of taste itself) in respect of its *principles*; for here concepts that contradict one another (as to the ground of the possibility of judgments of taste in general) naturally and unavoidably present themselves. The transcendental Kritik

---

[1] We may describe as a rationalising judgment (*judicium ratiocinans*) one which proclaims itself as universal, for as such it can serve as the major premise of a syllogism. On the other hand, we can only speak of a judgment as rational (*judicium ratiocinatum*) which is thought as the conclusion of a syllogism, and consequently as grounded *a priori*.

of taste will therefore contain a part which can bear the name of a Dialectic of the æsthetical Judgment, only if and so far as there is found an antinomy of the principles of this faculty which renders its conformity to law, and consequently also its internal possibility, doubtful.

§ 56. *Representation of the antinomy of Taste*

The first commonplace of taste is contained in the proposition, with which every tasteless person proposes to avoid blame : *every one has his own taste.* That is as much as to say that the determining ground of this judgment is merely subjective (gratification or grief), and that the judgment has no right to the necessary assent of others.

The second commonplace invoked even by those who admit for judgments of taste the right to speak with validity for every one is : *there is no disputing about taste.* That is as much as to say that the determining ground of a judgment of taste may indeed be objective, but that it cannot be reduced to definite concepts ; and that consequently about the judgment itself nothing can be *decided* by proofs, although much may rightly be *contested.* For *contesting* [quarrelling] and *disputing* [controversy] are doubtless the same in this, that by means of the mutual opposition of judgments they seek to produce their accordance ; but different in that the latter hopes to bring this about according to definite concepts as determining grounds, and consequently assumes *objective concepts* as grounds of the judgment. But where this is regarded as impracticable, controversy is regarded as alike impracticable.

We easily see that between these two commonplaces there is a proposition wanting, which, though it has not passed into a proverb, is yet familiar to every one, viz. *there may be a quarrel about taste* (although there can be no controversy). But this proposition involves the contradictory of the former one. For wherever quarrelling is permissible, there must be a hope of mutual reconciliation ; and consequently we can count on grounds of our judgment that have not merely private validity, and therefore are not merely subjective. And· to this the proposition, *every one has his own taste*, is directly opposed.

There emerges therefore in respect of the principle of taste the following Antinomy :—

(1) *Thesis.* The judgment of taste is not based upon concepts ; for otherwise it would admit of controversy (would be determinable by proofs).

(2) *Antithesis.* The judgment of taste is based on concepts ; for otherwise, despite its diversity, we could not quarrel about it (we could not claim for our judgment the necessary assent of others).

§ 57. *Solution of the antinomy of Taste*

There is no possibility of removing the conflict between these principles that underlie every judgment of taste (which are nothing else than the two peculiarities of the judgment of taste exhibited above in the Analytic), except by showing that the concept to which we refer the Object in this kind of judgment is not taken in the same sense in both maxims of the æsthetical Judgment. This twofold sense or twofold point of view is necessary to our transcendental Judgment ; but also the illusion

which arises from the confusion of one with the
other is natural and unavoidable.

The judgment of taste must refer to some concept; otherwise it could make absolutely no claim
to be necessarily valid for every one. But it is not
therefore capable of being proved from a concept;
because a concept may be either determinable or in
itself undetermined and undeterminable. The concepts of the Understanding are of the former kind;
they are determinable through predicates of sensible
intuition which can correspond to them. But the
transcendental rational concept of the supersensible,
which lies at the basis of all sensible intuition, is of
the latter kind, and therefore cannot be theoretically
determined further.

Now the judgment of taste is applied to objects
of Sense, but not with a view of determining a *concept* of them for the Understanding; for it is not a
cognitive judgment. It is thus only a private
judgment, in which a singular representation intuitively perceived is referred to the feeling of pleasure;
and so far would be limited as regards its validity
to the individual judging. The object is *for me* an
object of satisfaction; by others it may be regarded
quite differently—every one has his own taste.

Nevertheless there is undoubtedly contained in
the judgment of taste a wider reference of the
representation of the Object (as well as of the
subject), whereon we base an extension of judgments of this kind as necessary for every one. At
the basis of this there must necessarily be a concept
somewhere; though a concept which cannot be
determined through intuition. But through a concept of this sort we know nothing, and consequently
it can *supply no proof* for the judgment of taste.

Such a concept is the mere pure rational concept of the supersensible which underlies the Object (and also the subject judging it), regarded as an object of sense and thus as phenomenal.[1] For if we do not admit such a reference, the claim of the judgment of taste to universal validity would not hold good. If the concept on which it is based were only a mere confused concept of the Understanding, like that of perfection, with which we could bring the sensible intuition of the Beautiful into correspondence, it would be at least possible in itself to base the judgment of taste on proofs; which contradicts the thesis.

But all contradiction disappears if I say: the judgment of taste is based on a concept (viz. the concept of the general ground of the subjective purposiveness of nature for the Judgment); from which, however, nothing can be known and proved in respect of the Object, because it is in itself undeterminable and useless for knowledge. Yet at the same time and on that very account the judgment has validity for every one (though of course for each only as a singular judgment immediately accompanying his intuition); because its determining ground lies perhaps in the concept of that which may be regarded as the supersensible substrate of humanity.

The solution of an antinomy only depends on the possibility of showing that two apparently contradictory propositions do not contradict one another in fact, but that they may be consistent; although the explanation of the possibility of their concept may transcend our cognitive faculties. That this illusion is natural and unavoidable by human Reason, and

[1] [Cf. p. 241 infra.]

also why it is so, and remains so, although it ceases
to deceive after the analysis of the apparent contradiction, may be thus explained.

In the two contradictory judgments we take the
concept, on which the universal validity of a judgment must be based, in the same sense ; and yet we
apply to it two opposite predicates. In the Thesis
we mean that the judgment of taste is not based
upon *determinate* concepts ; and in the Antithesis
that the judgment of taste is based upon a concept,
but an *indeterminate* one (viz. of the supersensible
substrate of phenomena). Between these two there
is no contradiction.

We can do nothing more than remove this
conflict between the claims and counter-claims of
taste. It is absolutely impossible to give a definite
objective principle of taste, in accordance with
which its judgments could be derived, examined,
and established ; for then the judgment would not
be one of taste at all. The subjective principle,
viz. the indefinite Idea of the supersensible in us,
can only be put forward as the sole key to the
puzzle of this faculty whose sources are hidden
from us : it can be made no further intelligible.

The proper concept of taste, that is of a merely
reflective æsthetical Judgment, lies at the basis of
the antinomy here exhibited and adjusted. Thus
the two apparently contradictory principles are
reconciled—*both can be true* ; which is sufficient.
If, on the other hand, we assume, as some do,
pleasantness as the determining ground of taste (on
account of the singularity of the representation
which lies at the basis of the judgment of taste), or,
as others will have it, the principle of perfection (on
account of the universality of the same), and settle

the definition of taste accordingly ; then there arises
an antinomy which it is absolutely impossible to
adjust except by showing that *both* the contrary
(not merely contradictory) *propositions are false.*
And this would prove that the concept on which
they are based is self-contradictory.   Hence we see
that the removal of the antinomy of the æsthetical
Judgment takes a course similar to that pursued by
the Kritik in the solution of the antinomies of pure
theoretical Reason.   And thus here, as also in the
Kritik of practical Reason, the antinomies force us
against our will to look beyond the sensible and to
seek in the supersensible the point of union for all
our *a priori* faculties ; because no other expedient is
left to make our Reason harmonious with itself.

Remark I.

As we so often find occasion in Transcendental
Philosophy for distinguishing Ideas from concepts of
the Understanding, it may be of use to introduce
technical terms to correspond to this distinction.   I
believe that no one will object if I propose some.—
In the most universal signification of the word,
Ideas are representations referred to an object,
according to a certain (subjective or objective)
principle, but so that they can never become a
cognition of it.   They are either referred to an
intuition, according to a merely subjective principle
of the mutual harmony of the cognitive powers
(the Imagination and the Understanding), and they
are then called *æsthetical*; or they are referred to
a concept according to an objective principle,
although they can never furnish a cognition of the
object, and are called *rational Ideas.*   In the latter

case the concept is a *transcendent* one, which is different from a concept of the Understanding, to which an adequately corresponding experience can always be supplied, and which therefore is called *immanent*.

An *æsthetical Idea* cannot become a cognition, because it is an *intuition* (of the Imagination) for which an adequate concept can never be found. A *rational Idea* can never become a cognition, because it involves a concept (of the supersensible), corresponding to which an intuition can never be given.

Now I believe we might call the æsthetical Idea an *inexponible* representation of the Imagination, and a rational Idea an *indemonstrable* concept of Reason. It is assumed of both that they are not generated without grounds, but (according to the above explanation of an Idea in general) in conformity with certain principles of the cognitive faculties to which they belong (subjective principles in the one case, objective in the other).

Concepts of the Understanding must, as such, always be demonstrable [if by demonstration we understand, as in anatomy, merely *presentation*];[1] *i.e.* the object corresponding to them must always be capable of being given in intuition (pure or empirical); for thus alone could they become cognitions. The concept of *magnitude* can be given *a priori* in the intuition of space, *e.g.* of a right line, etc.; the concept of *cause* in impenetrability, in the collision of bodies, etc. Consequently both can be authenticated by means of an empirical intuition, *i.e.* the thought of them can be proved (demonstrated, verified) by an example; and this must be possible,

[1] [Second Edition.]

for otherwise we should not be certain that the concept was not empty, *i.e.* devoid of any *Object*.

In Logic we ordinarily use the expressions demonstrable or indemonstrable only in respect of *propositions*, but these might be better designated by the titles respectively of *mediately and immediately certain* propositions ; for pure Philosophy has also propositions of both kinds, *i.e.* true propositions, some of which are susceptible of proof and others not. It can, as philosophy, prove them on *a priori* grounds, but it cannot demonstrate them ; unless we wish to depart entirely from the proper meaning of this word, according to which *to demonstrate* (*ostendere*, *exhibere*) is equivalent to presenting a concept in intuition (whether in proof or merely in definition). If the intuition is *a priori* this is called construction ; but if it is empirical, then the Object is displayed by means of which objective reality is assured to the concept. Thus we say of an anatomist that he demonstrates the human eye, if by a dissection of this organ he makes intuitively evident the concept which he has previously treated discursively.

It hence follows that the rational concept of the supersensible substrate of all phenomena in general, or even of that which must be placed at the basis of our arbitrary will in respect of the moral law, viz. of transcendental freedom, is already, in kind, an indemonstrable concept and a rational Idea ; while virtue is so, in degree. For there can be given in experience, as regards its quality, absolutely nothing corresponding to the former ; whereas in the latter case no empirical product attains to the degree of that causality, which the rational Idea prescribes as the rule.

As in a rational Idea the *Imagination* with its intuitions does not attain to the given concept, so in an æsthetical Idea the *Understanding* by its concepts never attains completely to that internal intuition which the Imagination binds up with a given representation. Since, now, to reduce a representation of the Imagination to concepts is the same thing as to *expound* it, the æsthetical Idea may be called an *inexponible* representation of the Imagination (in its free play). I shall have occasion in the sequel to say something more of Ideas of this kind ; now I only note that both kinds of Ideas, rational and æsthetical, must have their principles ; and must have them in Reason—the one in the objective, the other in the subjective principles of its employment.

We can consequently explain *genius* as the faculty of *æsthetical Ideas* ; by which at the same time is shown the reason why in the products of genius it is the nature (of the subject) and not a premeditated purpose that gives the rule to the art (of the production of the beautiful). For since the beautiful must not be judged by concepts, but by the purposive attuning of the Imagination to agreement with the faculty of concepts in general, it cannot be rule and precept which can serve as the subjective standard of that æsthetical but unconditioned purposiveness in beautiful art, that can rightly claim to please every one. It can only be that in the subject which is nature and cannot be brought under rules or concepts, *i.e.* the supersensible substrate of all his faculties (to which no concept of the Understanding extends), and consequently that with respect to which it is the final purpose given by the intelligible [part] of our nature to harmonise all our cognitive faculties. Thus alone is it possible that there should be *a priori* at the basis of this purposiveness, for which we can prescribe no objective principle, a principle subjective and yet of universal validity.

Remark II.

The following important remark occurs here: There are *three kinds of Antinomies* of pure Reason, which, however, all agree in this, that they compel us to give up the otherwise very natural hypothesis—that objects of sense are things in themselves, and force us to regard them merely as phenomena, and to supply to them an intelligible substrate (something supersensible of which the concept is only an Idea, and supplies no proper knowledge). Without such antinomies Reason could never decide upon accepting a principle narrowing so much the field of its speculation, and could never bring itself to sacrifices by which so many otherwise brilliant hopes must disappear. For even now when, by way of compensation for these losses, a greater field in a practical aspect opens out before it, it appears not to be able without grief to part from those hopes, and disengage itself from its old attachment.

That there are three kinds of antinomies has its ground in this, that there are three cognitive faculties,—Understanding, Judgment, and Reason; of which each (as a superior cognitive faculty) must have its *a priori* principles. For Reason, in so far as it judges of these principles and their use, inexorably requires, in respect of them all, the unconditioned for the given conditioned; and this can never be found if we consider the sensible as belonging to things in themselves, and do not rather supply to it, as mere phenomenon, something supersensible (the intelligible substrate of nature both external and internal) as the reality in itself [Sache an sich selbst]. There are then : (1) *For the cognitive faculty* an antinomy of Reason in respect of the theoretical employment of the Understanding extended to the unconditioned ; (2) *for the feeling of pleasure and pain* an antinomy of Reason in respect of the æsthetical employment of the Judgment ; and (3) *for the faculty of desire* an antinomy in respect of the practical employment of the self-legislative Reason ; so far as all these faculties have their superior principles *a priori*, and, in conformity with an inevitable requirement of Reason, must judge and be able to determine their Object, *unconditionally* according to those principles.

As for the two antinomies of the theoretical and practical employment of the superior cognitive faculties, we have already shown their *unavoidableness*, if judgments of this kind are not referred to a supersensible substrate of the given Objects, as phenomena ; and also the *possibility of their solution*, as soon as this is done. And as for the antinomies in the employment of the Judgment, in conformity with the requirements of Reason, and their solution which is here given, there are only two ways of avoiding them. *Either*: we must deny that any *a priori* principle lies at the basis of the æsthetical judgment of taste ; we must maintain that all claim to necessary universal agreement is a groundless and vain fancy, and that a judgment of taste only deserves to be regarded as correct because *it happens* that many people agree about it ; and this,

not because we *assume* an *a priori* principle behind
this agreement, but because (as in the taste of the
palate) of the contingent similar organisation of the
different subjects. *Or*: we must assume that the
judgment of taste is really a disguised judgment of
Reason upon the perfection discovered in a thing
and the reference of the manifold in it to a purpose,
and is consequently only called æsthetical on
account of the confusion here attaching to our
reflection, although it is at bottom teleological. In
the latter case we could declare the solution of the
antinomies by means of transcendental Ideas to
be needless and without point, and thus could
harmonise these laws of taste with Objects of sense,
not as mere phenomena but as things in themselves.
But we have shown in several places in the exposition of judgments of taste how little either of
these expedients will satisfy.

However, if it be granted that our deduction at
least proceeds by the right method, although it be
not yet plain enough in all its parts, three Ideas
manifest themselves. *First*, there is the Idea of
the supersensible in general, without any further
determination of it, as the substrate of nature.
Secondly, there is the Idea of the same as the
principle of the subjective purposiveness of nature
for our cognitive faculty. And *thirdly*, there is the
Idea of the same as the principle of the purposes
of freedom, and of the agreement of freedom with
its purposes in the moral sphere.

§ 58. *Of the Idealism of the purposiveness of both
      Nature and Art as the unique principle of
      the æsthetical Judgment.*

To begin with, we can either place the principle

R

of taste in the fact that it always judges in accordance with grounds which are empirical and therefore
are only given *a posteriori* by sense, or concede
that it judges on *a priori* grounds.   The former
would be the *empiricism* of the Kritik of Taste ;
the latter its *rationalism*.   According to the *former*
the Object of our satisfaction would not differ from
the *pleasant* ; according to the latter, if the judgment
rests on definite concepts, it would not differ from
the *good*.   Thus all *beauty* would be banished from
the world, and only a particular name, expressing
perhaps a certain mingling of the two above-named
kinds of satisfaction, would remain in its place.   But
we have shown that there are also *a priori* grounds
of satisfaction which can subsist along with the
principle of rationalism, although they cannot be
comprehended in *definite concepts*.

On the other hand, the rationalism of the principle of taste is either that of the *realism* of the
purposiveness, or of its *idealism*.· Because a judgment of taste is not a cognitive judgment, and
beauty is not a characteristic of the Object, considered in itself, the rationalism of the principle of
taste can never be placed in the fact that the purposiveness in this judgment is thought as objective,
i.e. that the judgment theoretically, and therefore
also logically (although only in a confused way),
refers to the perfection of the Object.   It only refers
æsthetically to the agreement of the representation
of the Object in the Imagination with the essential
principles of Judgment in general in the subject.
Consequently, even according to the principle of
rationalism, the judgment of taste and the distinction between its realism and idealism can only be
settled thus.   Either in the first case, this subjective

purposiveness is assumed as an actual (designed) *purpose* of nature (or art) harmonising with our Judgment; or, in the second case, as a purposive harmony with the needs of Judgment, in respect of nature and its forms produced according to particular laws, which shows itself, without purpose, spontaneously, and contingently.

The beautiful formations in the kingdom of organised nature speak loudly for the 'Realism of the æsthetical purposiveness of nature; since we might assume that behind the production of the beautiful there is an Idea of the beautiful in the producing cause, viz. a *purpose* in respect of our Imagination. Flowers, blossoms, even the shapes of entire plants; the elegance of animal formations of all kinds, unneeded for their proper use, but, as it were, selected for our taste; especially the charming variety so satisfying to the eye and the harmonious arrangement of colours (in the pheasant, in shell-fish, in insects, even in the commonest flowers), which, as it only concerns the surface and not the figure of these creations (though perhaps requisite in regard of their internal purposes), seems to be entirely designed for external inspection; these things give great weight to that mode of explanation which assumes actual purposes of nature for our æsthetical Judgment.

On the other hand, not only is Reason opposed to this assumption in its maxims, which bid us always avoid as far as possible unnecessary multiplication of principles; but nature everywhere shows in its free formations much mechanical tendency to the productions of forms which seem, as it were, to be made for the æsthetical exercise of our Judgment, without affording the least ground for the supposition that there is need of anything more than its mechanism, merely as nature, according to which, without any Idea lying at their root, they can be purposive for our judgment. But I understand by *free formations* of nature *those* whereby from a *fluid at rest*, through the volatilisation or separation of a portion of its constituents (sometimes merely of caloric), the remainder in becoming solid assumes a definite shape or tissue (figure or texture), which is different according to the specific difference of the material, but in the same material is constant. Here it is always presupposed that we are speaking of a perfect fluid, *i.e.* that the material in it is completely dissolved, and that it is not a mere medley of solid particles in a state of suspension.

Formation, then, takes place by a *shooting together*, *i.e.* by a sudden solidification, not by a gradual transition from the fluid to the solid state, but all at once by a *saltus*; which transition is also called *crystallisation*. The commonest example of this kind of formation is the freezing of water, where first icicles are produced, which combine at angles of 60°, while others attach themselves to each vertex, until it all becomes ice ; and so that, while this is going on, the water does not gradually become viscous, but is as perfectly fluid as if its temperature were far higher, although it is absolutely ice-cold. The matter that disengages itself, which is dissipated suddenly at the moment of solidification, is a considerable quantum of caloric, the disappearance of which, as it was only required for preserving fluidity, leaves the new ice not in the least colder than the water which shortly before was fluid.

Many salts, and also rocks, of a crystalline figure, are produced thus from a species of earth dissolved in water, we do not exactly know how. Thus are formed the crystalline configurations of many minerals, the cubical sulphide of lead, the ruby silver ore, etc., in all probability in water and by the shooting together of particles, as they become forced by some cause to dispense with this vehicle and to unite in definite external shapes.

But also all kinds of matter, which have been kept in a fluid state by heat, and have become solid by cooling, show internally, when fractured, a definite texture. This makes us judge that if their own weight or the disturbance of the air had not prevented it, they would also have exhibited on the outer surface their specifically peculiar shapes. This has been observed in some metals on their inner surface, which have been hardened externally by fusion but are fluid in the interior, by the drawing off the internal fluid and the consequent undisturbed crystallisation of the remainder. Many of these mineral crystallisations, such as spars, hematite, arragonite, etc., often present beautiful shapes, the like of which art can only conceive : and the halo in the cavern of Antiparos[1] is merely produced by water trickling down strata of gypsum.

The fluid state is, to all appearance, older than the solid state, and plants as well as animal bodies are fashioned out of fluid nutritive matter, so far as this forms itself in a state of rest. This last of course primarily combines and forms itself in freedom according to a certain original disposition directed towards purposes (which, as will be shown in Part II., must not be judged æsthetically but teleologically according to the principle of realism).

[1] [Antiparos is a small island in the Cyclades, remarkable for a splendid stalactite cavern near the south coast.]

but also perhaps in conformity with the universal
law of the affinity of materials. Again, the watery
fluids dissolved in an atmosphere that is a mixture
of different gases, if they separate from the latter
on account of cooling, produce snow figures, which
in correspondence with the character of the special
mixture of gases, often seem very artistic and are
extremely beautiful. So, without detracting from
the teleological principle by which we judge of
organisation, we may well think that the beauty of
flowers, of the plumage of birds, or of shell-fish,
both in shape and colour, may be ascribed to nature
and its faculty of producing forms in an æsthetically
purposive way, in its freedom, without particular
purposes adapted thereto, according to chemical
laws by the arrangement of the material requisite
for the organisation in question.

But what shows the principle of the *Ideality* of
the purposiveness in the beauty of nature, as that
which we always place at the basis of an æsthetical
judgment, and which allows us to employ, as a
ground of explanation for our representative faculty,
no realism of purpose, is the fact that in judging
beauty we invariably seek its gauge in ourselves
a priori, and that our æsthetical Judgment is itself
legislative in respect of the judgment whether
anything is beautiful or not. This could not be, on
the assumption of the Realism of the purposiveness
of nature ; because in that case we must have
learned from nature what we ought to find beautiful,
and the æsthetical judgment would be subjected to
empirical principles. For in such an act of judging
the important point is not, what nature is, or even,
as a purpose, is in relation to us, but how we take
it. There would be an objective purposiveness in

nature if it had fashioned its forms for our satisfaction ; and not a subjective purposiveness which
depended upon the play of the Imagination in its
freedom, where it is we who receive nature with
favour, not nature which shows us favour. The
property of nature that gives us occasion to perceive the inner purposiveness in the relation of our
mental faculties in judging certain of its products
—a purposiveness which is to be explained on
supersensible grounds as necessary and universal—
cannot be a natural purpose or be judged by us as
such ; for otherwise the judgment hereby determined
would not be free, and would have at its basis
heteronomy, and not, as beseems a judgment of
taste, autonomy.

In beautiful Art the principle of the Idealism of
purposiveness is still clearer. As in the case of
the beautiful in Nature an æsthetical Realism of this
purposiveness cannot be perceived by sensations
(for then the art would be only pleasant, not beautiful). But that the satisfaction produced by æsthetical
Ideas must not depend on the attainment of definite
purposes (as in mechanically designed art), and that
consequently, in the very rationalism of the principle,
the ideality of the purposes and not their reality
must be fundamental, appears from the fact that
beautiful Art, as such, must not be considered as a
product of Understanding and Science, but of Genius,
and therefore must get its rule through *æsthetical*
Ideas, which are essentially different from rational
Ideas of definite purposes.

Just as the *ideality* of the objects of sense as
phenomena is the only way of explaining the possibility of their forms being susceptible of *a priori*
determination, so the *idealism* of purposiveness, in

judging the beautiful in nature and art, is the only
hypothesis under which Kritik can explain the
possibility of a judgment of taste which demands
a priori validity for every one (without grounding
on concepts the purposiveness that is represented in
the Object).

§ 59. *Of Beauty as the symbol of Morality*

Intuitions are always required to establish the
reality of our concepts. If the concepts are empirical, the intuitions are called *examples*. If they are
pure concepts of Understanding, the intuitions are
called *schemata*. If we desire to establish the
objective reality of rational concepts, *i.e.* of Ideas,
on behalf of theoretical cognition, then we are asking
for something impossible, because absolutely no
intuition can be given which shall be adequate to
them.

All *hypotyposis* (presentation, *subjectio sub ad-
spectum*), or sensible illustration, is twofold. It is
either *schematical*, when to a concept comprehended
by the Understanding the corresponding intuition is
given ; or it is *symbolical*. In the latter case to a
concept only thinkable by the Reason, to which no
sensible intuition can be adequate, an intuition is
supplied with which accords a procedure of the Judgment analogous to what it observes in schematism,
i.e. merely analogous to the rule of this procedure,
not to the intuition itself, consequently to the form
of reflection merely and not to its content.

There is a use of the word *symbolical* that has
been adopted by modern logicians, which is mis-
leading and incorrect, *i.e.* to speak of the *symbolical*
mode of representation as if it were opposed to the

intuitive; for the symbolical is only a mode of the intuitive. The latter (the intuitive), that is, may be divided into the *schematical* and the *symbolical* modes of representation. Both are hypotyposes, *i.e.* presentations (*exhibitiones*) ; not mere *characterisations*, or designations of concepts by accompanying sensible signs which contain nothing belonging to the intuition of the Object, and only serve as a means for reproducing the concepts, according to the law of association of the Imagination, and consequently in a subjective point of view. These are either words, or visible (algebraical, even mimetical) signs, as mere expressions for concepts.[1]

All intuitions, which we supply to concepts *a priori*, are therefore either *schemata* or *symbols*, of which the former contain direct, the latter indirect, presentations of the concept. The former do this demonstratively ; the latter by means of an analogy (for which we avail ourselves even of empirical intuitions) in which the Judgment exercises a double function ; first applying the concept to the object of a sensible intuition, and then applying the mere rule of the reflection made upon that intuition to a quite different object of which the first is only the symbol. Thus a monarchical state is represented by a living body, if it is governed by national laws, and by a mere machine (like a hand-mill) if governed by an individual absolute will ; but in both cases only *symbolically*. For between a despotic state and a hand-mill there is, to be sure, no similarity ; but there is a similarity in the rules according

---

[1] The intuitive in cognition must be opposed to the discursive (not to the symbolical). The former is either *schematical*, by *demonstration* ; or *symbolical*, as a representation in accordance with a mere *analogy*.

to which we reflect upon these two things and their causality. This matter has not been sufficiently ana-lysed hitherto, for it deserves a deeper investigation ; but this is not the place to linger over it. Our language [*i.e.* German] is full of indirect presenta-tions of this sort, in which the expression does not contain the proper schema for the concept, but merely a symbol for reflection. Thus the words *ground* (support, basis), *to depend* (to be held up from above), to *flow* from something (instead of, to follow), *substance* (as *Locke* expresses it, the support of accidents), and countless others, are not schematical but symbolical hypotyposes and expressions for con-cepts, not by means of a direct intuition, but only by analogy with it, *i.e.* by the transference of reflec-tion upon an object of intuition to a quite different concept to which perhaps an intuition can never directly correspond. If we are to give the name of cognition to a mere mode of representation (which is quite permissible if the latter is not a principle of the theoretical determination of what an object is in itself, but of the practical determination of what the Idea of it should be for us and for its purposive use), then all our knowledge of God is merely symbolical ; and he who regards it as schematical, along with the properties of Understanding, Will, etc., which only establish their objective reality in beings of this world, falls into Anthropomorphism, just as he who gives up every intuitive element falls into Deism, by which nothing at all is cognised, not even in a practical point of view.

Now I say the Beautiful is the symbol of the morally Good, and that it is only in this respect (a reference which is natural to every man and which every man postulates in others as a duty) that it gives pleasure with a claim for the agreement of every one else. ¶ By this the mind is made conscious of a certain ennoblement and elevation above the mere sensibility to pleasure received through sense, and the worth of others is estimated in accordance with a like maxim of their Judgment. That is the *intelligible*, to which, as pointed out in the preceding paragraph, Taste looks ; with which our higher cognitive faculties are in accord ; and without which a downright contradiction would arise between their nature and the claims made by taste. In this faculty the Judgment does not see itself, as in empirical judging, subjected to a heteronomy of empirical laws ; it gives the law to itself in respect of the objects of so pure a satisfaction, just as the Reason does in respect of the faculty of desire. Hence, both on account of this inner possibility in the subject and of the external possibility of a nature that agrees with it, it finds itself to be referred to something within the subject as well as without him, something which is neither nature nor freedom, but which yet is connected with the supersensible ground of the latter. In this supersensible ground, therefore, the theoretical faculty is bound together in unity with the practical, in a way which though common is yet unknown. We shall indicate some points of this analogy, while at the same time we shall note the differences.

(1) The beautiful pleases *immediately* (but only in reflective intuition, not, like morality, in its concept). (2) It pleases *apart from any interest* (the morally good is indeed necessarily bound up with an interest, though not with one which precedes the judgment upon the satisfaction, but with one which is first of all produced by it). (3) The

freedom of the Imagination (and therefore of the
sensibility of our faculty) is represented in judging
the beautiful as harmonious with the conformity to
law of the Understanding (in the moral judgment
the freedom of the will is thought as the harmony of
the latter with itself according to universal laws of
Reason). (4) The subjective principle in judging
the beautiful is represented as *universal, i.e.* as valid
for every man, though not cognisable through any
universal concept. (The objective principle of morality is also expounded as universal, *i.e.* for every
subject and for every action of the same subject, and
thus as cognisable by means of a universal concept).
Hence the moral judgment is not only susceptible of
definite constitutive principles, but is possible *only* by
grounding its maxims on these in their universality.

A reference to this analogy is usual even with
the common Understanding [of men], and we often
describe beautiful objects of nature or art by names
that seem to put a moral appreciation at their basis.
We call buildings or trees majestic and magnificent,
landscapes laughing and gay ; even colours are
called innocent, modest, tender, because they excite
sensations which have something analogous to the
consciousness of the state of mind brought about
by moral judgments. Taste makes possible the
transition, without any violent leap, from the charm
of Sense to habitual moral interest : as it represents
the Imagination in its freedom as capable of purposive determination for the Understanding, and so
teaches us to find even in objects of sense a free
satisfaction apart from any charm of sense.

APPENDIX

§ 60. *Of the method of Taste*

The division of a Kritik into Elementology and Methodology, as preparatory to science, is not applicable to the Kritik of taste, because there neither is nor can be a science of the Beautiful, and the judgment of taste is not determinable by means of principles. As for the scientific element in every art, which regards *truth* in the presentation of its Object, this is indeed the indispensable condition (*conditio sine qua non*) of beautiful art, but not beautiful art itself. There is therefore for beautiful art only a *manner* (*modus*), not a *method of teaching* (*methodus*). The master must show what the pupil is to do and how he is to do it; and the universal rules, under which at last he brings his procedure, serve rather for bringing the main points back to his remembrance when occasion requires, than for prescribing them to him. Nevertheless regard must be had here to a certain ideal, which art must have before its eyes, although it cannot be completely attained in practice. It is only through exciting the Imagination of the pupil to accordance with a given concept, by making him note the inadequacy of the expression for the Idea, to which the concept itself does not attain because it is an æsthetical Idea, and by severe Kritik, that he can be prevented from taking the examples set before him as types and models for imitation, to be subjected to no higher standard or independent judgment. It is thus that genius, and with it the freedom of the Imagination, is stifled by its very conformity to law ; and without these no beautiful art, and not even an accurately judging individual taste, is possible.

The propaedeutic to all beautiful art, regarded in the highest degree of its perfection, seems to lie, not in precepts, but in the culture of the mental powers by means of those elements of knowledge called *humaniora*, probably because *humanity* on the one side indicates the universal *feeling of sympathy*, and on the other the faculty of being able to *communicate* universally our inmost [feelings]. For these properties taken together constitute the characteristic social spirit [1] of humanity by which it is distinguished from the limitations of animal life. The age and peoples, in which the impulse towards a *law-abiding* social life, by which a people becomes a permanent community, contended with the great difficulties presented by the difficult problem of uniting freedom (and equality) with compulsion (rather of respect and submission from a sense of duty than of fear)—such an age and such a people naturally first found out the art of reciprocal communication of Ideas between the cultivated and uncultivated classes and thus discovered how to harmonise the large-mindedness and refinement of the former with the natural simplicity and originality of the latter. In this way they first found that mean between the higher culture and simple nature which furnishes that true standard for taste as a sense universal to all men which no general rules can supply.

With difficulty will a later age dispense with those models, because it will be always farther

---

[1] [I read *Geselligkeit* with Rosenkranz; Hartenstein and Kirchmann have *Glückseligkeit*.]

from nature ; and in fine, without having permanent
examples before it, a concept will hardly be possible,
in one and the same people, of the happy union of
the law-abiding constraint of the highest culture with
the force and truth of free nature which feels its own
proper worth.

Now taste is at bottom a faculty for judging of
the sensible illustration of moral Ideas (by means
of a certain analogy involved in our reflection upon
both these) ; and it is from this faculty also and
from the greater susceptibility grounded thereon
for the feeling arising from the latter (called moral
feeling), that that pleasure is derived which taste
regards as valid for mankind in general and not
merely for the private feeling of each.   Hence
it appears plain that the true propaedeutic for the
foundation of taste is the development of moral
Ideas and the culture of the moral feeling ; because
it is only when sensibility is brought into agreement
with this that genuine taste can assume a definite
invariable form.

THE KRITIK OF JUDGMENT

PART II

KRITIK OF THE TELEOLOGICAL JUDGMENT

S

We have on transcendental principles good
ground to assume a subjective purposiveness in
nature, in its particular laws, in reference to its
comprehensibility by human Judgment and to the
possibility of the connection of particular experiences
in a system.> This may be expected as possible in
many products of nature, which, as if they were
established quite specially for our Judgment, contain
a specific form conformable thereto, which through
their manifoldness and unity serve at once to
strengthen and to sustain the mental powers (that
come into play in the employment of this faculty),
and to these we therefore give the name of *beautiful*
forms.

But that the things of nature serve one another
as means to purposes, and that their possibility is
only completely intelligible through this kind of
causality—for this we have absolutely no ground in
the universal Idea of nature, as the complex of the
objects of sense. In the above-mentioned case, the
representation of things, because it is something in
ourselves, can be quite well thought *a priori* as
suitable and useful for the internally purposive
determination of our cognitive faculties; but that
purposes, which neither are our own nor belong to
nature (for we do not regard nature as an intelligent

being), could or should constitute a particular kind of causality, at least a quite special conformity to law, —this we have absolutely no *a priori* reason for presuming. Yet more, experience itself cannot prove to us the actuality of this; there must then have preceded a rationalising subtlety which only sportively introduces the concept of purpose into the nature of things, but which does not derive it from Objects or from their empirical cognition. To this latter it is of more service to make nature comprehensible according to analogy with the subjective ground of the connection of our representations, than to cognise it from objective grounds.

Further, objective purposiveness, as a principle of the possibility of things of nature, is so far removed from *necessary* connection with the concept of nature, that it is much oftener precisely that upon which one relies to prove the contingency of nature and of its form. When, *e.g.*, we adduce the structure of a bird, the hollowness of its bones, the disposition of its wings for motion and of its tail for steering, etc., we say that all this is contingent in the highest degree according to the mere *nexus effectivus* of nature, without calling in the aid of a particular kind of causality, namely that of purpose (*nexus finalis*). In other words, nature, considered as mere mechanism, can produce its forms in a thousand different ways without stumbling upon unity in accordance with such a principle. It is not in the concept of nature but quite apart from it that we can hope to find the least ground *a priori* for this.

Nevertheless the teleological act of judgment is rightly brought to bear, at least problematically, upon the investigation of nature; but only in order to bring it under principles of observation and inquiry according to the *analogy* with the causality of purpose, without any pretence to *explain* it thereby. It belongs therefore to the reflective and not to the determinant judgment. The concept of combinations and forms of nature in accordance with purposes is then at least *one principle more* for bringing its phenomena under rules where the laws of simply mechanical causality do not suffice. For we bring in a teleological ground, where we attribute causality in respect of an Object to the concept of an Object, as if it were to be found in nature (not in ourselves); or rather when we represent to ourselves the possibility of the Object after the analogy of that causality which we experience in ourselves, and consequently think nature technically as through a special faculty. If, on the other hand, we did not ascribe to it such a method of action, its causality would have to be represented as blind mechanism. If, on the contrary, we supply to nature causes acting *designedly*, and consequently place at its basis teleology, not merely as a *regulative* principle for the mere *judging* of phenomena, to which nature can be thought as subject in its particular laws, but as a *constitutive* principle of the *derivation* of its products from their causes; then would the concept of a natural purpose no longer belong to the reflective but to the determinant Judgment. Then, in fact, it would not belong specially to the Judgment (like the concept of beauty regarded as formal subjective purposiveness), but as a rational concept it would introduce into a natural science a new causality, which we only borrow from ourselves and ascribe to other beings, without meaning to assume them to be of the same kind with ourselves.

FIRST DIVISION

ANALYTIC OF THE TELEOLOGICAL JUDGMENT

§ 62. *Of the objective purposiveness which is merely formal as distinguished from that which is material*

All geometrical figures drawn on a principle display a manifold, oft admired, objective purposiveness; *i.e.* in reference to their usefulness for the solution of several problems by a single principle, or of the same problem in an infinite variety of ways. The purposiveness is here obviously objective and intellectual, not merely subjective and æsthetical. For it expresses the suitability of the figure for the production of many intended figures, and is cognised through Reason. But this purposiveness does not make the concept of the object itself possible. *i.e.* it is not regarded as possible merely with reference to this use.

In so simple a figure as the circle lies the key to the solution of a multitude of problems, each of which would demand various appliances; whereas their solution results of itself, as it were, as one of the infinite number of excellent properties of this figure. Are we, for example, asked to construct a triangle, being given the base and vertical angle? The problem is indeterminate, *i.e.* it can be solved in an infinite number of ways. But the circle embraces them all together as the geometrical locus

of the vertices of triangles satisfying the given
conditions. Again, suppose that two lines are to
cut one another so that the rectangle under the
segments of the one should be equal to the rectangle under the segments of the other ; the solution
of the problem from this point of view presents
much difficulty. But all chords intersecting inside
a circle divide one another in this *proportion*. Other
curved lines suggest other purposive solutions of
which nothing was thought in the rule that furnished
their construction. All conic sections in themselves
and when compared with one another are fruitful
in principles for the solution of a number of possible
problems, however simple is the definition which
determines their concept.— It is a true joy to see
the zeal with which the old geometers investigated
the properties of lines of this class, without allowing
themselves to be led astray by the questions of nar-
row-minded persons, as to what use this knowledge
would be. Thus they worked out the properties of
the parabola without knowing the law of gravitation,
which would have suggested to them its application
to the trajectory of heavy bodies (for the motion of
a heavy body can be seen to be parallel to the curve
of a parabola). Again, they found out the properties
of an ellipse without surmising that any of the
heavenly bodies had weight, and without knowing
the law of force at different distances from the point
of attraction, which causes it to describe this curve
in free motion. While they thus unconsciously
worked for the science of the future, they delighted
themselves with a purposiveness in the [essential]
being of things which yet they were able to present
completely *a priori* in its necessity. *Plato*, himself
master of this science, hinted at such an original

constitution of things in the discovery of which we
can dispense with all experience, and at the power
of the mind to produce from its supersensible principle the harmony of beings (where the properties
of number come in, with which the mind plays in
music). This [he touches upon] in the inspiration
that raised him above the concepts of experience to
Ideas, which seem to him to be explicable only
through an intellectual affinity with the origin of all
beings. No wonder that he banished from his
school the man who was ignorant of geometry, since
he thought he could derive from pure intuition,
which has its home in the human spirit, that which
Anaxagoras drew from empirical objects and their
purposive combination. For in the very necessity
of that which is purposive, and is constituted just as
if it were designedly intended for our use,—but at
the same time seems to belong originally to the
being of things without any reference to our use—
lies the ground of our great admiration of nature,
and that not so much external as in our own Reason.
It is surely excusable that this admiration should
through misunderstanding gradually rise to the
height of fanaticism.

But this intellectual purposiveness, although no
doubt objective (not subjective like æsthetical
purposiveness), is in reference to its possibility
merely formal (not real). It can only be conceived
as purposiveness in general without any [definite]
purpose being assumed as its basis, and consequently
without teleology being needed for it. The figure of
a circle is an intuition which is determined by means
of the Understanding according to a principle.
The unity of this principle which I arbitrarily
assume and use as fundamental concept, applied to

a form of intuition (space) which is met with in myself as a representation and yet *a priori*, renders intelligible the unity of many rules resulting from the construction of that concept, which are purposive for many possible designs.   But this purposiveness does not imply a *purpose* or any other ground whatever.   It is quite different if I meet with order and regularity in complexes of *things*, external to myself, enclosed within certain boundaries ; as, *e.g.*, in a garden, the order and regularity of the trees, flower-beds, and walks.   These I cannot expect to derive *a priori* from my bounding of space made after a rule of my own ; for this order and regularity are existing things which must be given empirically in order to be known, and not a mere representation in myself determined *a priori* according to a principle.   So then the latter (empirical) purposiveness, as *real*, is dependent on the concept of a purpose.

But the ground of admiration for a perceived purposiveness, although it be in the being of things (so far as their concepts can be constructed), may be very well involved and apprehended as rightful. The manifold rules whose unity (derived from a principle) excites admiration, are all synthetical and do not follow from the *concept* of the Object as in the case of the circle ; but require this Object to be given in intuition.   Hence this unity gets the appearance of having empirically an external basis of rules distinct from our representative faculty ; as if therefore the correspondence of the Object to that need of rules which is proper to the Understanding were contingent in itself, and therefore only possible by means of a purpose expressly directed thereto. Now because this harmony, notwithstanding all this purposiveness, is not cognised empirically but *a*

and that not only on account of the union being just of the kind that it is, but because it is enlarging for the mind to surmise the existence of something lying outside our sensible representations in which, although unknown to us, the ultimate ground of that agreement may be met with. We are, it is true, not necessitated to cognise this if we have only to do with the formal purposiveness of our representations; but the fact that we are compelled to look out beyond it inspires at the same time an admiration for the object that impels us thereto.

We are accustomed to speak of the above-mentioned properties of geometrical figures or of numbers as *beautiful*, on account of a certain *a priori* purposiveness they have for all kinds of cognitive uses, this purposiveness being quite unexpected on account of the simplicity of the construction. We speak *e.g.* of this or that *beautiful* property of the circle, which was discovered in this or that way. But there is no aesthetical act of judgement through which we find it purposive, no act of judgement without a concept which renders noticeable a mere *subjective* purposiveness in the free play of our cognitive faculties; but an intellectual act according to concepts which enables us clearly to cognise an objective purposiveness, *i.e.* availableness for all kinds of (infinitely manifold) purposes. We must rather call this *relative perfection* than a beauty of the mathematical figure. To speak thus of an *intellectual beauty* cannot in general be permitted; for otherwise the word beauty would lose all determinate significance, or the intellectual satisfaction all superiority over the sensible. We should rather call a *demonstration* of such properties beautiful

because through it the Understanding as the faculty
of concepts, and the Imagination as the faculty of
presenting them, feel themselves strengthened *a
priori.* (This, when viewed in connection with the
precision introduced by Reason, is spoken of as
elegant.) Here, however, the satisfaction, although
it is based on concepts, is subjective ; while perfection brings with itself an objective satisfaction.

§ 63. *Of the relative as distinguished from the inner purposiveness of nature*

Experience leads our Judgment to the concept of
an objective and material purposiveness, *i.e.* to the
concept of a purpose of nature, only when [1] we have
to judge of a relation of cause to effect which we
find ourselves able to apprehend as legitimate only
by presupposing the Idea of the effect of the
causality of the cause as the fundamental condition, in the cause, of the possibility of the effect.
This can take place in two ways. We may regard
the effect directly as an art product, or only as
material for the art of other possible natural beings ;
in other words, either as a purpose or as a means
towards the purposive employment of other causes.
This latter purposiveness is called utility (for man)
or mere advantage (for other creatures), and is
merely relative ; while the former is an inner purposiveness of the natural being.

For example, rivers bring down with them all
kinds of earth serviceable for the growth of plants

---

[1] As in pure mathematic we can never talk of the existence, but
only of the possibility of things, viz. of an intuition corresponding to
a concept, and so never of cause and effect, it follows that all
purposiveness observed there must be considered merely as formal
and never as a natural purpose.

which sometimes is deposited inland, often also at their mouths. The tide brings this mud to many coasts over the land or deposits it on the shore ; and so, more especially if men give their aid so that the ebb shall not carry it back again, the fruit-bearing land increases in area, and the vegetable kingdom gains the place which formerly was the habitation of fish and shells. In this way has nature itself brought about most of the extensions of the land, and still continues to do so, although very slowly.— Now the question is whether this is to be judged a purpose of nature, because it contains profit for men. We cannot put it down to the account of the vegetable kingdom, because just as much is subtracted from sea-life as is added to land-life.

Or, to give an example of the advantageousness of certain natural things as means for other creatures (if we suppose them to be means), no soil is more suitable to pine trees than a sandy soil. Now the deep sea, before it withdrew from the land, left behind large tracts of sand in our northern regions, so that on this soil, so unfavourable for all cultivation, widely extended pine forests were enabled to grow, for the unreasoning destruction of which we frequently blame our ancestors. We may ask if this original deposit of tracts of sand was a purpose of nature for the benefit of the possible pine forests ? So much is clear, that if we regard this as a purpose of nature, we must also regard the sand as a relative purpose, in reference to which the ocean strand and its withdrawal were means : for in the series of the mutually subordinated members of a purposive combination, every member must be regarded as a purpose (though not as a final purpose), to which its proximate cause is the means.

So too if cattle, sheep, horses, etc., are to exist, there must be grass on the earth, but there must also be saline plants in the desert if camels are to thrive; and again these and other herbivorous animals must be met with in numbers if there are to be wolves, tigers, and lions. Consequently the objective purposiveness, which is based upon advantage, is not an objective purposiveness of things in themselves; as if the sand could not be conceived for itself as an effect of a cause, viz. the sea, without attributing to the latter a purpose, and regarding the effect, namely the sand, as a work of art. It is a merely relative purposiveness contingent upon the thing to which it is ascribed; and although in the examples we have cited, the different kinds of grass are to be judged as in themselves organised products of nature, and consequently as artificial, yet are they to be regarded, in reference to the beasts which feed upon them, as mere raw material.

But above all, though man, through the freedom of his causality, finds certain natural things of advantage for his designs—designs often foolish, such as using the variegated plumage of birds to adorn his clothes, or coloured earths and the juices of plants for painting his face; often again reasonable as when the horse is used for riding, the ox or (as in Minorca) the ass or pig for ploughing—yet we cannot even here assume a relative natural purpose. For his Reason knows how to give things a conformity with his own arbitrary fancies for which he was not at all predestined by nature. Only, *if* we assume that men are to live upon the earth, then the means must be there without which they could not exist as animals, and even as rational animals (in however low a degree of rationality) ; and thereupon those natural things, which are indispensable in this regard, must be considered as natural purposes.

We can hence easily see that external purposiveness (advantage of one thing in respect of others) can be regarded as an external natural purpose only under the condition, that the existence of that [being], to which it is immediately or distantly advantageous, is in itself a purpose of nature. Since that can never be completely determined by mere contemplation of nature, it follows that relative purposiveness, although it hypothetically gives indications of natural purposes, yet justifies no absolute teleological judgment.

Snow in cold countries protects the crops from the frost ; it makes human intercourse easier (by means of sleighs). The Laplander finds in his country animals by whose aid this intercourse is brought about, *i.c.* reindeer, who find sufficient sustenance in a dry moss which they have to scratch out for themselves from under the snow, and who are easily tamed and readily permit themselves to be deprived of that freedom in which they could have remained if they chose. For other people in the same frozen regions marine animals afford rich stores ; in addition to the food and clothing which are thus supplied, and the wood which is floated in by the sea to their dwellings, these marine animals provide material for fuel by which their huts are warmed. Here is a wonderful concurrence of many references of nature to one purpose ; and all this applies to the cases of the Greenlander, the Lapp, the Samoyede, the inhabitant of Yakutsk, etc. But then we do not see why, generally, men must live there at all. Therefore to say that vapour falls out of the atmosphere in the form of snow, that the sea has its currents which float down wood that has grown in warmer lands, and that there are in it great sea monsters filled with oil, *because* the idea of advantage for certain poor creatures is fundamental for the cause which collects all these natural products, would be a very venturesome and arbitrary judgment. For even if there were none of this natural utility, we should miss nothing as regards the adequateness of natural causes to [man's] constitution; much more even to desire such a tendency in, and to attribute such a purpose to, nature would be the part of a presumptuous and inconsiderate fancy. For indeed it might be observed that it could only have been the greatest want of harmony among men which thus scattered them into such inhospitable regions.

§ 64. *Of the peculiar character of things as natural purposes*

In order to see that a thing is only possible as a purpose, that is to be forced to seek the causality of its origin not in the mechanism of nature but in a cause whose faculty of action is determined through concepts, it is requisite that its form be not possible according to mere natural laws, *i.e.* laws which can be cognised by us through the Understanding alone when applied to objects of Sense; but that even the empirical knowledge of it as regards its cause and effect presupposes concepts of Reason. This *contingency* of its form in all empirical natural laws in reference to Reason affords a ground for regarding its causality as possible only through Reason. For Reason, which must cognise the necessity of every form of a natural product in order to comprehend even the conditions of its genesis, cannot assume such [natural] necessity in that particular given form. The causality of its origin is then referred to the faculty of acting in accordance with purposes (a will); and the Object which can only thus be represented as possible is represented as a purpose.

If in a seemingly uninhabited country a man perceived a geometrical figure, say a regular hexagon, inscribed on the sand, his reflection busied with such a concept would attribute, although obscurely, the unity in the principle of its genesis to Reason, and consequently would not regard as a ground of the possibility of such a shape the sand, or the neighbouring sea, or the winds, or beasts with familiar footprints, or any other irrational cause. For the chance against meeting with such a concept, which is only possible through Reason, would seem so infinitely great, that it would be just as if there were no natural law, no cause in the mere mechanical working of nature capable of producing it; but as if only the concept of such an Object, as a concept which Reason alone can supply and with which it can compare the thing, could contain the causality for such an effect. This then would be regarded as a purpose, but as a product of *art*, not as a natural purpose (*vestigium hominis video*).[1]

But in order to regard a thing cognised as a natural product as a purpose also—consequently as a *natural purpose*, if this is not a contradiction—something more is required. I would say provisionally:

[1 The allusion is to Vitruvius *de Architectura*, Bk. vi. Praef. "Aristippus philosophus Socraticus, naufragio cum ejectus ad Rhodiensium litus animadvertisset geometrica schemata descripta, exclamavisse ad comites ita dicitur, Bene speremus, hominum enim vestigia video."]

a thing exists as a natural purpose, if it is [although in a double sense]¹ both *cause and effect of itself*. For herein lies a causality the like of which cannot be combined with the mere concept of a nature without attributing to it a purpose; it can certainly be thought without contradiction, but cannot be comprehended. We shall elucidate the determination of this Idea of a natural purpose by an example, before we analyse it completely.

In the first place, a tree generates another tree according to a known natural law. But the tree produced is of the same genus; and so it produces itself *generically*. On the one hand, as effect it is continually self-produced; on the other hand, as cause it continually produces itself, and so perpetuates itself generically.

Secondly, a tree produces itself as an *individual*. This kind of effect no doubt we call growth; but it is quite different from any increase according to mechanical laws, and is to be reckoned as generation, though under another name. The matter that the tree incorporates it previously works up into a specifically peculiar quality, which natural mechanism external to it cannot supply; and thus it develops itself by aid of a material which, as compounded, is its own product. No doubt, as regards the constituents got from nature without, it must only be regarded as an educt; but yet in the separation and recombination of this raw material we see such an originality in the separating and formative faculty of this kind of natural being, as is infinitely beyond the reach of art, if the attempt is made to reconstruct such vegetable products out of elements obtained by their dissection or material supplied by nature for their sustenance.

¹ [Second Edition.]

Thirdly, each part of a tree generates itself in such a way that the maintenance of any one part depends reciprocally on the maintenance of the rest. A bud of one tree engrafted on the twig of another produces in the alien stock a plant of its own kind, and so also a scion engrafted on a foreign stem. Hence we may regard each twig or leaf of the same tree as merely engrafted or inoculated into it, and so as an independent tree attached to another and parasitically nourished by it. At the same time, while the leaves are products of the tree they also in turn give support to it; for the repeated defoliation of a tree kills it, and its growth thus depends on the action of the leaves upon the stem. The self-help of nature in case of injury in the vegetable creation, when the want of a part that is necessary for the maintenance of its neighbours is supplied by the remaining parts; and the abortions or mal-formations in growth, in which certain parts, on account of casual defects or hindrances, form themselves in a new way to maintain what exists, and so produce an anomalous creature, I shall only mention in passing, though they are among the most wonderful properties of organised creatures.

§ 65. *Things regarded as natural purposes are organised beings*

According to the character alleged in the preceding section, a thing, which, though a natural product, is to be cognised as only possible as a natural purpose, must bear itself alternately as cause and as effect. This, however, is a somewhat inexact and indeterminate expression which needs derivation from a determinate concept.

Causal combination as thought merely by the Understanding is a connection constituting an ever-progressive series (of causes and effects) ; and things which as effects presuppose others as causes cannot be reciprocally at the same time causes of these. This sort of causal combination we call that of effective causes (*nexus effectivus*). But on the other hand, a causal combination according to a concept of Reason (of purposes) can also be thought, which regarded as a series would lead either forwards or backwards : in this the thing that has been called the effect may with equal propriety be termed the cause of that of which it is the effect. In the practical department of human art we easily find connections such as this ; *e.g.* a house, no doubt, is the cause of the money received for rent, but also conversely the representation of this possible income was the cause of building the house. Such a causal connection we call that of final causes (*nexus finalis*). We may perhaps suitably name the first the connection of real causes, the second of those which are ideal ; because from this nomenclature it is at once comprehended that there can be no more than these two kinds of causality.

For a thing to be a natural purpose in the *first* place it is requisite that its parts (as regards their presence and their form) are only possible through their reference to the whole. For the thing itself is a purpose and so is comprehended under a concept or an Idea which must determine *a priori* all that is to be contained in it. But so far as a thing is only thought as possible in this way, it is a mere work of art ; *i.e.* a product of one rational cause distinct from the matter (of the parts), whose causality (in the collection and combination of the

parts) is determined through its Idea of a whole
possible by their means (and consequently not
through external nature).

But if a thing as a natural product is to involve
in itself and in its internal possibility a reference to
purposes,—*i.e.* to be possible only as a natural purpose, and without the causality of the concepts of
rational beings external to itself,—then it is requisite
secondly that its parts should so combine in the unity
of a whole that they are reciprocally cause and effect
of each other's form. Only in this way can the Idea
of the whole conversely (reciprocally) determine the
form and combination of all the parts ; not indeed as
cause—for then it would be an artificial product—
but as the ground of cognition, for him who is
judging it, of the systematic unity and combination
of all the manifold contained in the given material.

For a body then which is to be judged in itself
and its internal possibility as a natural purpose, it
is requisite that its parts mutually depend upon each
other both as to their form and their combination,
and so produce a whole by their own causality ;
while conversely the concept of the whole may be
regarded as its cause according to a principle (in a
being possessing a causality according to concepts
adequate to such a product). In this case then the
connection of *effective causes* may be judged as an
effect through final causes.

In such a product of nature every part not only
exists *by means of* the other parts, but is thought as
existing *for the sake of* the others and the whole,
that is as an (organic) instrument. Thus, however,
it might be an artificial instrument, and so might be
represented only as a purpose that is possible in
general ; but also its parts are all organs reciprocally

producing each other. This can never be the case with artificial instruments, but only with nature which supplies all the material for instruments (even for those of art). Only a product of such a kind can be called a *natural purpose*, and this because it is an *organised* and *self-organising being*.

In a watch one part is the instrument for moving the other parts, but the wheel is not the effective cause of the production of the others; no doubt one part is for the sake of the others, but it does not exist by their means. In this case the producing cause of the parts and of their form is not contained in the nature (of the material), but is external to it in a being which can produce effects according to Ideas of a whole possible by means of its causality. Hence a watch wheel does not produce other wheels, still less does one watch produce other watches, utilising (organising) foreign material for that purpose; hence it does not replace of itself parts of which it has been deprived, nor does it make good what is lacking in a first formation by the addition of the missing parts, nor if it has gone out of order does it repair itself— all of which, on the contrary, we may expect from organised nature.—An organised being is then not a mere machine, for that has merely *moving* power, but it possesses in itself *formative* power of a self-propagating kind which it communicates to its materials though they have it not of themselves; it organises them, in fact, and this cannot be explained by the mere mechanical faculty of motion.

We say of nature and its faculty in organised products far too little if we describe it as an *analogon of art*; for this suggests an artificer (a rational being) external to it. Much rather does it organise itself and its organised products in every species, no doubt

after one general pattern but yet with suitable deviations, which self-preservation demands according to
circumstances. We perhaps approach nearer to this
inscrutable property, if we describe it as an *analogon
of life*; but then we must either endow matter, as
mere matter, with a property which contradicts
its very being (hylozoism), or associate therewith an
alien principle *standing in communion* with it (a
soul). But in the latter case we must, if such a
product is to be a natural product, either presuppose
organised matter as the instrument of that soul,
which does not make the soul a whit more comprehensible; or regard the soul as artificer of this
structure and so remove the product from (corporeal)
nature. To speak strictly, then, the organisation of
nature has in it nothing analogous to any causality
we know.[1] Beauty in nature can be rightly described
as an analogon of art, because it is ascribed to objects
only in reference to reflection upon their *external*
aspect, and consequently only on account of the
form of their external surface. But *internal natural
perfection*, as it belongs to those things which are
only possible as *natural purposes*, and are therefore
called organised beings, is not analogous to any
physical, *i.e.* natural, faculty known to us; nay even,
regarding ourselves as, in the widest sense, belong-

---

[1] We can conversely throw light upon a certain combination,
much more often met with in Idea than in actuality, by means of an
analogy to the so-called immediate natural purposes. In a recent
complete transformation. of a great people into a state the word
organisation for the regulation of magistracies, etc., and even of the
whole body politic, has often been fitly used. For in such a whole
every member should surely be purpose as well as means, and, whilst
all work together towards the possibility of the whole, each should
be determined as regards place and function by means of the Idea
of the whole. [Kant probably alludes here to the organisation of
the United States of America.]

ing to nature, it is not even thinkable or explicable by means of any exactly fitting analogy to human art.

The concept of a thing as in itself a natural purpose is therefore no constitutive concept of Understanding or of Reason, but it can serve as a regulative concept for the reflective Judgment, to guide our investigation about objects of this kind by a distant analogy with our own causality according to purposes generally, and in our meditations upon their ultimate ground. This latter use, however, is not in reference to the knowledge of nature or of its original ground, but rather to our own practical faculty of Reason, in analogy with which we considered the cause of that purposiveness.

Organised beings are then the only beings in nature which, considered in themselves and apart from any relation to other things, can be thought as possible only as purposes of nature. Hence they first afford objective reality to the concept of a *purpose of nature*, as distinguished from a practical purpose ; and so they give to the science of nature the basis for a teleology, *i.e.* a mode of judgment about natural Objects according to a special principle which otherwise we should in no way be justified in introducing (because we cannot see *a priori* the possibility of this kind of causality).

§ 66. *Of the principle of judging of internal purposiveness in organised beings*

This principle, which is at the same time a definition, is as follows : *An organised product of nature is one in which every part is reciprocally purpose* [end] *and means.* In it nothing is vain, with-

out purpose, or to be ascribed to a blind mechanism
of nature.

The principle is no doubt, as regards its occasion,
derived from experience, viz. from that methodised
experience called observation ; but on account of
the universality and necessity which it ascribes to
such purposiveness it cannot rest solely on empirical
grounds, but must have at its basis an *a priori*
principle, although it be merely regulative and
these purposes lie only in the idea of the judging
[subject] and not in an effective cause. We may
therefore describe the aforesaid principle as a *maxim*
for judging of the internal purposiveness of organised
beings.

It is an acknowledged fact that the dissectors
of plants and animals, in order to investigate their
structure and to find out the reasons, why and for
what end such parts, such a disposition and combination of parts, and just such an internal form
have been given them, assume as indisputably necessary the maxim that nothing in such a creature is
vain ; just as they lay down as the fundamental
proposition of the universal science of nature, that
nothing happens *by chance*. In fact, they can as little
free themselves from this teleological proposition
as from the universal physical proposition ; for as
without the latter we should have no experience
at all, so without the former we should have no
guiding thread for the observation of a species
of natural things which we have conceived teleologically under the concept of natural purposes.

Now this concept brings the Reason into a
quite different order of things from that of a mere
mechanism of nature, which is no longer satisfying
here. An Idea is to be the ground of the possibility

of the natural product. But because this is an absolute unity of representation, instead of the material being a plurality of things that can supply by itself no definite unity of composition,—if that unity of the Idea is to serve at all as the *a priori* ground of determination of a natural law of the causality of such a form of composition,—the purpose of nature must be extended to *everything* included in its product. For if we once refer action of this sort *on the whole* to any supersensible ground of determination beyond the blind mechanism of nature, we must judge of it altogether according to this principle; and we have then no reason to regard the form of such a thing as partly dependent on mechanism—for by such mixing up of disparate principles no certain rule of judging would be left.

For example, it may be that in an animal body many parts can be conceived as concretions according to mere mechanical laws (as the hide, the bones, the hair). And yet the cause which brings together the required matter, modifies it, forms it, and puts it in its appropriate place, must always be judged of teleologically; so that here everything must be considered as organised, and everything again in a certain relation to the thing itself is an organ.

§ 67. *Of the principle of the teleological judging of nature in general as a system of purposes*

We have already said above that the *external* purposiveness of natural things affords no sufficient warrant for using them as purposes of nature in order to explain their presence, and for regarding their contingently purposive effects as the grounds of their presence according to the principle of final causes.   Thus we cannot take for natural purposes, *rivers* because they promote intercourse among inland peoples, *mountains* because they contain the sources of the rivers and for their *maintenance* in rainless seasons have a store of snow, or the *slope* of the land which carries away the water and leaves the country dry ; because although this shape of the earth's surface be very necessary for the origin and maintenance of the vegetable and animal kingdoms, it has nothing in itself for the possibility of which we are forced to assume a causality according to purposes.   The same is true of plants which man uses for his needs or his pleasures ; of beasts, the camel, the ox, the horse, dog, etc., which are indispensable for him as well for food as because they are used in his service in many different ways.   In the case of things which we have no reason for regarding in themselves as purposes, such external relation can only be hypothetically judged as purposive.

To judge of a thing as a natural purpose on account of its internal form is something very different from taking the existence of that thing to be a purpose of nature.   For the latter assertion we require not merely the concept of a possible purpose, but the knowledge of the final purpose (*scopus*) of nature.   But this requires a reference of such knowledge to something supersensible far transcending all our teleological knowledge of nature, for the purpose of [the existence of][1] nature must itself be sought beyond nature.   The internal form of a mere blade of grass is sufficient to show that for our human faculty of judgment its origin is

[1] [These words are inserted by Rosenkranz, but omitted by Hartenstein and Kirchmann.]

possible only according to the rule of purposes.
But if we change our point of view and look to the
use which other natural beings make of it, abandon
the consideration of its internal organisation and
only look to its externally purposive references, we
shall arrive at no categorical purpose ; all this purposive reference rests on an ever more distant condition, which, as unconditioned (the presence of a
thing as final purpose), lies quite outside the physico-
teleological view of the world.   For example, grass
is needful for the ox, which again is needful for man
as a means of existence, but then we do not see why
it is necessary that men should exist (a question
this, which we shall not find so easy to answer if we
sometimes cast our thoughts on the New Hollanders
or the inhabitants of Tierra del Fuego).   So conceived, the thing is not even a natural purpose, for
neither it (nor its whole genus) is to be regarded as
a natural product.

Hence it is only so far as matter is organised
that it necessarily carries with it the concept of a
natural purpose, because this its specific form is at
the same time a product of nature.   But this concept leads necessarily to the Idea of collective
nature as a system in accordance with the rule of
purposes, to which Idea all the mechanism of nature
must be subordinated according to principles of
Reason (at least in order to investigate natural
phenomena in it).   The principle of Reason belongs
to it only as a subjective principle or a maxim : viz.
everything in the world is some way good for something ; nothing is vain in it.   By the example that
nature gives us in its organic products we are justified, nay called upon, to expect of it and of its laws
nothing that is not purposive on the whole.

It is plain that this is not a principle for the determinant but only for the reflective judgment; that it is regulative and not constitutive; and that we derive from it a clue by which we consider natural things in reference to an already given ground of determination according to a new law-abiding order; and extend our natural science according to a different principle, viz. that of final causes, but yet without prejudice to the principle of mechanical causality. Furthermore, it is in no wise thus decided, whether anything of which we judge by this principle, is a *designed* purpose of nature; whether the grass is for the ox or the sheep, or whether these and the other things of nature are here for men. It is well also from this side to consider the things which are unpleasant to us and are contrary to purpose in particular references. Thus, for example, we can say : The vermin that torment men in their clothes, their hair, or their beds, may be, according to a wise appointment of nature, a motive to cleanliness which is in itself an important means for the preservation of health. Or again the mosquitoes and other stinging insects that make the wildernesses of America so oppressive to the savages, may be so many goads to activity for these primitive men, [inducing them] to drain the marshes and bring light into the forests which intercept every breath of air, and in this way, as well as by cultivating the soil, to make their habitations more healthy. The same thing, which appears to men contradictory to nature in its inner organisation, if viewed in this light gives an entertaining, sometimes an instructive, outlook into a teleological order of things, to which, without such a principle, mere physical observation would not lead us by itself. Thus some persons regard the tapeworm as given to the men or animals in whom it resides, as a kind of set-off for some defect in their vital organs ; now I would ask if dreams (without which we never sleep, though we seldom remember them) may not be a purposive ordinance of nature ? For during the relaxation of all the moving powers of the body, they serve to inwardly excite the vital organs by the medium of the Imagination and its great activity (which in this state generally rises to the height of affection). During sleep the Imagination commonly is more actively at play when the stomach is overloaded, in which case this excitement is the more necessary. Consequently, then, without this internal power of motion and this fatiguing unrest, on account of which we complain about our dreams (though in fact they are rather remedies), sleep even in a sound state of health would be a complete extinction of life.

Also the beauty of nature, *i.e.* its connection with the free play of our cognitive faculties in apprehending and judging of its appearance, can be regarded as a kind of objective purposiveness of nature in its whole [content] as a system of which man is a member ; if once the teleological judging of the same by means of the natural purposes with which organised beings furnish us, has justified for us the Idea of a great system of purposes of nature. We can regard it as a favour [1] which nature has felt

---

[1] In the æsthetical part [§ 58, p. 247] it was said : *We view beautiful nature with favour*, whilst we have a quite free (disinterested) satisfaction in its form. For in this mere judgment of taste no consideration is given to the purpose for which these natural beauties exist ; whether to excite pleasure in us, or as purposes without any reference to us at all. But in a teleological judgment we pay attention to this reference, and here we can *regard it as a favour of nature* that it has been willing to minister to our culture by the exhibition of so many beautiful figures.

for us, that in addition to what is useful it has so profusely dispensed beauty and charm ; and we can therefore love it, as well as regard it with respect on account of its immensity, and feel ennobled ourselves by such regard ; just as if nature had established and adorned its splendid theatre precisely with this view.

We shall say only one thing more in this paragraph. If we have once discovered in nature a faculty of bringing forth products that can only be thought by us in accordance with the concept of final causes, we go further still. We venture to judge that things belong to a system of purposes, which yet do not (either in themselves or in their purposive relations) necessitate our seeking for any principle of their possibility beyond the mechanism of causes working blindly. For the first Idea, as concerns its ground, already brings us beyond the world of sense ; since the unity of the supersensible principle must be regarded as valid in this way not merely for certain species of natural beings, but for the whole of nature as a system.

§ 68. *Of the principle of Teleology as internal principle of natural science*

The principles of a science are either internal to it and are then called domestic (*principia domestica*), or are based on concepts that can only find their place outside it and so are *foreign* principles (*peregrina*). Sciences that contain the latter, place at the basis of their doctrines auxiliary propositions (*lemmata*), *i.e.* they borrow some concept, and with it a ground of arrangement, from another science.

Every science is in itself a system, and it is not

enough in it to build in accordance with principles
and thus to employ a technical procedure, but we
must go to work with it architectonically, as a
building subsisting for itself; we must not treat it as
an additional wing or part of another building, but as
a whole in itself, although we may subsequently
make a passage from it into that other or conversely.

If then we introduce into the context of natural
science the concept of God in order to explain the
purposiveness in nature, and subsequently use this
purposiveness to prove that there is a God, there is
no internal consistency in either science [*i.e.* either
in natural science or theology]; and a delusive
circle brings them both into uncertainty, because
they have allowed their boundaries to overlap.

The expression, a purpose of nature, already
sufficiently prevents the confusion of mixing up
natural science and the occasion that it gives for
judging *teleologically* of its objects, with the consideration of God, and so of a *theological* derivation
of them. We must not regard it as insignificant,
if one interchanges this expression with that of a
divine purpose in the ordering of nature, or gives
out the latter as more suitable and proper for a
pious soul, because it must come in the end to
deriving these purposive forms in nature from a
wise author of the world. On the contrary, we
must carefully and modestly limit ourselves to the
expression, a purpose of nature, which asserts exactly
as much as we know. Before we ask after the cause
of nature itself, we find in nature, and in the course
of its development, products of the same kind which
are developed in it according to known empirical
laws, in accordance with which natural science must
judge of its objects, and, consequently, must seek

in nature their causality according to the rule of purposes. So then it must not transgress its bounds in order to introduce into itself as a domestic principle that, to whose concept no experience can be commensurate, upon which we are only entitled to venture after the completion of natural science.

Natural characteristics which demonstrate themselves *a priori*, and consequently admit of insight into their possibility from universal principles without any admixture ·of experience, although they carry with them a technical purposiveness, yet cannot, because they are absolutely necessary, be referred to the Teleology of nature, as to a method belonging to Physic for solving its problems. Arithmetical or geometrical analogies, as well as universal mechanical laws,—however strange and admirable may seem to us the union of different rules, quite independent of one another according to all appearance, in a single principle,—possess on that account no claim to be teleological grounds of explanation in Physic. Even if they deserve to be brought into consideration in the universal theory of the purposiveness of things of nature, yet they belong to another [science], *i.e.* Metaphysic, and constitute no internal principle of natural science ; as with the empirical laws of natural purposes in organised beings, it is not only permissible but unavoidable to use the teleological *mode of judging* as a principle of the doctrine of nature in regard to a particular class of its objects.

So to the end that Physic may keep within its own bounds, it abstracts itself entirely from the question, whether natural purposes are *designed* or *undesigned* ; for that would be to meddle in an extraneous business, in Metaphysic. It is enough that there are objects, alone *explicable* according

U

to natural laws which we can only think by means of the Idea of purposes as principle, and also alone internally *cognisable* as concerns their internal form, in this way. In order, therefore, to remove the suspicion of the slightest assumption,—as if we wished to mix with our grounds of cognition something not belonging to Physic at all, viz. a supernatural cause,—we speak, indeed, in Teleology of nature as if the purposiveness in it were designed, but in such a way that this design is ascribed to nature, *i.e.* to matter. Now in this way there can be no misunderstanding, because no design in the proper meaning of the word can possibly be ascribed to inanimate matter; we thus give notice that this word here only expresses a principle of the reflective not of the determinant Judgment, and so is to introduce no particular ground of causality; but only adds for the use of the Reason a different kind of investigation from that according to mechanical laws, in order to supplement the inadequacy of the latter even for empirical research into all particular laws of nature. Hence we speak quite correctly in Teleology, so far as it is referred , to Physic, of the wisdom, the economy, the forethought, the beneficence of Nature, without either making an intelligent being of it, for that would be preposterous; or even without presuming to place another intelligent Being above it as its Architect, for that would be presumptuous.[1]   But there should

---

[1] The German word *vermessen* is a good word and full of meaning. A judgment in which we forget to consider the extent of our powers (our Understanding) may sometimes sound very humble, and yet make great pretensions, and so be very presumptuous. Of this kind are most of those by which we pretend to extol the divine wisdom by ascribing to it designs in the works of creation and preservation which are really meant to do honour to the private wisdom of the reasoner.

be only signified thereby a kind of causality of nature after the analogy of our own in the technical use of Reason, in order to have before us the rule according to which certain products of nature must be investigated.

But now why is it that Teleology usually forms no proper part of theoretical natural science, but is regarded as a propædeutic or transition to Theology? This is done in order to restrict the study of nature mechanically considered to that which we can so subject to observation or experiment that we are able to produce it ourselves as nature does, or at least by similar laws. For we see into a thing completely only so far as we can make it in accordance with our concepts and bring it to completion. But organisation, as an inner purpose of nature, infinitely surpasses all our faculty of presenting the like by means of art. And as concerns the external contrivances of nature regarded as purposive (wind, rain, etc.), Physic, indeed, considers their mechanism, but it cannot at all present their reference to purposes, so far as this is a condition necessarily belonging to cause; for this necessity of connection has to do altogether with the combination of our concepts and not with the constitution of things.

SECOND DIVISION

DIALECTIC OF THE TELEOLOGICAL JUDGMENT

§ 69. *What is an antinomy of the Judgment?*

The *determinant* Judgment has for itself no principles which are the foundation of *concepts of Objects*. It has no autonomy, for it *subsumes* only under given laws or concepts as principles. Hence it is exposed to no danger of an antinomy of its own or to a conflict of its principles. So [we saw that] the transcendental Judgment which contains the conditions of subsuming under categories was for itself not *nomothetic*, but that it only indicated the conditions of sensuous intuition, under which reality (application) can be supplied to a given concept, as law of the Understanding, whereby the Judgment could never fall into discord with itself (at least as far as its principles are concerned). •

But the *reflective* Judgment must subsume under a law, which is not yet given, and is therefore in fact only a principle of reflection upon objects, for which we are objectively quite in want of a law or of a concept of an Object that would be adequate as a principle for the cases that occur. Since now no use of the cognitive faculties can be permitted without principles, the reflective Judgment must in such cases serve as a principle for itself. This, because it is not objective and can supply no ground of cognition of the Object adequate for design, must serve as a mere subjective principle, for the purposive employment of our cognitive faculties, *i.e.* for reflecting upon a class of objects. Therefore in reference to such cases the reflective Judgment has its maxims—necessary maxims—on behalf of the cognition of natural laws in experience, in order to attain by their means to concepts, even concepts of Reason ; since it has absolute need of such in order to learn merely to cognise nature according to its empirical laws.— Between these necessary maxims of the reflective Judgment there may be a conflict and consequently an antinomy, upon which a Dialectic bases itself. If each of two conflicting maxims has its ground in the nature of the cognitive faculties, this may be called a natural Dialectic, and an unavoidable illusion which we must expose and resolve in our Kritik, to the end that it may not deceive us.

§ 70. *Representation of this antinomy*

So far as Reason has to do with nature, as the complex of objects of external sense, it can base itself partly upon laws which the Understanding itself prescribes *a priori* to nature, partly upon laws which it can extend indefinitely by means of the empirical determinations occurring in experience. To apply the former kind of laws, *i.e.* the *universal* laws of material nature in general, the Judgment needs no special principle of reflection, since it is there determinant because an objective principle is given to it through Understanding. But as regards the particular laws that can only be made known to us

through experience, there can be under them such
great manifoldness and diversity, that the Judgment
must serve as its own principle in order to investigate and search into the phenomena of nature
in accordance with a law.   Such a guiding thread is
needed, if we are only to hope for a connected
empirical cognition according to a thoroughgoing
conformity of nature to law, even its unity according
to empirical laws.   In this contingent unity of
particular laws it may very well happen that the
Judgment in its reflection proceeds from two maxims.
One of these is suggested to it *a priori* by the mere
Understanding ; but the other is prompted by particular experiences, which bring the Reason into
play in order to form a judgment upon corporeal
nature and its laws in accordance with a particular
principle.   Hence it comes about that these two
kinds of maxims seem not to be capable of existing·
together, and consequently a Dialectic arises which
leads the Judgment into error in the principle of its
reflection.

The *first maxim* of Judgment is the *proposition* :
all production of material things and their forms
must be judged to be possible according to merely
mechanical laws.

The *second maxim* is the *counter-proposition* :
some products of material nature cannot be judged
to be possible according to merely mechanical laws.
(To judge them requires quite a different law of
causality, namely, that of final causes.)

If these regulative principles of investigation be
converted into constitutive principles of the possibility of Objects, they will run thus :

Proposition : All production of material things is
possible according to merely mechanical laws.

Counter-proposition : Some production of material things is not possible according to merely mechanical laws.

In this latter aspect, as objective principles for the determinant judgment, they would contradict each other ; and consequently one of the two propositions must necessarily be false. We shall then, it is true, have an antinomy, but not of Judgment ; there will be a conflict in the legislation of Reason. Reason, however, can prove neither the one nor the other of these fundamental propositions, because we can have *a priori* no determinant principle of the possibility of things according to mere empirical laws of nature.

On the other hand, as regards the first-mentioned maxims of a reflective Judgment, they involve no contradiction in fact. For if I say, I must *judge*, according to merely mechanical laws, of the possibility of all events in material nature, and consequently of all forms regarded as its products, I do not therefore say: *They are possible in this way alone* (apart from any other kind of causality). All that is implied is *I must* always *reflect* upon them *according to the principle* of the mere mechanism of nature, and consequently investigate this as far as I can ; because unless this lies at the basis of investigation, there can be no proper knowledge of nature at all. But this does not prevent us, if opportunity offers, from following out the second maxim in the case of certain natural forms (and even by instigation of these in the whole of nature), in order to reflect upon them according to the principle of final causes, which is quite a different thing from explaining them according to the mechanism of nature. Reflection in accordance with the first maxim is thus not removed ; on the

contrary, we are told to follow it as far as we can.
Nor is it said that these forms would not be possible
in accordance with the mechanism of nature.   It is
only asserted that *human Reason* in following up this
maxim and in this way could never find the least
ground for that which constitutes the specific
[character] of a natural purpose, although it would
increase its knowledge of natural laws.   Thus it is
left undecided whether or not in the unknown inner
ground of nature, physico-mechanical and purposive
combination may be united in the same things in one
principle.   We only say that our Reason is not in a
position so to unite them ; and that therefore the
Judgment (as *reflective*—from subjective grounds,
not as determinant, in consequence of an objective
principle of the possibility of things in themselves)
is compelled to think a different principle from that
of natural mechanism as the ground of the possibility of certain forms in nature.

§ 71. *Preliminary to the solution of the above antinomy*

We can in no way prove the impossibility of the
production of organised natural products by the mere
mechanism of nature, because we cannot see into
the first inner ground of the infinite multiplicity of
the particular laws of nature, which are contingent
for us since they are only empirically known ; and so
we cannot arrive at the inner all-sufficient principle
of the possibility of a nature (a principle which lies
in the supersensible).   Whether therefore the productive faculty of nature is sufficient for that which
we judge to be formed or combined in accordance
with the Idea of purposes, as well as for that which

we believe to require merely a mechanical system [Maschinenwesen] of nature ; or whether there lies at the basis of things which we must necessarily judge as properly natural purposes, a quite different kind of original causality, which cannot be contained in material nature or in its intelligible substrate, viz. an architectonic Understanding—this is a question to which our Reason, very narrowly limited in respect of the concept of causality if it is to be specified *a priori*, can give no answer whatever.— But it is just as certain and beyond doubt that, in regard to our cognitive faculties, the mere mechanism of nature can furnish no ground of explanation of the production of organised beings. *For the reflective Judgment* it is therefore a quite correct fundamental proposition, that for that connection of things according to final causes which is so plain, there must be thought a causality distinct from that of mechanism, viz. that of an (intelligent) Cause of the world acting in accordance with purposes ; but *for the determinant Judgment* this would be a hasty and unprovable proposition. In the first case it is a mere maxim of the Judgment, wherein the concept of that causality is a mere Idea, to which we by no means undertake to concede reality, but which we use as a guide to reflection, which remains thereby always open to all mechanical grounds of explanation and does not withdraw out of the world of Sense. In the second case the proposition would be an objective principle prescribed by Reason, to which the determinant Judgment must subject itself, whereby however it withdraws beyond the world of Sense into the transcendent and perhaps is led into error.

All appearance of an antinomy between the maxims of the proper physical (mechanical) and the teleological (technical) methods of explanation rests therefore on this ; that we confuse a fundamental proposition of the reflective with one of the determinant Judgment, and the *autonomy* of the first (which has mere subjective validity for our use of Reason in respect of particular empirical laws) with the *heteronomy* of the second, which must regulate itself according to laws (universal or particular) given to it by the Understanding.

§ 72. Of the different systems which deal with the purposiveness of nature

No one has ever doubted the correctness of the proposition that judgment must be passed upon certain things of nature (organised beings) and their possibility in accordance with the concept of final causes, even if we only desire a *guiding thread* to learn how to cognise their constitution through observation, without aspiring to an investigation into their first origin. The question therefore can only be : whether this fundamental proposition is merely subjectively valid, *i.e.* is a mere maxim of our Judgment ; or whether it is an objective principle of nature, in accordance with which, apart from its mechanism (according to the mere laws of motion), quite a different kind of causality attaches to it, viz. that of final causes, under which these laws (of moving forces) stand only as intermediate causes.

We could leave this question or problem quite undecided and unsolved speculatively ; because if we content ourselves with speculation within the bounds of mere natural knowledge, we have enough in these maxims for the study of nature and for the tracking out of its hidden secrets, as far as human powers

reach.   There is then indeed a certain presentiment
of our Reason or a hint as it were given us by
nature, that, by means of this concept of final causes,
we go beyond nature, and could unite it to the
highest point in the series of causes, if we were to
abandon or at least to lay aside for a time the
investigation of nature (although we may not have
advanced far in it), and seek thenceforth to find out
whither this stranger in natural science, viz. the
concept of natural purposes, would lead us.

But here these undisputed maxims pass over
into problems opening out a wide field for difficulties.
Does purposive connection in nature *prove* a particular kind of causality?   Or is it not rather,
considered in itself and in accordance with objective
principles, similar to the mechanism of nature, resting on one and the same ground?   Only, as this
ground in many natural products is often hidden too
deep for our investigation, we make trial of a
subjective principle, that of art, *i.e.* of causality
according to Ideas, and we ascribe it to nature by
analogy.   This expedient succeeds in many cases,
but seems in some to mislead, and in no case does
it justify us in introducing into natural science a
particular kind of operation quite distinct from the
causality according to the mere mechanical laws of
nature.   We give the name of *Technic* to the procedure (the causality) of nature, on account of the
appearance of purpose that we find in its products ;
and we shall divide this into *designed* (*technica
intentionalis*) and *undesigned* (*technica naturalis*).
The first is meant to signify that the productive
faculty of nature according to final causes must be
taken for a particular kind of causality ; the second
that it is at bottom the same as the mechanism of

nature, and that its contingent agreement with our artistic concepts and their rules should be explained as a mere subjective condition of judging it, and not, falsely, as a particular kind of natural production.

If we now speak of systems explanatory of nature in regard of final causes, it must be remarked that they all controvert each other dogmatically, *i.e.* as to objective principles of the possibility of things, whether there are causes which act designedly or whether they are quite without design. They do not dispute as to the subjective maxims, by which we merely judge of the causes of such purposive products. In this latter case *disparate* principles could very well be unified; but in the former, contradictorily opposed laws annul each other and cannot subsist together.

There are two sorts of systems as to the Technic of nature, *i.e.* its productive power in accordance with the rule of purposes ; viz. *Idealism* or *Realism* of natural purposes. The first maintains that all purposiveness of nature is *undesigned*; the second that some (in organised beings) is *designed*. From this latter the hypothetical consequence can be deduced that the Technic of Nature, as concerns all its other products in reference to the whole of nature, is also designed, *i.e.* is a purpose.

(1) The *Idealism* of purposiveness (I always understand by this, objective purposiveness) is either that of the *casuality* or the *fatality* of the determination of nature in the purposive form of its products. The former principle treats of the reference of matter to the physical basis of its form, viz. the laws of motion ; the second, its reference to the *hyperphysical* basis of itself and of the whole of nature. The system of *casuality* that is ascribed to *Epicurus* or

Democritus is, taken literally, so plainly absurd that it need not detain us. Opposed to this is the system of fatality, of which *Spinoza* is taken as the author, although it is much older according to all appearance. This, as it appeals to something supersensible to which our insight does not extend, is not so easy to controvert; but that is because its concept of the original Being is not possible to understand. But so much is clear, that on this theory the purposive combination in the world must be taken as undesigned; for although derived from an original Being, it is not derived from His Understanding or from any design of His, but rather from the necessity of His nature and of the world-unity which emanates from Him. Consequently the Fatalism of purposiveness is at the same time an Idealism.

(2) The *Realism* of the purposiveness of nature is also either physical or hyperphysical. The *former* bases the purposes in nature, by the analogy of a faculty acting with design, on the *life of matter* (either its own or the life of an inner principle in it, a world-soul) and is called *Hylozoism*. The *latter* derives them from the original ground of the universe, as from an intelligent Being (originally living), who produces them with design, and is *Theism*.[1]

---

[1] We thus see that in most speculative things of pure Reason, as regards dogmatic assertions, the philosophical schools have commonly tried all possible solutions of a given question. To explain the purposiveness of nature men have tried either *lifeless matter* or a *lifeless God*, or again, *living matter* or a *living God*. It only remains for us, if the need should arise, to abandon all these objective *assertions* and to examine critically our judgment merely in reference to our cognitive faculties, in order to supply to their principle a value which, if not dogmatic, shall at least be that of a maxim sufficient for the sure employment of Reason.

§ 73. *None of the above systems give what they pretend*

What do all these systems desire ? They desire to explain our teleological judgments about nature, and they go so to work therewith that some deny their truth and, consequently, explain them as an Idealism of Nature (represented as Art) ; others recognise them as true, and promise to establish the possibility of a nature in accordance with the Idea of final causes.

(1) The systems which defend the Idealism of final causes in nature grant, it is true, on the one hand to their principle a causality in accordance with the laws of motion (through which [causality] natural things exist purposively) ; but they deny to it *intentionality*, *i.e.* that it designedly determines itself to this its purposive production ; in other words, they deny that the cause is a purpose. This is *Epicurus's* method of explanation, according to which the distinction between a Technic of nature and mere mechanism is altogether denied. Blind chance is taken as the explanatory ground not only of the agreement of the developed products with our concepts of the purpose, and consequently of [nature's] Technic ; but also of the determination of the causes of this production in accordance with the laws of motion, and consequently of their mechanism. Thus nothing is explained, not even the illusion in our teleological judgments, and consequently, the pretended Idealism of these in no way established.

On the other hand, *Spinoza* wishes to dispense with all inquiries into the ground of the possibility of purposes of nature, and to take away all reality

from this Idea.   He allows their validity in general
not as products but as accidents inhering in an
original Being ; and to this Being, as substrate of
those natural things, he ascribes in regard to them not
causality but mere subsistence.   On account of its
unconditioned necessity, and also that of all natural
things as accidents inhering in it, he secures, it is
true, to the forms of nature that unity of ground
which is requisite for all purposiveness ; but at the
same time he tears away their contingence, without
which no *unity of purpose* can be thought, and with
it all *design*, inasmuch as he takes away all
intelligence from the original ground of natural
things.

But Spinozism does not furnish what it wishes.
It wishes to afford an explanatory ground of the
purposive connection (which it does not deny) of
the things of nature, and it merely speaks of the
unity of the subject in which they all inhere.   But
even if we concede to it that the beings of the
world exist in this way, that ontological unity is not
therefore a *unity of purpose*, and does not make this
in any way comprehensible.   For this latter is a
quite particular kind of unity which does not follow
from the connection of things (the beings of the
world) in a subject (the original Being), but implies in
itself reference to a *cause* which has Understanding ;
and even if we unite all these things in a simple
subject, this never exhibits a purposive reference.
For we do not think of them, first, as the inner
effects of the substance, as if it were a *cause* ; nor,
secondly, of this cause as a cause producing effects
by means of its Understanding.   Without these
formal conditions all unity is mere natural necessity ;
and, if it is ascribed as well to things which we

represent as external to one another, blind necessity. But if we wish to give the name of purposiveness of nature to that which the schoolmen call the transcendental perfection of things (in reference to their proper being), according to which everything has in itself that which is requisite to make it one thing and not another, then we are only like children playing with words instead of concepts. For if all things must be thought as purposes, then to be a thing is the same as to be a purpose, and there is at bottom nothing which specially deserves to be represented as a purpose.

We hence see at once that Spinoza by his reducing our concepts of the purposive in nature to our own consciousness of existing in an all-embracing (though simple) Being, and by his seeking that form merely in the unity of this being, must have intended to maintain not the realism, but the idealism of its purposiveness. Even this he was not able to accomplish, because the mere representation of the unity of the substrate cannot bring about the Idea of a purposiveness, even that which is only undesigned.

(2) Those who not only maintain the *Realism* of natural purposes, but also set about explaining it, believe that they can comprehend, at least as regards its possibility, a practical kind of causality, viz. that of causes working designedly ; otherwise they could not undertake to supply this explanation. For to authorise even the most daring of hypotheses, at least the *possibility* of what we assume as basis must be *certain*, and we must be able to assure objective reality to its concept.

But the possibility of living matter cannot even be thought ; its concept involves a contradiction because lifelessness, *inertia*, constitutes the essential character of matter. The possibility of matter endowed with life, and of collective nature regarded as an animal, can only be used in an inadequate way (in regard to the hypothesis of purposiveness in the whole of nature), so far as it is manifested by experience in the organisation of nature on a small scale ; but in no way can its possibility be comprehended *a priori*. There must then be a circle in the explanation, if we wish to derive the purposiveness of nature in organised beings from the life of matter, and yet only know this life in organised beings, and can form no concept of its possibility without experience of this kind. Hylozoism, therefore, does not perform what it promises.

Finally, *Theism* can just as little establish dogmatically the possibility of natural purposes as a key to Teleology ; although it certainly is superior to all other grounds of explanation in that, through the Understanding which it ascribes to the original Being, it rescues in the best way the purposiveness of nature from Idealism, and introduces a causality acting with design for its production.

But we must first prove satisfactorily to the determinant Judgment the impossibility of the unity of purpose in matter resulting from its mere mechanism, before we are justified in placing the ground of this beyond nature in a determinate way. We can, however, advance no further than this. In accordance with the constitution and limits of our cognitive faculties (whilst we do not comprehend even the first inner ground of this mechanism) we must in no wise seek in matter a principle of determinate purposive references : but no other way of judging of the origination of its products as natural purposes remains to us than that by means of a supreme Understanding as cause of the world. But this is only a ground for the reflective, not for the determinant Judgment, and can justify absolutely no objective assertion.

§ 74. *The reason that we cannot treat the concept of a Technic of nature dogmatically is the fact that a natural purpose is inexplicable*

We deal with a concept dogmatically (even though it should be empirically conditioned) if we consider it as contained under another concept of the Object which constitutes a principle [1] of Reason, and determine it in conformity with this. But we deal with it merely critically, if we consider it only in reference to our cognitive faculties and consequently to the subjective conditions of thinking it, without undertaking to decide anything about its Object. Dogmatic procedure with a concept is then that which is conformable to law for the determinant Judgment, critical procedure for the reflective Judgment.

Now the concept of a thing as a natural purpose is a concept which subsumes nature under a causality only thinkable through Reason, in order to judge in accordance with this principle about that which is given of the Object in experience. But in order to use it dogmatically for the determinant Judgment, we must be assured first of the objective reality of this concept, because otherwise we could subsume no natural thing under it. Again, the

---

[1] [That is, the wider concept serves as a universal, under which the particular may be brought ; cognition from principles, in Kant's phrase, is the process of knowing the particular in the universal by means of concepts.]

concept of a thing as a natural purpose is, no doubt, empirically conditioned, *i.e.* only possible under certain conditions given in experience, though not to be abstracted therefrom ; but it is a concept only possible in accordance with a rational principle in the judgment about the object. Its objective reality, therefore (*i.e.* that an object in conformity with it is possible), cannot be comprehended and dogmatically established as such a principle ; and we do not know whether it is merely a sophistical and objectively empty concept (*conceptus ratiocinans*), or a rational concept, establishing a cognition and confirmed by Reason (*conceptus ratiocinatus*).[1] Therefore it cannot be dogmatically treated for the determinant Judgment, *i.e.* it is not only impossible to decide whether or not things of nature considered as natural purposes require for their production a causality of a quite peculiar kind (that acting on design) ; but the question cannot even be put, because the concept of a natural purpose is simply not susceptible of proof through Reason as regards its objective reality. That is, it is not constitutive for the determinant Judgment, but merely regulative for the reflective.

That it is not susceptible of proof is clear from the fact that as concept of a *natural product* it embraces in itself necessity and at the same time a contingency of the form of the Object (in reference to the mere laws of nature) in the selfsame thing regarded as purpose. Hence, if there is to be no contradiction here it must contain a ground for the possibility of the thing in nature, and also a ground of the possibility of this nature itself and of its

---

[1] [This distinction will be familiar to the student of the Kritik of *Pure Reason.* See Dialectic, bk. i., *Of the Concepts of Pure Reason.*]

reference to something which, not being empirically cognisable nature (supersensible), is therefore for us not cognisable at all. [This is requisite] if it is to be judged according to a different kind of causality from that of natural mechanism when we wish to establish its possibility. The concept of a thing, then, as a natural purpose, is transcendent *for the determinant Judgment*, if we consider the Object through Reason (although for the reflective Judgment it certainly may be immanent in respect of the objects of experience). Hence for determinant judgments objective reality cannot be supplied to it; and so it is intelligible how all systems that one may project for the dogmatic treatment of the concept of natural purposes and of nature itself [considered] as a whole connected together by means of final causes, can decide nothing either by objective affirmation or by objective denial. For if things be subsumed under a concept that is merely problematical, its synthetical predicates (*e.g.* in the question whether the purpose of nature which we conceive for the production of things is designed or undesigned) can furnish only problematical judgments of the Object, whether affirmative or negative; and we do not know whether we are judging about something or about nothing. The concept of a causality through purposes (of art) has at all events objective reality, and also the concept of a causality according to the mechanism of nature. But the concept of a causality of nature according to the rule of purposes, still more of a Being such as cannot be given us in experience, a Being who is the original cause of nature, though it can be thought without contradiction, yet is of no avail for dogmatic determinations. For, since it cannot be

derived from experience, and also is not requisite
for the possibility thereof, its objective reality can
in no way be assured.   But even if this could be
done, how can I number among the products of
nature things which are definitely accounted products
of divine art, when it is just the incapacity of nature
to produce such things according to its own laws
that made it necessary to invoke a cause different
from it ?

§ 75. *The concept of an objective purposiveness of
    nature is a critical principle of Reason for
    the reflective Judgment*

It is then one thing to say, "the production of
certain things of nature or that of collective nature
is only possible through a cause which determines
itself to action according to design"; and quite
another to say, " I can *according to the peculiar
constitution of my cognitive faculties* judge concerning the possibility of these things and their production, in no other fashion than by conceiving for this
a cause working according to design, *i.e.* a Being
which is productive in a way analogous to the
causality of an intelligence."   In the former case I
wish to establish something concerning the Object,
and am bound to establish the objective reality of
an assumed concept ; in the latter, Reason only
determines the use of my cognitive faculties, conformably to their peculiarities and to the essential
conditions of their range and their limits.   Thus
the former principle is an objective proposition for
the determinant Judgment, the latter merely a
subjective proposition for the reflective Judgment,
i.e. a maxim which Reason prescribes to it.

We are in fact indispensably obliged to ascribe the concept of design to nature if we wish to investigate it, though only in its organised products, by continuous observation; and this concept is therefore an absolutely necessary maxim for the empirical use of our Reason. It is plain that once such a guiding thread for the study of nature is admitted and verified, we must at least try the said maxim of Judgment in nature as a whole; because according to it many of nature's laws might discover themselves, which otherwise, on account of the limitation of our insight into its inner mechanism, would remain hidden. But though in regard to this latter employment that maxim of Judgment is certainly useful, it is not indispensable, for nature as a whole is not given as organised (in the narrow sense of the word above indicated). On the other hand, in regard to those natural products, which must be judged of as designed and not formed otherwise (if we are to have empirical knowledge of their inner constitution), this maxim of the reflective Judgment is essentially necessary; because the very thought of them as organised beings is impossible without combining therewith the thought of their designed production.

Now the concept of a thing whose existence or form we represent to ourselves as possible under the condition of a purpose is inseparably bound up with the concept of its contingency (according to natural laws). Hence the natural things that we find possible only as purposes supply the best proof of the contingency of the world-whole; to the common Understanding and to the philosopher alike they are the only valid ground of proof for its dependence on and origin from a Being existing out-

side the world—a Being who must also be intelligent
on account of its purposive form.   Teleology then
finds the consummation of its investigations only in
Theology.

But what now in the end does the most complete
Teleology prove ?   Does it prove that there is such
an intelligent Being ?   No.   It only proves that
according to the constitution of our cognitive faculties
and in the consequent combination of experience
with the highest principles of Reason, we can form
absolutely no concept of the possibility of such a
world [as this] save by thinking a *designedly-working*
supreme cause thereof.   Objectively we cannot therefore lay down the proposition, there is an intelligent
original Being ; but only subjectively, for the use of
our Judgment in its reflection upon the purposes in
nature, which can be thought according to no other
principle than that of a designing causality of a
highest Cause.

If we wished to establish on teleological grounds
the above proposition dogmatically we should be
beset with difficulties from which we could not
extricate ourselves.   For then the proposition must
at bottom be reduced to the conclusion, that the
organised beings in the world are no otherwise
possible than by a designedly-working cause.   And
we should unavoidably have to assert that, because
we can follow up these things in their causal combination only under the Idea of purposes, and cognise
them only according to their conformity to law, we
are thereby justified in assuming this as a condition
necessary for every thinking and cognising being—
a condition consequently attaching to the Object and
not merely to our subject.   But such an assertion
we do not succeed in sustaining.   For, since we do

not, properly speaking, *observe* the purposes in
nature as designed, but only in our reflection upon
its products *think* this concept as a guiding thread
for our Judgment, they are not given to us through
the Object.   It is quite impossible for us *a priori* to
vindicate, as capable of assumption, such a concept
according to its objective reality.   It remains therefore a proposition absolutely resting upon subjective
conditions alone, viz. of the Judgment reflecting in
conformity with our cognitive faculties.   If we expressed this proposition dogmatically as objectively
valid, it would be : " There is a God."   But for us
men there is only permissible the limited formula :
" We cannot otherwise think and make comprehensible the purposiveness which must lie at the
bottom of our cognition of the internal possibility of
many natural things, than by representing it and the
world in general as a product of an intelligent cause,
[a God]." [1]

Now if this proposition, based on an inevitably
necessary maxim of our Judgment, is completely
satisfactory from every *human* point of view for both
the speculative and practical use of our Reason, I
should like to know what we lose by not being able
to prove it as also valid for higher beings, from
objective grounds (which unfortunately are beyond
our faculties).   It is indeed quite certain that we
cannot adequately cognise, much less explain, organised beings and their internal possibility, according
to mere mechanical principles of nature ; and we can
say boldly it is alike certain that it is absurd for men
to make any such attempt or to hope that another
Newton will arise in the future, who shall make
comprehensible by us the production of a blade of

_____
[1] [Second Edition.]

grass according to natural laws which no design has ordered.[1] We must absolutely deny this insight to men. <But then how do we know that in nature, if we could penetrate to the principle by which it specifies the universal laws known to us, there cannot lie hidden (in its mere mechanism) a sufficient ground of the possibility of organised beings without supposing any design in their production ? would it not be judged by us presumptuous to say this ? Probabilities here are of no account when we have to do with judgments of pure Reason.— We cannot therefore judge objectively, either affirmatively or negatively, concerning the proposition : "Does a Being acting according to design lie at the basis of what we rightly call natural purposes, as the cause of the world (and consequently as its author) ?" So much only is sure, that if we are to judge according to what is permitted us to see by our own proper nature (the conditions and limitations of our Reason), we can place at the basis of the possibility of these natural purposes nothing else than an intelligent Being. This alone is in conformity with the maxim of our reflective Judgment and therefore with a ground which, though subjective, is inseparably attached to the human race.

§ 76. *Remark*

This consideration, which very well deserves to

---

[1] [This principle, that for our intellect, the conception of an organised body is impossible except by the aid of the Idea of design, is frequently insisted on by Kant. Professor Wallace points out (*Kant*, p. 110) that as far back as 1755, in his *General Physiogony and Theory of the Heavens*, Kant classed the origin of animals and plants with the secrets of Providence and the mystical number 666 "as one of the topics on which ingenuity and thought are occasionally wasted."]

be worked out in detail in Transcendental Philosophy, can come in here only in passing, by way of elucidation (not as a proof of what is here proposed).

Reason is a faculty of principles and proceeds in its furthest demand to the unconditioned; on the other hand, the Understanding stands at its service always only under a certain condition which must be given. But without concepts of Understanding, to which objective reality must be given, the Reason cannot form any objective (synthetical) judgment; and contains in itself, as theoretical Reason, absolutely no constitutive but merely regulative principles. We soon see that where the Understanding cannot follow, the Reason is transcendent, and shows itself in Ideas formerly established (as regulative principles), but not in objectively valid concepts. But the Understanding which cannot keep pace with Reason but yet is requisite for the validity of Objects, limits the validity of these Ideas to the subject, although [extending it] generally to all [subjects] of this kind. That is, the Understanding limits their validity to the condition, that according to the nature of our (human) cognitive faculties, or, generally, according to the concept which *we ourselves* can *make* of the faculty of a finite intelligent being, nothing else can or must be thought; though this is not to assert that the ground of such a judgment lies in the Object. We shall adduce some examples which, though they are too important and difficult to impose them on the reader as proved propositions, yet will give him material for thought and may serve to elucidate what we are here specially concerned with.

It is indispensably necessary for the human Understanding to distinguish between the possibility

and the actuality of things.   The ground for this
lies in the subject and in the nature of our cognitive
faculties.   Such a distinction (between the possible
and the actual) would not be given were there not
requisite for knowledge two quite different elements,
Understanding for concepts and sensible intuition
for Objects corresponding to them.   If our Understanding were intuitive it would have no objects but
those which are actual.   Concepts (which merely extend to the possibility of an object) and sensible intuitions (which give us something without allowing us
to cognise it thus as an object) would both disappear.
But now the whole of our distinction between the
merely possible and the actual rests on this, that the
former only signifies the positing of the representation of a thing in respect of our concept, and, in
general, in respect of the faculty of thought ; while
the latter signifies the positing of the thing in itself
outside this concept].[1]   The distinction, then, of
possible things from actual is one which has merely
subjective validity for the human Understanding,
because we can always have a thing in our thoughts
although it is [really] nothing, or we can represent a
thing as given although we have no concept of it.
The propositions therefore—that things can be
possible without being actual, and that consequently
no. conclusion can be drawn as to actuality from
mere possibility—are quite valid for human Reason,
without thereby proving that this distinction lies in
things themselves. _ That this does not follow,
and that consequently these propositions, though
valid of Objects (in so far as our cognitive faculty, as
sensuously conditioned, busies itself with Objects of
sense), do not hold for things in general, appears

<hr />

[1] [Second Edition.]

from the irrepressible demand of Reason to assume
something (the original ground) necessarily existing
as unconditioned, in which possibility and actuality
should no longer be distinguished, and for which
Idea our Understanding has absolutely no concept ;
i.e. it can find no way of representing such a thing
and its manner of existence.   For if the Understanding *thinks* such a thing (which it may do at pleasure),
the thing is merely represented as possible.   If it is
conscious of it as given in intuition, then is it actual ;
but nothing as to its possibility is thus thought.
Hence the concept of an absolutely necessary Being
is no doubt an indispensable Idea of Reason, but yet
it is a problematical concept unattainable by the
human Understanding.   It is indeed valid for the
employment of our cognitive faculties in accordance
with their peculiar constitution, but not valid of the
Object.   Nor is it valid for every knowing being,
because I cannot presuppose in every such being
thought and intuition as two distinct conditions of
the exercise of its cognitive faculties, and consequently as conditions of the possibility and actuality
of things.   An Understanding into which this distinction did not enter, might say : All Objects that I
know *are*, *i.e.* exist ; and the possibility of some,
which yet do not exist (*i.e.* the contingency or the
contrasted necessity of those which do exist), might
never come into the representation of such a being
at all.   But what makes it difficult for our Understanding to treat its concepts here as Reason does,
is merely that for it, as human Understanding, that
is transcendent (*i.e.* impossible for the subjective
conditions of its cognition) which Reason makes
into a principle appertaining to the Object.—   Here
the maxim always holds, that all Objects whose

cognition surpasses the faculty of the Understanding are thought by us according to the subjective conditions of the exercise of that faculty which necessarily attach to our (human) nature. If judgments laid down in this way (and there is no other alternative in regard to transcendent concepts) cannot be constitutive principles determining the Object as it is, they will remain regulative principles adapted to the human point of view, immanent in their exercise and sure.

Just as Reason in the theoretical consideration of nature must assume the Idea of an unconditioned necessity of its original ground, so also it presupposes in the practical [sphere] its own (in respect of nature) unconditioned causality, or freedom, in that it is conscious of its own moral command. Here the objective necessity of the act, as a duty, is opposed to that necessity which it would have as an event, if its ground lay in nature and not in freedom (*i.e.* in the causality of Reason). The morally absolutely necessary act is regarded as physically quite contingent, since that which *ought* necessarily to happen often does not happen. It is clear then that it is owing to the subjective constitution of our practical faculty that the moral laws must be represented as commands, and the actions conforming to them as duties; and that Reason expresses this necessity not by an "*is*" (happens), but by an "ought to be." This would not be the case were Reason considered as in its causality independent of sensibility (as the subjective condition of its application to objects of nature), and so as cause in an intelligible world entirely in agreement with the moral law. For in such a world there would be no distinction between "ought to do" and "does," between a practical law of that which is

possible through us, and the theoretical law of that
which is actual through us. Though, therefore, an
intelligible world in which everything would be
actual merely because (as something good) it is
possible, together with freedom as its formal condition, is for us a transcendent concept, not available
as a constitutive principle to determine an Object
and its objective reality; yet, because of the constitution of our (in part sensuous) nature and faculty it
is, so far as we can represent it in accordance with the
constitution of our Reason, for us and for all rational
beings that have a connection with the world of
sense, a universal *regulative principle*. This principle
does not objectively determine the constitution of
freedom, as a form of causality, but it makes the
rule of actions according to that Idea a command
for every one, with no less validity than if it did
so determine it.

In the same way we may concede thus much as
regards the case in hand. Between natural mechanism and the Technic of nature, *i.e.* its purposive
connection, we should find no distinction, were it not
that our Understanding is of the kind that must
proceed from the universal to the particular. The
Judgment then in respect of the particular can cognise no purposiveness and, consequently, can form no
determinant judgments, without having a universal
law under which to subsume that particular. Now
the particular, as such, contains something contingent
in respect of the universal, while yet Reason requires
unity and conformity to law in the combination of
particular laws of nature. This conformity of the
contingent to law is called purposiveness; and the
derivation of particular laws from the universal, as
regards their contingent element, is impossible *a*

priori through a determination of the concept of
the Object. ~~Hence, the concept of the purposiveness of nature in its products is necessary for human
Judgment in respect of nature, but has not to do
with the determination of objects. It is, therefore,
a subjective principle of Reason for the Judgment,
which as regulative (not constitutive) is just as
necessarily valid for our *human Judgment* as if it
were an objective principle.

§ 77. *Of the peculiarity of the human Understanding, by means of which the concept of a natural purpose is possible.*

We have brought forward in the *Remark*
peculiarities of our cognitive faculties (even the
higher ones) which we are easily led to transfer
as objective predicates to the things themselves. But
they concern Ideas, no object adequate to which
can be given in experience, and they could only
serve as regulative principles in the prosecution
of the latter. This is the case with the concept
of a natural purpose, which concerns the cause
of the possibility of such a predicate, which cause
can only lie in the Idea. But the result corresponding to it (*i.e.* the product) is given in nature; and
the concept of a causality of nature as of a being
acting according to purposes seems to make the
Idea of a natural purpose into a constitutive principle,
which Idea has thus something different from all
other Ideas.

This difference consists, however, in the fact
that the Idea in question is not a rational principle
for the Understanding but for the Judgment. It
is, therefore, merely the application of an Under-

standing in general to possible objects of experience, in cases where the judgment can only be reflective, not determinant, and where, consequently, the object, although given in experience, cannot be *determinately judged* in conformity with the Idea (not to say with complete adequacy), but can only be reflected on.

There emerges, therefore, a peculiarity of *our* (human) Understanding in respect of the Judgment in its reflection upon things of nature. But if this be so, the Idea of a possible Understanding different from the human must be fundamental here. (Just so in the Kritik of Pure Reason we must have in our thoughts another possible [kind of] intuition, if ours is to be regarded as a particular species for which objects are only valid as phenomena). And so we are able to say : Certain natural products, from the special constitution of our Understanding, *must be considered by us*, in regard to their possibility, as if produced designedly and as purposes. But we do not, therefore, demand that there should be actually given a particular cause which has the representation of a purpose as its determining ground ; and we do not deny that an Understanding, different from (*i.e.* higher than) the human, might find the ground of the possibility of such products of nature in the mechanism of nature, *i.e.* in a causal combination for which an Understanding is not explicitly assumed as cause.

We have now to do with the relation of *our* Understanding to the Judgment : viz. we seek for a certain contingency in the constitution of our Understanding, to which we may point as a peculiarity distinguishing it from other possible Understandings.

This contingency is found, naturally enough,

in the *particular*, which the Judgment is to bring
under the *universal* of the concepts of Understanding. For the universal of *our* (human) Understanding
does not determine the particular, and it is contingent
in how many ways different things which agree in
a common characteristic may come before our
perception.   Our Understanding is a faculty of
concepts, *i.e.* a discursive Understanding, for which
it obviously must be contingent of what kind and
how very different the particulars may be that
can be given to it in nature and brought under its
concepts.   But now intuition also belongs to knowledge, and a faculty of a *complete spontaneity of
intuition* would be a cognitive faculty distinct from
sensibility, and quite independent of it, in other
words, an Understanding in the most general sense.
⟨Thus we can think an *intuitive* Understanding
[negatively, merely as not discursive [1]], which does
not proceed from the universal to the particular,
and so to the individual (through concepts).⟩ For
it that contingency of the accordance of nature in
its products according to *particular* laws with the
Understanding would not be met with ; and it is
this contingency that makes it so hard for our
Understanding to reduce the manifold of nature
to the unity of knowledge.   This reduction our
Understanding can only accomplish by bringing
natural characteristics into correspondence which is
very contingent, with our faculty of concepts, and
of which an intuitive Understanding would have
no need.

Our Understanding has then this peculiarity as
concerns the Judgment, that in cognition by it the
particular is not determined by the universal and

[1] [Second Edition.]

Y

cannot therefore be derived from it ; but at the same time this particular in the manifold of nature must accord with the universal (by means of concepts and laws) that it may be capable of being subsumed under it.   This accordance under such circumstances must be very contingent and without definite principle as concerns the Judgment.

In order now to be able at least to think the possibility of such an accordance of things of nature with our Judgment (which accordance we represent as contingent and consequently as only possible by means of a purpose directed thereto), we must at the same time think of another Understanding, by reference to which and apart from any purpose ascribed to it, we may represent as *necessary* that accordance of natural laws with our Judgment, which for our Understanding is only thinkable through the medium of purposes.

In fact our Understanding has the property of proceeding in its cognition, *e.g.* of the cause of a product, from the *analytical-universal* (concepts) to the particular (the given empirical intuition).   Thus as regards the manifold of the latter it determines nothing, but must await this determination by the Judgment of the subsumption of the empirical intuition (if the object is a natural product) under the concept.   We can however think an Understanding which, being, not like ours, discursive, but intuitive, proceeds from the *synthetical-universal* (the intuition of a whole as such) to the particular, *i.e.* from the whole to the parts.   The *contingency* of the combination of the parts, in order that a definite form of the whole shall be possible, is not implied by such an Understanding and its representation of the whole.   Our Understanding requires this because it must proceed from the parts as universally con-

ceived grounds to different forms possible to be
subsumed under them, as consequences. According
to the constitution of our Understanding a real
whole of nature is regarded only as the effect of the
concurrent motive powers of the parts. Suppose
then that we wish not to represent the possibility of·
the whole as dependent on that of the parts (after
the manner of our discursive Understanding), but
according to the standard of the intuitive (original)
Understanding to represent the possibility of the
parts (according to their constitution and combination) as dependent on that of the whole. In accordance with the above peculiarity of our Understanding
it cannot happen that the whole shall contain the
ground of the possibility of the connection of the
parts (which would be a contradiction in discursive
cognition), but only that the *representation* of a
whole may contain the ground of the possibility of
its form and the connection of the parts belonging
to it. Now such a whole would be an effect (*product*)
the *representation* of which is regarded as the *cause*
of its possibility, but the product of a cause whose
determining ground is merely the representation of
its effect is called a purpose. Hence it is merely a
consequence of the particular constitution of our
Understanding, that it represents products of nature
as possible, according to a different kind of causality
from that of the natural laws of matter, namely, that
of purposes and final causes. Hence also this
principle has not to do with the possibility of such
things themselves (even when considered as phenomena) according to the manner of their production,
but merely with the judgment upon them which is
possible to our Understanding. Here we see at
once why it is that in natural science we are not

long contented with an explanation of the products of nature by a causality according to purposes. For there we desire to judge of natural production merely in a manner conformable to our faculty of judging, *i.e.* to the reflective Judgment, and not in reference to things themselves on behalf of the determinant Judgment. It is here not at all requisite to prove that such an *intellectus archetypus* is possible, but only that we are led to the Idea of it,—which too contains no contradiction,—in contrast to our discursive Understanding which has need of images (*intellectus ectypus*) and to the contingency of its constitution.

If we consider a material whole, according to its form, as a product of the parts with their powers and faculties of combining with one another (as well as of bringing in foreign materials), we represent to ourselves a mechanical mode of production of it. But in this way no concept emerges of a whole as purpose, whose internal possibility presupposes throughout the Idea of a whole on which depend the constitution and mode of action of the parts, as we must represent to ourselves an organised body. It does not follow indeed, as has been shown, that the mechanical production of such a body is impossible ; for to say so would be to say that it would be impossible (contradictory) for *any Understanding* to represent to itself such a unity in the connection of the manifold, without the Idea of the unity being at the same time its producing cause, *i.e.* without designed production. This, however, would follow in fact if we were justified in regarding material beings as things in themselves. For then the unity that constitutes the ground of the possibility of natural formations would be simply the unity of space. But space is no real ground of the products, but only their formal condition, although it has this similarity to the real ground which we seek that in it no part can be determined except in relation to the whole (the representation of which therefore lies at the ground of the possibility of the parts). But now it is at least possible to consider the material world as mere phenomenon, and to think as its substrate something like a thing in itself (which is not phenomenon), and to attach to this a corresponding intellectual intuition (even though it is not ours). Thus there would be, although incognisable by us, a supersensible real ground for nature, to which we ourselves belong. In this we consider according to mechanical laws what is necessary in nature regarded as an object of Sense ; but we consider according to teleological laws the agreement and unity of its particular laws and its forms—which in regard to mechanism we must judge contingent—regarded as objects of Reason (in fact the whole of nature as a system). Thus we should judge nature according to two different kinds of principles without the mechanical way of explanation being shut out by the teleological, as if they contradicted one another.

From this we are permitted to see what otherwise, though we could easily surmise it, could with difficulty be maintained with certainty and proved, viz. that the principle of a mechanical derivation of purposive natural products is consistent with the teleological, but in no way enables us to dispense with it. In a thing that we must judge as a natural purpose (an organised being) we can no doubt try all the known and yet to be discovered laws of mechanical production, and even hope to make good progress therewith ; but we can never get rid of the call for a

quite different ground of production for the possibility of such a product, viz. causality by means of
purposes. ⟨Absolutely no human Reason (in fact
no finite Reason like ours in quality, however much
it may surpass it in degree) can hope to understand
the production of even a blade of grass by mere
mechanical causes. As regards the possibility of
such an object, the teleological connection of causes
and effects is quite indispensable for the Judgment,
even for studying it by the clue of experience. For
external objects as phenomena an adequate ground
related to purposes cannot be met with; this, although
it lies in nature, must only be sought in the supersensible substrate of nature, from all possible insight
into which we are cut off. Hence it is absolutely
impossible for us to produce from nature itself
grounds of explanation for purposive combinations;
and it is necessary by the constitution of the human
cognitive faculties to seek the supreme ground of
these purposive combinations in an original Understanding as the cause of the world.

§ 78. *Of the union of the principle of the universal
mechanism of matter with the teleological principle in the Technic of nature.*

It is infinitely important for Reason not to let
slip the mechanism of nature in its products, and in
their explanation not to pass it by, because without
it no insight into the nature of things can be attained.
Suppose it admitted that a supreme Architect
immediately created the forms of nature as they
have been from the beginning, or that He predeter-
mined those which in the course of nature continually form themselves on the same model. Our

knowledge of nature is not thus in the least furthered, because we cannot know the mode of action of that Being and the Ideas which are to contain the principles of the possibility of natural beings, and we cannot by them explain nature as from above downwards (*a priori*). And if, starting from the forms of the objects of experience, from below upwards (*a posteriori*), we wish to explain the purposiveness, which we believe is met with in experience, by appealing to a cause working in accordance with purposes, then is our explanation quite tautological and we are only mocking Reason with words. Indeed when we lose ourselves with this way of explanation in the transcendent, whither natural knowledge cannot follow, Reason is seduced into poetical extravagance, which it is its peculiar destination to avoid.

On the other hand, it is just as necessary a maxim of Reason not to pass by the principle of purposes in the products of nature. For, although it does not make their mode of origination any more comprehensible, yet it is a heuristic principle for investigating the particular laws of nature ; supposing even that we wish to make no use of it for explaining nature itself, in which we still always speak only of natural purposes, although it apparently exhibits a designed unity of purpose,—*i.e.* without seeking the ground of their possibility beyond nature. But since we must come in the end to this latter question, it is just as necessary to think for nature a particular kind of causality which does not present itself in it, as the mechanism of natural causes which does. To the receptivity of several forms, different from those of which matter is susceptible by mechanism, must be added a spontaneity of a cause

(which therefore cannot be matter), without which no
ground can be assigned for those forms. No doubt
Reason, before it takes this step, must proceed with
caution, and not try to explain teleologically every
Technic of nature, *i.e.* every productive faculty of
nature which displays in itself (as in regular bodies)
purposiveness of figure to our mere apprehension ;
but must always regard such as so far mechanically
possible. But on that account to wish entirely to
exclude the teleological principle, and to follow
simple mechanism only—in cases where, in the
rational investigation of the possibility of natural
forms through their causes, purposiveness shows
itself quite undeniably as the reference to a different
kind of causality—to do this must make Reason
fantastic, and send it wandering among chimeras of
unthinkable natural faculties ; just as a mere teleological mode of explanation which takes no account
of natural mechanism makes it visionary.

In the same natural thing both principles cannot
be connected as fundamental propositions of explanation (deduction) of one by the other, *i.e.* they do not
unite for the determinant Judgment as dogmatical
and constitutive principles of insight into nature. If
I choose, *e.g.*, to regard a maggot as the product of
the mere mechanism of nature (of the new formation
that it produces of itself, when its elements are set
free by corruption), I cannot derive the same product
from the same matter as from a causality that acts
according to purposes. Conversely, if I regard the
same product as a natural purpose, I cannot count
on any mechanical mode of its production and regard
this as the constitutive principle of my judgment
upon its possibility, and so unite both principles.
One method of explanation excludes the other ;

even supposing that objectively both grounds of
the possibility of such a product rested on a single
ground, to which we did not pay attention. The
principle which should render possible the compatibility of both in judging of nature must be placed
in that which lies outside both (and consequently
outside the possible empirical representation of
nature), but yet contains their ground, *i.e.* in the
supersensible ; and each of the two methods of
explanation must be referred thereto. Now of this
we can have no concept but the indeterminate concept of a ground, which makes the judging of nature
by empirical laws possible, but which we cannot
determine more nearly by any predicate. Hence the
union of both principles cannot rest upon a ground
of *explanation* of the possibility of a product according to given laws, for the *determinant* Judgment, but
only upon a ground of its *exposition* for the *reflective*
Judgment.— To explain is to derive from a principle,
which therefore we must clearly know and of which
we can give an account. No doubt the principle of
the mechanism of nature and that of its causality
in one and the same natural product must coalesce
in a single higher principle, which is their common
source, because otherwise they could not subsist
side by side in the observation of nature. But if
this principle, objectively common to the two, which
therefore warrants the association of the maxims of
natural investigation depending on both, be such
that, though it can be pointed to, it cannot be
determinately known nor clearly put forward for use
in cases which arise, then can we from such a
principle draw no explanation, *i.e.* no clear and
determinate derivation of the possibility of a natural
product in accordance with those two heterogene-

ous principles. But now the principle common to the mechanical and teleological derivations is the *supersensible*, which we must place at the basis of nature, regarded as phenomenon. And of this, in a theoretical point of view, we cannot form the smallest positive determinate concept. It cannot, therefore, in any way be explained how, according to it as principle, nature (in its particular laws) constitutes for us one system, which can be cognised as possible either by the principle of physical development or by that of final causes. If it happens that objects of nature present themselves which cannot be thought by us, as regards their possibility, according to the principle of mechanism (which always has a claim on a natural being), without relying on teleological propositions, we can only make an hypothesis. Namely, we suppose that we may hopefully investigate natural laws with reference to both (according as the possibility of its product is cognisable by our Understanding by one or the other principle), without stumbling at the apparent contradiction which comes into view between the principles by which they are judged. For at least the possibility is assured that both may be united objectively in one principle, since they concern phenomena that presuppose a supersensible ground.

Mechanism, then, and the teleological (designed) Technic of nature, in respect of the same product and its possibility, may stand under a common supreme principle of nature in particular laws. But since this principle is *transcendent* we cannot, because of the limitation of our Understanding, unite both principles *in the explanation* of the same production of nature even if the inner possibility of this product is only *intelligible* [verständlich] through a causality

according to purposes (as is the case with organised
matter). We revert then to the above fundamental
proposition of Teleology. ⟨According to the constitution of the human Understanding, no other
than designedly working causes can be assumed
for the possibility of organised beings in nature ;
and the mere mechanism of nature cannot be
adequate to the explanation of these its products.
But we do not attempt to decide anything by this
fundamental proposition as to the possibility of such
things themselves.⟩

This is only a maxim of the reflective, not of
the determinant Judgment ; consequently only subjectively valid for us, not objectively for the possibility of things themselves of this kind (in which
both kinds of production may well cohere in one
and the same ground). Further, without any concept,—besides the teleologically conceived method
of production, — of a simultaneously presented
mechanism of nature, no judgment can be passed
on this kind of production as a natural product.
Hence the above maxim leads to the necessity of
an unification of both principles in judging of things
as natural purposes in themselves, but does not lead
us to substitute one for the other either altogether
or in certain parts. ⟨For in the place of what is
thought (at least by us) as possible only by design
we cannot set mechanism, and in the place of what
is cognised as mechanically necessary we cannot set
contingency, which would need a purpose as its
determining ground ; but we can only subordinate
the one (Mechanism) to the other (designed Technic), which may quite well be the case according to
the transcendental principle of the purposiveness of
nature.

For where purposes are thought as grounds of the possibility of certain things, we must assume a means [thereto] whose law of working requires *for itself* nothing presupposing a purpose, which law consequently can be mechanical and yet a cause subordinated to designed effects. Thus—in the organic products of nature, and also when prompted by their infinite number, we assume (at least as a permissible hypothesis) design in the combination of natural causes by particular laws as a *universal principle* of the reflective Judgment for the whole of nature (the world),—we can think a great and indeed universal combination of mechanical with teleological laws in the productions of nature, without interchanging the principles by which they are judged or putting one in the place of the other. For, in a teleological judgment, the matter, even if the form that it assumes be judged possible only by design, can also, conformably to the mechanical laws of its nature, be subordinated as a means to the represented purpose. But, since the ground of this compatibility lies in that which is neither one nor the other (neither mechanism nor purposive combination), but is the supersensible substrate of nature of which we know nothing, the two ways of representing the possibility of such Objects are not to be blended together by our (human) Reason. However, we cannot judge of their possibility otherwise than by judging them as ultimately resting on a supreme Understanding by the connection of final causes; and thus the teleological method of explanation is not eliminated.

Now it is quite indeterminate, and for our Understanding always indeterminable, how much the mechanism of nature does as a means towards each final design in nature.   However, on account of the above-mentioned intelligible principle of the possibility of a nature in general, it may be assumed that it is possible throughout according to the two kinds of universally accordant laws (the physical and those of final causes), although we cannot see into the way how this takes place. Hence we do not know how far the mechanical method of explanation which is possible for us may extend.   So much only is certain that, so far as we can go in this direction, it must always be inadequate for things that we once recognise as natural purposes ; and therefore we must, by the constitution of our Understanding, subordinate these grounds collectively to a teleological principle.

Hereon is based a privilege, and on account of the importance which the study of nature by the principle of mechanism has for the theoretical use of our Reason, also an appeal.   We should explain all products and occurrences in nature, even the most purposive, by mechanism as far as is in our power (the limits of which we cannot give an account of in this kind of investigation).   But at the same time we are not to lose sight of the fact that those things which we cannot even state for investigation except under the concept of a purpose of Reason, must, in conformity with the essential constitution of our Reason, and notwithstanding those mechanical causes, be subordinated by us finally to causality in accordance with purposes.

METHODOLOGY OF
THE TELEOLOGICAL JUDGMENT.[1]

§ 79. *Whether teleology must be treated as if it belonged to the doctrine of nature*

Every science must have its definite position in the encyclopaedia of all the sciences. If it is a philosophical science its position must be either in the theoretical or practical part. If again it has its place in the former of these, it must be either in the doctrine of nature, so far as it concerns that which can be an object of experience (in the doctrine of bodies, the doctrine of the soul, or the universal science of the world), or in the doctrine of God (the original ground of the world as the complex of all objects of experience).

Now the question is, what place is due to Teleology? Does it belong to Natural Science (properly so called) or to Theology? One of the two it must be; for no science belongs to the transition from one to the other, because this transition only marks the articulation or organisation of the system, and not a place in it.

That it does not belong to Theology as a part of it, although it may be made of the most important use therein, is self-evident. For it has as

---

[1] [This is marked as an *Appendix* in the Second Edition.]

its objects, natural productions, and their cause, and
although it refers at the same time to the latter as
to a ground lying outside of and beyond nature (a
Divine Author), yet it does not do this for the
determinant but only for the reflective Judgment in
the consideration of nature (in order to guide our
judgment on things in the world by means of such
an Idea as a regulative principle, in conformity with
the human Understanding).

But it appears to belong just as little to Natural
Science, which needs determinant and not merely
reflective principles in order to supply objective
grounds for natural effects.   In fact, nothing is
gained for the theory of nature or the mechanical
explanation of its phenomena by means of its
effective causes, by considering them as connected
according to the relation of purposes.   The
exhibition of the purposes of nature in its products,
so far as they constitute a system according to
teleological concepts, properly belongs only to a
description of nature which is drawn up in accordance with a particular guiding thread.   Here
Reason, no doubt, accomplishes a noble work,
instructive and practically purposive in many points
of view ; but it gives no information as to the
origin and the inner possibility of these forms,
which is the special business of theoretical Natural
Science.   Teleology, therefore, as science, belongs
to no Doctrine, but only to Kritik ; and to the
Kritik of a special cognitive faculty, viz. Judgment.
But so far as it contains principles *a priori*, it can
and must furnish the method by which nature must
be judged according to the principle of final causes.
Hence its Methodology has at least negative
influence upon the procedure in theoretical Natural

Science, and also upon the relation which this can have in Metaphysic to Theology as its propaedeutic.

§ 80. *Of the necessary subordination of the mechanical to the teleological principle in the explanation of a thing as a natural purpose.*

The *privilege of aiming at* a merely mechanical method of explanation of all natural products is in itself quite unlimited; but the *faculty of attaining* thereto is by the constitution of our Understanding, so far as it has to do with things as natural purposes, not only very much limited but also clearly bounded. For, according to a principle of the Judgment, by this process alone nothing can be accomplished towards an explanation of these things; and consequently the judgment upon such products must always be at the same time subordinated by us to a teleological principle.

It is therefore rational, even meritorious, to pursue natural mechanism, in respect of the explanation of natural products, so far as can be done with probability; and if we give up the attempt it is not because it is impossible *in itself* to meet in this path with the purposiveness of nature, but only because it is impossible *for us* as men. For there would be required for that an intuition other than sensuous, and a determinate knowledge of the intelligible substrate of nature from which a ground could be assigned for the mechanism of phenomena according to particular laws, which quite surpasses our faculties.

Hence if the naturalist would not waste his labour he must in judging of things, the concept of

any of which is indubitably established as a natural
purpose (organised beings), always lay down as basis
an original organisation, which uses that very
mechanism in order to produce fresh organised
forms or to develop the existing ones into new
shapes (which, however, always result from that
purpose and conformably to it).

It is praiseworthy by the aid of comparative
anatomy to go through the great creation of organised natures, in order to see whether there may not
be in it something similar to a system and also in
accordance with the principle of production. For
otherwise we should have to be content with the
mere principle of judgment (which gives no insight
into their production) and, discouraged, to give up
all claim to *natural insight* in this field. The agreement of so many genera of animals in a certain
common schema, which appears to be fundamental
not only in the structure of their bones but also in
the disposition of their remaining parts,—so that
with an admirable simplicity of original outline, a
great variety of species has been produced by the
shortening of one member and the lengthening of
another, the involution of this part and the evolution
of that,—allows a ray of hope, however faint, to
penetrate into our minds, that here something may
be accomplished by the aid of the principle of the
mechanism of nature (without which there can be no
natural science in general). This analogy of forms,
which with all their differences seem to have been
produced according to a common original type,
strengthens our suspicions of an actual relationship
between them in their production from a common
parent, through the gradual approximation of one
animal-genus to another—from those in which the

z

principle of purposes seems to be best authenticated,
i.e. from man, down to the polype, and again from
this down to mosses and lichens, and finally to the
lowest stage of nature noticeable by us, viz. to crude
matter. And so the whole Technic of nature, which
is so incomprehensible to us in organised beings
that we believe ourselves compelled to think a
different principle for it, seems to be derived from
matter and its powers according to mechanical laws
(like those by which it works in the formation of
crystals).

Here it is permissible for the *Archæologist* of
nature to derive from the surviving traces of its
oldest revolutions, according to all its mechanism
known or supposed by him, that great family of
creatures (for so we must represent them if the said
thoroughgoing relationship is to have any ground).
He can suppose the bosom of mother earth, as she
passed out of her chaotic state (like a great animal),
to have given birth in the beginning to creatures of
less purposive form, that these again gave birth to
others which formed themselves with greater adaptation to their place of birth and their relations to each
other ; until this womb becoming torpid and ossified,
limited its births to definite species not further
modifiable, and the manifoldness remained as it
was at the end of the operation of that fruitful
formative power.— Only he must still in the end
ascribe to this universal mother an organisation
purposive in respect of all these creatures ; otherwise
it would not be possible to think the possibility of
the purposive form of the products of the animal and
vegetable kingdoms.[1] He has then only pushed

[1] We may call a hypothesis of this kind a daring venture of
reason, and there may be few even of the most acute naturalists

further back the ground of explanation and cannot
pretend to have made the development of those two
kingdoms independent of the condition of final
causes.

Even as concerns the variation to which certain
individuals of organised genera are accidentally
subjected, if we find that the character so changed
is hereditary and is taken up into the generative
power, then we cannot pertinently judge the variation to be anything else than an occasional development of purposive capacities originally present in
the species with a view to the preservation of the
race. For in the complete inner purposiveness of
an organised being, the generation of its like is
closely bound up with the condition of taking
nothing up into the generative power which does
not belong, in such a system of purposes, to one of
its undeveloped original capacities. Indeed, if we
depart from this principle, we cannot know with
certainty whether several parts of the form which is
now apparent in a species have not a contingent and
unpurposive origin ; and the principle of Teleology,
to judge nothing in an organised being as unpur-

through whose head it has not sometimes passed. For it is not
absurd, like that *generatio æquivoca* by which is understood the
production of an organised being through the mechanics of crude
unorganised matter. It would always remain *generatio univoca* in the
most universal sense of the word, for it only considers one organic
being as derived from another organic being, although from one
which is specifically different ; *e.g.* certain water-animals transform
themselves gradually into marsh-animals and from these, after
some generations, into land-animals. *A priori*, in the judgment
of Reason alone, there is no contradiction here. Only experience
gives no example of it ; according to experience all generation
that we know is *generatio homonyma*. This is not merely
univoca in contrast to the generation out of unorganised material,
but in the organisation the product is of like kind to that which
produced it ; and *generatio heteronyma*, so far as our empirical
knowledge of nature extends, is nowhere found.

posive which maintains it in its propagation, would
be very unreliable in its application and would be
valid solely for the original stock (of which we have
no further knowledge).

Hume[1] takes exception to those who find it
requisite to assume for all such natural purposes a
teleological principle of judgment, *i.e.* an architectonic
Understanding.   He says that it may fairly be asked :
how is such an Understanding possible ?   How can
the manifold faculties and properties that constitute
the possibility of an Understanding, which has at the
same time executive might, be found so purposively
together in one Being ?   But this objection is without weight.   For the whole difficulty which surrounds
the question concerning the first production of a
thing containing in itself purposes and only comprehensible by means of them, rests on the further
question as to the unity of the ground of the combination in this product of the various elements [des
Mannichfaltigen] which are *external to one another*.
For if this ground be placed in the Understanding of
a producing cause as simple substance, the question,
so far as it is teleological, is sufficiently answered ;
but if the cause be sought merely in matter as an

---

[1] [It is probable that Kant alludes here to Hume's Essay *On a
Providence and a Future State*, § xi of the *Inquiry*. Hume argues
that though the inference from an effect to an intelligent cause may
be valid in the case of human contrivance, it is not legitimate to rise
by a like argument to Supreme Intelligence.   " In human nature
there is a certain experienced coherence of designs and inclinations :
so that when from any fact we have discovered one intention of any
man, it may often be reasonable from experience to infer another,
and draw a long chain of conclusions concerning his past or future
conduct.   But this method of reasoning can never have place with
regard to a being so remote and incomprehensible, who bears much
less analogy to any other being in the universe than the sun to
a waxen taper, and who discovers himself only by some faint traces
or outlines, beyond which we have no authority to ascribe to him
any attribute or perfection."]

aggregate of many substances external to one another, the unity of the principle is quite wanting for the internally purposive form of its formation, and the *autocracy* of matter in productions which can only be conceived by our Understanding as purposes is a word without meaning.

Hence it comes to pass that those who seek a supreme ground of possibility for the objectively-purposive forms of matter, without attributing to it Understanding, either make the world-whole into a single all-embracing substance (Pantheism), or (which is only a more determinate explanation of the former) into a complex of many determinations inhering in a single *simple substance* (Spinozism); merely in order to satisfy that condition of all purposiveness—the *unity* of ground. Thus they do justice indeed to *one* condition of the problem, viz. the unity in the purposive combination, by means of the mere ontological concept of a simple substance; but they adduce nothing for the *other* condition, viz. the relation of this substance to its result as *purpose*, through which relation that ontological ground is to be more closely determined in respect of the question at issue. Hence they answer *the whole* question in no way. It remains absolutely unanswerable (for our Reason) if we do not represent that original ground of things, as simple *substance*; its property which has reference to the specific constitution of the forms of nature grounded thereon, viz. its purposive unity, as the property of an intelligent substance; and the relation of these forms to this intelligence (on account of the contingency which we ascribe to everything that we think possible only as a purpose) as that of *causality*.

§ 81. *Of the association of mechanism with the teleological principle in the explanation of a natural
purpose as a natural product*

According to the preceding paragraphs the
mechanism of nature alone does not enable us to
think the possibility of an organised being ; but (at
least according to the constitution of our cognitive
faculty) it must be originally subordinated to a
cause working designedly. But, just as little is the
mere teleological ground of such a being sufficient
for considering it and judging it as a product of
nature, if the mechanism of the latter be not associated with the former, like the instrument of a cause
working designedly, to whose purposes nature is
subordinated in its mechanical laws. The possibility of such a unification of two quite different
kinds of causality,—of nature in its universal conformity to law with an Idea which limits it to a
particular form, for which it contains no ground in
itself—is not comprehended by our Reason. It lies
in the supersensible substrate of nature, of which we
can determine nothing positively, except that it is
the being in itself of which we merely know the
phenomenon. But the principle, "all that we assume as belonging to this nature (*phenomenon*) and
as its product, must be thought as connected with
it according to mechanical laws," has none the
less force, because without this kind of causality
organised beings (as purposes of nature) would not
be natural products.

Now if the teleological principle of the production of these beings be assumed (as is inevitable),
we can place at the basis of the cause of their

internally purposive form either *Occasionalism* or *Pre-established Harmony*.   According to the former the Supreme Cause of the world would, conformably to its Idea, furnish immediately the organic formation on the occasion of every union of intermingling materials.   According to the latter it would, in the original products of its wisdom, only have supplied the capacity by means of which an organic being produces another of like kind, and the species perpetually maintains itself; whilst the loss of individuals is continually replaced by that nature which at the same time works towards their destruction.   If we assume the Occasionalism of the production of organised beings, all nature is quite lost, and with it all employment of Reason in judging of the possibility of such products; hence we may suppose that no one will adopt this system, who has anything to do with philosophy.

[The theory of] *Pre-established Harmony* may proceed in two different ways.   It regards every organised being as generated by one of like kind, either as an *educt* or a *product*.   The system which regards generations as mere educts is called the theory of *individual preformation* or the theory of *evolution* : that which regards them as products is entitled the system of *epigenesis*.   This latter may also be entitled the system of *generic preformation*, because the productive faculty of the generator and consequently the specific form would be *virtually* preformed according to the inner purposive capacities which are part of its stock.   In correspondence with this the opposite theory of individual preformations would be better entitled the *theory of involution*.

The advocates of the *theory of evolution*, who remove every individual from the formative power

of nature, in order to make it come immediately
from the hand of the Creator, would, however, not
venture to regard this as happening according to
the hypothesis of Occasionalism.   For according
to this the union is a mere formality, *à propos* of
which a supreme intelligent Cause of the world has
concluded to immediately form a fruit, and only to
leave to its parent its development and nourishment.
They declare themselves for preformation ; as if it
were not all the same, whether a supernatural origin
is assigned to these forms in the beginning or in the
course of the world.   On the contrary, a great
number of supernatural arrangements would be
spared by occasional creation, which would be
requisite, in order that the embryo formed in the
beginning of the world might not be injured up to
[the moment of] its development by the destructive
powers of nature, and might keep itself unharmed ;
and there would also be requisite an incalculably
greater number of such preformed beings than would
ever be developed, and with them many creations
would be made without need and without purpose.
They would, however, be willing to leave at least
something to nature, so as not to fall into a complete Hyperphysic which can dispense with all
natural explanations.   It is true, they hold so fast
by their Hyperphysic that they find even in abortions
(which it is quite impossible to take for purposes of
nature) an admirable purposiveness ; though it be
only directed to the fact that an anatomist would
take exception to it as a purposeless purposiveness,
and would feel a disheartened wonder thereat.   But
the production of hybrids could absolutely not be
accommodated with the system of preformation ;
and to the seeds of the male creature, to which they

had attributed nothing but the mechanical property of serving as the first means of nourishment for the embryo, they must attribute in addition a purposive formative power, which in the case of the product of two creatures of the same genus they would concede to neither parent.

On the other hand, even if we do not recognise the great superiority which the theory of *Epigenesis* has over the former as regards the empirical grounds of its proof, still prior to proof Reason views this way of explanation with peculiar favour. For in respect of the things which we can only represent as possible originally according to the causality of purposes, at least as concerns their propagation, this theory regards nature as self-producing, not merely as self-evolving : and so with the least expenditure of the supernatural leaves to nature all that follows after the first beginning (though without determining anything about this first beginning by which Physic generally is thwarted, however it may essay its explanation by a chain of causes).

As regards this theory of Epigenesis, no one has contributed more either to its proof or to the establishment of the legitimate principles of its application,— partly by the limitation of a too presumptuous employment of it,—than Herr Hofr. *Blumenbach*.[1] In all physical explanations of these formations he starts from organised matter. That crude matter should have originally formed itself according to mechanical laws, that life should have sprung from the nature of what is lifeless, that matter should have been able to dispose itself into the form

---

[1] [J. F. Blumenbach (1752-1840), a German naturalist and professor at Göttingen ; the author of *Institutiones Physiologicæ* (1787) and other works.]

of a self-maintaining purposiveness—this he rightly
declares to be contradictory to Reason. But at the
same time he leaves to natural mechanism under
this to us indispensable *principle* of an original
organisation, an undeterminable but yet unmistake-
able element, in reference to which the faculty of
matter in an organised body is called by him a
formative impulse (in contrast to, and yet standing
under the higher guidance and direction of, that
merely mechanical *formative power* universally resident in matter).

§ 82. *Of the teleological system in the external relations of organised beings*

By external purposiveness I mean that by which
one thing of nature serves another as means to a
purpose. Now things which have no internal purposiveness and which presuppose none for their
possibility, *e.g.* earth, air, water, etc., may at the same
time be very purposive externally, *i.e.* in relation to
other beings. But these latter must be organised
beings, *i.e.* natural purposes, for otherwise the former
could not be judged as means to them. Thus water,
air, and earth cannot be regarded as means to the
raising of mountains, because mountains contain
nothing in themselves that requires a ground of
their possibility according to purposes, in reference to
which therefore their cause can never be represented
under the predicate of a means (as useful therefor).
External purposiveness is a quite different concept from that of internal purposiveness, which
is bound up with the possibility of an object irre-
spective of its actuality being itself a purpose. We
can ask about an organised being the question :

What is it for? But we cannot easily ask this
about things in which we recognise merely the
working of nature's mechanism. For in the
former, as regards their internal possibility, we represent a causality according to purposes, a creative
Understanding, and we refer this active faculty to *design*
its determining ground, viz. design. There is only
one external purposiveness which is connected with
the internal purposiveness of organisation, and yet
serves in the external relation of a means to a
purpose, without the question necessarily arising, as
to what end this being so organised must have
existed for. This is the organisation of both sexes
in their mutual relation for the propagation of their
kind ; since here we can always ask, as in the case
of an individual, why must such a pair exist? The
answer is: This pair first constitutes an *organising*
whole, though not an organised whole in a single
body.

If we now ask, wherefore anything is, the answer
is either: Its presence and its production have no
reference at all to a cause working according to
design, and so we always refer its origin to the
mechanism of nature, or : There is somewhere a designed ground of its presence (as a contingent natural
being). This thought we can hardly separate from
the concept of an organised thing ; for, since we
must place at the basis of its internal possibility a
causality of final causes and an Idea lying at the
ground of this, we cannot think the existence of this
product except as a purpose. ⟨For the represented   *find*
effect, the representation of which is at the same
time the determining ground of the intelligent cause
working towards its production, is called a *purpose.*⟩
In this case therefore we can either say: The

purpose of the existence of such a natural being is in itself; *i.e.* it is not merely a purpose but a *final purpose*, or : This is external to it in another natural being, *i.e.* it exists purposively not as a final purpose, but necessarily as a means.'

But if we go through the whole of nature we find in it, as nature, no being which could make claim to the eminence of being the final purpose of creation ; and we can even prove *a priori* that what might be for nature an *ultimate purpose*, according to all the thinkable determinations and properties wherewith one could endow it, could yet as a natural thing never be a *final purpose*.

If we consider the vegetable kingdom we might at first sight, on account of the immeasurable fertility with which it spreads itself almost on every soil, be led to take it for a mere product of that mechanism which nature displays in the formations of the mineral kingdom. But a more intimate knowledge of its indescribably wise organisation does not permit us to hold to this thought, but prompts the question : What are these things created for ? If it is answered : For the animal kingdom, which is thereby nourished and has thus been able to spread over the earth in genera so various, then the further question comes : What are these plant-devouring animals for ? The answer would be something like this : For beasts of prey, which can only be nourished by that which has life. Finally we have the question : What are these last, as well as the first-mentioned natural kingdoms, good for ? For man, in reference to the manifold use which his Understanding teaches him to make of all these creatures. He is the ultimate purpose of creation here on earth, because he is the only being upon it who can form a concept of purposes, and who can by his Reason make out of an aggregate of purposively formed things a system of purposes.

We might also with the chevalier *Linnæus* go the apparently opposite way and say : The herbivorous animals are there to moderate the luxurious growth of the vegetable kingdom, by which many of its species are choked. The carnivora are to set bounds to the voracity of the herbivora. Finally man, by his pursuit of these and his diminution of their numbers, preserves a certain equilibrium ﹅ between the producing and the destructive powers of nature. And so man, although in a certain reference he might be esteemed a purpose, yet in another has only the rank of a means.

If an objective purposiveness in the variety of the genera of creatures and their external relations to one another, as purposively constructed beings, be made a principle, then it is conformable to Reason to conceive in these relations a certain organisation and a system of all natural kingdoms according to final causes. Only here experience seems flatly to contradict the maxims of Reason, especially as concerns an ultimate purpose of nature, which is indispensable for the possibility of such a system and which we can put nowhere else but in man. For regarding him as one of the many animal genera, nature has not in the least excepted him from its destructive or its productive powers, but has subjected everything to a mechanism of its own without any purpose.

The first thing that must be designedly prepared in an arrangement for a purposive complex of natural beings on the earth would be their place

of habitation, the soil and the element on and in
which they are to thrive. But a more exact knowledge of the constitution of this basis of all organic
production indicates no other causes than those
working quite undesignedly, causes which rather
destroy than favour production, order, and purposes.
Land and sea not only contain in themselves
memorials of ancient mighty desolations which have
confounded them and all creatures that are in them ;
but their whole structure, the strata of the one
and the boundaries of the other have quite the
appearance of being the product of the wild and
violent forces of a nature working in a state of chaos.
Although the figure, the structure, and the slope of
the land might seem to be purposively ordered
for the reception of water from the air, for the
welling up of streams between strata of different
kinds (for many kinds of products), and for the
course of rivers—yet a closer investigation shows
that they are merely the effects of volcanic eruptions
or of inundations of the ocean, as regards not only
the first production of this figure, but, above all, its
subsequent transformation, as well as the disappearance of its first organic productions.[1] Now if the
place of habitation of all these creatures, the soil
(of the land) or the bosom (of the sea), indicates

---

[1] If the once adopted name *Natural history* is to continue for the
description of nature, we may in contrast with art, give the title of
Archaeology of nature to that which the former literally indicates, viz.
a representation of the *old* condition of the earth, about which,
although we cannot hope for certainty, we have good ground for
conjecture. As sculptured stones, etc., belong to the province of art,
so petrefactions belong to the archaeology of nature. And since work
is actually being done in this [science] (under the name of the Theory
of the Earth), constantly, although of course slowly, this name is
not given to a merely imaginary investigation of nature, but to one to
which nature itself leads and invites us.

nothing but a quite undesigned mechanism of its production, how and with what right can we demand and maintain a different origin for these latter products?   The closest examination, indeed (in *Camper's* judgment), of the remains of the aforesaid devastations of nature seems to show that man was not comprehended in these revolutions; but yet he is so dependent on the remaining creatures that, if a universally directing mechanism of nature be admitted in the case of the others, he must also be regarded as comprehended under it; even though his Understanding (for the most part at least) has been able to deliver him from these devastations.

But this argument seems to prove more than was intended by it.   It seems to prove not merely that man cannot be the ultimate purpose of nature, and that on the same grounds the aggregate of the organised things of nature on the earth cannot be a system of purposes; but also that the natural products formerly held to be natural purposes have no other origin than the mechanism of nature.

But in the solution given above of the Antinomy of the principles of the mechanical and teleological methods of production of organic beings of nature, we have seen that they are merely principles of the reflective Judgment in respect of nature as it produces forms in accordance with particular laws (for the systematic connection of which we have no key).   They do not determine the origin of these beings in themselves; but only say that we, by the constitution of our Understanding and our Reason, cannot conceive it in this kind of being except according to final causes.   The greatest possible effort, even intrepidity, in the attempt to explain them mechanically is not only permitted, but we

are invited to it by Reason ; notwithstanding that
we know from the subjective grounds of the particular
species and limitations of our Understanding (not
e.g. because the mechanism of production would
contradict in itself an origin according to purposes)
that we can never attain thereto.   Finally, the
compatibility of both ways of representing the
possibility of nature may lie in the supersensible
principle of nature (external to us, as well as in
us) ; whilst the method of representation according
to final causes may be only a subjective condition
of the use of our Reason, when it not merely wishes
to form a judgment upon objects as phenomena,
but desires to refer these phenomena together with
their principles to their supersensible substrate, in
order to find certain laws of their unity possible,
which it cannot represent to itself except through
purposes (of which the Reason also has such as
are supersensible).

§ 83. *Of the ultimate purpose of nature as a teleological system*

We have shown in the preceding that, though
not for the determinant but for the reflective
Judgment, we have sufficient cause for judging
man to be, not merely like all organised beings
a *natural purpose*, but also the *ultimate purpose* of
nature here on earth ; in reference to whom all
other natural things constitute a system of purposes
according to fundamental propositions of Reason.
If now that must be found in man himself, which
is to be furthered as a purpose by means of his
connection with nature, this purpose must either
be of a kind that can be satisfied by nature in

its beneficence ; or it is the aptitude and skill for all kinds of purposes for which nature (external and internal) can be used by him. The first purpose of nature would be man's *happiness*, the second his *culture*.

The concept of happiness is not one that man derives by abstraction from his instincts and so deduces from his animal nature ; but it is a mere *Idea* of a state, that he wishes to make adequate to the Idea under merely empirical conditions (which is impossible). This Idea he projects in such different ways on account of the complication of his Understanding with Imagination and Sense, and changes so often, that nature, even if it were entirely subjected to his elective will, could receive absolutely no determinate, universal and fixed law, so as to harmonise with this vacillating concept and thus with the purpose which each man arbitrarily sets before himself. And even if we reduce this to the true natural wants as to which our race is thoroughly agreed, or on the other hand, raise ever so high man's skill to accomplish his imagined purposes ; yet, even thus, what man understands by happiness, and what is in fact his proper, ultimate, natural purpose (not purpose of freedom), would never be attained by him. For it is not his nature to rest and be contented with the possession and enjoyment of anything whatever. On the other side, too, there is something wanting. Nature has not taken him for her special darling and favoured him with benefit above all animals. Rather, in her destructive operations,—plague, hunger, perils of waters, frost, assaults of other animals great and small, etc.,—in these things has she spared him as little as any other animal. Further, the inconsistency of his own *natural dispositions* drives him into self-devised torments, and also reduces others of his own race to misery, by the oppression of lordship, the barbarism of war, and so forth ; he, himself, as far as in him lies, works for the destruction of his own race ; so that even with the most beneficent external nature, its purpose, if it were directed to the happiness of our species, would not be attained in an earthly system, because our nature is not susceptible of it. Man is then always only a link in the chain of natural purposes ; a principle certainly in respect of many purposes, for which nature seems to have destined him in her disposition, and to which he sets himself, but also a means for the maintenance of purposiveness in the mechanism of the remaining links. As the only being on earth which has an Understanding and, consequently, a faculty of setting arbitrary purposes before itself, he is certainly entitled to be the lord of nature ; and if it be regarded as a teleological system he is, by his destination, the ultimate purpose of nature. But this is subject to the condition of his having an Understanding and the Will to give to it and to himself such a reference to purposes, as can be self-sufficient independently of nature, and, consequently, can be a final purpose ; which, however, must not be sought in nature itself.

But in order to find out where in man we have to place that *ultimate purpose* of nature, we must seek out what nature can supply to prepare him for what he must do himself in order to be a final purpose, and we must separate it from all those purposes whose possibility depends upon things that one can expect only from nature. Of the latter kind is earthly happiness, by which is under-

stood the complex of all man's purposes possible
through nature, whether external nature or man's
nature ; *i.e.* the matter of all his earthly purposes,
which, if he makes it his whole purpose, renders
him incapable of positing his own existence as a
final purpose, and being in harmony therewith.
There remains therefore of all his purposes in
nature only the formal subjective condition ; viz.
the aptitude of setting purposes in general before
himself, and (independent of nature in his purposive
determination) of using nature, conformably to the
maxims of his free purposes in general, as a means.
This nature can do in regard to the final purpose
that lies outside it, and it therefore may be regarded
as its ultimate purpose.   The production of the
aptitude of a rational being for arbitrary purposes
in general (consequently in his freedom) is *culture*.
Therefore, culture alone can be the ultimate purpose
which we have cause for ascribing to nature in
respect to the human race (not man's earthly happiness or the fact that he is the chief instrument
of instituting order and harmony in irrational nature
external to himself).

   But all culture is not adequate to this ultimate
purpose of nature. The culture of *skill* is indeed the
chief subjective condition of aptitude for furthering
one's purposes in general ; but it is not adequate to
furthering the *will*[1] in the determination and choice
of purposes, which yet essentially belongs to the
whole extent of an aptitude for purposes.   The
latter condition of aptitude, which we might call the
culture of training (discipline), is negative, and
consists in the freeing of the will from the despotism
of desires.   By these, tied as we are to certain

   [1] [First Edition has *freedom*.]

natural things, we are rendered incapable even of choosing, while we allow those impulses to serve as fetters, which Nature has given us as guiding threads that we should not neglect or injure the destination of our animal nature—we being all the time free enough to strain or relax, to extend or diminish them, according as the purposes of Reason require.

Skill cannot be developed in the human race except by means of inequality among men; for the great majority provide the necessities of life, as it were, mechanically, without requiring any art in particular, for the convenience and leisure of others who work at the less necessary elements of culture, science and art. In an oppressed condition they have hard work and little enjoyment, although much of the culture of the higher classes gradually spreads to them. Yet with the progress of this culture (the height of which is called luxury, reached when the propensity to what can be done without begins to be injurious to what is indispensable), their calamities increase equally in two directions, on the one hand through violence from without, on the other hand through internal discontent; but still this splendid misery is bound up with the development of the natural capacities of the human race, and the purpose of nature itself, although not our purpose, is thus attained. The formal condition under which nature can alone attain this its final design, is that arrangement of men's relations to one another, by which lawful authority in a whole, which we call a *civil community*, is opposed to the abuse of their conflicting freedoms; only in this can the greatest development of natural capacities take place. For this also there would be requisite,—if

men were clever enough to find it out and wise
enough to submit themselves voluntarily to its
constraint,—a *cosmopolitan* whole, *i.e.* a system of
all states that are in danger of acting injuriously
upon each other.[1]   Failing this, and with the
obstacles which ambition, lust of dominion, and
avarice, especially in those who have the authority
in their hands, oppose even to the possibility of
such a scheme, there is, inevitably, *war* (by
which sometimes states subdivide and resolve
themselves into smaller states, sometimes a state
annexes other smaller states and strives to form a
greater whole).   Though war is an undesigned
enterprise of men (stirred up by their unbridled
passions), yet is it [perhaps][2] a deep-hidden and
designed enterprise of supreme Wisdom for
preparing, if not for establishing, conformity to law
amid the freedom of states, and with this a unity of
a morally grounded system of those states.   In
spite of the dreadful afflictions with which it visits
the human race, and the perhaps greater afflictions
with which the constant preparation for it in time
of peace oppresses them, yet is it (although the
hope for a restful state of popular happiness is ever
further off) a motive for developing all talents serviceable for culture, to the highest possible pitch.[3]

As concerns the discipline of the inclinations,—
for which our natural capacity in regard of our

---

[1] [These views are set forth by Kant more fully in the essay
Zum ewigen Frieden (1795).]

[2] [Second Edition.]

[3] [Cf. *The Philosophical Theory of Religion*, Part i., *On the bad
principle in Human Nature*, III., where Kant remarks that although
war " is not so incurably bad as the deadness of a universal mon-
archy . . . yet, as an ancient observed, it makes more bad men than
it takes away."]

destination as an animal race is quite purposive, but
which render the development of humanity very
difficult,—there is manifest in respect of this second
requirement for culture a purposive striving of
nature to a cultivation which makes us receptive of
higher purposes than nature itself can supply. We
cannot strive against the preponderance of evil,
which is poured out upon us by the refinement of
taste pushed to idealisation, and even by the luxury
of science as affording food for pride, through the
insatiable number of inclinations thus aroused. But
yet we cannot mistake the purpose of nature—ever
aiming to win us away from the rudeness and violence of those inclinations (inclinations to enjoyment)
which belong rather to our animality, and for the
most part are opposed to the cultivation of our higher
destiny, and to make way for the development of
our humanity. The beautiful arts and the sciences
which, by their universally-communicable pleasure,
and by the polish and refinement of society, make
man more civilised, if not morally better, win us in
large measure from the tyranny of sense-propensions,
and thus prepare men for a lordship, in which
Reason alone shall have authority; whilst the evils
with which we are visited, partly by nature, partly
by the intolerant selfishness of men, summon,
strengthen, and harden the powers of the soul not
to submit to them, and so make us feel an
aptitude for higher purposes, which lies hidden
in us.¹

¹ The value of life for us, if it is estimated by that which we
enjoy (by the natural purpose of the sum of all inclinations, i.e.
happiness), is easy to decide. It sinks below zero; for who would
enter again upon life anew under the same conditions? who
would do so even according to a new, self-chosen plan, yet in conformity
to the course of nature, if it were merely directed to enjoyment?

§ 84. *Of the final purpose of the existence of a world. i.e. of creation itself*

A *final purpose* is that purpose which needs no other as condition of its possibility.

If the mere mechanism of nature be assumed as the ground of explanation of its purposiveness, we cannot ask: what are things[1] there for? For according to such an idealistic system it is only the physical possibility of things (to think which as purposes would be mere subtlety without any Object) that is under discussion; whether we refer this form of things to chance or to blind necessity, in either case the question would be vain. If, however, we assume the purposive combination in the world to be real and to be ⌐brought about⌐ by a particular kind of causality, viz. that of a *designedly working* cause, we cannot stop at the question: why have things of the world (organised beings) this or that form? why are they placed by nature in this or that relation to one another? But once an Understanding is thought that must be regarded as the cause of the possibility of such forms as they are actually found in things, it must be also asked on objective grounds: Who could have determined this productive Understanding to an operation of this kind?

We have shown above what value life has in virtue of what it contains in itself, when lived in accordance with the purpose that nature has along with us, and which consists in what we do not merely what we enjoy, in which however, we are always but means towards an undetermined final purpose. There remains then nothing but the value which we ourselves give our life, through what we can not only do, but do purposively in such independence of nature that the existence of nature itself can only be a purpose under this condition.

[1] [First Edition has *things in the world*.]

This being is then the final purpose in reference to which such things are there.

I have said above that the final purpose is not a purpose which nature would be competent to bring about and to produce in conformity with its Idea, because it is unconditioned. For there is nothing in nature (regarded as a sensible being) for which the determining ground present in itself would not be always conditioned ; and this holds not merely of external (material) nature, but also of internal (thinking) nature—it being of course understood that I only am considering that in myself which is nature. But a thing that is to exist necessarily, on account of its objective constitution, as the final purpose of an intelligent cause, must be of the kind that in the order of purposes it is dependent on no further condition than merely its Idea.

Now we have in the world only one kind of beings whose causality is teleological, *i.e.* is directed to purposes and is at the same time so constituted that the law according to which they have to determine purposes for themselves is represented as unconditioned and independent of natural conditions, and yet as in itself necessary. The being of this kind is man, but man considered as noumenon ; the only natural being in which we can recognise, on the side of its peculiar constitution, a supersensible faculty (*freedom*) and also the law of causality, together with the Object, which this faculty may propose to itself as highest purpose (the highest good in the world).

Now of man (and so of every rational creature in the world) as a moral being it can no longer be asked : why (*quem in finem*) he exists ? His existence involves the highest purpose to which, as far as is in his power, he can subject the whole of nature ; contrary to which at least he cannot regard himself as subject to any influence of nature.— If now things of the world, as beings dependent in their existence, need a supreme cause acting according to purposes, man is the final purpose of creation ; since without him the chain of mutually subordinated purposes would not be complete as regards its ground. Only in man, and only in him as subject of morality, do we meet with unconditioned legislation in respect of purposes, which therefore alone renders him capable of being a final purpose, to which the whole of nature is teleologically subordinated.[1]

[1] It would be possible that the happiness of rational beings in the world should be a purpose of nature, and then also this would be its *ultimate* purpose. At least we cannot see *a priori* why nature should not be so ordered, because by means of its mechanism this effect would be certainly possible, at least so far as we see. But morality, with a causality according to purposes subordinated thereto, is absolutely impossible by means of natural causes ; for the principle by which it determines to action is supersensible, and is therefore the only possible principle in the order of purposes that in respect of nature is absolutely unconditioned. Its subject consequently alone is qualified to be the *final purpose* of creation to which the whole of nature is subordinated.— *Happiness*, on the contrary, as has been shown in the preceding paragraphs by the testimony of experience, is not even a *purpose of nature* in respect of man in preference to other creatures ; much less a *final purpose of creation*. Men may of course make it their ultimate subjective purpose. But if I ask, in reference to the final purpose of creation, why must men exist ? then we are speaking of an objective supreme purpose, such as the highest Reason would require for creation. If we answer : These beings exist to afford objects for the benevolence of that Supreme Cause ; then we contradict the condition to which the Reason of man subjects even his inmost wish for happiness (viz. the harmony with his own internal moral legislation). This proves that happiness can only be a conditioned purpose, and that it is only as a moral being that man can be the final purpose of creation ; but that as concerns his state happiness is only connected with it as a consequence, according to the measure of his harmony with that purpose regarded as the purpose of his being.

§ 85. *Of Physico-theology*

Physico-theology is the endeavour of Reason to infer the Supreme Cause of nature and its properties from the *purposes* of nature (which can only be empirically known). *Moral theology* (ethico-theology) would be the endeavour to infer that Cause and its properties from the moral purpose of rational beings in nature (which can be known *a priori*).

The former naturally precedes the latter. For if we wish to infer a World Cause *teleologically* from the things in the world, purposes of nature must first be given, for which we afterwards have to seek a final purpose, and for this the principle of the causality of this Supreme Cause.

Many investigations of nature can and must be conducted according to the teleological principle, without our having cause to inquire into the ground of the possibility of purposive working which we meet with in various products of nature. But if we wish to have a concept of this we have absolutely no further insight into it than the maxim of the reflective Judgment affords : viz. if only a single organic product of nature were given to us, by the constitution of our cognitive faculty we could think no other ground for it than that of a cause of nature itself (whether the whole of nature or only this part) which contains the causality for it through Understanding. This principle of judging, though it does not bring us any further in the explanation of natural things and their origin, yet discloses to us an outlook over nature, by which perhaps we may be able to determine more closely the otherwise so unfruitful concept of an Original Being.

Now I say that Physico-theology, however far it
may be pursued, can disclose to us nothing of a *final*
purpose of creation ; for it does not even extend to
the question as to this.   It can, it is true, justify the
concept of an intelligent World Cause, as a subjective concept (only available for the constitution of
our cognitive faculty) of the possibility of things
that we can make intelligible to ourselves according to purposes ; but it cannot determine this concept
further, either in a theoretical or a practical point of
view.   Its endeavour does not come up to its design
of being the basis of a Theology, but it always
remains only a physical Teleology ; because the
purposive reference therein is and must be always
considered only as conditioned in nature, and it
consequently cannot inquire into the purpose for
which nature itself exists (for which the ground must
be sought outside nature),—notwithstanding that it
is upon the determinate Idea of this that the determinate concept of that Supreme Intelligent World
Cause, and the consequent possibility of a Theology,
depend.

What the things in the world are mutually
useful for ; what good the manifold in a thing does
for the thing ; how we have ground to assume that
nothing in the world is in vain, but that everything
in nature is good for something,—the condition being
granted that certain things are to exist (as purposes),
whence our Reason has in its power for the Judgment no other principle of the possibility of the
Object, which it inevitably judges teleologically,
than that of subordinating the mechanism of nature
to the Architectonic of an intelligent Author of the
world—all this the teleological consideration of the
world supplies us with excellently and to our extreme

admiration. But because the data, and so the principles, for *determining* that concept of an intelligent World Cause (as highest Artist) are merely empirical, they do not enable us to infer any of its properties beyond those which experience reveals in its effects. Now experience, since it can never embrace collective nature as a system, must often (apparently) happen upon this concept (and by mutually conflicting grounds of proof) ; but it can never, even if we had the power of surveying empirically the whole system as far as it concerns mere nature, raise us above nature to the purpose of its existence, and so to the determinate concept of that supreme Intelligence.

If we lessen the problem with the solution of which Physico-theology has to do, its solution appears easy. If we reduce the concept of a *Deity* to that of an intelligent being thought by us, of which there may be one or more, which possesses many and very great properties, but not all the properties which are requisite for the foundation of a nature in harmony with the greatest possible purpose ; or if we do not scruple in a theory to supply by arbitrary additions what is deficient in the grounds of proof, and so, where we have only ground for assuming *much* perfection (and what is "much" for us?), consider ourselves entitled to presuppose *all possible* perfection ; thus indeed physical Teleology may make weighty claims to the distinction of being the basis of a Theology. But if we are desired to point out what impels and moreover authorises us to add these supplements, then we shall seek in vain for a ground of justification in the principles of the theoretical use of Reason, which is ever desirous in the explanation of an Object of experience to ascribe to it no more properties than those for which empirical data of possibility are to be found. On closer examination we should see that properly speaking an Idea of a Supreme Being, which rests on a quite different use of Reason (the practical use), lies in us fundamentally *a priori*, impelling us to supplement the defective representation, supplied by a physical Teleology, of the original ground of the purposes in nature by the concept of a Deity; and we should not falsely imagine that we had worked out this Idea, and with it a Theology by means of the theoretical use of Reason in the physical cognition of the world—much less that we had proved its reality.

One cannot blame the ancients much, if they thought of their gods as differing much from each other both as regards their faculties and as regards their designs and volitions, but yet thought of all of them, the Supreme One not excepted, as always limited after human fashion. For if they considered the arrangement and the course of things in nature, they certainly found ground enough for assuming something more than mechanism as its cause, and for conjecturing behind the machinery of this world designs of certain higher causes, which they could not think otherwise than superhuman. But because they met with good and evil, the purposive and the unpurposive, mingled together (at least as far as our insight goes), and could not permit themselves to assume nevertheless that wise and benevolent purposes of which they saw no proof lay hidden at bottom, on behalf of the arbitrary Idea of a supremely perfect original Author, their judgment upon the supreme World Cause could hardly have been other than it was, so long as they proceeded

consistently according to maxims of the mere
theoretical use of Reason.   Others, who wished
to be theologians as well as physicists, thought to
find contentment for the Reason by providing for
the absolute unity of the principle of natural things
which Reason demands, the Idea of a Being of
which as sole Substance the things would be
all only inherent determinations.   This Substance
would not be Cause of the World by means of
intelligence, but in it all the intelligences of the
beings in the world would be comprised.   This
Being consequently would produce nothing according to purposes ; but in it all things, on account
of the unity of the subject of which they are mere
determinations, must necessarily relate themselves
purposively to one another, though without purpose
and design.   Thus they introduced the Idealism of
final causes, by changing the unity (so difficult to
explain) of a number of purposively combined
substances, from being the unity of causal dependence *on one* Substance to be the unity of inherence
in one.   This system—which in the sequel, considered on the side of the inherent world beings,
becomes *Pantheism*, and (later) on the side of the
Subject subsisting by itself as Original Being,
becomes *Spinozism*,—does not so much resolve as
explain away into nothing the question of the first
ground of the purposiveness of nature ; because this
latter concept, bereft of all reality, must be taken
for a mere misinterpretation of a universal ontological concept of a thing in general.

Hence the concept of a Deity, which would
be adequate for our teleological judging of nature,
can never be derived according to mere theoretical
principles of the use of Reason (on which Physico-

theology alone is based). For as one alternative we may explain all Teleology as a mere deception of the Judgment in its judging of the causal combination of things, and fly to the sole principle of a mere mechanism of nature, which merely seems to us, on account of the unity of the Substance of whose determinations nature is but the manifold, to contain a universal reference to purposes. Or if, instead of this Idealism of final causes, we wish to remain attached to the principle of the Realism of this particular kind of causality, we may set beneath natural purposes many intelligent original beings or- only a single one. But so far as we have for the basis of this concept [of Realism] only empirical principles derived from the actual purposive combination in the world, we cannot on the one hand find any remedy for the discordance that nature presents in many examples in respect of unity of purpose ; and on the other hand, as to the concept of a single intelligent Cause, so far as we are authorised by mere experience, we can never draw it therefrom in a manner sufficiently determined for any serviceable Theology whatever (whether theoretical or practical).

Physical Teleology impels us, it is true, to seek a Theology ; but it cannot produce one, however far we may investigate nature by means of experience and, in reference to the purposive combination apparent in it, call in Ideas of Reason (which must be theoretical for physical problems).—What is the use, one might well complain, of placing at the basis of all these arrangements a great Understanding incommensurable by us, and supposing it to govern the world according to design, if nature does not and cannot tell us anything of the final design ? For

without this we cannot refer all these natural purposes to any common point, nor can we form any
teleological principle, sufficient either for cognising
the purposes collected in a system, or for forming
a concept of the Supreme Understanding, as Cause
of such a nature, that could serve as a standard
for our Judgment reflecting teleologically thereon.
I should thus have an *artistic Understanding* for
scattered purposes, but no *Wisdom* for a final purpose, in which final purpose nevertheless must be
contained the determining ground of the said Understanding. But in the absence of a final purpose
which pure Reason alone can supply (because all
'purposes in the world are empirically conditioned,
and can contain nothing absolutely good but only
what is good for this or that regarded as a contingent design), and which alone would teach me
what properties, what degree, and what relation of
the Supreme Cause to nature I have to think in
order to judge of nature as a teleological system ;
how and with what right do I dare to extend at
pleasure my very limited concept of that original
Understanding (which I can base on my limited
knowledge of the world), of the Might of that
original Being in actualising its Ideas, and of its
Will to do so, and complete this into the Idea of
an Allwise, Infinite Being ? If this is to be done
theoretically, it would presuppose omniscience in
me, in order to see into the purposes of nature in
their whole connection, and in addition the power
of conceiving all possible plans, in comparison with
which the present plan would be with justice regarded as the best. For without this complete
knowledge of the effect I can arrive at no determinate concept of the Supreme Cause, which can

only be found in the concept of an Intelligence infinite in every respect, *i.e.* the concept of a Deity, and so I can supply no foundation for Theology.

Hence, with every possible extension of physical Teleology, according to the propositions above laid down we may say : By the constitution and the principles of our cognitive faculty we can think of nature, in its purposive arrangements which have become known to us, in no other way than as the product of an Understanding to which it is subject. But the theoretical investigation of nature can never reveal to us whether this Understanding may not also, with the whole of nature and its production, have had a final design (which would not lie in the nature of the sensible world). On the contrary, with all our knowledge of nature it remains undecided whether that Supreme Cause is its original ground according to a final purpose or not rather by means of an Understanding determined by the mere necessity of its nature to produce certain forms (according to the analogy of what we call the Art-instinct in animals); without it being necessary to ascribe to it even wisdom, much less the highest wisdom combined with all other properties requisite for the perfection of its product.

Hence Physico-theology is a misunderstood physical Teleology, only serviceable as a preparation (propædeutic) for Theology; and it is only adequate to this design by the aid of a foreign principle on which it can rely, and not in itself, as its name seems to indicate.

2 B

§ 86. *Of Ethico-theology*

The commonest Understanding, if it thinks over the presence of things in the world, and the existence of the world itself, cannot forbear from the judgment that all the various creatures, no matter how great the art displayed in their arrangement, and how various their purposive mutual connection,—even the complex of their numerous systems (which we incorrectly call worlds),—would be for nothing, if there were not also men (rational beings in general). Without men the whole creation would be a mere waste, in vain, and without final purpose. But it is not in reference to man's cognitive faculty (theoretical Reason) that the being of everything else in the world gets its worth; he is not there merely that there may be some one to *contemplate* the world. For if the contemplation of the world only afforded a representation of things without any final purpose, no worth could accrue to its being from the mere fact that it is known; we must presuppose for it a final purpose, in reference to which its contemplation itself has worth. Again it is not in reference to the feeling of pleasure, or to the sum of pleasures, that we think a final purpose of creation as given; *i.e.* we do not estimate that absolute worth by well-being or by enjoyment (whether bodily or mental), or in a word, by happiness. For the fact that man, if he exists, takes this for his final design, gives us no concept as to why in general he should exist, and as to what worth he has in himself to make his existence pleasant. He must, therefore, be supposed to be the final purpose of creation, in order to have a rational ground for holding that nature must harmonise with his happiness, if it is considered as an absolute whole according to principles of purposes.— Hence [that which we seek] is only the faculty of desire ; not, however, that which makes man dependent (through sensuous impulses) upon nature, nor that in respect of which the worth of his being depends upon what he receives and enjoys. But it is that worth which he alone can give to himself, and which consists in what he does, how and according to what principles he acts, and that not as a link in nature's chain but in the *freedom* of his faculty of desire. That·is, a good will is that whereby alone his being can have an absolute worth, and in reference to which the being of the world can have a *final purpose*.

The commonest judgment of healthy human Reason completely accords with this, that it is only as a moral being that man can be a final purpose of creation ; if we but direct men's attention to the question and incite them to investigate it. What does it avail, one will say, that this man has so much talent, that he is so active therewith, and that he exerts thereby a useful influence over the community, thus having a great worth both in relation to his own happy condition and to the advantage of others, if he does not possess a good will ? He is a contemptible Object considered in respect of his inner self ; and if the creation is not to be without any final purpose at all, he, who as man belongs to it, but as a bad man is in a world under moral laws, must conformably to these forfeit his subjective purpose (happiness), as the sole condition under which his existence can accord with the final purpose.

If now we meet with purposive arrangements in the world and, as Reason inevitably requires, subordinate the purposes that are only conditioned to an unconditioned, supreme, *i.e.* final, purpose; then we easily see in the first place that we are thus concerned not with a purpose of nature (internal to itself), so far as it exists, but with the purpose of its existence along with all its ordinances, and, consequently, with the ultimate *purpose of creation*, and specially with the supreme condition under which a final purpose (*i.e.* the determinining ground of a supreme Understanding for the production of beings of the world) can be allowed.

Since now it is only as a moral being that we recognise man as the purpose of creation, we have in the first place a ground (at least, the chief condition) for regarding the world as a whole connected according to purposes, and as a *system* of final causes. And, more especially, as regards the reference (necessary for us by the constitution of our Reason) of natural purposes to an intelligent World Cause, we have *one principle* enabling us to think the nature and properties of this First Cause as supreme ground in the kingdom of purposes, and to determine its concept. This physical Teleology could not do; it could only lead to indeterminate concepts of it, unserviceable alike in theoretical and in practical use.

From this so definite principle of the causality of the Original Being we must not think Him merely as Intelligence and as legislative for nature, but also as legislating supremely in a moral kingdom of purposes. In reference to the *highest good*, alone possible under His sovereignty, viz. the existence of rational beings under moral laws, we shall think this Original Being as *all-knowing* : thus our inmost dispositions (which constitute the proper moral worth of the actions of rational beings of the world) will not be hid from Him. We shall think Him as *all-mighty* : thus He will be able to make the whole of nature accord with this highest purpose. We shall think Him as *all-good*, and at the same time as *just* : because these two properties (which when united constitute *Wisdom*) are the conditions of the causality of a supreme Cause of the world, as highest good, under moral laws. So also all the other transcendental properties, such as *Eternity, Omnipresence*, etc. [for goodness and justice are moral properties[1]], which are presupposed in reference to such a final purpose, must be thought in Him.— In this way *moral Teleology* supplies the deficiency in *physical Teleology*, and first establishes a *Theology* ; because the latter, if it did not borrow from the former without being observed, but were to proceed consistently, could only found a *Demonology*, which is incapable of any definite concept.

But the principle of the reference of the world to a supreme Cause, as Deity, on account of the moral purposive determination of certain beings in it, does not accomplish this by completing the physico-teleological ground of proof and so taking this necessarily as its basis. It is sufficient *in itself* and directs attention to the purposes of nature and the investigation of that incomprehensible great art lying hidden behind its forms, in order to confirm incidentally by means of natural purposes the Ideas that pure practical Reason furnishes. For the concept of beings of the world under moral laws

---

[1] [Second Edition.]

is a principle (*a priori*) according to which man must
of necessity judge himself. Further, if there is
in general a World Cause acting designedly and
directed towards a purpose, this moral relation must
be just as necessarily the condition of the possibility
of a creation, as that in accordance with physical
laws (if, that is, that intelligent Cause has also a
final purpose). This is regarded *a priori* by
Reason as a necessary fundamental proposition for
it in its teleological judging of the existence of
things. It now only comes to this whether we
have sufficient ground for Reason (either speculative or practical) to ascribe to the supreme Cause
that acts in accordance with purposes a *final purpose*. For it may *a priori* be taken by us as
certain that this, by the subjective constitution of
our Reason and even of the Reason of other beings
as far as we can think it, can be nothing else than
man under moral laws: since otherwise the purposes of nature in the physical order could not be
known *a priori*, especially as it can in no way be
seen that nature could not exist without such purposes.

Remark

Suppose the case of a man at the moment when
his mind is disposed to a moral sensation. If surrounded by a beautiful nature, he is in a state of
restful, serene enjoyment of his being, he feels a
want, viz. to be grateful for this to some being or
other. Or if another time he finds himself in the
same state of mind when pressed by duties that
he can and will only competently perform by a
voluntary sacrifice, he again feels in himself a want,
viz. to have thus executed a command and obeyed

a Supreme Lord. Or, again ; if he has in some
heedless way transgressed his duty, but without
becoming answerable to men, his severe self-
reproach will speak to him with the voice of a judge
to whom he has to give account. In a word, he
needs a moral Intelligence, in order to have a Being
for the purpose of his existence, which may be,
conformably to this purpose, the cause of himself
and of the world. It is vain to assign motives
behind these feelings, for they are immediately
connected with the purest moral sentiment, because
gratitude, obedience, and *humiliation* (submission to
deserved chastisement) are mental dispositions that
make for duty ; and the mind which is inclined
towards a widening of its moral sentiment here only
voluntarily conceives an object that is not in the
world in order where possible to evince its duty
before such an One. It is therefore at least possible
and grounded too in our moral disposition to represent a pure moral need of the existence of a Being,
by which our morality gains strength or even (at
least according to our representation) more scope,
viz. a new object for its exercise. That is, [there is
a need] to assume a morally-legislating Being outside the world, without any reference to theoretical
proofs, still less to self-interest, from pure moral
grounds free from all foreign influence (and consequently only subjective), on the mere recommendation of a pure practical Reason legislating by itself
alone. And although such a mental disposition
might seldom occur or might not last long, but be
transient and without permanent effect, or might
even pass away without any meditation on the object
represented in such shadowy outline, or without care
to bring it under clear concepts—there is yet here

unmistakably the ground why our moral capacity, as a subjective principle, should not be contented in its contemplation of the world with its purposiveness by means of natural causes, but should ascribe to it a supreme Cause governing nature according to moral principles.— In addition, we feel ourselves constrained by the moral law to strive for a universal highest purpose which yet we, in common with the rest of nature, are incapable of attaining ; and it is only so far as we strive for it that we can judge ourselves to be in harmony with the final purpose of an intelligent World Cause (if such there be). Thus is found a pure moral ground of practical Reason for assuming this Cause (since it can be done without contradiction), in order that we may no more regard that effort of Reason as quite idle, and so run the risk of abandoning it from weariness.

With all this, so much only is to be said, that though *fear* first produces *gods* (demons), it is *Reason* by means of its moral principles that can first produce the concept of *God* (even when, as commonly is the case, one is very ignorant in the Teleology of nature, or is very doubtful on account of the difficulty of adjusting by a sufficiently established principle its mutually contradictory phenomena). Also, the inner *moral* purposive destination of man's being supplies that in which natural knowledge is deficient, by directing us to think, for the final purpose of the being of all things (for which no other principle than an *ethical* one is satisfactory to Reason), the supreme Cause [as endowed] with properties, whereby it is able to subject the whole of nature to that single design (for which nature is merely the instrument),—*i.e.* to think it as a *Deity*.

§ 87. *Of the moral proof of the Being of God*

There is a *physical Teleology*, which gives
sufficient ground of proof to our theoretical reflective Judgment to assume the being of an
intelligent World-Cause. But we find also in ourselves and still more in the concept of a rational
being in general endowed with freedom (of his
causality) a *moral Teleology*. However, as the
purposive reference, together with its law, is determined *a priori* in ourselves and therefore can be
cognised as necessary, this internal conformity to
law requires no intelligent cause external to us ;
any more than we need look to a highest Understanding as the source of the purposiveness (for
every possible exercise of art) that we find in the
geometrical properties of figures. But this moral
Teleology concerns us as beings of the world, and
therefore as beings bound up with other things in
the world ; upon which latter, whether as purposes
or as objects in respect of which we ourselves are
final purpose, the same moral laws require us to
pass judgment. This moral Teleology, then, has
to do with the reference of our own causality to
purposes and even to a final purpose that we must
aim at in the world, as well as with the reciprocal
reference of the world to that moral purpose, and
the external possibility of its accomplishment (to
which no physical Teleology can lead us). Hence
the question necessarily arises, whether it compels
our rational judgment to go beyond the world and
seek an intelligent supreme principle for that reference of nature to the moral in us ; in order to
represent nature as purposive even in reference to

our inner moral legislation and its possible accomplishment. There is therefore certainly a moral Teleology, which is connected on the one hand with the *nomothetic* of freedom and on the other with that of nature ; just as necessarily as civil legislation is connected with the question where the executive authority is to be sought, and in general in every case [with the question] wherein Reason is to furnish a principle of the actuality of a certain regular order of things only possible according to Ideas.— We shall first set forth the progress of Reason from that moral Teleology and its reference to physical, to *Theology*; and then make some observations upon the possibility and the validity of this way of reasoning.

If we assume the being of certain things (or even only certain forms of things) to be contingent and so to be possible only through something else which is their cause, we may seek for the unconditioned ground of this causality of the supreme (and so of the conditioned) either in the physical or the teleological order (either according to the *nexus effectivus* or the *nexus finalis*). That is, we may either ask, what is the supreme productive cause of these things ; 'or what is their supreme (absolutely unconditioned) purpose, *i.e.* the final purpose of that cause in its production of this or all its products generally ? In the second case it is plainly pre-supposed that this cause is capable of representing purposes to itself, and consequently is an intelligent Being ; at least it must be thought as acting in accordance with the laws of such a being.

If we follow the latter order, it is a FUNDA-MENTAL PROPOSITION, to which even the commonest human Reason is compelled to give immediate assent, that if there is to be in general a *final purpose* furnished *a priori* by Reason, this can be no other than *man* (every rational being of the world) *under moral laws.*[1] For (and so every one judges) if the world consisted of mere lifeless, or even in part of living but irrational, beings, its existence would have no worth because in it there would be no being who would have the least concept of what worth is. Again, if there were intelligent beings, whose Reason were only able to place the worth of the existence of things in the relation of

---

[1] I say deliberately under moral laws. It is not man *in accordance with* moral laws, *i.e.* a being who behaves himself in conformity with them, who is the final purpose of creation. For by using the latter expression we should be asserting more than we know ; viz. that it is in the power of an Author of the world to cause man always to behave himself in accordance with moral laws. But this presupposes a concept of freedom and of nature (of which latter we can only think an external author), which would imply an insight into the supersensible substrate of nature and its identity with that which causality through freedom makes possible in the world. And this far surpasses the insight of our Reason. Only of *man under moral laws* can we say, without transgressing the limits of our insight : his being constitutes the final purpose of the world. This harmonises completely with the judgment of human Reason reflecting morally upon the course of the world. We believe that we perceive in the case of the wicked the traces of a wise purposive reference, if we only see that the wanton criminal does not die before he has undergone the deserved punishment of his misdeeds. According to our concepts of free causality, our good or bad behaviour depends on ourselves ; we regard it the highest wisdom in the government of the world to ordain for the first, opportunity, and for both, their consequence, in accordance with moral laws. In the latter properly consists the glory of God, which is hence not unsuitably described by theologians as the ultimate purpose of creation.— It is further to be remarked that when we use the word creation, we understand nothing more than we have said here, viz. the cause of the *being* of the world or of the things in it (substances). This is what the concept properly belonging to this word involves (*actuatio substantiæ est creatio*) ; and consequently there is not implied in it the supposition of a freely working, and therefore intelligent, cause (whose being we first of all desire to prove).

nature to themselves (their well-being), but not to
furnish of itself an original worth (in freedom), then
there would certainly be (relative) purposes in the
world, but no (absolute) final purpose, because the
existence of such rational beings would be always
purposeless.   But the moral laws have this peculiar
characteristic that they prescribe to Reason something as a purpose without any condition, and
consequently exactly as the concept of a final purpose requires.   The existence of a Reason that can
be for itself the supreme law in the purposive reference, in other words the existence of rational beings
under moral laws, can therefore alone be thought as
the final purpose of the being of a world.   If on the
contrary this be not so, there would be either no
purpose at all in the cause of its being, or there
would be purposes, but no final purpose.

The moral law as the formal rational condition
of the use of our freedom obliges us by itself alone,
without depending on any purpose as material
condition ; but it nevertheless determines for us,
and indeed *a priori*, a final purpose towards which
it obliges us to strive ; and this purpose is the
highest good in the world possible through freedom.

The subjective condition under which man (and,
according to all our concepts, every rational finite
being) can set a final purpose before himself under
the above law is happiness.   Consequently, the
highest physical good possible in the world, to be
furthered as a final purpose as far as in us lies, is
happiness, under the objective condition of the
harmony of man with the law of *morality* as worthiness to be happy.

But it is impossible for us in accordance with all
our rational faculties to represent these two

requirements of the final purpose proposed to us by the moral law, as *connected* by merely natural causes, and yet as conformable to the Idea of that final purpose. Hence the concept of the *practical necessity* of such a purpose through the application of our powers does not harmonise with the theoretical concept of the *physical possibility* of its performance, if we connect with our freedom no other causality (as a means) than that of nature.

Consequently, we must assume a moral World-Cause (an Author of the world), in order to set before ourselves a final purpose consistently with the moral law ; and in so far as the latter is necessary, so far (*i.c.* in the same degree and on the same ground) the former also must be necessarily assumed ; *i.c.* we must admit that there is a God.[1]

This proof, to which we can easily give the form of logical precision, does not say : it is as necessary to assume the Being of God as to recognise the validity of the moral law ; and consequently he who cannot convince himself of the first, can judge himself free from the obligations of the second. No ! there must in such case only be given up the *aiming at* the final purpose in the world, to be brought about by the pursuit of the second (viz. a happiness of rational beings in harmony with the pursuit of moral laws, regarded as the highest

---

[1] [Note added in Second Edition.] This moral argument does not supply any *objectively-valid* proof of the Being of God ; it does not prove to the sceptic that there is a God, but proves that if he wishes to think in a way consonant with morality, he must admit the *assumption* of this proposition under the maxims of his practical Reason.— We should therefore not say : it is necessary *for morals* [Sittlichkeit], to assume the happiness of all rational beings of the world in proportion to their morality [Moralität] ; but rather, this is necessitated *by* morality. Accordingly, this is a *subjective* argument sufficient for moral beings.

good).   Every rational being would yet have to
cognise himself as straitly bound by the precepts
of morality, for its laws are formal and command
unconditionally without respect to purposes (as the
matter of volition).   But the one requisite of the
final purpose, as practical Reason prescribes it to
beings of the world, is an irresistible purpose
imposed on them by their nature (as finite beings),
which Reason wishes to know as subject only to the
moral law as inviolable *condition*, or even as
universally set up in accordance with it.   Thus
Reason takes for final purpose the furthering of
happiness in harmony with morality.   To further
this so far as is in our power (*i.e.* in respect of
happiness) is commanded us by the moral law ; be
the issue of this endeavour what it may.   The
fulfilling of duty consists in the form of the earnest
will, not in the intermediate causes of success.

Suppose then that partly through the weakness
of all the speculative arguments so highly extolled,
and partly through many irregularities in nature and
the world of sense which come before him, a man
is persuaded of the proposition, There is no God ;
he would nevertheless be contemptible in his own
eyes if on that account he were to imagine the
laws of duty as empty, invalid and inobligatory,
and wished to resolve to transgress them boldly.
Such an one, even if he could be convinced in the
sequel of that which he had doubted at the first,
would always be contemptible while having such a
disposition, although he should fulfil his duty as
regards its [external] effect as punctiliously as could
be desired, for [he would be acting] from fear or
from the aim at recompense, without the sentiment
of reverence for duty.   If, conversely, as a believer

[in God] he performs his duty according to his conscience, uprightly and disinterestedly, and nevertheless believes that he is free from all moral obligation so soon as he is convinced that there is no God, this could accord but badly with an inner moral disposition.

We may then suppose the case of a righteous man [*e.g. Spinoza*],[1] who holds himself firmly persuaded that there is no God, and also (because in respect of the Object of morality a similar consequence results) no future life ; how is he to judge of his own inner purposive destination, by means of the moral law, which he reveres in practice ?   He desires no advantage to himself from following it, either in this or another world ; he wishes, rather, disinterestedly to establish the good to which that holy law directs all his powers. But his effort is bounded ; and from nature, although he may expect here and there a contingent accordance, he can never expect a regular harmony agreeing according to constant rules (such as his maxims are and must be, internally), with the purpose that he yet feels himself obliged and impelled to accomplish.   Deceit, violence, and envy will always surround him, although he himself be honest, peaceable, and kindly ; and the righteous men with whom he meets will, notwithstanding all their worthiness of happiness, be yet subjected by nature which regards not this, to all the evils of want, disease, and untimely death, just like the beasts of the earth.   So it will be until one wide grave engulfs them together (honest or not, it makes no difference), and throws them back—who were able to believe themselves the final purpose of creation

---

[1] [Second Edition.]

—into the abyss of the purposeless chaos of matter from which they were drawn.— The purpose, then, which this well-intentioned person had and ought to have before him in his pursuit of moral laws, he must certainly give up as impossible. Or else, if he wishes to remain dependent upon the call of his moral internal destination, and not to weaken the respect with which the moral law immediately inspires him, by assuming the nothingness of the single, ideal, final purpose adequate to its high demand (which cannot be brought about without a violation of moral sentiment), he must, as he well can—since there is at least no contradiction from a practical point of view in forming a concept of the possibility of a morally prescribed final purpose—assume the being of a *moral* author of the world, that is, a God.

§ 88. *Limitation of the validity of the moral proof*

Pure Reason, as a practical faculty, *i.e.* as the faculty of determining the free use of our causality by Ideas (pure rational concepts), not only comprises in the moral law a regulative principle of our actions, but supplies us at the same time with a subjective constitutive principle in the concept of an Object which Reason alone can think, and which is to be actualised by our actions in the world according to that law. The Idea of a final purpose in the employment of freedom according to moral laws has therefore subjective *practical* reality. We are *a priori* determined by Reason to promote with all our powers the *summum bonum* [Weltbeste] which consists in the combination of the greatest welfare of rational beings with the highest condition of the good in itself, *i.e.* in universal happiness conjoined with morality most accordant to law. In this final purpose the possibility of one part, happiness, is empirically conditioned, *i.e.* dependent on the constitution of nature (which may or may not agree with this purpose) and is in a theoretical aspect problematical ; whilst the other part, morality, in respect of which we are free from the effects of nature, stands fast *a priori* as to its possibility, and is dogmatically certain.   It is then requisite for the objective theoretical reality of the concept of the final purpose of rational beings, that we should not only have *a priori* presupposed to ourselves a final purpose, but also that the creation, *i.e.* the world itself, should have as regards its existence a final purpose, which if it could be proved *a priori* would add objectivity to the subjective reality of the final purpose [of rational beings].   For if the creation has on the whole a final purpose, we cannot think it otherwise than as harmonising with the moral purpose (which alone makes the concept of a purpose possible).   Now we find without doubt purposes in the world, and physical Teleology exhibits them in such abundance, that if we judge in accordance with Reason, we have ground for assuming as a principle in the investigation of nature that nothing in nature is without a purpose ; but the final purpose of nature we seek there in vain.   This can and must therefore, as its Idea only lies in Reason, be sought as regards its objective possibility only in rational beings.   And the practical Reason of these latter not only supplies this final purpose ; it also determines this concept in respect of the conditions under which alone a final purpose of creation can be thought by us.

The question is now, whether the objective

reality of the concept of a final purpose of creation cannot be exhibited adequately to the theoretical requirements of pure Reason—if not apodictically for the determinant Judgment yet adequately for the maxims of the theoretical reflective Judgment? This is the least one could expect from theoretical philosophy, which undertakes to combine the moral purpose with natural purposes by means of the Idea of one single purpose; but yet this little is far more than it can accomplish.

According to the principle of the theoretical reflective Judgment we should say : if we have ground for assuming for the purposive products of nature a supreme Cause of nature —whose causality in respect of the actuality of creation is of a different kind from that required for the mechanism of nature, *i.e.* must be thought as the causality of an Understanding— we have also sufficient ground for thinking in this original Being not merely the purposes everywhere in nature but also a final purpose. This is not indeed a final purpose by which we can explain the presence of such a Being, but one of which we may at least convince ourselves (as was the case in physical Teleology) that we can make the possibility of such a world conceivable, not merely according to purposes, but only through the fact that we ascribe to its existence a final purpose.

But a final purpose is merely a concept of our practical Reason, and can be inferred from no data of experience for the theoretical judging of nature, nor can it be applied to the cognition of nature. No use of this concept is possible except its use for practical Reason according to moral laws ; and the final purpose of creation is that constitution of the world which harmonises with that which alone we

can put forward definitely according to laws, viz. the
final purpose of our pure practical Reason, in so far
as it is to be practical.— Now we have in the moral
law which enjoins on us in a practical point of view
the application of our powers to the accomplishment
of this final purpose, a ground for assuming its
possibility and practicability, and consequently too
(because without the concurrence of nature with a
condition not in our power, its accomplishment
would be impossible) a nature of things harmonious
with it.   Hence we have a moral ground for thinking in a world also a final purpose of creation.

We have not yet advanced from moral Teleology
to a Theology, *i.e.* to the being of a moral Author
of the world, but only to a final purpose of creation
which is determined in this way.   But in order to
account for this creation, *i.e.* the existence of things,
in accordance with a *final purpose*, we must assume
not only first an intelligent Being (for the possibility
of things of nature which we are compelled to judge
of as *purposes*), but also a *moral* Being, as author of
the world, *i.e.* a *God*.   This second conclusion is of
such a character that we see it holds merely for
the Judgment according to concepts of practical
Reason, and as such for the reflective and not the
determinant Judgment.   It is true that in us morally
practical Reason is essentially different in its principles from technically practical Reason.   But we
cannot assume that it must be so likewise in the
supreme World-Cause, regarded as Intelligence,
and that a peculiar mode of its causality is requisite
for the final purpose, different from that which is
requisite merely for purposes of nature.   We cannot
therefore assume that in our final purpose we have
not merely a *moral ground* for admitting a final

purpose of creation (as an effect), but also for admitting a _moral Being_ as the original ground of creation. But we may well say, that, _according to the constitution of our rational faculty_, we cannot comprehend the possibility of such a purposiveness _in respect of the moral law_, and its Object, as there is in this final purpose, apart from an Author and Governor of the world, who is at the same time its moral Lawgiver.

The actuality of a highest morally-legislating Author is therefore sufficiently established merely _for the practical use_ of our Reason, without determining anything theoretically as regards its being. For Reason requires, in respect of the possibility of its purpose, which is given to us independently by its own legislation, an Idea through which the inability to follow up this purpose, according to the mere natural concepts of the world, is removed (sufficiently for the reflective Judgment). Thus this Idea gains practical reality, although all means of creating such for it in a theoretical point of view, for the explanation of nature and determination of the supreme Cause, are entirely wanting for speculative cognition. For the theoretical reflective Judgment physical Teleology sufficiently proves from the purposes of nature an intelligent World-Cause : for the practical Judgment moral Teleology establishes it by the concept of a final purpose, which it is forced to ascribe to creation in a practical point of view. The objective reality of the Idea of God, as moral Author of the world, cannot, it is true, be established by physical purposes _alone_. But nevertheless, if the cognition of these purposes is combined with that of the moral purpose, they are, by virtue of the maxim of pure Reason which bids us seek unity of principles so far as is possible, of great importance for the practical reality of that Idea, by bringing in the reality which it has for the Judgment in a theoretical point of view.

To prevent a misunderstanding which may easily arise, it is in the highest degree needful to remark that, in the first place, we can *think* these properties of the highest Being only according to analogy. How indeed could we investigate [directly] the nature of that, to which experience can show us nothing similar? Secondly, in this way we only think the supreme Being; we cannot thereby *cognise* Him and ascribe anything theoretically to Him. It would be needful for the determinant Judgment in the speculative aspect of our Reason, to consider what the supreme World-Cause is in Himself. But here we are only concerned with the question what concept we can form of Him, according to the constitution of our cognitive faculties; and whether we have to assume His existence in order merely to furnish practical reality to a purpose, which pure Reason without any such presupposition enjoins upon us *a priori* to bring about with all our powers, *i.e.* in order to be able to think as possible a designed effect. Although that concept may be transcendent for the speculative Reason, and the properties which we ascribe to the Being thereby thought may, objectively used, conceal an anthropomorphism in themselves; yet the design of its use is not to determine the nature of that Being which is unattainable by us, but to determine ourselves and our will accordingly. We may call a cause after the concept which we have of its effect (though only in reference to this relation), without thereby meaning to determine internally its inner constitution, by means of the properties which can be made known

to us solely by similar causes and must be given in
experience.   For example, amongst other properties
we ascribe to the soul a *vis locomotiva* because
bodily movements actually arise whose cause lies in
the representation of them ; without therefore meaning to ascribe to it the only mode [of action] that we
know in moving forces (viz. by attraction, pressure,
impulse, and consequently motion, which always
presuppose an extended being).   Just so we must
assume *something*, which contains the ground of the
possibility and practical reality, *i.e.* the practicability,
of a necessary moral final purpose ; but we can think
of this, in accordance with the character of the effect
expected of it, as a wise Being governing the world
according to moral laws, and, conformably to the
constitution of our cognitive faculties, as a cause of
things distinct from nature, only in order to express
the *relation* of this Being which transcends all our
cognitive faculties to the Objects of *our* practical
Reason.   We do not pretend thus to ascribe to it
theoretically the only causality of this kind known to
us, viz. an Understanding and a Will : we do not
even pretend to distinguish objectively the causality
thought in this Being, as regards what is *for us*
final purpose, from the causality thought in it as
regards nature (and its purposive determinations in
general).   We can only assume this distinction as
subjectively necessary by the constitution of our
cognitive faculties, and as valid for the reflective, not
for the objectively determinant Judgment.   But if we
come to practice, then such a *regulative* principle (for
prudence or wisdom) [commanding us] to act conformably to that as purpose, which by the constitution of our cognitive faculties can only be thought as
possible in a certain way, is at the same *constitutive*,

i.e. practically determinant.   Nevertheless, as a principle for judging of the objective possibility of things, it is no way theoretically determinant (*i.e.* it does not say that the only kind of possibility which belongs to the Object is that which belongs to our thinking faculty), but is a mere *regulative* principle for the reflective Judgment.

Remark

This moral proof is not one newly discovered, although perhaps its basis is newly set forth ; since it has lain in man's rational faculty from its earliest germ, and is only continually developed with its advancing cultivation.   So soon as men begin to reflect upon right and wrong—at a time when, quite indifferent as to the purposiveness of nature, they avail themselves of it without thinking anything more of it than that it is the accustomed course of nature—this judgment is inevitable, viz. that the issue cannot be the same, whether a man has behaved fairly or falsely, with equity or with violence, even though up to his life's end, as far as can be seen, he has met with no happiness for his virtues, no punishment for his vices.   It is as if they perceived a voice within [saying] that the issue must be different.   And so there must lie hidden in them a representation, however obscure, of something after which they feel themselves bound to strive ; with which such a result would not agree,— with which, if they looked upon the course of the world as the only order of things, they could not harmonise that inner purposive determination of their minds.   Now they might represent in various rude fashions the way in which such an irregularity

could be adjusted (an irregularity which must be
far more revolting to the human mind than the
blind chance that we sometimes wish to use as a
principle for judging of nature). But they could
never think any other principle of the possibility of
the unification of nature with its inner ethical laws,
than a supreme Cause governing the world according to moral laws ; because a final purpose in them
proposed as duty, and a nature without any final
purpose beyond them in which that purpose might
be actualised, would involve a contradiction. As to
the [inner][1] constitution of that World-Cause they
could contrive much nonsense. But that moral
relation in the government of the world would
remain always the same, which by the uncultivated
Reason, considered as practical, is universally
comprehensible, but with which the speculative
Reason can make far from the like advance.—
And in all probability attention would be directed
first by this moral interest to the beauty and the
purposes in nature, which would serve excellently
to strengthen this Idea though they could not be
the foundation of it. Still less could that moral
interest be dispensed with, because it is only in
reference to the final purpose that the investigation of the purposes of nature acquires that immediate interest which displays itself in such a
great degree in the admiration of them without any
reference to the advantage to be derived from them.

§ 89. *Of the use of the moral argument*

The limitation of Reason in respect of all our
Ideas of the supersensible to the conditions of its

---

[1] [Second Edition.]

practical employment has, as far as the Idea of God is concerned, undeniable uses. For it prevents *Theology* from rising into THEOSOPHY (into transcendent concepts which confound Reason), or from sinking into DEMONOLOGY (an anthropomorphic way of representing the highest Being). And it also prevents *Religion* from turning into *Theurgy* (a fanatical belief that we can have a feeling of other supersensible beings and can reciprocally influence them), or into *Idolatry* (a superstitious belief that we can please the Supreme Being by other means than by a moral sentiment).[1]

For if we permit the vanity or the presumption of sophistry to determine the least thing theoretically (in a way that extends our knowledge) in respect of what lies beyond the world of sense, or if we allow any pretence to be made of insight into the being and constitution of the nature of God, of His Understanding and Will, of the laws of both and of His properties which thus affect the world, I should like to know where and at what point we will bound these assumptions of Reason. For wherever such insight can be derived, there may yet more be expected (if we only strain our reflection, as we have a mind to do). Bounds must then be put to such claims according to a certain principle, and not merely because we find that all attempts of the sort have hitherto failed, for that proves nothing against the possibility of a better result.

---

[1] In a practical sense that religion is always idolatry which conceives the Supreme Being with properties, according to which something else besides morality can be a fit condition for that which man can do being in accordance with His Will. For however pure and free from sensible images the concept that we have formed may be in a theoretical point of view, yet it will be in a practical point of view still represented as an *idol*, *i.e.* in regard to the character of His Will, anthropomorphically.

But here no principle is possible, except either to
assume that in respect of the supersensible absolutely
nothing can be theoretically determined (except
mere negations); or else that our Reason contains
in itself a yet unused mine of cognitions, reaching
no one knows how far, stored up for ourselves and
our posterity.— But as concerns Religion, *i.e.*
morals in reference to God as legislator, if the
theoretical cognition of Him is to come first, morals
must be adjusted in accordance with Theology;
and not only is an external arbitrary legislation
of a Supreme Being introduced in place of an
internal necessary legislation of Reason, but also
whatever is defective in our insight into the nature
of this Being must extend to ethical precepts, and
thus make Religion immoral and perverted.

As regards the hope of a future life, if instead of
the final purpose we have to accomplish in conformity with the precept of the moral law, we ask
of our theoretical faculty of cognition a clue for the
judgment of Reason upon our destination (which
clue is only considered as necessary or worthy of
acceptance in a practical reference), then in this
aspect Psychology, like Theology, gives no more
than a negative concept of our thinking being.
That is, none of its actions or of the phenomena
of the internal sense can be explained materialistic-
ally; and hence of its separate nature and of the
continuance or non-continuance of its personality
after death absolutely no ampliative determinant
judgment is possible on speculative grounds by
means of our whole theoretical cognitive faculty.
Here then everything is handed over to the
teleological judging of our existence in a practically
necessary aspect, and to the assumption of our

continuance as a condition requisite for the final purpose absolutely furnished by Reason. And so this advantage (which indeed at first glance seems to be a loss) is apparent; that, as Theology for us can never be Theosophy, or rational *Psychology* become *Pneumatology*—an ampliative science—so on the other hand this latter is assured of never falling into *Materialism*. Psychology, rather, is a mere anthropology of the internal sense, *i.e.* is the knowledge of our thinking self *in life*; and, as theoretical cognition, remains merely empirical. On the other hand, rational Psychology, as far as it is concerned with questions as to our eternal existence, is not a theoretical science at all, but rests on a single conclusion of moral Teleology; as also its whole use is necessary merely on account of the latter, *i.e.* on account of our practical destination.

§ 90. *Of the kind of belief in a teleological proof of the Being of God*

The first requisite for every proof, whether it be derived from the immediate empirical presentation (as in the proof from observation of the object or from experiment) of that which is to be proved, or by Reason *a priori* from principles, is this. It should not *persuade*, but *convince*,[1] or at least should tend to conviction. *I.e.* the ground of proof or the conclusion should not be merely a subjective (æsthetical) determining ground of assent (mere illusion), but objectively valid and a logical ground

---

[1] [Cf. *Introd. to Logic*, ix. p. 63, "Conviction is opposed to Persuasion, which is a belief from inadequate reasons, of which we do not know whether they are only subjective or are also objective."]

of cognition ; for otherwise the Understanding is
ensnared, but not convinced.   Such an illusory
proof is that which, perhaps with good intent but
yet with wilful concealment of its weaknesses, is
adduced in Natural Theology.   In this we bring
in the great number of indications of the origin
of natural things according to the principle of
purposes, and take advantage of the merely
subjective basis of human Reason, viz. its special
propensity to think only one principle instead of
several, whenever this can be done without contradiction ; and, when in this principle only one or
more requisites for determining a concept are
furnished, to add in our thought these additional
[features] so as to complete the concept of the
thing by arbitrarily supplementing it.   For, in truth,
when we meet with so many products in nature
which are to us marks of an intelligent cause, why
should we not think One cause rather than many ;
and in this One, not merely great intelligence,
power, etc., but rather Omniscience, and Omnipotence—in a word, think it as a Cause that contains the sufficient ground of such properties in all
possible things ?   Further, why should we not
ascribe to this unique, all-powerful, original Being
not only intelligence for natural laws and products,
but also, as to a moral Cause of the world, supreme,
ethical, practical Reason ?   For by this completion
of the concept a sufficient principle is furnished
both for insight into nature and for moral wisdom ;
and no objection grounded in any way can be made
against the possibility of such an Idea.   If now
at the same time the moral motives of the mind are
aroused, and a lively interest in the latter is added
by the force of eloquence (of which they are indeed

very worthy), then there arises therefrom a persuasion of the objective adequacy of the proof; and also (in most cases of its use) a wholesome illusion which quite dispenses with all examination of its logical strictness, and even on the contrary regards this with abhorrence and dislike as if an impious doubt lay at its basis.— Now against this there is indeed nothing to say, so long as we only have regard to its popular usefulness. But then the division of the proof into the two dissimilar parts involved in the argument — belonging to physical and moral Teleology respectively—cannot and must not be prevented. For the blending of these makes it impossible to discern where the proper force of the proof lies, and in what part and how it must be elaborated in order that its validity may be able to stand the strictest examination (even if we should be compelled to admit in one part the weakness of our rational insight). Thus it is the duty of the philosopher (supposing even that he counts as nothing the claims of sincerity) to expose the above illusion, however wholesome it is, which such a confusion can produce; and to distinguish what merely belongs to persuasion from that which leads to conviction (for these are determinations of assent which differ not merely in degree but in kind), in order to present plainly the state of the mind in this proof in its whole clearness, and to be able to subject it frankly to the closest examination.

But a proof which is intended to convince, can again be of two kinds; either deciding what the object is *in itself*, or what it is *for us* (for men in general) according to our necessary rational principles of judgment (proof κατ᾽ ἀλήθειαν or κατ᾽ ἄνθρωπον,

the last word being taken in its universal signification of man in general).   In the first case it is based
on adequate principles for the determinant Judgment,
in the second for the reflective Judgment.   In the
latter case it can never, when resting on merely
theoretical principles, tend to conviction ; but if
a practical principle of Reason (which is therefore
universally and necessarily valid) lies at its basis,
it may certainly lay claim to conviction adequate
in a pure practical point of view, *i.e.* to moral
conviction.   But a proof *tends to conviction*, though
without convincing, if it is [merely]¹ brought on the
way thereto ; *i.e.* if it contains in itself only objective
grounds, which although not attaining to certainty
are yet of such a kind that they do not serve merely
for persuasion as subjective grounds of the judgment.²

All theoretical grounds of proof resolve themselves either into : (1) Proofs by logically strict
Syllogisms of Reason ; or where this is not the case,
(2) *Conclusions* according to *analogy* ; or where this
also has no place, (3) *Probable opinion* ; or finally,
which has the least weight, (4) Assumption of a
merely possible ground of explanation, *i.e. Hypothesis.*— Now I say that all grounds of proof in
general, which tend to theoretical conviction, can
bring about no belief of this kind from the highest to
the lowest degree, if there is to be proved the
proposition of the *existence* of an original Being, as
a God, in the signification adequate to the whole
content of this concept ; viz. a *moral* Author of the
world, by whom the final purpose of creation is at
the same time supplied.

¹ [Second Edition.]
² [*I.e. Urtheils.*   First Edition had *Urtheilens,* the judging
subject.]

(1.) As to the *logically accurate* proof proceeding from universal to particular, we have sufficiently established in the Kritik the following : Since no intuition possible for us corresponds to the concept of a Being that is to be sought beyond nature—whose concept therefore, so far as it is to be theoretically determined by synthetical predicates, remains always problematical for us—there is absolutely no cognition of it to be had (by which the extent of our theoretical knowledge is in the least enlarged). The particular concept of a supersensible Being cannot be subsumed under the universal principles of the nature of things, in order to conclude from them to it, because those principles are valid simply for nature, as an object of sense.

(2.) We can indeed *think* one of two dissimilar things, even in the very point of their dissimilarity, in accordance with the *analogy* [1] of the other ; but

---

[1] *Analogy* (in a qualitative signification) is the identity of the relation between reasons and consequences (causes and effects), so far as it is to be found, notwithstanding the specific difference of the things or those properties in them which contain the reason for like consequences (*i.e.* considered apart from this relation). Thus we conceive of the artificial constructions of beasts by comparing them with those of men ; by comparing the ground of those effects brought about by the former, which we do not know, with the ground of similar effects brought about by men (reason), which we do know ; *i.e.* we regard the ground of the former as an analogon of reason. We then try at the same time to show that the ground of the artisan faculty of beasts, which we call instinct, specifically different as it is in fact from reason, has yet a similar relation to its effect (the buildings of the beaver as compared with those of men).— But then I cannot therefore conclude that because man uses *reason* for his building, the beaver must have the like, and call this a *conclusion* according to analogy. But from the similarity of the mode of operation of beasts (of which we cannot immediately perceive the ground) to that of men (of which we are immediately conscious), we can quite rightly conclude *according to analogy*, that beasts too act in accordance with *representations* (not as *Descartes* has it, that they are machines), and that despite their specific distinction they are yet (as living beings) of the same genus as

we cannot, from that wherein they are dissimilar,
conclude from the one to the other by analogy, *i.e.*
transfer from the one to the other this sign of
specific distinction. Thus I can, according to the
analogy of the law of the equality of action and
reaction in the mutual attraction and repulsion of
bodies, also conceive of the association of the
members of a commonwealth according to rules of
right ; but I cannot transfer to it those specific
determinations (material attraction or repulsion), and
ascribe them to the citizens in order to constitute a
system called a state.— Just so we can indeed
conceive of the causality of the original Being in
respect of the things of the world, as natural
purposes, according to the analogy of an Understanding, as ground of the forms of certain products
which we call works of art (for this only takes place
on behalf of the theoretical or practical use that
we have to make by our cognitive faculty of this
concept in respect of the natural things in the world
according to a certain principle). But we can in
no way conclude according to analogy, because in
the case of beings of the world Understanding must

man. The principle of our right so to conclude consists in the
sameness of the ground for reckoning beasts in respect of the said
determination in the same genus with men, regarded as men, so far
as we can externally compare them with one another in accordance
with their actions. There is *par ratio*. Just so I can conceive,
according to the analogy of an Understanding, the causality of the
supreme World-Cause, by comparing its purposive products in the
world with the artificial works of men ; but I cannot conclude
according to analogy to those properties in it [which are in man],
because here the principle of the possibility of such a method of
reasoning entirely fails, viz. the *paritas rationis* for counting the
Supreme Being in one and the same genus with man (in respect of
the causality of both). The causality of the beings of the world,
which is always sensibly conditioned (as is causality through Understanding) cannot be transferred to a Being which has in common with
them no generic concept save that of Thing in general.

be ascribed to the cause of an effect which is judged artificial, that in respect of nature the same causality which we perceive in men attaches also to the Being which is quite distinct from nature. For this concerns the very point of dissimilarity which is thought between a cause sensibly conditioned in respect of its effects and the supersensible original Being itself in our concept of it, and which therefore cannot be transferred from one to the other.— In the very fact that I must conceive the divine causality only according to the analogy of an Understanding (which faculty we know in no other being than in sensibly-conditioned man) lies the prohibition to ascribe to it this Understanding in its proper signification.[1]

(3.) *Opinion* finds in *a priori* judgments no place whatever, for by them we either cognise something as quite certain or else cognise nothing at all. But if the given grounds of proof from which we start (as here from the purposes in the world) are empirical, then we cannot even with their aid form any opinion as to anything beyond the world of sense, nor can we concede to such venturesome judgments the smallest claim to probability. For probability is part of a certainty possible in a certain series of grounds (its grounds compare with the sufficient ground as parts with a whole), the insufficient ground of which must be susceptible of completion. But since, as determining grounds of one and the same judgment, they must be of the same kind, for otherwise they would not together constitute a whole (such as certainty is), one part of them cannot lie within

---

[1] We thus miss nothing in the representation of the relations of this Being to the world, as far as the consequences, theoretical or practical, of this concept are concerned. To wish to investigate what it is in itself, is a curiosity as purposeless as it is vain.

the bounds of possible experience and another outside
all possible experience. Consequently, since merely
empirical grounds of proof lead to nothing supersensible, and since what is lacking in the series of
them cannot in any way be completed, we do not
approach in the least nearer in our attempt to attain
by their means to the supersensible and to a cognition
thereof. Thus in any judgment about the latter by
means of arguments derived from experience, probability has no place.

(4.) If an *hypothesis* is to serve for the explanation
of the possibility of a given phenomenon, at least its
possibility must be completely certain.[1] It is sufficient
that in an hypothesis I disclaim any cognition of
actuality (which is claimed in an opinion given out
as probable); more than this I cannot give up. The
possibility of that which I place at the basis of my
explanation, must at least be exposed to no doubt;
otherwise there would be no end of empty chimeras.
But to assume the possibility of a supersensible
Being determined according to certain concepts
would be a completely groundless supposition. For
here none of the conditions requisite for cognition,
as regards that in it which rests upon intuition, is
given, and so the sole criterion of possibility remaining is the mere principle of Contradiction
(which can only prove the possibility of the thought,
not of the object thought).

The result then is this. For the existence
[Dasein] of the original Being, as a Godhead, or of
the soul as an immortal spirit, absolutely no proof
in a theoretical point of view is possible for the

---

[1] [Cf. *Introd. to Logic*, p. 76, where the conditions of a legitimate
hypothesis are laid down. See also Kritik of *Pure Reason*, Methodology, c. i. § 3.]

human Reason, which can bring about even the
least degree of belief.   The ground of this is quite
easy to comprehend.   For determining our Ideas
of the supersensible we have no material whatever,
and we must derive this latter from things in the
world of sense, which is absolutely inadequate for
such an Object.   Thus, in the absence of all determination of it, nothing remains but the concept of a
non-sensible something which contains the ultimate
ground of the world of sense, but which does not
furnish any knowledge (any amplification of the
concept) of its inner constitution.

§ 91. *Of the kind of belief produced by a practical faith*

If we look merely to the way in which anything
can be *for us* (according to the subjective constitution of our representative powers) an Object of
knowledge (*res cognoscibilis*), then our concepts will
not be confronted with Objects, but merely with our
cognitive faculties and the use which they can make
of a given representation (in a theoretical or practical
point of view).   Thus the question whether anything is or is not a cognisable being is not a question
concerning the possibility of things but of our
knowledge of them.

Cognisable things are of three kinds : *things of
opinion* (*opinabile*) ; *things of fact* (*scibile*) ; and *things
of faith* (*mere credibile*).

(1.) Objects of mere rational Ideas, which for
theoretical knowledge cannot be presented in any
possible experience, are so far not *cognisable* things,
and consequently in respect of them we can form no
opinion ; for to form an opinion *a priori* is absurd in

itself and the straight road to mere chimeras. Either then our proposition is certain *a priori* or it contains nothing for belief. Therefore *things of opinion* are always Objects of an empirical cognition at least possible in itself (objects of the world of sense); but which, on account merely of the [low] degree of this faculty that we possess, is *for us* impossible. Thus the ether of the new physicists,[1] an elastic fluid pervading all other material (mingled intimately with it) is a mere thing of opinion, yet is such that, if our external senses were sharpened to the highest degree, it could be perceived; though it can never be presented in any observation or experiment. To assume [the existence of] rational inhabitants of other planets is a thing of opinion; for if we could come closer to them, which is in itself possible, we should decide by experience whether they did or did not exist; but as we shall never come so near, it remains in the region of opinion. But to hold the opinion that there are in the material universe pure thinking spirits without bodies (viz. if we dismiss as unworthy of our notice certain phenomena which have been published as actual[2]) is to be called poetic fiction. This is no thing of opinion, but a mere Idea which remains over, when we

---

[1] [This illustration is also given in the *Logic* (p. 57); where the three *modi* of belief, Opinion, Faith, and Knowledge, are distinguished from each other. Cf. Kritik of *Pure Reason*, Methodology, c. ii. § 3.]

[2] [The speculations of Swedenborg seem to have always had a strange fascination for Kant. In an early essay, *Dreams of a Visionary explained by Dreams of Metaphysics*, he avows his scepticism as to the value of the information which "psychical research" can supply about the spirit-world, though he is careful not to commit himself to any dogmatic statement on the subject of ghosts. In the Kritik of *Pure Reason* (when discussing the Postulates of Empirical Thought) he gives, as an instance of a concept inconsistent with the canons of possibility, "a power of being in a community of thought with other men, however distant from us."]

remove from a thinking being everything material, and only leave thought to it. Whether then the latter (which we know only in man, that is, in combination with a body) does survive, we cannot decide. Such a thing is a *sophistical being* (*ens rationis ratiocinantis*), not a *rational being* (*ens rationis ratiocinatæ*)[1]; of which latter it is possible to show conclusively, the objective reality of its concept; at least for the practical use of Reason, because this which has its peculiar and apodictically certain principles *a priori*, demands (postulates) it.

(2.) Objects for concepts, whose objective reality can be proved (whether through pure Reason or through experience, and, in the first case, from its theoretical or practical data, in all cases by means of a corresponding intuition) are *things of fact* (*res facti*).[2] Of this kind are the mathematical properties of magnitudes (in geometry), because they are susceptible of a *presentation a priori* for the theoretical use of Reason. Further, things or their characteristics, which can be exhibited in experience (either our own or that of others through the medium of testimony) are likewise things of fact. — And, what is very remarkable, there is one rational Idea (which is susceptible in itself of no presentation in intuition, and consequently, of no theoretical proof of its possibility) which also comes under things of fact. This is the Idea of *freedom*,

---

[1] [Cf. *supra*, p. 229.]

[2] I here extend, correctly as it seems to me, the concept of a thing of fact beyond the usual signification of this word. For it is not needful, not even feasible, to limit this expression merely to actual experience, if we are talking of the relation of things to our cognitive faculties; for an experience merely possible is quite sufficient in order that we may speak of them merely as objects of a definite kind of cognition.

whose reality, regarded as that of a particular kind
of causality (of which the concept, theoretically
considered, would be transcendent), may be exhibited
by means of practical laws of pure Reason, and
conformably to this, in actual actions, and, consequently, in experience.— This is the only one
of all the Ideas of pure Reason, whose object is a
thing of fact, and to be reckoned under the *scibilia*.

(3.) Objects, which in reference to the use of
pure practical Reason that is in conformity with
duty must be thought *a priori* (whether as consequences or as grounds), but which are transcendent
for its theoretical use, are mere *things of faith*. Of
this kind is the *highest good* in the world, to be
brought about by freedom.[1] The concept of this
cannot be established as regards its objective reality
in any experience possible for us and thus adequately
for the theoretical use of Reason ; but its use is
commanded by practical pure Reason [in reference
to the best possible working out of that purpose],[2]
and it consequently must be assumed possible. This
commanded effect, *together with the only conditions
of its possibility thinkable by us*, viz. the Being of
God and the immortality of the soul, are *things of
faith (res fidei)*, and of all objects are the only ones
which can be so called.[3] For though what we learn
by *testimony* from the experience of others must be
believed by us, yet it is not therefore a thing of

---

[1] [Cf. *Introduction to Logic*, p. 59 note.]

[2] [Second Edition.]

[3] Things of faith are not therefore *articles of faith* ; if we
understand by the latter things of faith to the *confession* of which
(internal or external) we can be bound. Natural theology contains nothing like this. For since they, as things of faith (like
things of fact) cannot be based on theoretical proofs, [they are
accepted by] a belief which is free and which only as such is compatible
with the morality of the subject.

faith ; for it was the proper experience of some *one* witness and so a thing of fact, or is presupposed as such.   Again it must be possible by this path (that of historical faith) to arrive at knowledge ; and the Objects of history and geography, like everything in general which it is at least possible to know by the constitution of our cognitive faculties, belong not to things of faith but to things of fact.   It is only objects of pure Reason which can be things of faith at all, though not as objects of the mere pure speculative Reason : for then they could not be reckoned with certainty among things, *i.e.* Objects of that cognition which is possible for us.   They are Ideas, *i.e.* concepts of the objective reality of which we cannot theoretically be certain.   On the other hand, the highest final purpose to be worked out by us, by which alone we can become worthy of being ourselves the final purpose of creation, is an Idea which has in a practical reference objective reality for us, and is also a thing.   But because we cannot furnish such reality to this concept in a theoretical point of view, it is a mere thing of faith of the pure Reason, along with God and Immortality, as the conditions under which alone we, in accordance with the constitution of our (human) Reason, can conceive the possibility of that effect of the use of our freedom in conformity with law.   But belief in things of faith is a belief in a pure practical point of view, *i.e.* a moral faith, which proves nothing for theoretical pure rational cognition, but only for that which is practical and directed to the fulfilment of its duties; it in no way extends speculation or the practical rules of prudence in accordance with the principle of self-love.   If the supreme principle of all moral laws is a postulate, so is also the possibility of its highest

Object; and consequently, too, the condition under which we can think this possibility is postulated along with it and by it. Thus the cognition of the latter is neither knowledge nor opinion of the being and character of these conditions, regarded as theoretical cognition; but is a mere assumption in a reference which is practical and commanded for the moral use of our Reason.

If we were able also with some plausibility to base upon the purposes of nature, which physical Teleology presents to us in such rich abundance, a *determinate* concept of an intelligent World-Cause, then the existence [Dasein] of this Being would not be a thing of faith. For since this would not be assumed on behalf of the performance of my duty, but only in reference to the explanation of nature, it would be merely the opinion and hypothesis most conformable to our Reason. Now such Teleology leads in no way to a determinate concept of God: on the contrary, this can only be found in the concept of a moral Author of the World, because this alone furnishes the final purpose to which we can only reckon ourselves [as attached] if we behave conformably to what the moral law prescribes as final purpose and consequently obliges us [to do]. Hence it is only by its reference to the Object of our duty, as the condition of the possibility of attaining the final purpose of the same, that the concept of God attains the advantage of being [reckoned as] valid in our belief as a thing of faith; but on the other hand, this same concept cannot make its Object valid as a thing of fact. For, although the necessity of duty is very plain for practical Reason, yet the attainment of its final purpose, so far as it is not altogether in our own power, is only assumed on behalf of the practical use of Reason, and therefore is not so practically necessary as duty itself.[1]

Faith (as *habitus*, not as *actus*) is the moral attitude of Reason as to belief in that which is unattainable by theoretical cognition. It is therefore the permanent principle of the mind, to assume as true, on account of the obligation in reference to it, that which it is necessary to presuppose as condition of the possibility of the highest moral final purpose[2];

---

[1] The final purpose which the moral law enjoins upon us to further, is not the ground of duty; since this lies in the moral law, which, as formal practical principle, leads categorically, independently of the Objects of the faculty of desire (the material of the will) and consequently of any purpose whatever. This formal characteristic of my actions (their subordination under the principle of universal validity), wherein alone consists their inner moral worth, is quite in our power; and I can quite well abstract from the possibility or the unattainableness of purposes which I am obliged to promote in conformity with that law (because in them consists only the external worth of my actions) as something which is never completely in my power, in order only to look to that which is of my doing. But then the design of promoting the final purpose of all rational beings (happiness so far as it is possible for it to be accordant with duty) is even yet prescribed by the law of duty. The speculative Reason, however, does not see at all the attainableness of this (neither on the side of our own physical faculty nor on that of the co-operation of nature). It must rather, so far as we can judge in a rational way, hold the derivation, by the aid of such causes, of such a consequence of our good conduct from mere nature (internal and external) without God and immortality, to be an ungrounded and vain, though well-meant, expectation; and if it could have complete certainty of this judgment, it would regard the moral law itself as the mere deception of our Reason in a practical aspect. But since the speculative Reason fully convinces itself that the latter can never take place, but that on the other hand those Ideas whose object lies outside nature can be thought without contradiction, it must for its own practical law and the problem prescribed thereby, and therefore in a moral aspect, recognise those Ideas as real in order not to come into contradiction with itself.

[2] It is a trust in the promise of the moral law; [not however such as is contained in it, but such as I put into it and that on morally adequate grounds.[3]] For a final purpose cannot be commanded by any law of Reason without this latter at the same time

---

[3] [Second Edition.]

although its possibility or impossibility be alike impossible for us to see into. Faith (absolutely so called) is trust in the attainment of a design, the promotion of which is a duty, but the possibility of the fulfilment of which (and consequently also that of the only conditions of it thinkable by us) is not to be *comprehended* by us. Faith, then, that refers to particular objects, which are not objects of possible knowledge or opinion (in which latter case it ought to be called, especially in historical matters, credulity and not faith), is quite moral. It is a free belief, not in that for which dogmatical proofs for the theoretically determinant Judgment are to be found, or in that to which we hold ourselves bound, but in that which we assume on behalf of a design in accordance with laws of freedom. This, however, is not, like opinion, without any adequate ground; but, is grounded as in Reason (although only in respect of its practical employment), and *adequately for its design.* For without this, the moral attitude of thought in its repudiation of the claim of the theoretical Reason for proofs (of the possibility of the Objects of morality) has no permanence; but wavers between practical commands and theoretical doubts. To be *incredulous* means to cling to

promising, however uncertainly, its attainableness; and thus justifying our belief in the special conditions under which alone our Reason can think it as attainable. The word *fides* expresses this; and it can only appear doubtful, how this expression and this particular Idea came into moral philosophy, since it first was introduced with Christianity, and the adoption of it perhaps might seem to be only a flattering imitation of Christian terminology. But this is not the only case in which this wonderful religion with its great simplicity of statement has enriched philosophy with far more definite and purer concepts of morality, than it had been able to furnish before; but which, once they are there, are *freely* assented to by Reason and are assumed as concepts to which it could well have come of itself and which it could and should have introduced.

maxims, and not to believe testimony in general ; but he is *unbelieving*, who denies all validity to rational Ideas, because there is wanting a *theoretical* ground of their reality.[1]   He judges therefore dogmatically.   A dogmatical *unbelief* cannot subsist together with a moral maxim dominant in the mental attitude (for Reason cannot command one to follow a purpose, which is cognised as nothing more than a chimera) ; but a *doubtful faith* can.   To this the absence of conviction by grounds of speculative Reason is only a hindrance ; and for this a critical insight into the limits of this faculty can remove its influence upon conduct, while it substitutes by way of compensation a paramount practical belief.

If, in place of certain mistaken attempts, we wish to introduce a different principle into philosophy and to procure influence for it, it produces great contentment if we can see how and why those attempts must have disappointed us.

God, freedom, and *immortality*, are the problems at the solution of which all the preparations of Metaphysic aim, as their ultimate and unique purpose. Now it was believed that the doctrine of freedom is needed for practical philosophy only as its negative condition ; but that on the other hand the doctrine of God and of the constitution of the soul, as belonging to theoretical philosophy, must be established for themselves and separately, in order afterwards to unite both with that which the moral law (possible only under the condition of freedom) commands, and so to constitute a religion.   But we can easily

---

[1] [Cf. *Introd. to Logic*, ix. p. 60, "That man is morally *unbelieving* who does not accept that which though *impossible* to know is *morally necessary* to suppose."]

see that these attempts must fail.   For from mere
ontological concepts of things in general, or of the
existence of a necessary Being, it is possible to
form absolutely no determinate concept of an
original Being by means of predicates which can
be given in experience and can therefore serve for
cognition.   Again a concept based on experience
of the physical purposiveness of nature could furnish
no adequate proof for morality, or consequently for
cognition of a Deity.   Just as little could the cognition of the soul by means of experience (which we
only apply in this life) supply us with a concept of
its spiritual immortal nature, a concept which would
thus be adequate for morality.   *Theology* and
Pneumatology, regarded as problems of the sciences
of a speculative Reason, can be established by no
empirical data and predicates, because the concept
of them is transcendent for our whole cognitive
faculty.—   The determination of both predicates,
God and the soul (in respect of its immortality)
alike, can only take place by means of predicates,
which, although they are only possible from a supersensible ground, must yet prove their reality in
experience ; for thus alone can they make possible
a cognition of a quite supersensible Being.—   The
only concept of this kind to be met with in human
Reason is that of the freedom of men under moral
laws, along with the final purpose which Reason
prescribes by these laws.   Of these two [the moral
laws and the final purpose] the first are useful for
ascribing to the Author of Nature, the second for
ascribing to man, those properties which contain
the necessary condition of the possibility of both
[God and the soul] ; so that from this Idea we can
conclude as to the existence and constitution of

these beings which are otherwise quite hidden from us.

Thus the ground of the failure of the attempt to prove God and immortality by the merely theoretical path lies in this, that no cognition whatever is possible of the supersensible in this way (of natural concepts). The ground of its success by the moral way (of the concept of freedom) is as follows. Here the supersensible (freedom), which in this case is fundamental, by a determinate law of causality that springs from it, not only supplies material for cognition of other supersensibles (the moral final purpose and the conditions of its attainability), but also establishes its reality in actions as a fact; though at the same time it can furnish a valid ground of proof in no other than a practical point of view (the only one, however, of which Religion has need).

It is thus very remarkable that of the three pure rational Ideas, *God, freedom,* and *immortality,* that of freedom is the only concept of the supersensible which (by means of the causality that is thought in it) proves its objective reality in nature by means of the effects it can produce there; and thus renders possible the connection of both the others with nature, and of all three together with Religion. We have therefore in us a principle capable of determining the Idea of the supersensible within us, and thus also that of the supersensible without us, for knowledge, although only in a practical point of view; a principle this of which mere speculative philosophy (which could give a merely negative concept of freedom) must despair. Consequently the concept of freedom (as fundamental concept of all unconditioned practical laws) can extend Reason beyond those bounds, within which every natural (theoretical) concept must remain hopelessly limited.

General remark on Teleology

If the question is, what rank the moral argument, which proves the Being of God only as a thing of faith for the practical pure Reason, maintains among the other arguments in philosophy, it is easy to count up the whole possessions of this last; by which it appears that there is here no choice, but that our theoretical faculty must give up all its pretensions before an impartial Kritik.

All belief must in the first place be grounded upon facts, if it is not to be completely groundless; and therefore the only distinction in proofs that there can be is that belief in the consequence derived therefrom can either be grounded on this fact as *knowledge* for theoretical cognition, or merely as *faith* for practical. All facts belong either to the *natural concept* which proves its reality in the objects of sense, given (or which may possibly be given) before all natural concepts; or to the *concept of freedom*, which sufficiently establishes its reality through the causality of Reason in regard of certain effects in the world of sense, possible through it, which it incontrovertibly postulates in the moral law. The natural concept (merely belonging to theoretical cognition) is now either metaphysical and thinkable completely *a priori*, or physical, *i.e.* thinkable *a posteriori* and only necessary through determinate experience. The metaphysical natural concept (which presupposes no determinate experience) is therefore ontological.

The *ontological* proof of the being of God from the concept of an original Being is either that which from ontological predicates, by which alone it can be thought as completely determined, infers absolutely necessary being ; or that which, from the absolute necessity of the being somewhere of some thing, whatever it be, infers the predicates of the original Being.   For there belongs to the concept of an original Being, inasmuch as it is not derived from anything, the unconditioned necessity of its presence, and (in order to represent this) its complete determination by its [mere]¹ concept.   It was believed that both requirements were found in the concept of the ontological Idea of a *Being the most real of all*; and thus two metaphysical proofs originated.

The proof (properly called ontological) resting upon a merely metaphysical natural concept concludes from the concept of the Being the most real of all, its absolutely necessary existence ; for (it is said), if it did not exist, a reality would be wanting to it, viz. existence.—   The other (which is also called the metaphysico-*cosmological* proof) concludes from the necessity of the existence somewhere of a thing (which must be conceded, for a being is given to us in self-consciousness), its complete determination as that of a Being the most real of all ; for everything existing must be completely determined, but the absolutely necessary (*i.e.* that which *we* ought to cognise as such and consequently *a priori*) must be completely determined *by means of its own concept*.   But this is only the case with the concept of a thing the most real of all. It is not needful to expose here the sophistry in

¹ [First Edition.]

both arguments, which has been already done elsewhere;[1] it is only needful to remark that neither
proof, even if they could be defended by all
manner of dialectical subtlety, could ever pass from
the schools into the world, or have the slightest
influence on the mere sound Understanding.

The proof, which rests on a natural concept
that can only be empirical and yet is to lead us
beyond the bounds of nature regarded as the
complex of the objects of sense, can be no other
than that derived from the *purposes* of nature. The
concept of these cannot, it is true, be given *a priori*
but only through experience; but yet it promises
such a concept of the original ground of nature as
alone, among all those which we can conceive, is
suited to the supersensible, viz. that of a highest
Understanding as Cause of the world. This, in fact,
it completely performs in accordance with principles
of the reflective Judgment, *i.e.* in accordance with
the constitution of our (human) faculty of cognition.— But whether or not it is in a position to
supply from the same data this concept of a *supreme*,
i.e. independent intelligent Being, in short of a God
or Author of a world under moral laws, and consequently as sufficiently determined for the Idea of a
final purpose of the being of the world—this is the
question upon which everything depends, whether
we desire a theoretically adequate concept of the
Original Being on behalf of our whole knowledge of
nature, or a practical concept for religion.

This argument derived from physical Teleology
is worthy of respect. It produces a similar effect
in the way of conviction upon the common Understanding as upon the subtlest thinker; and a

[1] [In the Kritik of *Pure Reason*, Dialectic, bk. II. c. iii. §§ 4, 5.]

Reimarus[1] has acquired immortal honour in his
work (not yet superseded), in which he abundantly
develops this ground of proof with his peculiar
thoroughness and lucidity. — But how does this
proof acquire such mighty influence upon the mind,
especially in a judgment by cold reason (for we
might refer to persuasion the emotion and elevation
of reason produced by the wonders of nature) upon
a calm and resigned assent? It is not the physical
purposes, which all indicate in the World Cause
an unfathomable intelligence; these are inadequate
thereto, because they do not content the want of the
inquiring Reason. For, wherefore (it asks) are all
those natural things that exhibit art? Wherefore
is man himself, whom we must regard as the ultimate purpose of nature thinkable by us? Wherefore
is this collective Nature here, and what is the final
purpose of such great and manifold art? Reason
cannot be contented with enjoyment or with contemplation, observation, and admiration (which, if
it stops there, is only enjoyment of a particular kind)
as the ultimate final purpose for the creation of the
world and of man himself; for this presupposes a
personal worth, which man alone can give himself,
as the condition under which alone he and his being
can be the final purpose. Failing this (which alone
is susceptible of a definite concept), the purposes of
nature do not satisfactorily answer our questions;
especially because they cannot furnish any *determinate* concept of the highest Being as an all-
sufficient (and therefore unique and so properly

---

[1] [H. S. Reimarus (1694-1768), the author of the famous
Wolfenbüttel Fragments, published after the death of Reimarus by
Lessing. The book alluded to by Kant is probably the *Abhand-
lungen von den vornehmsten Wahrheiten der natürlichen Religion*
(1754), which had great popularity in its day.]

called *highest*) being, and of the laws according to which an Understanding is Cause of the world.

Hence that the physico-teleological proof convinces, just as if it were a theological proof, does not arise from our availing ourselves of the Ideas of purposes of nature as so many empirical grounds of proof of a *highest* Understanding. But it mingles itself unnoticed with that moral ground of proof, which dwells in every man and influences him secretly, in the conclusion by which we ascribe to the Being, which manifests itself with such incomprehensible art in the purposes of nature, a final purpose and consequently wisdom (without however being justified in doing so by the perception of the former); and by which therefore we arbitrarily fill up the lacunas of the [design] argument. In fact it is only the moral ground of proof which produces conviction, and that only in a moral reference with which every man feels inwardly his agreement. But the physico-teleological proof has only the merit of leading the mind in its consideration of the world by the way of purposes and through them to an *intelligent* Author of the world; for the moral reference to purposes and the Idea of a moral legislator and Author of the world, as a theological concept, seem to be developed of themselves out of that ground of proof, although they are in truth pure additions.

From this on we may allow the customary statement to stand. For it is generally difficult (if the distinction requires much reflection) for ordinary sound Understanding to distinguish from one another as heterogeneous the different principles which it confuses, and from one of which alone it actually draws conclusions with correctness. The

moral ground of proof of the Being of God, properly
speaking, does not merely *complete* and render
perfect the physico-teleological proof; but it is a
special proof that *supplies* the conviction which is
wanting in the latter.   This latter in fact can do
nothing more than guide Reason, in its judgments
upon the ground of nature and that contingent but
admirable order of nature only known to us by
experience, to the causality of a Cause containing
the ground of the same in accordance with purposes
(which we by the constitution of our cognitive
faculties must think as an intelligent cause); and
thus by arresting the attention of Reason it makes
it more susceptible of the moral proof.   For what
is requisite to the latter concept is so essentially
different from everything which natural concepts
contain and can teach, that there is need of a particular ground of proof quite independent of the
former, in order to supply the concept of the
original Being adequately for Theology and to
infer its existence.— The moral proof (which it
is true only proves the Being of God in a practical
though indispensable aspect of Reason) would preserve all its force, if we found in the world no
material, or only that which is doubtful, for physical
Teleology.   It is possible to conceive rational beings
surrounded by a nature which displayed no clear
trace of organisation but only the effects of a mere
mechanism of crude matter ; on behalf of which and
amid the changeability of some merely contingent
purposive forms and relations there would appear
to be no ground for inferring an intelligent Author.
In such case there would be no occasion for a
physical Teleology ; and yet Reason, which here
gets no guidance from natural concepts, would

find in the concept of freedom and in the moral
Ideas founded thereon a practically sufficient ground
for postulating the concept of the original Being
in conformity with these, *i.e.* as a Deity, and for
postulating nature (even the nature of our own
being) as a final purpose in accordance with freedom
and its laws—and all this in reference to the indispensable command of practical Reason.— However the fact that there is in the actual world for
the rational beings in it abundant material for
physical Teleology (even though this is not necessary) serves as a desirable confirmation of the
moral argument, as far as nature can exhibit anything analogous to the (moral) rational Ideas.   For
the concept of a supreme Cause possessing intelligence (though not reaching far enough for a
Theology) thus acquires sufficient reality for the
reflective Judgment, but it is not required as the
basis of the moral proof ; nor does this latter serve
to complete as a proof the former, which does not
by itself point to morality at all, by means of an
argument developed according to a single principle.
Two such heterogeneous principles as nature and
freedom can only furnish two different kinds of
proof ; and the attempt to derive one from the
other is found unavailing as regards that which is
to be proved.

If the physico-teleological ground of proof
sufficed for the proof which is sought, it would
be very satisfactory for the speculative Reason ;
for it would furnish the hope of founding a Theosophy (for so we must call the theoretical cognition
of the divine nature and its existence which would
suffice at once for the explanation of the constitution
of the world and for the determination of moral laws).

In the same way if Psychology enabled us to arrive at a cognition of the immortality of the soul it would make Pneumatology possible, which would be just as welcome to the speculative Reason. But neither, agreeable as they would be to the arrogance of our curiosity, would satisfy the wish of Reason in respect of a theory which must be based on a cognition of the nature of things. Whether the first, as Theology, and the second, as Anthropology, when founded on the moral principle, *i.e.* the principle of freedom, and consequently in accordance with the practical use [of Reason] do not better fulfil their objective final design, is another question which we need not here pursue.

The physico-teleological ground of proof does not reach to Theology, because it does not and cannot give any determinate concept, sufficient for this design, of the original Being; but we must derive this from quite another quarter, or must supply its lacuna by an arbitrary addition. You infer, from the great purposiveness of natural forms and their relations, an intelligent Cause of the world; but what is the degree of this intelligence [Verstand]? Without doubt you cannot assume that it is the highest possible intelligence; because for that it would be requisite that you should see that a greater intelligence than that of which you perceive proofs in the world, is not thinkable; and this would be to ascribe Omniscience to yourself.[1] In the same way, if you infer from the magnitude of the world the very great might of its Author, you must be content with this having only a comparative significance for your faculty of comprehen-

---

[1] [These arguments are advanced by Hume, *Inquiry*, § vii. Cf. also Kritik of *Pure Reason*, Dialectic, bk. II. c. iii. § 6, and Kritik of *Practical Reason*, Dialectic, c. ii. § vii.]

sion ; for since you do not know all that is possible,
so as to compare it with the magnitude of the world
as far as you know it, you cannot infer the Almightiness of its Author from so small a standard, and so on.
Now you arrive in this way at no definite concept
of an original Being available for a Theology ; for
this can only be found in the concept of the totality
of perfections compatible with intelligence, and you
cannot help yourself to this by merely *empirical* data.
But without such a definite concept you cannot infer
a *unique* intelligent original Being ; you can only
assume it (with whatever motive).— Now it may
certainly be conceded that you should arbitrarily
add (for Reason has nothing fundamental to say
to the contrary) : Where so much perfection is
found, we may well assume that all perfection is
united in a unique Cause of the world, because
Reason succeeds better both theoretically and practically with a principle thus definite. But then
you cannot regard this concept of the original Being
as proved by you, for you have only assumed it on
behalf of a better employment of Reason. Hence
all lamentation or impotent anger on account of
the alleged mischief of rendering doubtful the
coherency of your chain of reasoning, is vain pre-
tentiousness, which would fain have us believe that
the doubt here freely expressed as to your argument
is a doubting of sacred truth, in order that under
this cover the shallowness of your argument may
pass unnoticed.

Moral Teleology, on the other hand, which is
not less firmly based than physical,—which, indeed,
rather deserves the preference because it rests
a priori on principles inseparable from our Reason
—leads to that which is requisite for the possibility

of a Theology, viz. to a determinate *concept* of the
supreme Cause, as Cause of the world according
to moral laws, and, consequently, to the concept
of such a cause as satisfies our moral final purpose.
For this are required, as natural properties belonging to it, nothing less than Omniscience, Omnipotence, Omnipresence, and the like, which must be
thought as bound up with the moral final purpose
which is infinite and thus as adequate to it. Hence
moral Teleology alone can furnish the concept of
a *unique* Author of the world, which is available
for a Theology.

In this way Theology leads immediately to
*Religion, i.e. the recognition of our duties as divine
commands*[1]; because it is only the recognition of
our duty and of the final purpose enjoined upon
us by Reason which brings out with definiteness
the concept of God. This concept, therefore, is
inseparable in its origin from obligation to that
Being. On the other hand, even if the concept
of the original Being could be also found determinately by the merely theoretical path (viz. the
concept of it as mere Cause of nature), it would
afterwards be very difficult — perhaps impossible
without arbitrary interpolation [of elements] — to
ascribe to this Being by well-grounded proofs
a causality in accordance with moral laws; and
yet without this that quasi-theological concept
could furnish no foundation for religion. Even if
a religion could be established by this theoretical
path, it would actually, as regards sentiment
(wherein its essence lies) be different from that in
which the concept of God and the (practical)
conviction of His Being originate from the funda-

[1] [Cf. Kritik of *Practical Reason*, Dialectic, c. ii. § v.]

mental Ideas of morality.   For if we must suppose
the Omnipotence, Omniscience, etc., of an Author
of the world as concepts given to us from another
quarter, in order afterwards only to apply our
concepts of duties to our relation to Him, then
these latter concepts must bear very markedly the
appearance of compulsion and forced submission.
If, instead of this, the respect for the moral law,
quite freely, in virtue of the precept of our own
Reason, represents to us the final purpose of our
destination, we admit among our moral views a
Cause harmonising with this and with its accomplishment, with the sincerest reverence, which is quite
distinct from pathological fear ; and we willingly
submit ourselves thereto.[1]

If it be asked why it is incumbent upon us to
have any Theology at all, it appears clear that
it is not needed for the extension or correction of
our cognition of nature or in general for any theory,
but simply in a subjective point of view for Religion,
i.e. the practical or moral use of our Reason.   If
it is found that the only argument which leads to
a definite concept of the object of Theology is itself
moral, it is not only not strange, but we miss
nothing in respect of its final purpose as regards
the sufficiency of belief from this ground of proof,
provided that it be admitted that such an argument

---

[1] The admiration for beauty, and also the emotion aroused by
the manifold purposes of nature, which a reflective mind is able
to feel even prior to a clear representation of a rational Author of the
world, have something in themselves like *religious* feeling.   They
seem in the first place by a method of judging analogous to moral
to produce an effect upon the moral feeling (gratitude to, and
veneration for, the unknown Cause) ; and thus by exciting moral
Ideas to produce an effect upon the mind, when they inspire that
admiration which is bound up with far more interest than mere
theoretical observation can bring about.

only establishes the Being of God sufficiently for
our moral destination, *i.e.* in a practical point of
view, and that here speculation neither shows its
strength in any way, nor extends by means of it
the sphere of its domain. Our surprise and the
alleged contradiction between the here asserted
possibility of a Theology and that which the Kritik
of speculative Reason said of the Categories—viz.
that they can only produce knowledge when applied
to objects of sense, but in no way when applied
to the supersensible—vanish, if we see that they
are here used for a cognition of God not in a
theoretical point of view (in accordance with what
His own nature, which is inscrutable by us, may
be) but simply in a practical.—— In order then
at this opportunity to make an end of the misinterpretation of that very necessary doctrine of
the Kritik, which, to the chagrin of the blind
dogmatist, refers Reason to its bounds, I add here
the following elucidation.

If I ascribe to a body *motive force* and thus
think it by means of the category of *causality*,
then I at the same time *cognise* it by that [category];
i.e. I determine the concept of it, as of an Object in
general, by means of what belongs to it by itself
(as the condition of the possibility of that relation)
as an object of sense. If the motive force ascribed
to it is repulsive, then there belongs to it (although
I do not place near it any other body upon which
it may exert force) a place in space, and moreover
extension, *i.e.* space in itself, besides the filling
up of this by means of the repulsive forces of
its parts. In addition there is the law of this
filling up (that the ground of the repulsion of the
parts must decrease in the same proportion as the

extension of the body increases, and as the space, which it fills with the same parts by means of this force, is augmented).— On the contrary, if I think a supersensible Being as the first *mover*, and thus by the category of causality as regards its determination of the world (motion of matter), I must not think it as existing in any place in space nor as extended ; I must not even think it as existing in time or simultaneously with other beings. Hence I have no determinations whatever, which could make intelligible to me the condition of the possibility of motion by means of this Being as its ground. Consequently, I do not in the very least cognise it by means of the predicate of Cause (as first mover), for itself; but I have only the representation of a something containing the ground of the motions in the world ; and the relation of the latter to it as their cause, since it does not besides furnish me with anything belonging to the constitution of the thing which is cause, leaves its concept quite empty. The reason of this is, that by predicates which only find their Object in the world of sense I can indeed proceed to the being of something which must contain their ground, but not to the determination of its concept as a supersensible being, which excludes all those predicates. By the category of causality, then, if I determine it by the concept of a *first mover*, I do not in the very least cognise what God is. Perhaps, however, I shall have better success if I start from the order of the world, not merely to *think* its causality as that of a supreme *Understanding*, but to *cognise* it by means of this determination of the said concept ; because here the troublesome condition of space and of extension disappears.— At all events

the great purposiveness in the world compels us
to *think* a supreme cause of it, and to *think* its
causality as that of an Understanding; but we are
not therefore entitled to *ascribe* this to it. (*E.g.*
we think of the eternity of God as presence in
all time, because we can form no other concept
of mere being as a quantum, *i.e.* as duration;
or we think of the divine Omnipresence as presence
in all places in order to make comprehensible to
ourselves His immediate presence in things which
are external to one another; without daring to
ascribe to God any of these determinations, as something cognised in Him.)   If I determine the causality of a man, in respect of certain products which are
only explicable by designed purposiveness, by thinking it as that of Understanding, I need not stop
here, but I can ascribe to him this predicate as a
well-known property and cognise him accordingly.
For I know that intuitions are given to the senses
of men and are brought by the Understanding
under a concept and thus under a rule; that this
concept only contains the common characteristic
(with omission of the particular ones) and is thus
discursive; and that the rules for bringing given
representations under a consciousness in general
are given by Understanding before those intuitions,
etc.   I therefore ascribe this property to man as a
property by means of which I *cognise* him.   However, if I wish to *think* a supersensible Being (God)
as an intelligence, this is not only permissible in a
certain aspect of my employment of Reason—it is
unavoidable; but to ascribe to Him Understanding
and to flatter ourselves that we can *cognise* Him by
means of it as a property of His, is in no way permissible.   For I must omit all those conditions

under which alone I know an Understanding, and
thus the predicate which only serves for determining
man cannot be applied at all to a supersensible
Object ; and therefore by a causality thus determined,
I cannot cognise what God is. And so it is
with all Categories, which can have no significance
for cognition in a theoretical aspect, if they are not
applied to objects of possible experience.— However, according to the analogy of an Understanding
I can in a certain other aspect think a supersensible
being, without at the same time meaning thereby to
cognise it theoretically ; viz. if this determination of
its causality concerns an effect in the world, which
contains a design morally necessary but unattainable
by a sensible being. For then a cognition of God
and of His Being (Theology) is possible by means
of properties and determinations of His causality
merely thought in Him according to analogy, which
has all requisite reality in a practical reference
though *only in respect of this* (as moral).— An
Ethical Theology is therefore possible ; for though
morality can subsist without theology as regards its
rule, it cannot do so as regards the final design
which this proposes, unless Reason in respect of
it is to be renounced. But a Theological Ethic
(of pure Reason) is impossible ; for laws which
Reason itself does not give and whose observance it
does not bring about as a pure practical faculty,
cannot be moral. In the same way a Theological
Physic would be a nonentity, for it would propose no
laws of nature but ordinances of a Highest Will ;
while on the other hand a physical (properly speaking a physico-teleological) Theology can serve at
least as a propædeutic to Theology proper, by giving
occasion for the Idea of a final purpose which

nature cannot present by the observation of natural purposes of which it offers abundant material. It thus makes felt the need of a Theology which shall determine the concept of God adequately for the highest practical use of Reason, but it cannot develop this and base it satisfactorily on its proofs.

THE END

Printed by R. & R. CLARK, *Edinburgh.*

MESSRS. MACMILLAN & CO.'S
STANDARD PHILOSOPHICAL WORKS.

KANT'S CRITIQUE OF PURE REASON.

2 Vols. 8vo. 16s. each.

CRITIQUE OF PURE REASON. By IMMANUEL KANT. Translated by F. MAX MÜLLER. With Introduction by LUDWIG NOIRÉ.

Vol. I. HISTORICAL INTRODUCTION.
Vol. II. CRITIQUE OF PURE REASON.

A NEW AND COMPLETE EDITION.

2 Vols. Crown 8vo. Vol. I. 7s. 6d. Vol. II. 6s.

KANT'S CRITICAL PHILOSOPHY FOR ENGLISH READERS. By J. P. MAHAFFY, D.D., Professor of Ancient History in the University of Dublin, and JOHN H. BERNARD, B.D., Fellow of Trinity College, Dublin.

Vol. I. THE KRITIK OF PURE REASON EXPLAINED AND DEFENDED.
Vol. II. THE PROLEGOMENA. Translated with Notes and Appendices.

BY PROFESSOR CALDERWOOD.

Crown 8vo. 6s.

HANDBOOK OF MORAL PHILOSOPHY. By Rev. HENRY CALDERWOOD, LL.D., Professor of Moral Philosophy in the University of Edinburgh. 14th Edition, largely rewritten.

BY THE LATE PROFESSOR CLIFFORD.

Crown 8vo. 3s. 6d.

SEEING AND THINKING. By the late Prof. W. K. CLIFFORD, F.R.S. With Diagrams.

BY THE LATE PROFESSOR JEVONS.

18mo. 1s.

PRIMER OF LOGIC. By W. STANLEY JEVONS, F.R.S., formerly Professor of Political Economy in University College.

Fcap. 8vo. 3s. 6d.

ELEMENTARY LESSONS IN LOGIC, Deductive and Inductive, with Copious Questions and Examples, and a Vocabulary of Logical Terms. By the Same.

Crown 8vo. 12s. 6d.

THE PRINCIPLES OF SCIENCE. A Treatise on Logic and Scientific Method. By the Same. New and Revised Edition.

Crown 8vo. 6s.

STUDIES IN DEDUCTIVE LOGIC. By the Same. 2nd Edition.

8vo. 10s. 6d.

PURE LOGIC: AND OTHER MINOR WORKS. By the Same. Edited by R. ADAMSON, M.A., LL.D., Professor of Logic at Owens College, Manchester, and HARRIET A. JEVONS. With a Preface by Prof. ADAMSON.

MACMILLAN AND CO., LONDON.

MESSRS. MACMILLAN & CO.'S
STANDARD PHILOSOPHICAL WORKS.

BY J. N. KEYNES, M.A.

Crown 8vo. 10s. 6d.

FORMAL LOGIC, Studies and Exercises in. Including a Generalisation of Logical Processes in their Application to Complex Inferences. By JOHN NEVILLE KEYNES, M.A. 2nd Edition, Revised and Enlarged.

BY PRESIDENT JAMES McCOSH, D.D.

Extra Crown 8vo. 9s.

FIRST AND FUNDAMENTAL TRUTHS: being a Treatise on Metaphysics. By JAMES McCOSH, D.D., President of Princeton College.

BY THE LATE PROFESSOR MAURICE.

4th Edition. 2 vols. 8vo. 16s.

MORAL AND METAPHYSICAL PHILOSOPHY. By F. D. MAURICE, M.A., late Professor of Moral Philosophy in the University of Cambridge.

Vol. I. ANCIENT PHILOSOPHY AND THE FIRST TO THE THIRTEENTH CENTURIES.

Vol. II. FOURTEENTH CENTURY AND THE FRENCH REVOLUTION, WITH A GLIMPSE INTO THE NINETEENTH CENTURY.

BY PROFESSOR RAY. *1)*

Globe 8vo. 4s. 6d.

A TEXT-BOOK OF DEDUCTIVE LOGIC FOR THE USE OF STUDENTS. By P. K. RAY, D.Sc., Professor of Logic and Philosophy, Presidency College, Calcutta. 4th Edition.

BY HENRY SIDGWICK, LL.D., D.C.L.

4th Edition. 8vo. 14s.

THE METHODS OF ETHICS. By HENRY SIDGWICK, LL.D., D.C.L., Knightbridge Professor of Moral Philosophy in the University of Cambridge.

. *A Supplement to the 2nd Edition, containing all the important Additions and Alterations in the 3rd Edition.* 8vo. 6s.

8vo. 14s. net.

THE ELEMENTS OF POLITICS. By HENRY SIDGWICK, Litt.D.

TIMES—"No serious student of politics can afford to neglect it, and none can read it without deriving instruction and profit from almost every page. . . . An important contribution to the higher political thought of our time."

SATURDAY REVIEW—"Taking his own conception of his book, we have almost unqualified admiration for it."

Just ready. 3rd Edition. Crown 8vo. 3s. 6d.

OUTLINES OF THE HISTORY OF ETHICS, for English Readers. By the Same. 3rd Edition, Revised.

BY JOHN VENN, F.R.S.

Crown 8vo. 10s. 6d.

THE LOGIC OF CHANCE. An Essay on the Foundations and Province of the Theory of Probability, with special Reference to its Logical Bearings and its Application to Moral and Social Science. By JOHN VENN, M.A., F.R.S., late Fellow of Caius College, Cambridge. 3rd Edition, Rewritten and greatly Enlarged.

Crown 8vo. 10s. 6d.

SYMBOLIC LOGIC. By the Same.

8vo. 18s.

THE PRINCIPLES OF EMPIRICAL OR INDUCTIVE LOGIC. By the Same.

MACMILLAN AND CO., LONDON.

Druck:
Canon Deutschland Business Services GmbH
im Auftrag der KNV-Gruppe
Ferdinand-Jühlke-Str. 7
99095 Erfurt